QUIET TITLE: TRANSFERRING YOUR HOME TO A LIVING TRUST WITH A QUITCLAIM DEED

First edition. November 8, 2025.

ISBN: 979-8232629335

Written by janice green.

Table of Contents

Quiet Title:

Transferring Your Home to a Living Trust with a Quitclaim Deed

By

Janice Green

Dedication

To every homeowner who dared to take control of their legacy— This book is for you.

To the families navigating property transfers with courage, clarity, and conviction— May your trust be protected, your title secured, and your future empowered.

And to my mentors, colleagues, and loved ones who believed in the power of accessible legal knowledge— Your support made this possible.

Acknowledgements

This guide would not exist without the insight and encouragement of many professionals who dedicate their lives to simplifying estate planning and protecting families through education.

To the estate attorneys, title agents, and financial advisors who generously shared their expertise—thank you for helping demystify the process and elevate the standard of trust administration.

To my editorial team and design collaborators—your precision, creativity, and commitment to clarity brought this book to life.

To the readers who asked the hard questions, challenged assumptions, and demanded practical answers—your voices shaped every chapter.

And finally, to those who continue to advocate for transparency, equity, and empowerment in property law—this work is a tribute to your mission.

About the Author

Janice Green is a legal educator and estate planning advocate with a passion for making complex property processes simple, accessible, and empowering for everyday homeowners. With over two decades of experience in real estate documentation, trust administration, and title coordination, she has helped thousands of families protect their homes, preserve their legacies, and navigate the legal landscape with confidence.

Janice specializes in instructional writing that bridges the gap between legal jargon and practical action. Her guides are known for their clarity, precision, and step-by-step structure—making them trusted resources for individuals, families, and professionals alike. Whether teaching workshops, consulting on trust transfers, or writing manuals like *Quiet Title*, Janice is committed to demystifying the law and equipping readers with tools they can actually use.

When she's not writing or consulting, Janice enjoys mentoring new homeowners, collaborating with estate professionals, and developing resources that support financial literacy and long-term planning. Her work reflects a deep belief in empowerment through education—and a dedication to helping others secure what matters most.

Introduction

Introduction: Securing Your Legacy with Wisdom and Care

For a homeowner, the decision of how to manage and transfer their most valuable asset is an act of profound stewardship. This book serves as a practical guide to help you navigate a specific, powerful strategy for this purpose: transferring real estate into a living trust using a quitclaim deed. Our purpose is to provide a clear, step-by-step pathway to help you understand this process and its primary benefit—the ability to plan for the future of your family and your assets with a focus on privacy and discretion.

In a world where legal processes can be public and complicated, many are seeking ways to ensure their legacy is handled discreetly and efficiently. Homeowners often consider transferring property into a trust to avoid the lengthy and public probate process, maintain control of their assets, and provide for their loved ones in a private manner. The Bible speaks to the importance of leaving a legacy, with Proverbs 13:22 stating, "A good man leaves an inheritance to his children's children". This act of wise planning is not merely a legal transaction, but a fulfillment of a generational responsibility to steward what we have been given.

This book will provide an overview of the two key tools in this strategy: the living trust and the quitclaim deed. A living trust is a foundational estate planning tool that allows you to manage assets for your own benefit during your lifetime and then distribute them to your heirs without public court involvement. The quitclaim deed is the mechanism for this transfer, a simple and common document used to move property from an individual's name into the name of their trust, often between related parties. While God is the ultimate owner of all things, we are entrusted with the role of faithful stewards (Psalm 24:1). This guide is designed to empower you with the knowledge to manage your earthly possessions wisely, ensuring that your property is transferred in a way that honors this principle.

While this book provides a comprehensive overview of the process, it is not a substitute for professional counsel. We will explore the critical legal and ethical considerations to be mindful of, including the importance of consulting with a qualified attorney and tax advisor. Such counsel helps ensure your actions align with all applicable laws and do not create unintended consequences. Ultimately, by approaching this process with diligence and wisdom, you can secure your legacy and confidently fulfill your responsibility as a faithful steward of the resources entrusted to you.

Introduction: Stewardship, Legacy, and Trust

In a world where financial stewardship and legacy planning are increasingly important, this book serves as a guide for homeowners seeking to transfer their property into a living trust using a quitclaim deed. The purpose is not merely legal—it is spiritual. Scripture reminds us, "A good man leaves an inheritance to his children's children" (Proverbs 13:22), and this book is written to help believers honor that principle with wisdom and integrity. By understanding the tools available and the responsibilities involved, readers can take meaningful steps toward protecting their families and preserving their values.

Homeowners often consider transferring property to a trust for reasons that go beyond convenience. A living trust offers privacy, avoids probate, and ensures that assets are distributed according to one's wishes. It reflects the biblical call to plan diligently: "Be sure you know the condition of your flocks, give careful attention to your herds" (Proverbs 27:23). In modern terms, our "flocks" may be our homes, finances, and possessions—resources entrusted to us by God to manage wisely.

As previously stated, this book will also explore the role of quitclaim deeds and living trusts in estate planning. A quitclaim deed is a simple legal instrument that allows a property owner to transfer their interest in real estate to another party—often to a trust—without warranties. A living trust, particularly a revocable one, allows the owner to maintain control while designating beneficiaries. These tools, when used properly, can reflect the biblical principle of order and foresight: "Let all things be done decently and in order" (1 Corinthians 14:40).

Finally, we must address the legal and ethical considerations of such transfers. While some may seek discretion in handling their affairs, it is essential to act with integrity. Scripture warns, "Better is a poor man who walks in his integrity than a rich man who is crooked in his ways" (Proverbs 28:6). This book will not only provide practical steps but also encourage readers to align their actions with biblical values—ensuring that their legacy is built on both wisdom and righteousness.

Chapter 1:
Understanding Living Trusts

In the journey of biblical stewardship and legacy planning, understanding the role of a living trust is foundational. A living trust is a legal arrangement that allows an individual (the grantor) to transfer ownership of assets—such as a home—into a trust during their lifetime. The trust is managed by a trustee for the benefit of designated beneficiaries. This structure reflects the wisdom of Proverbs 21:5: "The plans of the diligent lead surely to abundance." A living trust is one such diligent plan, designed to protect, preserve, and pass on what God has entrusted to us.

What Is a Living Trust?

A living trust is created while the grantor is still alive, allowing them to maintain control over their assets while setting clear instructions for how those assets should be handled upon death or incapacitation. It serves as a private, flexible tool for estate planning. Unlike a will, which becomes public and must go through probate, a living trust operates outside the court system, offering discretion and efficiency. This aligns with the biblical principle of order: "Let all things be done decently and in order" (1 Corinthians 14:40).

A living trust (specifically, a Revocable Living Trust or RLT, unless structured otherwise for specific irrevocable purposes) is the cornerstone of a discreet and efficient estate plan. It is a legal document that, once executed, creates a separate entity to hold title to your assets, such as your home. Unlike a will, which only takes effect after your death and must go through a public probate court process, a living trust is effective immediately upon creation. It allows you, as the "grantor" or "settlor," to name yourself as the initial "trustee" to maintain complete control over your property during your lifetime. Upon your incapacity or death, a named "successor trustee" steps in seamlessly to manage and distribute the assets according to your private instructions, avoiding court intervention entirely.

The process of "funding" the trust—transferring the title of your home and other assets into the name of the trust—is crucial for its effectiveness. A trust has no power over assets not legally titled in its name. When transferring your home, precision is paramount. The names on the current title must match exactly the names used in the transfer deed; avoid adding or removing names without proper legal consultation. Once the quitclaim deed is signed and notarized, it must be officially filed with the county recorder's office to make the transfer legally valid.

Beyond the legal filing, practical steps are necessary to ensure the smooth administration of your home within the trust framework. You must contact your insurance provider and add the trust as an "additional insured" or "named insured" on your homeowner's policy. Failing to do so could jeopardize coverage in the event of a claim. Furthermore, when establishing your trust, you name beneficiaries who will inherit the home after you are gone. It is a wise and loving decision to identify your children or other heirs as successor beneficiaries early on. Proactive planning, while you are healthy and able, prevents future family disputes and ensures your intentions are honored efficiently. Utilizing a living trust with diligence is a prudent way to safeguard your legacy and provide for the generations that follow.

Revocable vs Irrevocable Trusts

There are two primary types of living trusts: revocable and irrevocable. A revocable trust allows the grantor to modify or dissolve the trust at any time. It offers flexibility and control, making it ideal for those who want to retain access to their assets. However, it provides limited protection from creditors and lawsuits.

An irrevocable trust, on the other hand, is permanent. Once assets are transferred, the grantor relinquishes control, and the terms cannot be easily changed. This structure offers stronger asset protection and is often used to shield property from future claims. It reflects the biblical call to surrender and trust: “Commit your way to the Lord; trust in Him, and He will act” (Psalm 37:5). By surrendering control, the grantor creates a fortress of protection for their legacy.

***

Section 1: Revocable vs Irrevocable Trusts: Understanding the Difference

When it comes to estate planning and protecting your assets, trusts serve as powerful legal instruments that allow you to manage your wealth according to your wishes. The two primary categories of trusts—revocable and irrevocable—offer distinct advantages and limitations that every person should understand before making important financial decisions. Just as we are called to be wise stewards of the resources God has entrusted to us, choosing the right type of trust reflects thoughtful planning and responsible management. Proverbs 21:5 reminds us, "The plans of the diligent lead to profit as surely as haste leads to poverty." This wisdom applies not only to our daily work but also to how we structure our financial affairs for the benefit of our families and future generations.

What is a Revocable Trust?

A revocable trust, often called a living trust, is a flexible estate planning tool that allows you to maintain complete control over your assets during your lifetime. As the name suggests, this type of trust can be changed, amended, or completely revoked at any time while you are alive and mentally competent. You can add or remove assets, change beneficiaries, or dissolve the trust entirely if your circumstances change. This flexibility makes revocable trusts attractive to many people who want to maintain control while still enjoying the benefits of trust planning, such as avoiding probate and ensuring privacy in asset distribution.

The concept of maintaining stewardship while planning for the future aligns with biblical principles of wisdom and foresight. In Luke 14:28, Jesus teaches, "Suppose one of you wants to build a tower. Won't you first sit down and estimate the cost to see if you have enough money to complete it?" Just as careful planning is essential in construction, thoughtful estate planning through a revocable trust demonstrates prudence in managing what God has given us. The revocable trust allows us to adapt our plans as life circumstances change, showing both wisdom and flexibility in our stewardship.

Benefits and Limitations of Revocable Trusts

Revocable trusts offer several key advantages that make them popular among families seeking to simplify estate administration. First, assets held in a revocable trust avoid the probate process, which can be lengthy, expensive, and public. This means your loved ones can access their inheritance more quickly and privately after your passing. Second, a revocable trust provides continuity if you become incapacitated, as your successor trustee can immediately step in to manage the trust assets without court intervention. Third, these trusts offer privacy since they don't become public record like wills do when filed with probate courts.

However, revocable trusts have important limitations that must be understood. Because you retain control over the assets, they remain part of your taxable estate for estate tax purposes. Additionally, assets in a revocable trust are not protected from creditors or lawsuits during your lifetime, since you can access and control them freely. The trust does not provide asset protection benefits while you're alive. Understanding these limitations helps us make informed decisions, echoing the wisdom found in Proverbs 4:7: "The beginning of wisdom is this: Get wisdom. Though it cost all you have, get understanding."

What is an Irrevocable Trust?

An irrevocable trust represents a more permanent commitment in estate planning. Once you create and fund an irrevocable trust, you generally cannot change its terms, remove assets, or dissolve it without the permission of the beneficiaries or a court order. By transferring assets into an irrevocable trust, you are effectively giving up ownership and control of those assets. While this may seem like a significant sacrifice, irrevocable trusts offer substantial benefits that revocable trusts cannot provide, particularly in the areas of asset protection and tax planning.

The act of placing assets into an irrevocable trust reflects a profound trust in God's provision and a commitment to blessing future generations. This mirrors the biblical concept of laying up treasures and planning for our children's children. Proverbs 13:22 states, "A good person leaves an inheritance for their children's children, but a sinner's wealth is stored up for the righteous." By creating an irrevocable trust, you demonstrate faith that your needs will be met even without direct control over certain assets, while ensuring your family's future security. This requires both courage and trust in God's faithfulness.

Benefits of Irrevocable Trusts

Irrevocable trusts provide powerful advantages that can significantly benefit your estate planning strategy. First and foremost, because you no longer own the assets in the trust, they are typically removed from your taxable estate, potentially reducing or eliminating estate taxes for your heirs. Second, assets in an irrevocable trust are generally protected from creditors, lawsuits, and long-term care costs, since you no longer legally own them. Third, irrevocable trusts can be used for Medicaid planning, as assets transferred into the trust may not count toward Medicaid's asset limits after a certain waiting period. Fourth, these trusts can provide for special needs beneficiaries without disqualifying them from government benefits.

The protection and provision that irrevocable trusts offer reflect God's design for caring for our families with intentionality and sacrifice. In 1 Timothy 5:8, Scripture teaches, "Anyone who does not provide for their relatives, and especially for their own household, has denied the faith and is worse than an unbeliever." Establishing an irrevocable trust demonstrates this kind of provision—taking permanent steps to ensure your family's security even when it requires giving up personal control. It's an act of love and responsibility that honors both God and family.

Drawbacks and Considerations of Irrevocable Trusts

Despite their benefits, irrevocable trusts come with significant drawbacks that require careful consideration. The most obvious limitation is the loss of control and flexibility. Once assets are transferred into an irrevocable trust, you typically cannot access them for your own use, change the beneficiaries, or alter the trust terms if your circumstances change. This permanence can be problematic if unexpected financial needs arise or family dynamics shift. Additionally, irrevocable trusts are more complex and expensive to establish and maintain than revocable trusts, often requiring ongoing legal and accounting fees.

Tax implications also require careful attention. While removing assets from your estate can reduce estate taxes, the trust itself may need to file tax returns and could face higher income tax rates on retained income.

Furthermore, beneficiaries may receive less favorable capital gains treatment on inherited assets compared to assets that receive a step-up in basis at death. These complexities remind us of the need for wise counsel in our planning. Proverbs 15:22 advises, "Plans fail for lack of counsel, but with many advisers they succeed." Working with experienced estate planning attorneys, financial advisors, and tax professionals is essential when considering an irrevocable trust.

Choosing Between Revocable and Irrevocable Trusts

The choice between a revocable and irrevocable trust depends on your specific circumstances, goals, and priorities. If your primary objectives are avoiding probate, maintaining control and flexibility, and ensuring smooth asset management during incapacity, a revocable trust is likely the better choice. This option works well for people with estates below the estate tax exemption threshold who don't have significant asset protection concerns. On the other hand, if you're focused on reducing estate taxes, protecting assets from creditors or long-term care costs, or planning for Medicaid eligibility, an irrevocable trust may be more appropriate despite the loss of control.

Many people actually benefit from using both types of trusts as part of a comprehensive estate plan. You might maintain a revocable trust for assets you want to control and access during your lifetime, while using one or more irrevocable trusts for specific purposes like life insurance, charitable giving, or special needs planning. This hybrid approach allows you to balance flexibility with protection and tax efficiency. The key is seeking godly wisdom and professional guidance in making these decisions. James 1:5 promises, "If any of you lacks wisdom, you should ask God, who gives generously to all without finding fault, and it will be given to you." Prayer and counsel should guide your estate planning process.

Conclusion: Stewardship Through Wise Planning

Understanding the differences between revocable and irrevocable trusts empowers you to make informed decisions about protecting and distributing your assets. Both types of trusts serve valuable purposes in estate planning, and the right choice depends on your unique situation, values, and goals. What matters most is that you approach these decisions with intentionality, seeking to honor God through wise stewardship of the resources He has entrusted to you. Whether you choose the flexibility of a revocable trust or the protection of an irrevocable trust, your planning should reflect both practical wisdom and faith in God's provision.

Ultimately, estate planning through trusts is about more than just legal documents and tax strategies—it's about caring for the people you love and managing God's resources responsibly. As you consider these options, remember the words of Proverbs 16:3: "Commit to the Lord whatever you do, and he will establish your plans." With prayer, wise counsel, and careful planning, you can create a trust structure that provides for your family, protects your assets, and honors God. Take the time to educate yourself, consult with qualified professionals, and make decisions that bring both earthly wisdom and heavenly peace to your financial legacy.

***

Section 2: Benefits of Placing Your Home in a Trust

Your Home as a Sacred Stewardship

Your home is likely the most valuable asset you own, representing not just financial investment but also shelter, security, and a place where memories are made with loved ones. For many families, the family home is the cornerstone of their wealth and legacy, making it essential to protect and plan for its future wisely. Placing your home in a trust is a strategic estate planning decision that can provide numerous benefits for you during your lifetime and for your family after you're gone. This act of careful planning reflects the biblical principle of wise stewardship, as we are reminded in 1 Corinthians 4:2 that "it is required that those who have been given a trust must prove faithful." When God blesses us with property and possessions, we have a responsibility to manage them wisely for the benefit of our families and to honor Him.

The decision to place your home in a trust should not be made hastily or without proper understanding of the implications and benefits. Like building a house on a solid foundation rather than on sand, as Jesus taught in Matthew 7:24-25, establishing a trust for your home creates a firm foundation for your estate plan. This article explores the many advantages of this important decision, from avoiding probate to protecting your family's inheritance, all while reflecting on how biblical wisdom guides us toward responsible stewardship of our earthly possessions.

Avoiding the Probate Process

One of the most significant benefits of placing your home in a trust is avoiding the probate process entirely. Probate is the court-supervised procedure for distributing a deceased person's assets, and it can be time-consuming, expensive, and emotionally draining for grieving families. Without a trust, your home will likely go through probate, which can take anywhere from several months to over a year depending on your state's laws and the complexity of your estate. During this time, your family cannot sell, refinance, or fully access the property without court approval, creating frustration and potential financial hardship during an already difficult period.

By transferring your home into a revocable living trust, you ensure that ownership passes immediately to your beneficiaries upon your death without any court involvement. This smooth transition means your loved ones can access and use the property right away, whether they choose to live in it, sell it, or rent it out. The probate process also involves court fees, attorney costs, and executor fees that can consume three to seven percent of your estate's value. Avoiding these expenses means more of your wealth goes directly to your family rather than to legal proceedings. Proverbs 13:22 reminds us that "a good person leaves an inheritance for their children's children," and by avoiding probate, you maximize the inheritance you leave behind while minimizing the burden on your heirs.

Maintaining Privacy and Confidentiality

When your home goes through probate, the proceedings become part of the public record. This means anyone can access information about your property's value, who inherits it, and details about your overall estate. This loss of privacy can expose your family to unwanted attention, potential scams targeting heirs, or simply uncomfortable public scrutiny during a vulnerable time. For families who value discretion or have concerns about privacy, this public exposure can be particularly troubling.

A trust, however, is a private document that does not need to be filed with any court or become part of public records. When your home is held in a trust, the transfer to your beneficiaries happens privately without public disclosure of your property's value or your family's personal business. This confidentiality protects your family's financial information and shields them from opportunists who might target grieving heirs. The Bible speaks to the value of discretion and wisdom in managing our affairs. Proverbs 11:13 states, "A gossip betrays a confidence, but a trustworthy person keeps a secret." While transparency is important in many contexts, maintaining appropriate privacy in family financial matters demonstrates wisdom and protects those we love from potential exploitation or unwanted intrusion.

Providing for Incapacity and Continuity of Management

Life is unpredictable, and any of us could face a time of physical or mental incapacity due to illness, injury, or aging. If you become unable to manage your affairs and your home is in your individual name, your family may need to go through a costly and public guardianship or conservatorship proceeding to gain legal authority to manage your property. This court process can be emotionally difficult, expensive, and time-consuming, adding stress to an already challenging situation.

When your home is placed in a trust, you name a successor trustee who can immediately step in to manage the property if you become incapacitated, without any court involvement. This person can handle necessary maintenance, pay the mortgage and property taxes, make repairs, or even sell the property if needed to cover your care costs. This seamless transition ensures your home continues to be managed properly during your incapacity, protecting both the asset and your interests. This planning reflects the wisdom found in Ecclesiastes 11:2, which advises, "Invest in seven ventures, yes, in eight; you do not know what disaster may come upon the land." We cannot predict when we might face incapacity, but we can prepare for that possibility by establishing structures that protect our interests and ease the burden on our families.

Simplifying Estate Distribution and Reducing Family Conflict

Real estate often becomes a source of conflict among heirs, particularly when multiple children or beneficiaries have different ideas about what should happen to the family home. Should it be sold and the proceeds divided? Should one child live in it while others receive equivalent value from other assets? These disagreements can strain relationships and even lead to legal disputes that tear families apart. When property passes through a will, unhappy heirs may contest the distribution, leading to expensive litigation that depletes the estate and creates lasting family divisions.

A properly structured trust provides clear instructions about what should happen to your home and can include specific provisions to minimize conflict. You might direct that the home be sold and proceeds divided equally, or you might give one child the right to purchase it from the trust at fair market value, or you might allow a surviving spouse to live there for life before it passes to children. Whatever your wishes, expressing them clearly in a trust and discussing them with your family while you're alive can prevent misunderstandings and disputes. Additionally, trust administration is generally less adversarial than probate, as it doesn't invite the same opportunities for legal challenges. The Bible calls us to pursue peace and unity within our families. Romans 12:18 instructs, "If it is possible, as far as it depends on you, live at peace with everyone." By creating clear, fair plans for distributing your home through a trust, you promote family harmony and reduce the likelihood of conflict that could damage relationships for generations.

Protecting Your Home from Creditors and Legal Claims

Depending on the type of trust you establish, placing your home in a trust may offer some protection from creditors and legal claims. While a revocable living trust doesn't provide asset protection during your lifetime (since you maintain control over the property), it can offer some benefits after your death. Once you pass away and the trust becomes irrevocable, the assets may be protected from your beneficiaries' creditors, depending on how the trust is structured and your state's laws. This means if your child inherits your home through a trust and later faces a lawsuit, bankruptcy, or divorce, the property may be shielded from those claims.

For those with significant asset protection concerns, an irrevocable trust offers even stronger safeguards. By transferring your home into an irrevocable trust, you give up direct ownership and control, but the property is generally protected from your own creditors and may not be counted as an available asset for long-term care costs or Medicaid eligibility after a required waiting period. This protection can be invaluable for preserving your family's inheritance and ensuring the home you worked so hard to purchase remains within the family rather than being seized by creditors or consumed by healthcare expenses. The concept of protecting resources for future generations aligns with biblical teaching about provision and stewardship. Proverbs 21:20 observes, "The wise store up choice food and olive oil, but fools gulp theirs down." Wise planning through trusts allows us to preserve assets rather than seeing them depleted by unforeseen circumstances.

Maintaining Eligibility for Government Benefits

For elderly individuals or those with disabilities who may need to qualify for Medicaid or other government benefits, proper planning with trusts becomes especially important. Medicaid has strict asset limits, and if your home is counted as an available asset, you may be disqualified from receiving benefits or the state may place a lien on your property to recover costs after your death. This can result in your family home being sold to repay the government, leaving nothing for your heirs.

Certain types of trusts, such as Medicaid Asset Protection Trusts or Special Needs Trusts, allow you to remove your home from your countable assets while still potentially maintaining some benefits from the property. These irrevocable trusts must be established well in advance of needing benefits (typically at least five years before applying for Medicaid due to look-back periods), but they can protect your home from being consumed by long-term care costs. For families with special needs members, a Special Needs Trust can hold the home while allowing the beneficiary to continue receiving government assistance without disqualification. This careful planning reflects responsible stewardship and care for vulnerable family members, echoing the heart of James 1:27, which says, "Religion that God our Father accepts as pure and faultless is this: to look after orphans and widows in their distress and to keep oneself from being polluted by the world." While this verse speaks specifically of orphans and widows, the principle extends to caring for all vulnerable family members through wise planning.

Facilitating Multi-Generational Planning

Placing your home in a trust opens up possibilities for sophisticated multi-generational planning that benefits not just your immediate children but also your grandchildren and beyond. You can structure the trust so that your home passes to your children for their lifetime, and then automatically to your grandchildren, keeping the property within the family for multiple generations. This type of dynasty planning ensures that the home you worked hard to purchase remains a family asset that provides stability and security for descendants you may never meet.

Trusts can also be structured to address different family situations, such as blended families where you want to ensure your current spouse can live in the home for life but the property ultimately goes to your children from a previous marriage. Without a trust, these complex family dynamics often lead to conflict and legal battles, but a well-drafted trust can balance competing interests fairly and clearly. This kind of forward-thinking planning reflects the biblical value of generational blessing and legacy. Psalm 78:4 speaks of declaring God's works "to the next generation," and in a similar way, we can create structures that bless and provide for generations to come. By placing your home in a trust with multi-generational provisions, you create a lasting legacy that extends your stewardship and care far beyond your own lifetime.

Providing Flexibility While Maintaining Control

One of the most appealing aspects of placing your home in a revocable living trust is that you can maintain complete control over the property during your lifetime while still enjoying all the benefits mentioned above. As the trustee of your own trust, you can continue living in the home, sell it if you choose, refinance it, rent it out, or make any other decisions just as you could before. The trust doesn't change your day-to-day relationship with your property at all—you're simply changing the legal ownership structure to provide future benefits.

This flexibility means you're not locked into permanent decisions, unlike with an irrevocable trust. If your circumstances change, you can amend the trust, add or remove beneficiaries, or even dissolve it entirely and take the property back into your individual name. This adaptability is particularly valuable in our changing world where family situations, financial needs, and personal goals can shift over time. The ability to maintain control while planning wisely reflects the balanced approach to stewardship that Scripture encourages. In the parable of the talents in Matthew 25:14-30, Jesus commends the servants who actively managed and multiplied what was entrusted to them, not those who simply buried their resources. A revocable trust allows you to remain an active manager of your property while simultaneously preparing for the future—a balance between present control and future provision.

Potential Tax Benefits and Estate Planning Advantages

While placing your home in a revocable living trust doesn't provide income tax or estate tax benefits during your lifetime, it can be structured to work in conjunction with other trusts and estate planning strategies that do offer tax advantages. For example, after your death, your home can be held in a trust for your spouse that qualifies for the unlimited marital deduction, deferring estate taxes until the second spouse's death. Or it can be divided between different trusts to maximize the use of both spouses' estate tax exemptions.

For high-net-worth families, more sophisticated strategies might involve transferring the home into an irrevocable trust, such as a Qualified Personal Residence Trust (QPRT), which removes the home's future appreciation from your taxable estate while allowing you to continue living there for a specified period. These advanced strategies require careful planning with experienced professionals but can result in significant tax savings. Additionally, homes held in properly structured trusts may be easier to value and divide among heirs in a tax-efficient manner. The biblical principle of wise financial stewardship includes making intelligent use of available legal strategies to maximize what we leave to our families. Jesus himself taught about shrewd management in Luke 16:8-9, noting that "the people of this world are more shrewd in dealing with their own kind than are the people of the light." While we must always act ethically and legally, there is nothing wrong with using lawful strategies to minimize taxes and maximize the inheritance we leave to loved ones.

Ensuring Your Home Aligns with Your Values and Legacy

Beyond the practical and financial benefits, placing your home in a trust allows you to attach conditions and guidelines that reflect your values and ensure your property is used in ways that honor your legacy. You might include provisions that the home must remain available for family gatherings, that it cannot be sold for a certain period to preserve family connections, or that it must be offered first to family members before being sold to outsiders. You could even attach charitable provisions, such as requiring that a portion of sale proceeds be donated to your church or favorite ministry.

These value-based provisions transform your home from merely a financial asset into a vehicle for expressing your faith, priorities, and hopes for future generations. Your trust can be a document that not only distributes property but also communicates important family values, shares wisdom you've gained, and encourages behaviors you want to see continue in your family line. This approach to estate planning recognizes that our earthly possessions are tools for advancing kingdom purposes and blessing others. As Jesus taught in Luke 12:34, "For where your treasure is, there your heart will be also." By thoughtfully planning how your home will be used and distributed, you ensure that this significant treasure reflects your heart and values, pointing your family toward what truly matters most.

Conclusion: Building Your Legacy on a Solid Foundation

The decision to place your home in a trust is an act of love, wisdom, and responsible stewardship that benefits both you and your family. From avoiding probate and maintaining privacy to protecting against incapacity and reducing family conflict, the advantages are numerous and significant. Whether you choose a revocable trust for flexibility and control or an irrevocable trust for asset protection and tax benefits, taking this step demonstrates your commitment to caring for those you love and managing God's blessings responsibly.

As you consider this important decision, remember that estate planning is not just about legal documents and tax strategies—it's about values, relationships, and legacy. It's about ensuring that the home where you've lived, loved, and created memories continues to bless your family long after you're gone. Proverbs 24:27 advises, "Put your outdoor work in order and get your fields ready; after that, build your house." This verse speaks to the importance of proper planning and laying foundations before building, and that's exactly what placing your home in a trust accomplishes. You're building a legal and financial foundation that will support your family for years to come, demonstrating the kind of foresight and care that honors God and blesses generations. Take the time to consult with experienced estate planning professionals, pray for wisdom in your decisions, and create a plan that protects your home while reflecting your faith and values.

Benefits of Placing Your Home in a Trust

Placing your home in a living trust offers several benefits:

Avoids probate, saving time and legal costs

Preserves privacy, as trust documents are not public

Ensures continuity, allowing the trustee to manage the property if the grantor becomes incapacitated

Clarifies inheritance, reducing family disputes

These benefits reflect the biblical value of peace and foresight: "A wise man thinks ahead; a fool doesn't and even brags about it" (Proverbs 13:16,

NLT). A trust is a wise step forward, ensuring that your home and legacy are handled with care.

How Trusts Protect Assets and Simplify Probate

Trusts, especially irrevocable ones, can protect assets from creditors, lawsuits, and even certain taxes. By removing the asset from the grantor's personal ownership, the trust creates a legal barrier that is difficult to penetrate. Additionally, because the trust owns the property, there is no need for probate—a court-supervised process that can be lengthy and costly. This simplifies the transition of ownership and honors the biblical principle of stewardship: "Moreover, it is required of stewards that they be found faithful" (1 Corinthians 4:2).

In summary, living trusts are not just legal tools—they are instruments of faith, foresight, and family protection. Whether revocable or irrevocable, they offer a path to secure your home, honor your values, and leave a legacy that reflects your walk with God.

***

Section 3: How Trusts Protect Assets and Simplify Probate

The Shield and the Bridge

In our modern world, protecting what God has blessed us with and ensuring smooth transitions for our loved ones requires both wisdom and careful planning. Trusts serve as powerful legal instruments that accomplish two critical objectives: they shield your assets from various threats and they create a seamless bridge for transferring wealth to the next generation without the complications of probate court. These dual functions make trusts indispensable tools in comprehensive estate planning, offering peace of mind that your hard-earned resources will be preserved and distributed according to your wishes. The Bible consistently emphasizes the importance of wise stewardship and planning ahead, as we see in Proverbs 27:12, which states, "The prudent see danger and take refuge, but the simple keep going and pay the penalty." Establishing a trust is precisely this kind of prudent action—recognizing potential dangers to your estate and taking refuge in legal protections before problems arise.

Understanding how trusts function to protect assets and simplify probate is essential for anyone seeking to build a lasting legacy and provide for their family's future. These benefits are not merely technical legal advantages but practical expressions of love and responsibility toward those who depend on us. When we take steps to protect our resources and make inheritance easier for our heirs, we demonstrate the kind of forward-thinking care that reflects God's own providential nature. As we explore the mechanisms by which trusts accomplish these goals, we'll see how ancient biblical wisdom about stewardship finds practical application in contemporary estate planning strategies.

The Probate Problem: Why It Matters

Before we can fully appreciate how trusts simplify probate, we must understand why probate poses such significant challenges for families. Probate is the legal process through which a deceased person's estate is administered under court supervision, ensuring debts are paid and assets are distributed according to the will or state law. While this process serves legitimate purposes, it has become increasingly burdensome, expensive, and time-consuming in most jurisdictions. Probate can take anywhere from six months to two years or more, during which time assets are essentially frozen. Your family cannot access bank accounts, sell property, or make significant financial decisions without court approval, creating hardship for those who may depend on these resources for their daily needs.

The costs associated with probate can be staggering, typically consuming between three and seven percent of the estate's total value. These expenses include court filing fees, attorney fees, executor compensation, appraisal costs, and various administrative charges that quickly accumulate. For an estate worth $500,000, this could mean $15,000 to $35,000 or more in probate costs—money that could otherwise go directly to your beneficiaries. Additionally, probate is entirely public, meaning anyone can access court records to learn about your assets, their values, and who inherits them. This lack of privacy can expose your family to unwanted attention, scams targeting heirs, or simply uncomfortable scrutiny during an already difficult time. The burden and expense of probate reflect the very kind of unnecessary difficulty that wise planning can prevent. Proverbs 22:3 teaches, "The prudent see danger and take refuge, but the simple keep going and suffer for it." Recognizing probate as a potential danger allows us to take refuge in trust planning before it becomes a problem for our families.

How Trusts Bypass Probate Entirely

The most significant way trusts simplify the inheritance process is by bypassing probate completely. When you transfer assets into a properly established trust, you change the legal ownership from your individual name to the trust itself. Upon your death, these trust assets do not form part of your probate estate because you technically no longer own them—the trust does. Since probate only governs assets owned in your individual name at death, everything held in the trust passes directly to your beneficiaries according to the trust's terms without any court involvement whatsoever.

This bypass mechanism works immediately and automatically. The moment you pass away, your designated successor trustee steps into your role and begins distributing assets according to your instructions. There are no court filings, no waiting periods, no judge's approval required, and no public notices. Your beneficiaries can receive their inheritance within days or weeks rather than months or years, and they can access it privately without the entire community knowing the details of your estate. This streamlined process is particularly valuable for families who need quick access to funds for living expenses, or for business owners whose enterprises need uninterrupted management. The peace and efficiency that trusts provide reflect God's desire for order and smooth transitions. As 1 Corinthians 14:33 reminds us, "God is not a God of disorder but of peace." By creating orderly plans through trusts, we minimize chaos and confusion for our grieving families, giving them the gift of clarity and simplicity during difficult times.

Asset Protection During Your Lifetime

While avoiding probate is perhaps the most well-known benefit of trusts, their asset protection capabilities during your lifetime and beyond are equally important. The type and degree of protection depends on whether you establish a revocable or irrevocable trust. A revocable living trust, where you maintain control and can modify terms at any time, provides limited asset protection during your life since you still effectively own and control the assets. However, even a revocable trust offers some protection by adding a layer of separation between you personally and the assets, which can discourage frivolous lawsuits and provide some privacy from those who might investigate your personal holdings.

Irrevocable trusts, on the other hand, offer robust asset protection precisely because you surrender ownership and control of the assets you transfer into them. Once property is placed in a properly structured irrevocable trust, it generally cannot be reached by your personal creditors, lawsuits, or judgments because you no longer legally own it. This protection extends to various threats including business liabilities, malpractice claims, divorce proceedings, and even long-term care costs in some circumstances. The trust becomes a separate legal entity that shields assets from your personal financial risks. This principle of separation for protection has biblical precedent in the concept of setting apart or consecrating resources for specific purposes. In the Old Testament, certain properties and possessions were dedicated to God and thus protected from common use or seizure. Similarly, when we set aside assets in an irrevocable trust for the benefit of our families, we create a protected space that shields these resources from threats. Proverbs 21:20 observes, "The wise store up choice food and olive oil, but fools gulp theirs down," teaching us the value of preserving resources rather than allowing them to be consumed carelessly or seized by external forces.

Protection from Beneficiaries' Creditors and Life Challenges

Beyond protecting assets from your own creditors, trusts can also shield your beneficiaries' inheritances from their creditors, lawsuits, divorces, and poor financial decisions. When you leave assets outright to heirs through a will or by beneficiary designation, those assets become their personal property the moment they receive them, exposing the inheritance to whatever financial or legal problems your beneficiaries face. If your child is going through a divorce, gets sued, declares bankruptcy, or simply makes poor spending choices, the inheritance you worked so hard to build could be lost within months.

Trusts solve this problem by allowing you to leave inheritances in continuing trust for your beneficiaries rather than distributing everything outright. These beneficiary trusts can provide your heirs with access to funds for their needs while keeping the principal protected from creditors and legal claims. You might direct that your trustee can distribute funds for your child's health, education, maintenance, and support, but the assets remain in the trust rather than passing into their personal ownership where they could be seized or squandered. This structure is particularly valuable if you have concerns about a beneficiary's financial maturity, substance abuse issues, disability, or vulnerability to manipulation. It's also wise planning even for responsible beneficiaries, as none of us can predict what challenges our children might face in the future. This kind of protective planning reflects parental love that extends beyond the grave, continuing to provide and protect even when you're no longer there to guide and help. It mirrors God's own protective nature toward His children, as we see in Psalm 121:7-8, "The Lord will keep you from all harm—he will watch over your life; the Lord will watch over your coming and going both now and forevermore." While we cannot protect our children from every danger, we can establish structures that shield their inheritance and provide ongoing support through whatever challenges life brings.

Protecting Against Long-Term Care Costs and Medicaid Recovery

One of the most significant financial threats facing elderly Americans is the astronomical cost of long-term care, whether in nursing homes, assisted living facilities, or through home health services. These expenses can easily exceed $100,000 per year, and they can rapidly deplete a lifetime of savings, leaving nothing for your spouse or heirs. Medicaid can help cover these costs, but it has strict income and asset limits, and states often seek to recover benefits paid by placing liens on your home or other assets after your death. Without proper planning, your estate could be entirely consumed by healthcare costs and Medicaid recovery claims.

Certain types of irrevocable trusts, particularly Medicaid Asset Protection Trusts (MAPTs), can shield assets from being counted toward Medicaid eligibility requirements and protect them from estate recovery after death. By transferring your home and other assets into such a trust, you remove them from your personal ownership while still potentially maintaining some benefits, such as the right to live in your home. However, these trusts must be established well in advance of needing care—typically at least five years before applying for Medicaid benefits due to look-back period rules. This requirement makes early planning essential. While no one wants to think about becoming incapacitated or needing institutional care, acknowledging this possibility and planning for it is an act of wisdom and realism. Ecclesiastes 7:2 observes, "It is better to go to a house of mourning than to go to a house of feasting, for death is the destiny of everyone; the living should take this to heart." Similarly, considering the possibility of needing long-term care and planning accordingly is better than ignoring reality until it's too late. Proper trust planning can mean the difference between preserving your life's work for your family or seeing it entirely consumed by healthcare costs.

Maintaining Privacy and Confidentiality

In our increasingly public world where personal information is easily accessible online, privacy has become a precious commodity. The probate process strips away privacy from estate matters, creating public records that anyone can access. When your will goes through probate, it becomes a public document filed with the court, detailing your assets, their values, your debts, who inherits what, and sometimes even family relationships and disputes. These records are often published in legal notices, posted online, and accessible to identity thieves, scam artists, distant relatives seeking a share, or simply curious neighbors.

Trusts provide a shield of privacy around your estate and family affairs. A trust is a private contract between you and your trustee that never needs to be filed with any court or become part of public records. When assets transfer through a trust, the transactions happen privately without public disclosure of values, beneficiaries, or terms. This confidentiality protects your family from unwanted attention, reduces the likelihood of inheritance disputes by disappointed parties who might not even know what they didn't receive, and shields vulnerable beneficiaries from being targeted by those who might learn of their inheritance. The value of appropriate discretion in financial matters is supported throughout Scripture. While we're called to be generous and open-hearted, we're not required to broadcast our private affairs to the world. Proverbs 11:13 states, "A gossip betrays a confidence, but a trustworthy person keeps a secret," and Matthew 6:3-4 teaches about giving in secret: "When you give to the needy, do not let your left hand know what your right hand is doing, so that your giving may be in secret." These passages affirm that privacy in certain matters is not only acceptable but can be wise and even spiritually appropriate. Trusts allow you to maintain appropriate confidentiality around family financial matters while still being transparent with those who need to know.

Simplifying Multi-State Property Administration

For individuals who own property in multiple states—perhaps a primary residence in one state, a vacation home in another, and rental property in a third—probate becomes exponentially more complicated and expensive. Without a trust, you would need to open separate probate proceedings in each state where you own real property, a process called ancillary probate. This means multiple sets of court filings, multiple attorneys, multiple executor appointments, and multiple sets of fees and costs. The administrative burden and expense can be overwhelming for your family, and the timeline extends even further as they navigate different states' laws and procedures simultaneously.

A trust elegantly solves this multi-state property problem by consolidating all real estate under one legal ownership structure. Regardless of where properties are located, they're all owned by your trust and will be administered according to the trust's terms by a single trustee without any probate proceedings in any state. This consolidation saves enormous time, money, and frustration for your heirs. It also simplifies management if you become incapacitated, as your successor trustee can handle all properties under one authority rather than needing separate legal proceedings in multiple jurisdictions. This principle of unity and consolidation for efficiency reflects biblical wisdom about organization and stewardship. When Jesus fed the five thousand in Mark 6:39-40, he had the people sit down in organized groups, bringing order to what could have been chaos. Similarly, organizing multiple properties under one trust brings order and efficiency to what would otherwise be a chaotic multi-state probate nightmare. The peace this brings to families dealing with loss cannot be overstated.

Protecting Special Needs Beneficiaries

Families with members who have disabilities face unique estate planning challenges. If you leave assets outright to a disabled individual who receives government benefits such as Supplemental Security Income (SSI) or Medicaid, that inheritance could disqualify them from these essential programs, creating a terrible dilemma. The inheritance might not be enough to cover their lifetime needs without government assistance, yet receiving it costs them the very benefits that provide for their care. Without proper planning, what was meant as a blessing becomes a crisis.

Special Needs Trusts (also called Supplemental Needs Trusts) solve this problem by holding assets for the benefit of disabled individuals while preserving their eligibility for needs-based government benefits. These trusts are carefully structured to provide supplemental support—enhancing quality of life through therapies, entertainment, education, travel, and other expenses—without replacing government benefits that cover basic necessities like food, shelter, and medical care. The trustee manages the assets and distributes them in ways that don't jeopardize benefit eligibility, ensuring your loved one is cared for throughout their lifetime. This specialized form of trust protection represents profound love and stewardship, ensuring that your most vulnerable family members are provided for in appropriate ways. It reflects the heart of God toward those who need special care, as we see in Matthew 25:40, "The King will reply, 'Truly I tell you, whatever you did for one of the least of these brothers and sisters of mine, you did for me.'" When we establish Special Needs Trusts to care for disabled family members, we're providing protection and dignity for those who are vulnerable, honoring both them and the God who values every person.

Providing for Minor Children with Wisdom

If you have minor children and you pass away before they reach adulthood, leaving assets to them outright creates numerous problems. Minors cannot legally own significant property or manage financial accounts in their own names. Courts will typically require establishment of a guardianship or conservatorship, appointing someone to manage the children's inheritance until they reach legal age—usually eighteen. However, most eighteen-year-olds lack the maturity and financial wisdom to responsibly manage significant inheritances, and studies show that sudden wealth at young ages often leads to squandering, exploitation, or poor decisions that leave young adults with nothing by their mid-twenties.

Trusts allow you to provide for minor children with protection and wisdom. You can establish trusts that hold inheritances until your children reach ages when they're more likely to use funds responsibly—perhaps distributing portions at ages twenty-five, thirty, and thirty-five rather than everything at eighteen. You can also give your trustee discretion to provide for education, health needs, and appropriate support while preserving principal for the future. This structure protects your children from their own immaturity, from predatory individuals who might take advantage of young heirs, and from the sudden wealth syndrome that ruins so many young lives. It's an expression of parental wisdom that continues guiding your children even after you're gone. This approach reflects the biblical principle of stewarding resources wisely and preparing the next generation to handle them appropriately. Proverbs 1:8-9 begins the book of Proverbs with, "Listen, my son, to your father's instruction and do not forsake your mother's teaching. They are a garland to grace your head and a chain to adorn your neck." Through a well-structured trust, your teaching and wisdom continue guiding your children in financial matters, helping them navigate wealth responsibly and building character alongside providing resources.

Business Succession and Asset Protection

For business owners, trusts offer invaluable tools for both succession planning and asset protection. Operating a business exposes you to significant liability risks—lawsuits from customers, employees, vendors, or competitors could threaten not just your business assets but also your personal wealth. Without proper structure, a judgment against your business could reach your personal assets, including your home, savings, and investments. Additionally, when business owners die without proper planning, the business often gets caught in probate, potentially disrupting operations, causing value to plummet, or even forcing liquidation at unfavorable prices.

Trusts can hold business interests, separating them from your personal assets and creating a clear succession plan. You might establish one trust to hold your operating business (protecting it from personal creditors) and another trust to hold key business assets like real estate or intellectual property. Upon your death or incapacity, your successor trustee can immediately step in to manage the business or execute your succession plan without probate delays. You can structure the trust to provide income to your spouse while transitioning management to your children, or to hold business interests until children are mature enough to take over. This continuity planning ensures that the business you built continues operating smoothly, preserving both its value and its ability to provide for your family. This kind of thoughtful business planning honors the work God has blessed and ensures it continues serving its purpose. The parable of the talents in Matthew 25:14-30 emphasizes the importance of wisely managing and multiplying what we've been given. By structuring your business within trusts that protect it and ensure smooth succession, you're acting as a faithful steward who ensures the enterprise continues producing fruit rather than being destroyed by poor planning.

Reducing Family Conflict and Inheritance Disputes

One of the most heartbreaking consequences of poor estate planning is the family conflict that erupts when parents die. Siblings who were once close become estranged over inheritances, fighting about who gets the family home, whether business interests should be sold or operated, or whether distributions were fair. These disputes often stem from ambiguity, lack of communication, or structures that inadvertently pit family members against each other. Probate proceedings, being adversarial in nature and open to challenges, provide fertile ground for these conflicts to escalate into expensive litigation that depletes the estate and destroys relationships.

Trusts significantly reduce the likelihood and severity of inheritance disputes through several mechanisms. First, trust administration is generally less adversarial than probate because it's a private matter managed by the trustee according to clear written instructions rather than a court process open to multiple parties filing competing claims. Second, trusts can include specific provisions that address potential conflict areas—perhaps giving one child who worked in the family business the right to purchase it, or creating separate shares for children from different marriages, or establishing objective criteria for distributions that remove trustee discretion. Third, certain trust provisions like no-contest clauses can discourage frivolous challenges by penalizing beneficiaries who unsuccessfully contest the trust. Finally, the very act of creating a comprehensive trust and discussing it with your family while you're alive opens conversations that prevent misunderstandings and manage expectations before they become disputes. The biblical value of family unity and peace cannot be overstated. Jesus himself prayed in John 17:21 "that all of them may be one," emphasizing the importance of unity among believers. In our families, pursuing peace and taking steps to prevent conflict honors God and protects the relationships He values. Establishing clear, fair trust arrangements is a practical expression of the peace-making that Jesus blessed in Matthew 5:9, "Blessed are the peacemakers, for they will be called children of God."

Flexibility to Adapt to Changing Circumstances

Unlike wills, which only take effect at death and cannot be modified thereafter, trusts—particularly revocable living trusts—offer remarkable flexibility to adapt to life's changes. As circumstances evolve, you can amend your trust to add or remove beneficiaries, change distribution provisions, replace trustees, add new assets, or modify any other terms.

This adaptability is crucial because life rarely unfolds exactly as we plan. Children's circumstances change, beneficiaries develop problems or prove themselves particularly responsible, family relationships shift, tax laws change, and your own needs and priorities evolve with age and experience.

This flexibility allows your estate plan to remain current and relevant throughout your life without requiring expensive legal proceedings or starting over from scratch. You simply execute amendments to your trust as needed, ensuring your plan continues reflecting your wishes and your family's reality. Some people revise their trusts multiple times over decades, fine-tuning provisions as they gain wisdom about their family dynamics and observe how their children develop. This ongoing refinement capacity means your final plan benefits from a lifetime of learning and observation rather than being frozen at one moment in time. The ability to adapt and adjust reflects biblical wisdom about seasons and change. Ecclesiastes 3:1 teaches, "There is a time for everything, and a season for every activity under the heavens." Recognizing that different seasons require different approaches, and having the flexibility to modify your plans accordingly, demonstrates both wisdom and realism. A trust that can grow and change with you is far superior to rigid arrangements that become outdated and inappropriate over time.

***

Section 4: How Trusts Protect Assets and Simplify Probate

Trusts create a legal separation between the person and the property, and that separation is the heart of how they protect assets. When you transfer a home or other asset into a properly funded trust, the trust becomes the legal owner while you (if it is a revocable trust) or the trustee (if irrevocable) continue to manage or benefit from the property according to the trust's terms. This legal ownership barrier makes it far more difficult for personal creditors to reach those assets, because the asset is no longer held in the grantor's individual name. The Bible commends wise stewardship and prudent protection of provision: "The prudent see danger and take refuge, but the simple keep going and pay the penalty" (Proverbs 27:12), and a trust is a practical refuge for God's provision placed under careful management.

Irrevocable trusts raise the protection to another level by permanently removing ownership and control from the grantor, which is often why they are used for asset protection planning. Because the grantor gives up legal title, creditors generally cannot claim trust property as the grantor's personal asset, and structured provisions—like spendthrift clauses—further prevent a beneficiary's creditors from attaching distributions before they are paid. This permanence is a heavy but purposeful step that mirrors biblical themes of surrender and faithful covenant: "Commit your way to the Lord; trust in him and he will act" (Psalm 37:5). The sacrifice of immediate control is balanced by long-term security for the family and future heirs.

Trusts also simplify and often avoid probate, and that simplification is both practical and pastoral. Probate is the court-supervised process for settling an estate, which can be slow, public, and costly. Assets owned by the trust generally pass to beneficiaries according to the trust instrument without the need for probate court intervention, preserving privacy and accelerating distribution. This efficiency honors the biblical call to order and care for one's household: "Let all things be done decently and in order" (1 Corinthians 14:40). Avoiding probate reduces stress on surviving family members at a time when they need space to grieve and steward what remains.

While trusts provide strong protections, they are not unconditional shields; courts may unwind transfers made with fraudulent intent or in active collusion to defeat existing creditors. Therefore integrity and proper timing are essential—do not use trusts to hide assets from legitimate obligations. Scripture warns against dishonest gain and counsels uprightness: "Better is a poor person who walks in his integrity than one who is crooked in speech and is a fool" (Proverbs 19:1). Sound trust planning should be guided by both legal counsel and moral clarity so that protection does not become deception.

Practical steps enhance a trust's protective and probate-avoiding functions: properly funding the trust (transferring deeds and titles), including clear trustee succession plans, adding spendthrift or distribution provisions where appropriate, and keeping records current. These actions create a durable framework so the trust can serve its intended purpose when circumstances change. The value of careful preparation is echoed in Scripture: "For which of you, desiring to build a tower, does not first sit down and count the cost?" (Luke 14:28). Thoughtful steps now spare family members legal entanglements and preserve the legacy you intend to leave.

Conclusion: The Wisdom of Preparation and Protection

The evidence is clear: trusts provide superior asset protection and dramatically simplify the process of transferring wealth to the next generation compared to relying on wills and probate. From avoiding the time, expense, and publicity of court proceedings to shielding assets from creditors, lawsuits, and poor decisions, trusts offer comprehensive solutions to the most significant challenges facing estate planning. They represent the practical application of biblical stewardship principles—protecting what God has entrusted to us and ensuring it blesses those we love rather than being consumed by unnecessary costs or lost to preventable threats.

As you consider whether to establish trusts as part of your estate plan, remember that this decision is not merely about legal technicalities or saving money, though those benefits are real and substantial. More fundamentally, it's about demonstrating love for your family by sparing them unnecessary burdens during grief, protecting vulnerable members who need special care, preventing conflicts that could destroy relationships, and ensuring your life's work accomplishes the purposes you intended. It's about being a faithful steward of everything God has blessed you with, managing it wisely during your lifetime and planning thoughtfully for its use after you're gone. Proverbs 13:22 reminds us that "a good person leaves an inheritance for their children's children," and trusts are powerful tools for ensuring you truly can leave that inheritance rather than seeing it depleted by probate costs, creditors, taxes, or family conflict. Take the time to consult with experienced estate planning professionals, pray for wisdom in your decisions, and establish trust structures that protect your assets and simplify your legacy. Your family will thank you, and you'll have the peace of knowing you've been a faithful steward of all that God entrusted to your care.

***

Side Note: There is important information to consider in this book which applies to transferring your home into a living trust.

So, the material we've covered — the nature and purpose of living trusts, the role of quitclaim deeds, how quitclaim deeds differ from warranty deeds, and how trusts protect assets and simplify probate — directly pertains to transferring a home into a living trust. Which at its core it explains the legal mechanics (re-titling the property into the trust), the practical benefits (probate avoidance, privacy, continuity), and the tradeoffs and risks (title risk with quitclaims, lender issues, loss of control for irrevocable trusts). Nevertheless, Proverbs reminds us to plan wisely: "For which of you, desiring to build a tower, does not first sit down and count the cost?" (Luke 14:28). That wisdom undergirds careful trust planning.

What this means practically for a home transfer

The typical technique for funding a revocable living trust is re-recording the deed so the trust becomes the legal owner; a quitclaim deed is commonly used for this because it is simple and fast.

For revocable trusts where the grantor remains trustee, day-to-day control usually doesn't change, but title is in the trust name so the property bypasses probate after your death.

For irrevocable trusts, transferring the home removes it from your personal ownership and offers stronger creditor protection, but you give up control and flexibility.

A quitclaim deed conveys whatever interest you have without title warranties; it is suitable for transfers between known parties (you to your trust) but not usually for sales to third parties without additional protections.

Key risks and contract issues to remember

Mortgage or lender clauses (due-on-sale) can be triggered by transfers; federal law often allows transfers into a grantor's revocable trust for estate planning, but lender policies vary.

Transfers made to defraud creditors or during active litigation can be set aside by courts. Integrity matters: "The integrity of the upright guides them" (Proverbs 11:3).

Quitclaim deeds do not cure latent title defects; if clear title assurance is important, a warranty deed and title insurance are preferable.

Compact checklist for transferring a house into a living trust

Confirm trust document exists and the trust name matches exactly.

Prepare a deed (commonly a quitclaim deed) naming the trust as grantee: "Your Name, Trustee of the [Trust Name] dated [date]."

Use the exact legal description from your current deed.

Sign per state law (notary and witnesses if required).

Record the deed at the county recorder's office and obtain a recorded copy.

Update homeowner's insurance and notify your title insurance company if applicable.

Keep copies of trust and recorded deed with your estate plan documents and notify successor trustee where documents are kept.

Consult an estate planning attorney and, if there is a mortgage, discuss lender implications with counsel or your loan servicer.

Final practical guidance

The materials you've read form a correct and useful foundation for transferring a home into a living trust, but they are not a substitute for state-specific legal advice. As Proverbs counsels, seek counsel: "Plans fail for lack of counsel, but with many advisers they succeed" (Proverbs 15:22). If you'd like, I can turn this checklist into a printable step-by-step form or draft a sample quitclaim deed wording tailored to a revocable trust format for your state.

Chapter 2:
The Role of the Quitclaim Deed

A quitclaim deed is a simple legal instrument that transfers whatever interest the grantor has in a parcel of real property to another party without making any promises or warranties about clear title. Unlike warranty deeds, which guarantee that the grantor holds good title and will defend it against claims, a quitclaim deed simply conveys whatever interest exists at the moment of signing. This plainness makes the quitclaim deed a quick, inexpensive tool for shifting ownership into a trust, for correcting title defects, or for moving property between family members. The simplicity reflects a biblical humility about stewardship: we act honestly and plainly in our arrangements, heeding Proverbs 11:3, "The integrity of the upright guides them."

Because a quitclaim deed offers no title guarantees, it carries both usefulness and risk. Its greatest advantage is speed and minimal formality—many united states county offices accept a properly completed quitclaim deed for recording with little delay—so it is often the tool of choice when the goal is to transfer property into a living trust efficiently. At the same time, because there are no covenants as to title, buyers or subsequent owners dealing with property conveyed by quitclaim must accept the possibility of existing liens, encumbrances, or competing claims. The practical wisdom of this choice is captured in Proverbs 22:3: "The prudent sees danger and hides himself; but the simple go on and suffer for it."

In the context of funding a trust, the quitclaim deed's role is usually procedural: it names the trust (for example, "John Doe, Trustee of the John Doe Living Trust dated January 1, 20XX") as the grantee and conveys the grantor's interest into that trust. For a revocable living trust where the grantor and trustee are the same person, this method typically does not change day-to-day control but re-titles the asset so it can pass to beneficiaries outside probate. The transfer should always use the exact legal description from the current deed, and the trust name used on the deed should match the trust document precisely to avoid later challenges. This attention to detail echoes the call to careful planning in Scripture: "For which of you, desiring to build a tower, does not first sit down and count the cost?" (Luke 14:28).

There are common situations where quitclaim deeds are particularly appropriate: transferring property into a trust you control, clearing up a misspelled name on title, moving property between spouses after marriage, or transferring between family members when no sale occurs. Conversely, quitclaim deeds are generally inappropriate for arms-length sales where the buyer expects title protections, or when serious title defects may exist; in those cases a warranty deed and title insurance are usually prudent. The balance between convenience and protection mirrors biblical counsel to exercise discernment: "Behold, I send you out as sheep in the midst of wolves; be ye therefore wise as serpents, and harmless as doves" (Matthew 10:16).

Executing a quitclaim deed properly involves several technical steps that protect the transfer's validity. The deed must correctly name the grantor and grantee, include the legal property description, state consideration (often nominal), and be signed in accordance with state law—typically in the presence of a notary and sometimes witnessed. After execution, the deed must be recorded in the county recorder's office where the property is located; recording puts the world on notice of the change in ownership. Skipping any of these steps can create confusion, legal exposure, or clouded title. The need for careful, lawful action parallels the biblical imperative to obey civil authorities and act responsibly: "Let every person be subject to the governing authorities" (Romans 13:1).

Ethical and relational considerations must accompany legal formality. When property is mortgaged, transferring title without addressing lender requirements can trigger contractual clauses (such as a due-on-sale provision) or strain relationships if heirs or co-owners feel excluded. Transparency with co-owners, counsel from competent attorneys, and honesty in intent preserve both legal safety and Christian witness. Proverbs 10:9 reminds us, "Whoever walks in integrity walks securely," and that security includes how we treat others in estate planning.

Finally, while a quitclaim deed is a practical mechanism for trust funding, it is only one piece of a broader estate plan. Proper trust funding includes updating insurance, beneficiary designations, mortgage awareness, and keeping records of deeds and trust documents. Combining technical competence with moral responsibility and spiritual discernment produces a plan that is both effective and honoring: "Commit your works to the Lord, and your plans will be established" (Proverbs 16:3).

***

Section 1: Using a Quitclaim Deed to Transfer Your Home into a Living Trust

The Foundation of Trust Funding

One of the most common and appropriate uses of a quitclaim deed is transferring your primary residence into your revocable living trust, a process known as "funding" the trust. This transfer is a critical step in making your living trust effective, as an unfunded trust is essentially an empty container that accomplishes nothing. Many people go through the effort and expense of creating a comprehensive living trust only to fail at this crucial step of actually transferring their home into it, leaving their most valuable asset to go through probate despite their planning efforts. Understanding how to properly use a quitclaim deed for this transfer, why this particular deed type is appropriate for this purpose, and what considerations arise in the process is essential knowledge for anyone establishing a living trust as part of their estate plan.

The act of transferring your home into your living trust represents a practical expression of stewardship and planning that honors biblical principles of wisdom and preparation. When we take steps to organize our affairs and create structures that will benefit our families after we're gone, we demonstrate the kind of foresight that Scripture commends. Proverbs 27:23-24 instructs us, "Be sure you know the condition of your flocks, give careful attention to your herds; for riches do not endure forever, and a crown is not secure for all generations." While most of us no longer tend flocks and herds, we do have homes and assets that require our careful attention and proper organization. Transferring your home into your trust through a quitclaim deed is precisely this kind of careful attention to your estate's condition, ensuring that your most significant asset is properly positioned to pass smoothly to your loved ones according to your wishes.

Why a Quitclaim Deed Works Perfectly for Trust Transfers

The quitclaim deed's lack of warranties, which makes it inappropriate for most purchases between unrelated parties, actually makes it ideal for transferring property into your own living trust. When you transfer your home from yourself as an individual to yourself as trustee of your trust, you're not really selling the property to someone else—you're simply changing the form of ownership while retaining complete control. Since you already know everything about your property's ownership history, title condition, and any encumbrances, you don't need anyone to make warranties to you about these matters. You're both the grantor and the grantee in the transaction, just wearing different legal hats, so promising things to yourself would be meaningless.

The simplicity and low cost of quitclaim deeds make them particularly attractive for trust funding. Since no money changes hands in this transfer—you're not selling your home, just reorganizing how you hold title to it—there's no need for the more complex and expensive warranty deed process that protects buyers in actual sales. Most title companies and attorneys charge significantly less to prepare a quitclaim deed than a warranty deed, and the recording fees are typically the same regardless of deed type. This cost efficiency matters when you may be transferring multiple properties into your trust, as many people do. Additionally, quitclaim deeds are straightforward documents that can be prepared quickly without the extensive title work and negotiations that accompany warranty deeds in sales transactions. This efficiency allows you to fund your trust promptly without unnecessary delay or expense. The appropriateness of using simple means for appropriate purposes reflects biblical wisdom about matching methods to situations. When Jesus sent his disciples out in Matthew 10:9-10, he instructed them to take nothing for the journey—no gold, silver, copper, extra tunic, sandals, or staff—because simplicity was appropriate for their mission. Similarly, when the mission is simply transferring your home from one pocket to another (from individual ownership to trust ownership), the simple quitclaim deed is the appropriate tool rather than the more complex warranty deed designed for protecting buyers in adversarial transactions.

The Basic Process of Transferring Your Home to Your Trust

Transferring your home into your living trust using a quitclaim deed follows a straightforward process, though attention to detail is important to ensure everything is done correctly. The first step is ensuring your trust actually exists—you must have a signed and properly executed trust document before you can transfer property into it. The trust document establishes the trust's existence and terms, creating the legal entity that will hold your property. Once your trust is established, you prepare a quitclaim deed with specific information. The grantor (the person transferring the property) should be listed exactly as your name appears on your current deed—if your current deed shows "John Robert Smith," use that exact name, not "John R. Smith" or "John Smith," as variations can create title problems.

The grantee (the person or entity receiving the property) should be yourself as trustee of your trust, using the exact trust name and date from your trust document. A typical grantee designation might read: "John Robert Smith, as Trustee of the John Robert Smith Revocable Living Trust dated January 15, 2024." Some attorneys prefer adding "and his successors in trust" after the trustee designation to clarify that future trustees will also have authority over the property. The deed must include a complete legal description of your property, which you can obtain from your current deed, recent title report, or county property records. Never use just the street address, as legal descriptions are required for real estate transfers. The consideration statement might simply say "for good and valuable consideration" or even "transfer to living trust" since no money is changing hands. After preparing the deed with all required information, you sign it as the grantor in the presence of a notary public, who verifies your identity and notarizes your signature. Finally, you record the executed deed with the county recorder's office where your property is located, paying the applicable recording fees. Once recorded, your home is officially owned by your trust rather than by you individually, accomplishing the goal of trust funding. This careful attention to proper procedure reflects the biblical principle of doing things decently and in order. As 1 Corinthians 14:40 instructs, "But everything should be done in a fitting and orderly way." Properly executing and recording your quitclaim deed ensures your trust funding is done correctly, avoiding future problems and confusion about your property's ownership.

Maintaining Your Property Tax Exemptions and Benefits

One of the most common concerns people have about transferring their home into a living trust is whether they'll lose important property tax benefits, particularly homestead exemptions, senior citizen exemptions, or other property tax reductions they currently enjoy. The good news is that in most states, transferring your primary residence into your own revocable living trust does not cause you to lose these benefits or trigger property tax reassessment. This is because you retain complete control over the trust and the property, you still live in the home as your primary residence, and the transfer is recognized as a mere change in the form of ownership rather than a true change in beneficial ownership.

However, the specific rules vary by state and even by county, so it's essential to verify your jurisdiction's rules before transferring property. Some states require you to file a form with the county assessor's office notifying them that the property has been transferred into your trust and requesting continuation of your homestead or other exemptions. Other states automatically continue the exemptions without requiring any action on your part. A few states have specific statutes that explicitly protect homestead and other exemptions when property is transferred to revocable living trusts, while others rely on administrative policies or practices. To ensure you don't inadvertently lose valuable tax benefits, contact your county property tax assessor's office before transferring your home and ask about their specific requirements for maintaining exemptions after a trust transfer. If any forms or notifications are required, complete them promptly after recording your quitclaim deed. Most assessor's offices are helpful and can provide the necessary information and forms. Additionally, keep copies of your trust document, the quitclaim deed, and any forms you file with the assessor's office in your records to document that you've complied with all requirements. This diligence in preserving your tax benefits while accomplishing your estate planning goals reflects wise stewardship of resources. Proverbs 21:5 teaches that "the plans of the diligent lead to profit as surely as haste leads to poverty." Taking time to understand and comply with property tax rules demonstrates the kind of diligence that protects your financial interests while still accomplishing your trust funding objectives. Don't let haste or assumptions cause you to lose valuable tax benefits that you've earned and that reduce your ongoing expenses.

Impact on Your Mortgage and Homeowner's Insurance

If your home has a mortgage, transferring it into your living trust raises important questions about whether this violates your loan agreement and what you should do about it. Many mortgages contain "due-on-sale" clauses that technically give the lender the right to demand full payment if the property is transferred to someone else. However, federal law—specifically the Garn-St. Germain Act of 1982—explicitly protects transfers into revocable living trusts from triggering due-on-sale clauses, as long as the borrower remains a beneficiary of the trust and continues living in the property as their primary residence. This means lenders cannot accelerate your loan or call it due simply because you transferred your home into your own living trust.

Despite this legal protection, it's still wise practice to notify your mortgage lender about the transfer, though not legally required in most cases. Some loan documents specifically require notification of any ownership changes, and maintaining good relationships with your lender is prudent. You can send a simple letter informing them that you've transferred the property into your revocable living trust for estate planning purposes, including a copy of the recorded quitclaim deed and perhaps the relevant pages of your trust document showing you as trustee and beneficiary. Most lenders will simply note this in their records without taking any action, though some might require you to provide periodic documentation that the trust remains revocable and you remain the beneficiary. Regarding homeowner's insurance, you should also notify your insurance company about the ownership change and request that the policy be updated to show the trust as the named insured. The typical designation would be "John Robert Smith, Trustee of the John Robert Smith Revocable Living Trust dated January 15, 2024." Most insurance companies make this change routinely without increasing premiums or changing coverage, but failing to update your policy could create claim problems if you have a loss and the property ownership doesn't match the policy. Some insurance companies require a copy of the trust document or at least the relevant pages showing the trust's name, date, and your role as trustee and beneficiary. This attention to keeping your mortgage and insurance properly aligned with your property's ownership demonstrates integrity and thoroughness in managing your affairs. Colossians 3:23 instructs, "Whatever you do, work at it with all your heart, as working for the Lord, not for human masters." Notifying your lender and insurer about the trust transfer and ensuring all documentation is properly updated is exactly this kind of thoroughness—doing things right and completely, not cutting corners or leaving loose ends that could create problems later.

***

Section 2: Coordinating with Title Insurance Considerations

When you purchased your home, you likely obtained owner's title insurance that protects you against title defects and claims that existed at the time of purchase. An important question is whether transferring your home into your trust via quitclaim deed affects this title insurance coverage. The good news is that most title insurance policies automatically continue covering property after it's transferred into the insured person's revocable living trust without requiring an endorsement or policy modification. This is because you remain the beneficial owner of the property—you just hold it through your trust rather than individually—and the trust is revocable, meaning you can take the property back out at any time.

However, it's still good practice to notify your title insurance company about the transfer and verify that coverage continues. Some title companies issue an endorsement confirming coverage for the trust, while others simply note the transfer in their records. If you have a particularly thorough estate planning attorney, they may arrange for this title insurance notification as part of the trust funding process. If not, you can contact the title company yourself, provide them with a copy of the recorded quitclaim deed and relevant trust pages, and request written confirmation that your title insurance remains in effect with the property now held in trust. This confirmation provides peace of mind and documentation if questions arise later. It's worth noting that title insurance companies generally don't view quitclaim deeds used for trust funding the same way they view quitclaim deeds in purchase transactions. When you acquire property via quitclaim deed from an unrelated seller, title companies often refuse to issue new insurance or require extensive additional work. But when you transfer your own property into your own trust via quitclaim deed, they recognize this as a non-threatening administrative change rather than a red flag suggesting title problems. This distinction is one reason why quitclaim deeds are appropriate for trust funding but inappropriate for purchases. The diligence of confirming your title insurance continues protecting your property after the trust transfer reflects responsible stewardship of your assets. Proverbs 27:12 warns, "The prudent see danger and take refuge, but the simple keep going and pay the penalty." While transferring to your trust shouldn't create title insurance problems, the prudent person verifies this rather than assuming everything is fine, thereby taking refuge against potential problems before they become costly penalties.

Handling Joint Ownership and Community Property Situations

If you own your home jointly with someone else, such as your spouse, transferring it into a living trust requires additional consideration about how the transfer should be structured. In most cases where spouses jointly own property, both spouses should sign the quitclaim deed as grantors, transferring the property from both of them individually to both of them as co-trustees of their trust. If you and your spouse have a joint trust (one trust established together by both of you), the grantee designation would typically read something like "John Robert Smith and Mary Ann Smith, as Trustees of the Smith Family Trust dated January 15, 2024." This transfers both ownership interests into the one shared trust.

In community property states (Arizona, California, Idaho, Louisiana, Nevada, New Mexico, Texas, Washington, and Wisconsin), special considerations arise regarding how property should be titled when transferred to a trust. Community property has unique tax benefits, particularly the "double step-up" in basis when one spouse dies, which can significantly reduce capital gains taxes if the surviving spouse later sells the property. To preserve community property character when transferring to a trust in community property states, the deed should include language stating that the property is being transferred as community property. The grantee designation might read "John Robert Smith and Mary Ann Smith, as Trustees of the Smith Family Trust dated January 15, 2024, as community property." This preserves the important tax benefits of community property ownership even though the property is now held in trust. If spouses have separate trusts rather than one joint trust, you have options about how to structure the transfer. You could transfer the property to both trusts, with each spouse's interest going into their respective trust, or you might transfer the entire property into one spouse's trust with provisions in that trust for how to handle it. Your estate planning attorney can advise on the best structure for your specific situation, considering both estate planning and tax implications. This attention to proper structure in joint ownership situations reflects wisdom about coordinating interests and protecting all parties appropriately. Ecclesiastes 4:9-10 observes, "Two are better than one, because they have a good return for their labor: If either of them falls down, one can help the other up. But pity anyone who falls and has no one to help them up." In marriage and estate planning, coordinating your plans and properly structuring joint property ownership ensures you truly benefit from partnership, with both spouses protected appropriately in all circumstances.

What Happens to Your Home When You Die

The entire purpose of transferring your home into your living trust via quitclaim deed is to ensure smooth transfer to your beneficiaries when you die, and understanding how this works helps appreciate why the effort of trust funding is worthwhile. When you pass away with your home properly titled in your trust, the property does not go through probate. Instead, your designated successor trustee (the person you named to take over trust management after your death) steps into your role immediately and has legal authority to manage and distribute the property according to your trust's instructions. There are no court proceedings required, no judge's approval needed, and no public filing of your estate information.

Your trust document specifies what should happen to your home—perhaps it directs the successor trustee to distribute it outright to your children, or to allow your spouse to live there for life before it passes to children, or to sell it and distribute the proceeds, or any other arrangement you've specified. The successor trustee follows these instructions, transferring the property to beneficiaries by deed (usually a trustee's deed) or selling it if directed, all without probate involvement. This process typically takes weeks or a few months rather than the year or more that probate often requires, and it's accomplished privately without public disclosure of your estate's details. Your beneficiaries receive their inheritance faster, with less expense, and with greater privacy than if the home had been in your individual name and forced through probate. Additionally, if you become incapacitated before death—perhaps due to dementia, stroke, or other serious illness—having your home in your trust means your successor trustee can immediately step in to manage the property, pay bills, arrange for maintenance, or even sell it to fund your care if necessary, all without requiring a court-appointed conservator or guardian. This seamless transition at death or incapacity is the payoff for the effort of transferring your home into your trust during your life. It reflects the biblical principle of planning ahead to benefit those we love. Proverbs 13:22 teaches that "a good person leaves an inheritance for their children's children," and by funding your trust properly, you ensure that inheritance actually reaches your descendants rather than being consumed by probate costs and delays. You transform your estate plan from mere words in a document into an effective structure that accomplishes your goals and blesses your family.

Common Mistakes to Avoid When Transferring Property to Your Trust

While using a quitclaim deed to transfer your home into your living trust is generally straightforward, several common mistakes can create problems if you're not careful. One frequent error is using your name inconsistently—if your current deed shows your name one way, you must use that exact name as the grantor on the quitclaim deed, even if it includes middle names, initials, or variations you don't normally use. Inconsistencies can create title problems that may require legal work to clean up later. Another common mistake is failing to include the complete legal description of your property, relying instead on just the street address. Street addresses aren't sufficient for real estate transfers and can make the deed legally ineffective.

Some people make the error of improperly naming the trust as grantee, perhaps leaving out the date of the trust, using an informal name instead of the official trust name, or forgetting to designate themselves as trustee. The grantee must be the trustee of the trust, not the trust itself (which is not a legal entity that can hold title), and the designation must be precise to avoid ambiguity. Another mistake is failing to record the deed after execution—some people prepare and sign the quitclaim deed but never take it to the county recorder's office, leaving their home's ownership technically unchanged despite their belief that they've funded their trust. Until the deed is recorded, the transfer isn't complete and won't be recognized by title companies, lenders, or courts. Some people also fail to notify their mortgage lender and homeowner's insurance company about the transfer, potentially creating problems if they need to refinance or file an insurance claim. A particularly serious mistake is transferring property subject to special programs or restrictions without checking whether the transfer is allowed—for example, some affordable housing programs, homesteading programs, or agricultural property tax programs prohibit transfers even to your own trust, and violating these restrictions could result in losing benefits or facing penalties. Always check program rules before transferring property with special status. Finally, some people transfer their primary residence into their trust but forget about other real property they own, leaving vacation homes, rental properties, or vacant land in their individual names where these assets will still go through probate despite having established a trust. Make sure you fund your trust with all significant assets, not just your primary residence. These mistakes reflect the danger of attempting complex legal procedures without adequate knowledge or professional guidance. Proverbs 11:14 wisely counsels, "For lack of guidance a nation falls, but victory is won through many advisers." While transferring property to a trust may seem simple, the many details and potential pitfalls make professional guidance valuable. Working with an experienced estate planning attorney ensures your transfer is done correctly, avoiding mistakes that could undermine your entire estate plan.

The Cost and Timeline for Transferring Your Home to Your Trust

Understanding the practical aspects of cost and timing helps set realistic expectations for the trust funding process. The costs associated with using a quitclaim deed to transfer your home into your living trust are generally modest, particularly compared to the expense of probate that you're avoiding by taking this step. If you work with an estate planning attorney to prepare your living trust, the cost of preparing the quitclaim deed to fund the trust is often included in the overall fee for trust preparation, which typically ranges from $1,500 to $4,000 or more depending on complexity and your location. If you already have a trust and just need a deed prepared later, attorneys typically charge $150 to $500 to prepare a quitclaim deed, depending on your area's rates.

The county recording fees for filing the deed are usually modest, ranging from $15 to $200 depending on the county and state, with most falling in the $20 to $50 range. Some states charge transfer taxes when property changes hands, but most specifically exempt transfers into revocable living trusts from such taxes, recognizing that no actual sale is occurring. However, verify your state's rules to avoid surprises. Title companies may charge a small fee if you request an endorsement to your title insurance policy confirming coverage continues with the property in trust, though many don't charge for this or include it in their estate planning services if they're handling your title work. Overall, you should expect total costs of $150 to $500 in most cases if you're just preparing and recording a deed for an existing trust, or costs included in your overall trust preparation fees of $1,500 to $4,000 if you're establishing a new trust. Regarding timeline, preparing a quitclaim deed takes very little time once you provide the necessary information—your attorney or title company can typically prepare the deed within a few days or even same-day in some cases. Execution simply requires scheduling a time to sign before a notary, which can happen immediately if your attorney has a notary in-office.

Recording the deed after execution typically happens within a few days of dropping it off at the county recorder's office, though some counties are faster than others. Overall, the entire process from deciding to transfer your home into your trust to having the recorded deed back in hand typically takes one to three weeks, with most of that time being scheduling and processing rather than actual work. This modest cost and short timeline makes procrastination inexcusable—if you've established a trust but haven't funded it yet, there's no good reason to delay this critical step. The biblical principle of not delaying in matters of importance applies here. Proverbs 3:27-28 instructs, "Do not withhold good from those to whom it is due, when it is in your power to act. Do not say to your neighbor, 'Come back tomorrow and I'll give it to you'—when you already have it with you." Your trust accomplishes nothing until it's funded, and funding it is in your power to accomplish quickly and inexpensively. Don't withhold this good from your family by procrastinating what you have the power to complete today.

Reversing the Transfer: Taking Property Back Out of Your Trust

One of the advantages of using a revocable living trust is that it's not permanent—you can always change your mind and take property back out of the trust if circumstances change or you decide you no longer want the trust structure. Removing property from your trust is essentially the reverse of the funding process and is also typically accomplished with a quitclaim deed. To transfer your home out of your trust back to your individual ownership, you prepare a quitclaim deed where you (as trustee of your trust) are the grantor, and you (as an individual) are the grantee. The deed might show the grantor as "John Robert Smith, Trustee of the John Robert Smith Revocable Living Trust dated January 15, 2024" and the grantee as simply "John Robert Smith."

You sign the deed in your capacity as trustee, have it notarized, and record it with the county just as you did when transferring property into the trust. Once recorded, you again own the property individually rather than through your trust. You would want to notify your mortgage lender and homeowner's insurance company about this change just as you did when you initially transferred to the trust, though the same federal law protection against triggering due-on-sale clauses applies in reverse—lenders cannot accelerate your loan when you transfer property out of your revocable trust back to yourself individually. Common reasons for taking property out of a trust include deciding to dissolve the trust entirely, refinancing your mortgage with a lender who insists property be in your individual name for underwriting purposes (though you can transfer it back into the trust after closing the refinance), or selling your home to a buyer whose title company or lender has concerns about purchasing from a trust. In the sale situation, you would transfer the property out of your trust back to yourself individually shortly before closing, then complete the sale as an individual to the buyer. This reversibility provides flexibility and ensures you're never locked into the trust structure if it no longer serves your needs. However, most people who transfer homes into trusts leave them there permanently, as the estate planning benefits typically outweigh any disadvantages, and the few situations requiring removal are usually temporary. This flexibility reflects the wisdom of structures that can adapt to changing circumstances. Proverbs 24:3-4 teaches, "By wisdom a house is built, and through understanding it is established; through knowledge its rooms are filled with rare and beautiful treasures." Part of wisdom in estate planning is building flexible structures that can be established when needed, adapted when circumstances change, and adjusted as understanding increases. A revocable trust funded with a quitclaim deed that can be reversed through another quitclaim deed exemplifies this adaptable wisdom, providing benefits while not permanently locking you into decisions that may need revision.

Conclusion: Making Your Trust Effective Through Proper Funding

Using a quitclaim deed to transfer your home into your living trust is one of the most important steps in the entire estate planning process, transforming your trust from merely words on paper into an effective legal structure that will actually accomplish your goals. This simple act of funding your trust with your most valuable asset—your home—ensures that your family will benefit from the probate avoidance, privacy, efficiency, and continuity that motivated you to establish the trust in the first place. The quitclaim deed is the perfect tool for this transfer precisely because its limitations don't matter when you're transferring property to yourself, while its simplicity and low cost make the funding process accessible and affordable.

As you move forward with transferring your home into your trust, remember that this act of planning and preparation is not merely a legal formality but an expression of love and responsibility toward those you care about. You're taking steps to ensure that when you're gone, your family won't face unnecessary delays, expenses, or complications in receiving their inheritance. You're providing for smooth management if you become incapacitated, protecting your interests when you can no longer protect them yourself. And you're demonstrating the kind of faithful stewardship that God calls us to exercise over everything He entrusts to our care. Luke 16:10 teaches, "Whoever can be trusted with very little can also be trusted with much, and whoever is dishonest with very little will also be dishonest with much." By faithfully executing the seemingly small task of properly funding your trust with a quitclaim deed, you demonstrate trustworthiness in stewardship that honors God and blesses your family. Don't let this critical step remain undone—if you have a living trust but haven't yet transferred your home into it, make this a priority. Contact your estate planning attorney or title company, have the quitclaim deed prepared, execute it properly, and record it with your county. Complete the funding process so your trust can fulfill its intended purpose of protecting and providing for those you love, both now and in the generations to come.

***

Section 3: How It Differs from Warranty Deeds

A warranty deed contains express promises from the grantor that they hold clear title to the property and that they will defend that title against any lawful claims. These covenants typically include assurances that the grantor has the right to convey the property, that the property is free of undisclosed encumbrances, and that the grantor will protect the grantee against future claims. This level of protection gives the buyer confidence and is especially important in sale transactions, reflecting the biblical value of honest assurance: "Let your 'Yes' be 'Yes,' and your 'No,' 'No'" (Matthew 5:37).

By contrast, a quitclaim deed conveys only whatever interest the grantor then possesses without any promises about the state of the title. If the grantor has perfect title, the quitclaim will transfer that interest; if the grantor's interest is limited, defective, or non-existent, the grantee receives only that limited interest and has no contractual warranty to rely upon. This absence of warranty makes the quitclaim deed faster and simpler for transfers between familiar parties but riskier for purchasers who need assurance. Scripture urges prudence in dealings: "The prudent sees danger and takes refuge; the simple go on and suffer for it" (Proverbs 27:12).

A warranty deed commonly leads to purchase situations where title searches and title insurance are standard practice, giving the buyer legal and financial recourse if a claim later arises. A quitclaim deed is often used for non-sale transfers—such as into a trust, between spouses, or among family members—where parties already know the title history and are less concerned about guarantees. The difference in customary practice underscores the biblical principle of stewardship and responsibility: when we represent or transfer what belongs to others, we must do so faithfully and transparently (Colossians 3:23).

Recording and post-transfer remedies also differ in practical effect. Recording a warranty deed places public notice of both the transfer and the warranties backing it, which reassures third parties and lenders. Recording a quitclaim deed gives public notice of the change in record title but carries no promise that the title is clear, leaving the grantee to resolve any latent defects. Because the law treats these instruments differently, careful documentation and appropriate protections—such as title insurance in sales—are acts of wise preparation: "For which of you, desiring to build a tower, does not first sit down and count the cost?" (Luke 14:28).

Ethically, choosing between the two deeds should reflect the nature of the transaction and the relationship among parties. Using a quitclaim deed to conceal defects or to mislead a buyer violates both civil law and moral integrity; honest dealing honors God and neighbors: "Whoever walks in integrity walks securely, but he who makes his ways crooked will be found out" (Proverbs 10:9). In short, warranty deeds offer promise and protection appropriate for arm's-length transfers, while quitclaim deeds offer speed and simplicity appropriate for transfers where warranties are unnecessary or undesired.

***

Section 4: When and Why Quitclaim Deeds Are Used in Trust Transfers

A quitclaim deed is most commonly used in trust transfers when the parties involved already have a relationship of trust and knowledge about the property's history—most typically when an owner is retitling a home into their own revocable living trust. The quitclaim deed's simplicity makes it an efficient procedural tool: it conveys whatever interest the grantor holds at the moment without the formal warranties of a sale. For homeowners who are funding their estate plan, this straightforward transfer aligns with the biblical call to orderly stewardship and preparation: "The plans of the diligent lead surely to abundance" (Proverbs 21:5). When the parties are the same person acting as grantor and trustee, the quitclaim deed is often the least cumbersome way to place the asset under the trust's ownership.

Practically, quitclaim deeds are used when speed, cost, and minimal formality matter—such as correcting clerical errors in a name on title, moving property between spouses after marriage, or transferring property into a trust the grantor controls. Because there is no exchange of value in these contexts and the parties typically understand the title history, the absence of warranties is acceptable. This pragmatism echoes Scripture's encouragement to act with wisdom and prudence: "For which of you, desiring to build a tower, does not first sit down and count the cost?" (Luke 14:28). Using the appropriate instrument for the right circumstance honors both legal sense and moral responsibility.

Quitclaim deeds are also favored when the goal is to avoid probate and ensure continuity of management if the grantor becomes incapacitated. By re-recording title in the name of the trust—often phrased as "Jane Doe, Trustee of the Jane Doe Living Trust dated [date]"—the property is positioned to pass according to the trust terms without court involvement. This preserves privacy for the family and reduces administrative burden for survivors, which reflects the biblical concern for protecting and providing for household affairs: "Let all things be done decently and in order" (1 Corinthians 14:40). The deed serves the trust's larger purpose of orderly transition and care.

However, the quitclaim deed's lack of warranties also explains when it is not appropriate: arm's-length sales or transfers where a buyer needs assurance of clear title should use a warranty deed and often involve title searches and insurance. Similarly, when substantial title problems or unknown encumbrances might exist, relying solely on a quitclaim could expose the grantee to risk. The biblical mandate for integrity and honesty in our dealings cautions against shortcuts that could harm others: "Whoever walks in integrity walks securely" (Proverbs 10:9). Choose instruments that reflect both the legal realities and the moral duty to do no harm.

Finally, timing and intent matter. Courts may set aside transfers intended to defraud creditors or evade legitimate obligations—so quitclaim transfers should never be used to conceal assets dishonestly. Proper timing, full disclosure where required, and consultation with competent counsel ensure that the deed fulfills its rightful purpose: to place assets into a trust as part of faithful stewardship and legacy planning. The wisdom of seeking good counsel is underscored in Scripture: "Plans fail for lack of counsel, but with many advisers they succeed" (Proverbs 15:22). When used rightly, a quitclaim deed is a humble but powerful instrument in stewarding what God has entrusted to us.

***

Section 5: Risks and Limitations

Transferring property into a trust and using instruments like quitclaim deeds can offer powerful benefits, but they also carry real risks that require sober consideration. One significant risk is title uncertainty: a quitclaim deed conveys only whatever interest the grantor has at the moment, without warranty. If there are undisclosed liens, easements, or defects in title, those problems remain and can surface later to disrupt your plans. Scripture calls us to prudence in planning: "The prudent sees danger and takes refuge" (Proverbs 27:12), and careful title review is that refuge.

Another limitation involves mortgages and lender rights. Most mortgages contain due-on-sale or acceleration clauses that, though often not enforced for transfers into a grantor's revocable living trust, can be triggered in some circumstances. Failure to address mortgage terms can create loan default risk or unexpected demands from a lender. The Bible urges responsible stewardship of obligations: "Let every person be fully responsible for their own conduct" (Galatians 6:5), which includes honoring contract terms and seeking counsel before transfer.

There is also the danger of transfers being set aside as fraudulent conveyances when done to defeat known creditors or during imminent litigation. Courts will unwind transfers made with dishonest intent, and statutes of limitations and look-back periods can expose late attempts to shield assets. Integrity is paramount: "Better is a poor person who walks in his integrity than one who is crooked in speech and is a fool" (Proverbs 19:1), so protective planning must never be a cover for evasion.

Tax and eligibility consequences are often overlooked. Moving assets into certain trusts can create gift tax implications, change estate tax exposure, or affect Medicaid or bankruptcy eligibility depending on timing and structure. Irrevocable trusts in particular can alter your taxable position and must be drafted with tax counsel. The wisdom of seeking advice is biblical: "Plans fail for lack of counsel, but with many advisers they succeed" (Proverbs 15:22).

Loss of control is a deliberate trade-off with irrevocable trusts: once assets are transferred, you generally cannot reclaim them or change terms without significant legal steps. For those who need flexibility, that permanence can be a hardship rather than a help. Scripture acknowledges the weight of commitment and the need for discernment: "Let your 'Yes' be 'Yes,' and your 'No,' 'No'" (Matthew 5:37), reminding us to choose covenantal steps intentionally.

Administrative errors and procedural missteps are practical limitations. Mistakes in naming the trust, using an incorrect legal description, failing to notarize or properly record the deed, or neglecting to update insurance and title records can negate the intended benefits and create confusion for heirs. Careful attention to detail mirrors the biblical call to stewardship: "For which of you, desiring to build a tower, does not first sit down and count the cost?" (Luke 14:28).

Finally, interpersonal and relational risks arise when family members or co-owners feel excluded or surprised by transfers. Beneficiary disputes, unclear successor trustee directions, or poor communication can fracture relationships and lead to litigation. The Scriptures encourage peaceable conduct and clear communication in family matters: "If possible, so far as it depends on you, live peaceably with all" (Romans 12:18). Transparent conversation and documented intent help preserve both legacy and relationships.

In sum, trusts and quitclaim deeds are useful instruments but not cure-alls. They require careful legal, tax, and relational planning; honest motives; and meticulous execution. When pursued with wisdom, counsel, and integrity, they become faithful tools for stewardship rather than sources of unintended harm.

Chapter 3:
Preparing for the Transfer

Preparing to transfer your home into a living trust begins with prayerful intention and careful organization. Before any document is signed, pause to clarify your goals for the trust: who will manage the property if you are unable, who will inherit it, and what conditions or protections you wish to include. This posture of thoughtful preparation echoes Scripture's counsel to plan wisely: "For which of you, desiring to build a tower, does not first sit down and count the cost?" (Luke 14:28). Clear purpose makes every subsequent step more faithful and effective.

Gathering the necessary documents is the next practical step. Collect the current deed, the mortgage note and statement if applicable, any existing title insurance policy, property tax records, homeowners insurance policy, and surveys or plats that describe the land. Also locate personal identification, Social Security numbers for relevant parties, and any prior estate planning documents such as wills or power of attorney forms. Having those papers on hand prevents delays and ensures the deed you prepare uses the exact legal description required for recording. The Bible values orderly stewardship: "The plans of the diligent lead surely to abundance" (Proverbs 21:5).

Choosing the trustee and naming beneficiaries demands both wisdom and humility. For revocable living trusts many grantors name themselves as trustee so they retain control during life, with a trusted successor trustee designated to step in on incapacity or death. Beneficiaries should be named clearly and with contingencies—alternate beneficiaries, splits between heirs, and instructions for minors or vulnerable recipients. This careful naming secures continuity and honors the command to provide for family: "If anyone does not provide for his relatives, and especially for members of his household, he has denied the faith" (1 Timothy 5:8).

Drafting the trust document requires precision and legal expertise. While templates can illustrate common provisions, a well-drafted trust tailored to your state's law, family dynamics, and tax considerations will avoid pitfalls. Important provisions to consider include trustee powers, incapacity management, distribution schedules, spendthrift protections, and successor trustee instructions. The drafting process should reflect honesty and foresight: "Commit your work to the Lord, and your plans will be established" (Proverbs 16:3). Seek counsel so that the trust's language aligns with your intentions and is enforceable where you live.

Ensuring the trust will be properly funded is a practical but often overlooked step. A trust exists only to the extent assets are titled in its name; merely drafting the trust without re-recording deeds leaves the property outside the trust and subject to probate. Plan the exact method of transfer—commonly a quitclaim or warranty deed naming the trust as grantee—confirm the trust name and date match the deed language precisely, and prepare to update related accounts (insurance, utilities, HOA records) to reflect the trust ownership where appropriate. The necessity of complete follow-through echoes the counsel to finish what you begin: "Whoever is slack in his work is a brother to him who destroys" (Proverbs 18:9).

Addressing mortgage, tax, and insurance implications rounds out preparation. Review mortgage documents for due-on-sale clauses and consult your lender or legal counsel about transfers into a revocable trust; update homeowner's insurance to list the trust or trustee as insured interest; notify your title insurance carrier if necessary; and understand any potential tax reporting or local transfer fee consequences. Being proactive avoids surprises and models integrity in obligations: "Let every person be subject to the governing authorities" (Romans 13:1). Practical, up-front attention protects both your estate plan and your witness.

Finally, assemble a clear, accessible file and communicate your plan to the successor trustee and key family members. Leave recorded copies of the trust and deed in a safe but retrievable place, and ensure the successor trustee knows where to find them and whom to contact for legal and financial matters. Transparent communication preserves relationships and eases transitions: "If possible, so far as it depends on you, live peaceably with all" (Romans 12:18). Thoughtful preparation now becomes a gift of order, peace, and provision for those who follow.

***

Section 1: Gathering Necessary Documents for Transferring Your Home into a Living Trust

The Foundation of a Smooth Transfer

Gathering the necessary documents is the practical foundation for a smooth transfer of your home into a living trust. While the concept of trust funding may seem straightforward, the actual execution requires careful assembly of various legal, financial, and administrative documents that establish current ownership, verify your identity, reveal any encumbrances or restrictions, and provide the information needed to prepare an accurate quitclaim deed. Approaching this document-gathering phase with thoroughness and organization sets the stage for a successful transfer that accomplishes your estate planning goals without creating problems or requiring later corrections. This preparatory work, though sometimes tedious, represents responsible stewardship and careful planning that will benefit your family for years to come.

Scripture commends orderly preparation and diligent planning in all our endeavors. Proverbs 21:5 teaches that "the plans of the diligent lead surely to abundance, but everyone who is hasty comes only to poverty." This wisdom applies directly to the document-gathering phase of trust funding—taking time to diligently locate, organize, and review all necessary papers leads to abundant benefits (a properly funded trust that avoids probate and protects your family), while hasty or incomplete preparation leads to poverty (problems, delays, expenses, and potentially a trust that fails to accomplish its purpose). As we explore each category of documents you'll need to gather, remember that this organizational work is not merely bureaucratic busywork but rather an expression of love for your family and faithfulness in managing what God has entrusted to your care.

Locating Your Current Deed: The Primary Document

Begin by locating the current deed to your property—this is the primary document that shows legal description and current ownership. Your deed is the legal instrument that transferred property ownership to you when you acquired it, and it contains essential information that must be replicated exactly in your new quitclaim deed. The most critical element is the legal description, which is a precise technical description of your property's boundaries and location that goes far beyond a simple street address. Legal descriptions might reference metes and bounds (measurements and directional bearings from a starting point), lot and block numbers in a recorded subdivision plat, or government survey descriptions using townships, ranges, and sections. Whatever form your legal description takes, it must be copied exactly onto your quitclaim deed, as even minor errors can create ambiguity about which property is being transferred or render the deed legally insufficient.

Your deed also shows exactly how your name appears on title—including full legal names, middle names or initials, and any variations. This is important because when you prepare your quitclaim deed, you must list yourself as grantor using the exact same name that appears on your current deed. Variations or inconsistencies can create title problems that require legal work to resolve later. If you purchased your home recently, you likely received your deed at closing or shortly thereafter. If you've owned your home for many years, you may need to search for the deed among your important papers, in a safe deposit box, or in your filing system. If you cannot locate your original deed, don't worry—you can obtain a certified copy from the county recorder's office or register of deeds where your property is located. Most counties now offer online access to recorded documents, allowing you to search by your name or property address and download or print copies of your deed. Some counties charge small fees for certified copies while others provide access free or for minimal cost. Without the exact legal description from the recorded deed, any new deed can be rejected by the recording office or create ambiguity about what property is being transferred, so treat the recorded deed as the authoritative source rather than relying on property tax statements, insurance policies, or other documents that may contain abbreviated or informal property descriptions.

This careful attention to getting the foundational document right reflects biblical principles about building on solid foundations. Jesus concluded the Sermon on the Mount with the parable of two builders in

Matthew 7:24-27, contrasting the wise builder who constructed his house on rock with the foolish builder who built on sand. When storms came, the house on rock stood firm while the house on sand collapsed. Your current deed is the rock foundation for your trust transfer—building your quitclaim deed on accurate information from the recorded deed ensures your transfer will stand firm, while building on incomplete or inaccurate information creates a foundation that may fail when tested later.

Collecting Mortgage Documents and Loan Statements

Next, collect mortgage documents and loan statements if the property carries a mortgage. The mortgage note and the recorded mortgage or deed of trust show lender rights and clauses (such as due-on-sale provisions) that may affect how and when you transfer title. Your mortgage note is the promissory note you signed when borrowing money, detailing the loan amount, interest rate, payment terms, and your promise to repay. The mortgage or deed of trust is the security instrument that gives the lender a lien on your property as collateral for the loan. While federal law (the Garn-St. Germain Act) protects transfers to revocable living trusts from triggering due-on-sale clauses, having your mortgage documents available allows your attorney to verify this protection applies to your specific loan and to advise whether any lender notification is required by your loan agreement.

Having recent loan statements ready allows counsel to advise whether lender notification or other steps are advisable. Current statements show your loan balance, payment status, and lender contact information. Some attorneys recommend notifying lenders about trust transfers even though it's not legally required, as a matter of transparency and to maintain good relationships. Your loan documents and statements make this communication straightforward if you choose to pursue it. Additionally, if you're considering refinancing in the future, knowing your current loan terms helps evaluate whether any mortgage complications might arise from the trust transfer. Most lenders have no issue with properties held in revocable living trusts, but having documentation ready addresses any questions before they become problems.

Honoring obligations is a matter of integrity, as Galatians 6:5 reminds us: "Each one should carry their own load." Your mortgage represents a financial obligation you've undertaken, and maintaining awareness of its terms and status while making ownership changes demonstrates responsibility and integrity. Romans 13:7-8 similarly instructs, "Give to everyone what you owe them: If you owe taxes, pay taxes; if revenue, then revenue; if respect, then respect; if honor, then honor. Let no debt remain outstanding, except the continuing debt to love one another." Gathering your mortgage documents and ensuring your trust transfer doesn't create loan complications is part of giving what you owe—honoring your commitment to your lender by maintaining transparency and ensuring the transfer doesn't violate your loan agreement. This integrity in financial matters honors God and maintains your reputation and relationships.

Obtaining Title Insurance Policies and Prior Title Work

Title insurance policies, surveys or plats, and any recent title search reports are also essential documents to gather. Title insurance reveals whether prior title issues, liens, easements, or exceptions exist that must be addressed before or after transfer. When you purchased your home, you likely obtained an owner's title insurance policy that protects you against title defects that existed at the time of purchase but weren't discovered during the title search. This policy remains valuable and should be located and reviewed. The policy's Schedule B lists exceptions to coverage—items like easements, covenants, restrictions, and other matters that affect your title but aren't covered by the insurance. Understanding these exceptions helps you know what encumbrances will transfer with the property into your trust.

Additionally, your title insurance policy provides important contact information for the title company that issued it, which you'll want to notify about your trust transfer to confirm that coverage continues with the property now held in trust rather than in your individual name. Most title companies routinely continue coverage when property is transferred into the owner's revocable living trust, but obtaining written confirmation provides documentation and peace of mind. If you've had any title work done more recently than your original purchase—perhaps when refinancing or for other purposes—gather those title search reports or title commitments as well, as they may reveal more current information about liens, judgments, or other title matters. Surveys and plats confirm boundary lines and recorded easements that could affect use or value. A survey is a professional measurement and mapping of your property showing boundary lines, improvements, easements, encroachments, and other physical features. A plat is a recorded map of a subdivision showing lot lines, streets, and common areas. These documents help verify that the legal description on your deed accurately describes the physical property and reveal any boundary issues, easement locations, or encroachments that might affect your property's value or use.

Addressing these items up front prevents surprises and models the biblical wisdom to foresee pitfalls. Proverbs 27:12 teaches, "The prudent see danger and take refuge, but the simple keep going and pay the penalty." Reviewing your title insurance and survey before transferring property to your trust is exactly this kind of prudent seeing of danger—discovering any title defects, boundary problems, or other issues while you can address them proactively rather than having them surface later as penalties paid through complications, disputes, or reduced property value. Proverbs 22:3 makes the same point: "The prudent see danger and take refuge, but the simple keep going and suffer for it." Being prudent with your property transfer means gathering and reviewing title documents to identify any dangers or complications before they create suffering for you or your family.

Assembling Administrative and Identity Documents

Administrative and identity documents matter too: bring photo identification, Social Security numbers for relevant parties, homestead or property tax records, utility bills, homeowners association contact information, and the current homeowners insurance policy. These items help with notarization, recording, insurance updates, and verifying ownership details. Photo identification—such as a driver's license or passport—is required for notarization of your signature on the quitclaim deed. The notary must verify your identity before notarizing, and acceptable forms of identification vary by state but typically include government-issued photo IDs. If your spouse or other co-owners will also sign the deed, they'll need their identification as well.

Social Security numbers may be required for certain recording offices, particularly if you're claiming exemption from transfer taxes or documenting that the transfer qualifies for special treatment. Having Social

Security numbers readily available expedites paperwork completion. Homestead or property tax records serve multiple purposes. If you currently claim a homestead exemption or other property tax benefits, you'll want to ensure these continue after transferring property to your trust. Many jurisdictions automatically continue homestead exemptions when property is transferred to revocable living trusts, but some require filing updated forms. Having your current property tax information available allows you to verify what exemptions you're receiving and what steps are necessary to maintain them post-transfer. Property tax records also provide your property's parcel number or tax identification number, which may be needed for recording purposes.

Utility bills, homeowners association contact information, and the current homeowners insurance policy are administrative matters that need updating after your trust transfer. Your homeowners insurance policy must be updated to reflect that the property is now owned by your trust rather than by you individually. The typical updated designation would be "[Your Name], Trustee of [Trust Name] dated [Date]." Failing to update your insurance policy could create claim complications if you have a loss and the property ownership on the policy doesn't match the actual ownership per county records. Updating insurance to reflect trust ownership is a crucial step to keep coverage intact, reflecting the call to be faithful stewards of what is entrusted to us. As 1 Corinthians 4:2 states, "Moreover, it is required of stewards that they be found faithful." Maintaining proper insurance coverage by ensuring your policy accurately reflects property ownership demonstrates faithful stewardship—protecting what God has entrusted to your care rather than allowing gaps or errors that could jeopardize your family's security. Similarly, notifying utility companies and homeowners associations about the ownership change, while not legally required, demonstrates thoroughness and prevents confusion about billing, communications, or association matters.

Reviewing Prior Estate Planning Documents

If you have prior estate planning documents—wills, powers of attorney, prior trusts, or marital agreements—include them in your packet. These documents reveal competing provisions or beneficiary designations that could conflict with the trust's goals and should be reconciled before recording a deed. Your will, for instance, might contain provisions about who should inherit your home that differ from or contradict the beneficiary designations in your trust. Since your trust now owns the home (after transfer), your will's provisions about the home become inapplicable, but reviewing both documents together ensures you're aware of any discrepancies and can make intentional decisions about which provisions should govern.

Powers of attorney grant someone authority to act on your behalf in financial or health care matters, and reviewing these documents helps clarify who has authority to do what. Once your home is in your trust, your successor trustee will have authority to manage it if you become incapacitated, but your financial power of attorney might also grant someone authority over trust assets. Understanding how these documents interact prevents confusion and conflict if incapacity occurs. If you previously established a trust—even years ago—that you're now replacing or modifying, having that prior trust available helps ensure you're properly revoking or amending it and that no conflicting provisions remain. Some people establish multiple trusts for different purposes, and reviewing all of them together helps ensure they work harmoniously rather than creating contradictions. Marital agreements such as prenuptial or postnuptial agreements may contain provisions about property ownership, division, or inheritance that affect how you should hold property in trust. These agreements might require certain property to remain in individual names, to be divided in specific ways, or to pass to particular beneficiaries. Reviewing them before transferring property ensures your trust transfer doesn't violate any marital agreement obligations.

Legal harmony avoids family confusion later and exemplifies careful counsel. Proverbs 15:22 teaches, "Plans fail for lack of counsel, but with many advisers they succeed." Gathering and reviewing all your estate planning documents together with qualified counsel ensures your various planning instruments work together harmoniously rather than creating contradictions that undermine your goals. This comprehensive approach demonstrates the kind of careful planning that leads to success rather than the fragmented approach that leads to failure. Additionally, Proverbs 11:14 states, "For lack of guidance a nation falls, but victory is won through many advisers." Having legal counsel review your various estate planning documents together provides the guidance that prevents your plan from falling apart and achieves victory in your estate planning goals. Don't assume all your documents automatically work together simply because they exist—actively review them to ensure harmony and address any conflicts.

Preparing Practical Closing Materials and Organization

Finally, prepare practical closing materials: a checklist of required signatures, notary requirements for your state, and the address and recording rules of the county recorder's office where the property sits. Different states have varying requirements for deed execution. Some require only the grantor's signature to be notarized, while others require witness signatures in addition to notarization. Some states have specific forms or language that must be included on deeds. Researching your state's requirements and preparing a checklist ensures nothing is overlooked when you execute the quitclaim deed. Your attorney or title company will typically know these requirements, but being informed yourself provides an additional check.

County recorder's offices also have specific requirements about document formatting, fee schedules, and submission procedures. Some counties accept only certain paper sizes or ink colors, require specific margins, charge different fees based on page count, or have particular indexing requirements. Some now accept electronic recording while others require physical document submission. Knowing these requirements in advance prevents your deed from being rejected and having to be resubmitted with corrections. Most county recorder websites provide detailed information about recording requirements and fees, or you can call their office for guidance. Keep digital scans and physical copies organized, and provide the successor trustee with a clear copy of the trust document and the planned recording steps. Create both digital and physical filing systems for all documents related to your trust and property transfer. Scan every document and organize digital copies in clearly labeled folders on your computer or cloud storage. This provides backup if physical copies are lost and makes it easy to share documents electronically with attorneys, title companies, or successor trustees when needed.

Physical copies should be organized in binders or file folders with clear labeling and tab dividers for easy reference. Store originals securely but make sure a trusted successor knows access procedures so the family is not left scrambling. Your original trust document, recorded quitclaim deed, title insurance policy, and other critical documents should be stored in a secure location such as a fireproof safe in your home, a safe deposit box at a bank, or with your attorney. However, security must be balanced with accessibility—if documents are so secure that your family can't access them when needed, you've created problems rather than solved them. Make sure your successor trustee, spouse, or trusted family member knows where original documents are stored and has the necessary keys, combinations, or access permissions to retrieve them if you die or become incapacitated. Consider leaving a detailed letter of instruction that lists where all important documents are located and how to access them, along with contact information for your attorney, financial advisor, and other professionals who can assist your family.

The care you take in these preparations is an act of love and provision for those you care about most. Proverbs 13:22 reminds us, "A good person leaves an inheritance for their children's children, but a sinner's wealth is stored up for the righteous." Organizing your documents thoroughly and ensuring your family can access them when needed is part of leaving that inheritance—not just the property itself, but also the organized information and clear instructions that make it easy for your family to benefit from what you've provided. This practical expression of love reflects God's own careful provision for His children, as Jesus taught in Matthew 6:25-26: "Therefore I tell you, do not worry about your life, what you will eat or drink; or about your body, what you will wear. Is not life more than food, and the body more than clothes? Look at the birds of the air; they do not sow or reap or store in barns, and yet your heavenly Father feeds them. Are you not much more valuable than they?" God carefully provides for even the birds, and we who are made in His image should likewise carefully provide for our families through diligent planning and thorough preparation.

Creating a Master Document Checklist

To ensure you've gathered everything necessary for a smooth trust transfer, create a master checklist that you can work through systematically. Under "Property Documents," include: current recorded deed to the property, prior deeds if there were multiple transfers, legal description verification from county records, recent property survey or plat if available, and property tax statements showing assessed value and exemptions. Under "Mortgage and Lien Information," include: mortgage note and deed of trust or mortgage document, recent mortgage statements, information about any home equity loans or lines of credit, documentation of any other liens such as mechanic's liens or judgment liens, and payoff information if you plan to satisfy loans before transfer.

Under "Title Insurance and Title Work," include: owner's title insurance policy from when you purchased, any endorsements to the title policy issued over the years, title commitment or preliminary title report if you have recent title work, title search reports or abstracts of title if available, and contact information for the title insurance company. Under "Trust and Estate Planning Documents," include: the executed original trust document with all amendments, any prior trusts that are being revoked or replaced, your current will, durable power of attorney for financial matters, health care power of attorney and living will, and any marital agreements that address property rights. Under "Administrative and Personal Information," include: government-issued photo identification for all parties who will sign, Social Security numbers for relevant parties, homeowners insurance policy and agent contact information, utility account information and contact details, homeowners association documents if applicable, and proof of residence such as recent utility bills.

Under "Recording and Processing," include: contact information and recording requirements for the county recorder's office, fee schedule for recording deeds in your county, notary requirements for your state, forms required by your county or state for claiming transfer tax exemptions if applicable, and checklist of all required signatures and notarizations. Finally, under "Communication and Updates," include: contact information for your attorney or legal counsel, contact information for your financial advisor or accountant, contact information for your successor trustee, list of all entities that need to be notified of the ownership change such as mortgage lender and insurance company, and timeline for completing each step of the process. Working through this comprehensive checklist systematically ensures you don't overlook any necessary documents and provides a clear roadmap for completing the trust transfer efficiently. This organized approach reflects the biblical principle of doing things orderly and properly. As 1 Corinthians 14:40 instructs, "But everything should be done in a fitting and orderly way." Creating and following a systematic checklist is exactly this kind of orderly approach that ensures important details aren't missed and the process proceeds smoothly to successful completion.

The Role of Professional Assistance in Document Gathering

While you can gather many documents yourself, don't hesitate to seek professional assistance when needed. Estate planning attorneys typically provide document checklists as part of their trust preparation services and can help you understand what's needed and where to find it. They may also order title searches or surveys on your behalf, obtaining documents you might not know how to access. Title companies are experienced in gathering property-related documents and can often pull copies of your deed, mortgage information, and prior title work from their records or county databases. They can verify legal descriptions, confirm current ownership, and identify any title issues that need addressing before transfer.

Real estate professionals, while not typically involved in trust funding, can sometimes provide copies of documents from when you purchased your home if you worked with them on the transaction. Your mortgage lender can provide copies of loan documents and current statements, and most lenders have online portals where you can access and download this information yourself. County offices—including the recorder's office, assessor's office, and treasurer's office—are public service agencies that can help you obtain copies of recorded documents, property tax information, and other public records. Most county offices are helpful to citizens seeking information about their own properties, and many now offer online access to records that you can search and print yourself. The investment in professional assistance for document gathering is often money well spent. While it costs more than doing everything yourself, professionals can complete the work faster, with greater accuracy, and with less stress on your part. They know what to look for, where to find it, and how to interpret what they find. This frees you to focus on decision-making rather than getting bogged down in document searches.

The biblical principle of using skilled workers for important tasks supports seeking professional help. In Exodus 31:1-6, God specifically called Bezalel and filled him with skill, ability, and knowledge for crafting the tabernacle. God chose to work through skilled craftsmen rather than having everyone attempt complex work they weren't equipped to do well. Similarly, estate planning involves legal and financial complexities where skilled professionals can ensure work is done correctly. Proverbs 12:15 teaches, "The way of fools seems right to them, but the wise listen to advice." Seeking professional assistance in gathering and interpreting documents is listening to advice rather than assuming you know everything needed. This wisdom can save you from costly mistakes that arise from misunderstanding documents or overlooking important information.

Conclusion: Building on a Strong Documentary Foundation

Gathering the necessary documents for transferring your home into your living trust may feel tedious or overwhelming, but this preparatory work is absolutely essential for a successful transfer. These documents provide the information needed to prepare an accurate quitclaim deed, reveal any issues that must be addressed before or during the transfer, enable you to update insurance and other administrative matters properly, and create an organized record for your successor trustee and family. The time and effort you invest in thorough document gathering will pay dividends in the form of a smooth transfer process, proper legal protections, and peace of mind that everything has been done correctly.

As you work through this document-gathering phase, remember that you're not just collecting papers—you're demonstrating faithful stewardship of the resources God has entrusted to you and expressing love for the family you'll eventually leave behind. The diligence you show in organizing these documents, the care you take in reviewing them for accuracy and completeness, and the wisdom you exercise in seeking professional guidance when needed all reflect a heart committed to responsible management of blessings and intentional provision for loved ones. Proverbs 24:27 counsels, "Put your outdoor work in order and get your fields ready; after that, build your house." Gathering your documents is precisely this kind of preparatory work—getting your fields ready before building. Only after you've assembled the necessary information should you proceed to the actual deed preparation and execution. This patient, thorough approach to foundation-building ensures that what you construct will stand firm and accomplish its intended purposes for generations to come. Take the time to gather documents carefully, organize them systematically, and review them thoroughly. Your family will thank you for the clarity, completeness, and care reflected in your preparation.

***

Section 2: Documents and Instructional Process for Transferring a Home into a Living Trust

Required documents

Original recorded deed (to copy legal description exactly).

Proposed deed to record (quitclaim or warranty deed form drafted with trust as grantee).

Living trust document (certified copy or trustee certification if you prefer not to record the entire trust).

Mortgage statement and note (to check lender clauses).

Title insurance policy and title report (to identify liens, exceptions, easements).

Homeowners insurance policy (for updating insured party).

Property tax records / parcel number (for recorder's office and tax authority).

Photo ID for grantor(s) (required for notary).

Notary acknowledgment or jurat form (state-specific notarization block).

Any required witness signature forms (if your state requires witnesses).

Power of attorney (if applicable) (if someone signs on grantor's behalf).

Closing/transfer checklist (internal checklist of steps, contacts, and deadlines).

Step-by-step instructional process

Confirm trust is valid and up to date

Verify the trust name, date, grantor and trustee language exactly match what will appear on the deed.

If you plan to remain trustee of a revocable trust, ensure the trust expressly allows you to hold real property.

Obtain the exact legal description from the recorded deed

Use the recorded deed or county recorder's copy; do not rely on street address alone.

Choose the appropriate deed form

For retitling to your own revocable trust, a quitclaim deed is common; for other transfers consider a warranty deed.

Draft grantee wording precisely: for example, "Jane Doe, Trustee of the Jane Doe Revocable Trust dated January 1, 20XX."

Draft the deed and have it reviewed

Prepare deed with correct grantor/grantee names, legal description, consideration clause (often nominal), and signing blocks.

Have an estate attorney or title professional review for state-specific requirements and to confirm no conflicting provisions.

Check mortgage/lender implications

Review mortgage documents for due-on-sale provisions and consult lender if uncertain. Federal law often permits transfers to a revocable living trust for estate planning, but lender policies vary.

Arrange execution and notarization

Sign the deed in front of a notary; obtain any required witness signatures per state law.

If signing by power of attorney, ensure the POA document is valid for real estate transfers and is presented to the notary.

Record the deed at the county recorder's office

Submit the original signed and notarized deed to the recorder in the county where the property is located.

Pay recording fees and any transfer taxes or documentary stamp requirements.

Request a certified or stamped copy of the recorded instrument for your trust file.

Update related records and insurance

Notify your homeowners insurance company and update the policy to reflect the trust or trustee as an insured interest.

Notify your title insurance company if applicable; confirm continued coverage.

Update HOA records, utility accounts, and tax billing address if needed.

Verify successful funding of the trust

Confirm the county records show the trust as owner and keep the stamped recorded deed with your trust documents.

Ensure the property is listed in your trust schedules (if you maintain one).

Provide successor trustee access and documentation

Place a copy of the trust, the recorded deed, contact details for your attorney and financial advisor, and instructions in a secure location known to the successor trustee.

Follow up with professional reviews

Have an attorney confirm the transfer is complete and consistent with estate tax, Medicaid planning, or other financial goals.

Periodically (every 3–5 years or after major life events) review trust funding and beneficiary designations.

Practical tips and common pitfalls

Always use the exact trust name and date on the deed; small errors can create problems when administering the trust.

Do not cancel homeowners insurance before confirming the trust is recorded and accepted by the insurer.

If there is an active lien, pending litigation, or known creditor, consult counsel—transfers can be challenged if done to defraud creditors.

Keep digital scans plus original recorded copies in a secure place and provide clear instructions to your successor trustee.

Step-by-Step Instructional Process for Transferring Your Home into a Living Trust

A Clear Roadmap for Trust Funding

Transferring your home into a living trust requires more than just good intentions and assembled documents—it demands a systematic, step-by-step process that ensures each critical element is addressed properly and in the correct sequence. While the overall concept is straightforward, the practical execution involves numerous details that, if overlooked or performed incorrectly, can undermine your entire estate plan or create complications for your family later. This comprehensive instructional process provides a clear roadmap from beginning to end, guiding you through each phase of the transfer with attention to both legal requirements and practical wisdom. Following this structured approach protects you from common pitfalls, ensures compliance with applicable laws and regulations, and gives you confidence that your trust funding has been completed correctly and completely.

The biblical principle of careful, orderly work applies powerfully to this process. Proverbs 21:5 teaches that "the plans of the diligent lead to profit as surely as haste leads to poverty." Transferring your home into your trust is precisely the kind of undertaking where diligence—careful attention to each step in proper sequence—leads to profitable results, while haste that skips steps or rushes through details leads to poverty in the form of legal problems, family confusion, or failed estate planning. Similarly, Luke 14:28-30 records Jesus teaching about counting the cost before building: "Suppose one of you wants to build a tower. Won't you first sit down and estimate the cost to see if you have enough money to complete it? For if you lay the foundation and are not able to finish it, everyone who sees it will ridicule you, saying, 'This person began to build and wasn't able to finish.'" Following this systematic process is your way of counting the cost and ensuring you can complete what you've started, avoiding the metaphorical ridicule of a trust that was established but never properly funded and therefore fails to protect your family as intended.

Step One: Confirm Your Trust is Valid and Up to Date

The first critical step in transferring your home into your living trust is to verify that the trust itself is properly established, legally valid, and current with your wishes. Before you can transfer property into a trust, the trust must actually exist as a legal entity, created through a properly executed trust document that meets your state's legal requirements. Verify the trust name, date, grantor and trustee language exactly as they appear in the trust document, because these precise details must be replicated on your quitclaim deed. Any discrepancies between the trust document and the deed can create confusion about whether the property is truly held in the intended trust, potentially causing problems when your successor trustee tries to administer the trust after your death or incapacity.

If you plan to remain trustee of a revocable trust (which is typical), ensure the trust document expressly allows you to hold real property. Most living trusts include broad language authorizing the trustee to acquire, hold, manage, and dispose of real estate, but reviewing this provision confirms your trust has the necessary authority. Additionally, review the trust's beneficiary designations to confirm they still reflect your current wishes. Life circumstances change—marriages, divorces, births, deaths, estrangements, and reconciliations all affect who you want to inherit your property. If your trust was established years ago but your family situation has changed significantly, this is the time to amend the trust to reflect current realities before transferring your most valuable asset into it. Also verify that your trust hasn't been inadvertently revoked or superseded by later documents. If you created a will after establishing your trust, check whether the will contains language that might revoke prior trusts or conflict with trust provisions. Finally, ensure all required signatures, notarizations, and witness signatures were properly completed when the trust was originally established. A trust document that wasn't properly executed may not be legally valid, and transferring property into an invalid trust accomplishes nothing.

This foundational verification step reflects the biblical principle of building on solid ground. In Matthew 7:24-26, Jesus contrasts two builders: "Therefore everyone who hears these words of mine and puts them into practice is like a wise man who built his house on the rock. The rain came down, the streams rose, and the winds blew and beat against that house; yet it did not fall, because it had its foundation on the rock. But everyone who hears these words of mine and does not put them into practice is like a foolish man who built his house on sand." Your trust document is the rock foundation for your estate plan. Verifying its validity and current relevance before building the rest of your plan on it is the wise approach that ensures your estate plan will withstand future storms rather than collapsing when tested.

Step Two: Obtain the Exact Legal Description from Your Recorded Deed

Once you've confirmed your trust is valid and current, the next critical step is obtaining the exact legal description from your recorded deed. Use the recorded deed or a certified copy from the county recorder's office as your authoritative source; do not rely on street address alone or on property descriptions from tax statements, insurance policies, or other informal sources. Street addresses are convenient for mail delivery and general identification, but they're legally insufficient for real estate transfers. Properties are legally identified through technical descriptions that might reference lot and block numbers in recorded subdivisions, metes and bounds descriptions using precise measurements and compass directions, or government survey descriptions using townships, ranges, sections, and quarter-sections.

Your legal description might be several paragraphs long and include technical language about bearings, distances, monuments, and reference points. Every word, number, punctuation mark, and formatting detail matters—even seemingly minor variations can create ambiguity about which property is being transferred or render the deed legally defective. When you prepare your quitclaim deed, you'll copy this legal description exactly, character for character, from the recorded deed onto the new deed. Some people find it helpful to type the legal description separately first, then carefully proofread it against the original before incorporating it into the deed form. Others prefer to scan the legal description from the recorded deed and have it digitally inserted into the new deed to eliminate transcription errors, though you must still verify the digital copy matches the original exactly.

If your recorded deed contains obvious errors in the legal description—perhaps referencing the wrong lot number or containing mathematical inconsistencies in a metes and bounds description—consult with an attorney about whether a corrective deed should be recorded before transferring to your trust. It's better to address title issues now while you're actively working on the property rather than leaving problems for your successor trustee to discover and resolve after you're gone. This meticulous attention to accurate legal descriptions reflects the biblical principle of precision in important matters. In the Old Testament, detailed specifications were given for constructing the tabernacle and temple, with precise measurements, materials, and instructions. Exodus 25:9 records God saying, "Make this tabernacle and all its furnishings exactly like the pattern I will show you." While copying a legal description may seem less spiritually significant than building God's house, the principle applies—in matters of importance, exact adherence to specifications prevents problems and ensures the intended result is achieved.

Step Three: Choose the Appropriate Deed Form and Draft Precisely

With your trust confirmed and legal description in hand, you're ready to choose the appropriate deed form for your transfer. For retitling property to your own revocable living trust, a quitclaim deed is the common and appropriate choice, as discussed extensively in previous sections. The quitclaim deed's lack of warranties isn't problematic when you're transferring property to yourself in a different legal capacity, and its simplicity and lower cost make it ideal for this purpose. For transfers to others or in situations requiring warranties, you would consider warranty deeds or grant deeds instead, but for typical trust funding, a quitclaim deed is standard.

Draft the grantee wording precisely, using the exact trust name and date from your trust document. The typical format is: "[Your Name], Trustee of the [Trust Name] dated [Month Day, Year]." For example: "Jane Doe, Trustee of the Jane Doe Revocable Living Trust dated January 1, 2024." Some attorneys add "and his/her successors in trust" after the trustee designation to clarify that future successor trustees will also have authority over the property, though this is optional. The grantor designation should match exactly how your name appears on the current recorded deed. If your current deed shows "Jane Marie Doe," use that exact name as grantor even if you normally go by "Jane Doe" or "Jane M. Doe." This consistency prevents title companies and future buyers from questioning whether "Jane Doe" and "Jane Marie Doe" are the same person.

Draft the complete deed including all required elements: a title or heading identifying it as a quitclaim deed, the grantor's name exactly as shown on current title, the grantee designation with precise trust name and date, a consideration clause (often stating "for good and valuable consideration" or "transfer to living trust" since no money is changing hands), the complete legal description copied exactly from your recorded deed, a granting clause using appropriate quitclaim language such as "does hereby quitclaim and convey," any required state-specific language or clauses, the grantor's signature line, a notary acknowledgment block appropriate for your state, and witness signature lines if required by your state. Different states have different requirements for deed language and execution, so use a form appropriate for your jurisdiction or have an attorney prepare the deed to ensure compliance. This careful drafting reflects the principle from Colossians 3:23: "Whatever you do, work at it with all your heart, as working for the Lord, not for human masters." Preparing your deed carefully and precisely, treating this work as though you're doing it for the Lord rather than merely as a bureaucratic task, ensures you do it right and honors both God and your family.

Step Four: Have the Deed Reviewed by a Professional

After drafting your deed, resist the temptation to immediately execute and record it. Instead, have an estate attorney or title professional review it for state-specific requirements and to confirm no conflicting provisions exist. Even if you used a form from a reputable source or a deed preparation service, professional review provides an additional layer of protection against errors. An experienced attorney will verify that the deed includes all elements required by your state's laws, that the language is legally sufficient to accomplish the intended transfer, that the legal description is accurate and complete, that the grantor and grantee designations are proper, that the notary block and witness requirements match your state's formalities, and that the transfer doesn't conflict with other estate planning documents or create unintended consequences.

The attorney can also advise on any special considerations for your situation. For instance, if you're in a community property state, the deed might need specific language preserving community property character. If you have a spouse and are transferring jointly-owned property, the attorney will ensure both spouses are properly designated as grantors. If there are unusual circumstances—such as life estate interests, rights of first refusal, or other encumbrances—the attorney will address how these affect the transfer. This professional review typically costs a few hundred dollars, a modest investment compared to the cost of correcting problems later or the disaster of discovering after your death that the transfer was never legally effective. Many estate planning attorneys include deed review as part of their overall trust preparation fees, so if you had an attorney prepare your trust, they should review the funding deed as well.

The biblical wisdom of seeking counsel strongly supports this professional review step. Proverbs 15:22 teaches, "Plans fail for lack of counsel, but with many advisers they succeed." Having your deed reviewed by an experienced professional is precisely the kind of counsel that causes plans to succeed rather than fail. Proverbs 11:14 similarly states, "For lack of guidance a nation falls, but victory is won through many advisers." While you're not leading a nation, you are stewarding your family's future, and victory in that stewardship comes through seeking skilled advisers who can identify problems you might miss. Proverbs 12:15 adds, "The way of fools seems right to them, but the wise listen to advice." Even if your deed looks perfect to you, the wise approach is listening to professional advice rather than relying solely on your own judgment in matters requiring specialized knowledge.

Step Five: Check Mortgage and Lender Implications

Before executing your deed, carefully review your mortgage documents for due-on-sale provisions and consider whether you should notify your lender of the transfer. Federal law—specifically the Garn-St. Germain Depository Institutions Act of 1982—protects certain transfers from triggering due-on-sale clauses, including transfers to a revocable living trust where the borrower remains a beneficiary and continues occupying the property as their principal residence. This means your lender cannot legally accelerate your loan or demand full payment simply because you transferred your home into your own living trust for estate planning purposes. However, reviewing your specific mortgage documents confirms this protection applies and helps you understand any notification requirements your loan agreement might contain.

Some mortgage documents require borrowers to notify the lender of any ownership changes, even those protected by federal law. While violating this notification requirement typically doesn't give the lender grounds to accelerate the loan (thanks to federal protection), maintaining a good relationship with your lender and complying with contractual obligations reflects integrity. Consider sending a brief letter to your lender informing them that you're transferring your property into your revocable living trust for estate planning purposes, that you remain the trustee and beneficiary and will continue occupying the property as your principal residence, and that this transfer is protected under federal law from triggering any due-on-sale provisions. Include a copy of the recorded deed and relevant pages of your trust showing you as trustee and beneficiary.

Most lenders will acknowledge the notification and note it in their files without taking any action regarding your loan.

If you have any concerns about your lender's potential reaction or if your loan documents contain unusual provisions, consult with your attorney before proceeding. In very rare cases where mortgage documents contain problematic clauses or lenders have reputations for causing difficulties despite federal protections, your attorney can advise on the best approach—whether to proceed with notification, transfer without notification (if no notification requirement exists in the loan documents), or address the situation differently. This careful attention to contractual obligations reflects biblical teaching about integrity and honoring commitments. Romans 13:8 instructs, "Let no debt remain outstanding, except the continuing debt to love one another." While this verse addresses paying off debts generally, it reflects a principle of taking financial obligations seriously. Your mortgage is a debt, and honoring its terms by understanding how your trust transfer affects it demonstrates the integrity Scripture calls us to maintain. Psalm 15:4 praises those who keep their oaths "even when it hurts," and while transferring to your trust shouldn't hurt, the principle of keeping commitments regardless of convenience applies to reviewing loan obligations and complying with notification requirements even when doing so takes extra effort.

Step Six: Arrange Proper Execution and Notarization

Once your deed has been professionally reviewed and any lender considerations addressed, you're ready for the formal execution. Sign the deed in front of a notary public who will verify your identity, witness your signature, and complete the notarial certificate (acknowledgment or jurat) on the deed. Bring valid government-issued photo identification such as a driver's license or passport—the notary cannot notarize without verifying your identity. If your spouse or other co-owners are also grantors on the deed, they must also appear before the notary with identification and sign. Some states require witness signatures in addition to notarization. If your state has this requirement, arrange for the required number of witnesses (typically two) to be present, observe your signing, and sign in the appropriate locations on the deed. Witnesses should be adults who are not related to you and will not benefit from the transfer—essentially disinterested third parties who can later testify if necessary that they witnessed you signing voluntarily.

If you're signing through a power of attorney—perhaps because you're physically unable to appear or for other reasons—ensure the power of attorney document is valid for real estate transfers (some POAs specifically exclude real estate transactions) and present the original POA to the notary along with your identification. The person holding your power of attorney will sign your name on the deed and then sign their own name indicating they're acting as attorney-in-fact. The notary will notarize the attorney-in-fact's signature, and the POA document typically must be recorded along with the deed. Take time during the signing to read through the entire deed one final time, verifying all information is correct before signing. Once signed and notarized, the deed becomes a legal instrument, and correcting errors requires preparing and recording corrective documents, so careful final review before signing prevents problems.

This formal execution process reflects biblical principles about the seriousness of commitments and the importance of witnesses. Deuteronomy 19:15 establishes, "One witness is not enough to convict anyone accused of any crime or offense they may have committed. A matter must be established by the testimony of two or three witnesses." While you're not being accused of anything, the principle that important legal matters should be witnessed by multiple parties applies. The notary serves as an official witness to your signature, and additional witnesses in states requiring them provide further testimony that the signing was voluntary and proper. This solemnity in execution ensures the document's validity and protects against later challenges about whether you truly signed it or whether you were under duress or lacked capacity when signing. Taking this step seriously rather than treating it casually honors both the law and the importance of what you're accomplishing.

Step Seven: Record the Deed at the County Recorder's Office

After proper execution and notarization, your next critical step is recording the deed at the county recorder's office in the county where your property is located. Submit the original signed and notarized deed (not a copy) to the recorder, either in person, by mail, or through electronic recording if your county offers that option. Pay the required recording fees, which vary by county but typically range from $15 to $50 for a standard deed, though some jurisdictions charge more if the document exceeds a certain number of pages. Some states also charge transfer taxes or documentary stamp taxes when property changes hands, but most specifically exempt transfers to revocable living trusts from such taxes. Verify whether your county requires any additional forms to claim exemption from transfer taxes, and submit those forms along with the deed if required.

When submitting the deed for recording, include your return address so the recorder can mail the stamped recorded deed back to you after processing. Request a certified or stamped copy of the recorded instrument for your trust file—this recorded copy is your proof that the transfer was completed and should be kept with your trust documents permanently. Recording typically takes anywhere from a few days to a few weeks depending on the county's workload and procedures. Once recorded, your deed becomes part of the public record, and the county's online records (if available) will show your trust as the current owner of the property. The recording date establishes the priority of your trust's ownership interest, protecting it against later claims or transfers.

Recording is essential—without it, your transfer may not be legally effective against third parties, and future title problems could arise. Even though the deed may be valid between you and your trust from the moment of signing, it's not effective against the world until recorded. For example, if someone later obtained a judgment against you personally and tried to place a lien on your property, they might succeed if the transfer to your trust wasn't recorded because they would have no public notice that you no longer owned the property individually. This requirement of public recording reflects biblical principles about transparency and public witness. In Ruth 4:9-11, when Boaz acquired property rights, he made the transaction public before the elders and all the people at the gate, declaring "Today you are witnesses!" The public nature of the transaction established its validity beyond question. Similarly, recording your deed makes your transfer public record, establishing witnesses through the county's official records that the ownership change occurred.

Step Eight: Update Related Records and Insurance

After successfully recording your deed, your work isn't quite finished—you must update various related records and policies to reflect the ownership change. Most importantly, notify your homeowners insurance company immediately and request that the policy be updated to reflect the trust or trustee as the named insured. The typical updated designation would be "[Your Name], Trustee of [Trust Name] dated [Date]." For example: "Jane Doe, Trustee of the Jane Doe Revocable Living Trust dated January 1, 2024." Most insurance companies make this change routinely without affecting premiums or coverage, but some may request documentation such as a copy of the recorded deed or relevant pages of your trust document. This update is critical because if your property ownership doesn't match your insurance policy, claims could be complicated or even denied if the insurance company argues the policy doesn't cover the actual property owner.

Notify your title insurance company if you have an owner's policy, and request written confirmation that coverage continues with the property now held in trust. Most title insurance policies automatically continue covering property transferred to the insured's revocable living trust, but obtaining written confirmation provides documentation and peace of mind. Update HOA records if your property is in a homeowners association. Provide the HOA with a copy of the recorded deed and updated contact information if needed, ensuring they understand the trust now owns the property but you remain living there and responsible for all association obligations. Some HOAs charge fees for updating ownership records, so be prepared to pay any required charges.

Update utility accounts if necessary, though many people continue utility accounts in their individual names even after transferring property to trust because utilities don't typically require ownership verification and changing account names creates unnecessary administrative work. Update your property tax billing address if needed, and verify with the county assessor that any homestead exemptions or other property tax benefits continue after the transfer. Most jurisdictions automatically continue exemptions when property is transferred to revocable living trusts, but some require filing updated forms, so verify requirements and comply promptly to avoid losing valuable tax benefits. Finally, if you have a mortgage, send a courtesy notification to your lender as discussed in Step Five, providing a copy of the recorded deed and confirming you remain living in the property as your principal residence.

This thorough updating of records demonstrates faithful stewardship in completing what you've started. James 1:22-25 teaches about being doers of the word and not merely hearers, comparing incomplete action to someone who looks in a mirror and immediately forgets what they look like. Transferring your property to your trust but failing to update insurance and other records is like looking in the mirror and walking away without acting on what you've seen—the work is incomplete and problems remain unaddressed. Completing these administrative updates finishes the work properly and protects your interests comprehensively.

Step Nine: Verify Successful Trust Funding and Maintain Records

After recording the deed and updating insurance and other records, take time to verify that trust funding was completed successfully. Confirm that county records show the trust as owner by accessing the county recorder's online database (if available) or requesting a copy of the current ownership information from the assessor's office. Ensure the recorded deed was properly indexed under your name and your trust's name so both are searchable in county records. Keep the stamped recorded deed with your trust documents in a secure location, as this is your permanent proof that the transfer was completed. If you maintain a schedule of trust assets (a list of property held by the trust, though not all trusts include formal schedules), update it to show your home is now trust property, including the property address, legal description, approximate value, and recording information for the deed.

Create a complete trust administration file that includes the original trust document and all amendments, the recorded deed transferring your home into the trust, deeds for any other real property transferred to the trust, documentation of financial accounts transferred to trust ownership, insurance policies showing the trust as owner or beneficiary, and a list of contact information for your attorney, financial advisor, insurance agents, and other professionals who can assist your successor trustee. This comprehensive file should be stored securely but accessibly, with your successor trustee knowing its location and how to access it. Consider creating both physical and digital copies—a binder with physical documents stored in a fireproof safe or attorney's office, plus scanned PDF copies organized in clearly labeled folders on your computer or cloud storage.

This verification and record-keeping reflects the biblical principle of faithful stewardship that includes accountability and documentation. In Luke 16:2, when the master calls his steward to account, he says "Give an account of your management, because you cannot be manager any longer." While this is a parable about spiritual matters, it illustrates that good stewardship includes being able to give account—to document and demonstrate what you've done with what was entrusted to you. Maintaining clear records of your trust funding allows you (or your successor trustee after your death) to give account of your faithful stewardship, showing that you completed the work properly and protected your family's inheritance. Proverbs 27:23 similarly instructs, "Be sure you know the condition of your flocks, give careful attention to your herds." In modern application, this means knowing the condition of your assets—and you can't know their condition without maintaining records that document ownership, value, and status.

Step Ten: Provide Successor Trustee Access and Clear Instructions

With trust funding completed and verified, ensure your successor trustee (the person you've designated to manage the trust after your death or incapacity) has the access and information needed to fulfill their role when the time comes. Place a copy of your trust document, the recorded deed, and contact details for your attorney and financial advisor in a secure location that your successor trustee knows about and can access when needed. Some people provide their successor trustee with a copy of these documents immediately, while others prefer to keep everything secure but inform the successor trustee of the location and how to access it (combination to a safe, location of a key, contact information for the attorney holding documents, etc.).

Create a letter of instruction—an informal document that explains to your successor trustee what they need to know and do. This letter might include an overview of your trust's purpose and main provisions, location of important documents including the trust, recorded deeds, insurance policies, and financial records, contact information for all relevant professionals including attorney, financial advisor, accountant, insurance agents, and banker, list of trust assets including your home and any other property held in the trust, usernames and passwords for online accounts (stored securely), instructions for any special circumstances or wishes not fully detailed in the trust document, and personal messages you want your successor trustee to have. This letter isn't a legal document and doesn't override your trust's provisions, but it provides practical guidance that makes the successor trustee's job easier and ensures nothing is overlooked.

Update this information whenever significant changes occur—if you change attorneys, refinance your mortgage, switch insurance companies, or make other substantial changes, update the documents and information you've provided your successor trustee so they always have current information. This provision for your successor trustee reflects the biblical principle of equipping others for the work they'll need to do. In 2 Timothy 2:2, Paul instructs Timothy to "entrust to reliable people who will also be qualified to teach others." While Paul is addressing teaching Christian truth, the principle applies broadly—equipping those who will continue work after you. Providing your successor trustee with clear documentation, access, and instructions equips them to faithfully administer your trust when you can no longer do so, ensuring your estate plan accomplishes its purposes even after your death.

Step Eleven: Follow Up with Periodic Professional Reviews

Trust funding is not a one-time event but an ongoing responsibility. After successfully transferring your home into your trust, commit to periodic professional reviews to ensure your trust remains properly funded and aligned with your goals. Have an attorney confirm the transfer is complete and consistent with your broader estate planning, tax planning, Medicaid planning, or other financial goals. Sometimes trust transfers create unintended tax consequences, affect eligibility for certain programs, or conflict with other planning strategies. A comprehensive review by an attorney who understands your complete situation ensures the trust transfer fits properly within your overall plan.

Schedule periodic reviews every three to five years, or after major life events such as marriage, divorce, birth of children or grandchildren, death of a beneficiary or trustee, significant changes in asset values, retirement, serious illness, or major changes in tax or estate planning laws. These reviews provide opportunities to amend your trust if your wishes have changed, update beneficiary designations to reflect current family circumstances, add newly acquired assets to the trust, remove assets you've sold or given away, replace trustees if circumstances warrant, and ensure your plan remains coordinated with current laws and best practices. Many estate planning attorneys offer periodic review services at reduced rates for existing clients, recognizing that estate plans require maintenance over time to remain effective.

This commitment to ongoing review and maintenance reflects biblical teaching about faithful stewardship over time. In the parable of the talents (Matthew 25:14-30), the faithful servants didn't just receive resources and put them away—they actively managed them, invested them, and increased them over time. Similarly, establishing and funding a trust is just the beginning; faithful stewardship requires ongoing attention, periodic review, and adjustments as circumstances change. Luke 12:42 asks, "Who then is the faithful and wise manager, whom the master puts in charge of his servants to give them their food allowance at the proper time?" The faithful and wise manager doesn't just take charge once but continues faithfully managing over time, giving attention at proper intervals. Periodic reviews of your trust funding and estate plan are exactly this kind of faithful, ongoing management that characterizes wise stewardship.

Conclusion: The Satisfaction of Completed Stewardship

Following this comprehensive step-by-step process for transferring your home into your living trust may require significant time and effort, but the result—a properly funded trust that will protect your family and accomplish your estate planning goals—makes every step worthwhile. By systematically working through each phase from confirming trust validity to recording the deed to updating insurance and establishing ongoing review practices, you ensure that your trust isn't merely words on paper but a functional legal structure that will serve your family well both during your life and after your death. The peace of mind that comes from knowing you've completed this important work properly is itself a valuable reward, though the greater reward comes in the future when your family experiences the smooth, private, efficient transfer of your home without probate complications.

As you complete this process, take satisfaction in the knowledge that you've been a faithful steward of what God entrusted to your care. You've taken the time to learn what needed to be done, assembled the necessary resources and documents, sought professional guidance where needed, executed each step carefully and in proper sequence, and established structures to ensure ongoing maintenance and review. This level of intentionality and thoroughness honors both God and your family, demonstrating love through practical provision and wisdom through careful planning. Proverbs 31:27-28 describes the excellent person: "She watches over the affairs of her household and does not eat the bread of idleness. Her children arise and call her blessed." By watching carefully over the affairs of your household through proper trust funding, you position yourself to be called blessed by your children who will benefit from your diligent work. Rest in the assurance that you've completed an important task well, and encourage others in your circle to do likewise, sharing your knowledge and experience so that families throughout your community can benefit from the protection and peace that proper estate planning provides.

***

Section 3: Sample Quitclaim Deed Wording and Recording Instructions

Below is a clear, adaptable quitclaim deed template you can use to transfer a home into a revocable living trust. Replace the bracketed placeholders with your exact information (trust name, dates, legal description, county, etc.). Use the exact trust name and date as they appear in the trust document. Doing this task carefully is an act of stewardship: "The plans of the diligent lead surely to abundance" (Proverbs 21:5).

Sample Quitclaim Deed Wording

THIS QUITCLAIM DEED, made this [Day] day of [Month], [Year], between [Grantor Full Legal Name], whose address is [Grantor Address] (hereinafter called "Grantor"), and [Grantee Trust Name], by [Grantor Full Legal Name], as Trustee of the [Full Trust Name] dated [Trust Date], whose address is [Trust/Trustee Address] (hereinafter called "Grantee").

WITNESSETH, that Grantor, for and in consideration of the sum of [$10.00] and other good and valuable consideration, the receipt of which is hereby acknowledged, does hereby remise, release and quitclaim to Grantee all of Grantor's rights, title, interest, and claim in and to the following described real property located in the County of [County Name], State of [State Name], to wit:

[Insert full legal description exactly as shown on the recorded deed; include parcel number if available.]

TO HAVE AND TO HOLD the same, together with all and singular the tenements, hereditaments and appurtenances thereunto belonging, to the Grantee and Grantee's successors and assigns forever.

IN WITNESS WHEREOF, Grantor has executed this instrument the day and year first above written.

[Grantor Full Legal Name], Grantor

State of [State] County of [County]

On this [Day] day of [Month], [Year], before me, [Notary Name], personally appeared [Grantor Full Legal Name], known to me (or satisfactorily proven) to be the person whose name is subscribed to this instrument, and acknowledged that he/she executed the same for the purposes therein contained.

WITNESS my hand and official seal.

Notary Public for [State] My Commission Expires: [Date] (Seal)

Recording Acknowledgment: After notarization, deliver the original deed to the Recorder/Clerk of [County Name] for recording. Pay applicable recording fees and request a stamped/certified copy for the trust file.

Practical Recording and Follow-Up Steps

Verify trust name and date. Confirm the exact trust name and execution date match the trust document and use that exact phrasing on the deed. Small errors can create administrative confusion.

Use the exact legal description. Copy the property's legal description verbatim from the recorded deed; do not rely on the street address alone.

Decide consideration language. Many transfers to a revocable trust use nominal consideration (e.g., $10.00) or "for no consideration." Check local recording requirements; some counties expect a value for tax purposes.

Sign before a notary. The grantor must sign the deed in the presence of a notary public; some states also require witness signatures—confirm your state requirements before execution.

Record in the correct county. File the original signed and notarized deed with the county recorder or clerk where the property is located. Keep the stamped recorded copy with your trust documents.

Notify and update related parties. Contact the homeowner's insurance carrier to list the trust or trustee as an insured interest; notify your mortgage servicer only if required or advised by counsel; update HOA records and property tax mailing address if needed.

Keep copies and inform successor trustee. Maintain the recorded original in a secure place and provide a copy (or location information) to the successor trustee and your estate attorney.

Cautions and Scriptural Reminder

Do not use this transfer to evade creditors or during active litigation—courts can set aside transfers made with fraudulent intent. Seek counsel if liens, active claims, or complex tax issues exist. The Scripture's call to integrity guides this work: “Better is a poor person who walks in his integrity than one who is crooked in his ways” (Proverbs 28:6).

***

Section 4: Drafting the Trust Document: Creating Your Estate Planning Foundation

Introduction: Translating Intentions into Enforceable Instructions

Drafting the trust document is the cornerstone of effective estate planning; it translates your intentions into enforceable instructions that will govern management, distribution, and stewardship of your home and other assets long after you're no longer able to direct these matters personally. While gathering documents and executing deeds are important practical steps, the trust document itself is the legal foundation upon which everything else rests. This carefully crafted instrument establishes the rules that will govern your property, names the people who will manage it, identifies who will ultimately receive it, and provides guidance for countless situations that may arise over the years or decades the trust remains in existence. A well-drafted trust document brings clarity, prevents disputes, protects vulnerable beneficiaries, and ensures your values and priorities continue influencing how your property is used even after your death.

Doing this work thoughtfully honors the biblical call to wise planning. Jesus taught in Luke 14:28, "For which of you, desiring to build a tower, does not first sit down and count the cost, whether he has enough to complete it?" Drafting a trust document is precisely this kind of counting the cost—carefully considering all the elements needed for your estate plan to succeed, anticipating potential problems, and creating structures to address them before they arise. Just as a builder who fails to count the cost may start a tower but be unable to finish it, becoming an object of ridicule, a person who establishes a trust without careful drafting may create a document that fails to accomplish its purposes, leaving family members with confusion, conflict, and expensive legal problems. The time and thought invested in proper trust drafting is the counting of cost that ensures your estate planning tower will be completed successfully, standing as a testament to your wisdom and care for generations to come.

Essential Elements: What Every Trust Document Must Include

A carefully drafted trust must include certain essential elements to be legally valid and practically effective. First, the document must clearly identify the grantor (also called settlor or trustor)—the person creating the trust and transferring property into it. This identification should include your full legal name as it appears on official documents, and in some cases your Social Security number or date of birth for identification purposes. Second, the document must name the initial trustee—the person or institution responsible for managing trust property according to the trust's terms. In revocable living trusts, you typically serve as initial trustee, maintaining complete control during your lifetime. The document should state explicitly that you're serving as trustee and clarify what powers you have in that role.

Third, the trust must describe the trust property, at least in general terms. Some trusts include detailed schedules listing every asset held in trust, while others use general language like "all property transferred to this trust by deed, assignment, or beneficiary designation." Both approaches are valid, though schedules provide clarity about what's intended to be in the trust. Fourth, the document must specify successor trustees—who will take over management if you die or become incapacitated. This might be one person, multiple co-trustees, or a succession of individuals with clear instructions about the order of succession and circumstances triggering each succession. Fifth, the trust must identify beneficiaries—the people or organizations who will benefit from trust property. For revocable living trusts, you're typically the primary beneficiary during your lifetime, with other beneficiaries (usually children or other family members) receiving property after your death. The document should clearly name all beneficiaries, describing their relationship to you and providing sufficient information to identify them unambiguously.

Sixth, the document must specify distribution conditions—the circumstances under which trust property will be distributed to beneficiaries and any conditions that must be met. This might include specific ages at which children receive distributions, requirements that beneficiaries complete education or maintain sobriety, or discretionary standards allowing trustees to distribute based on beneficiaries' needs. Seventh, the trust should clearly state whether it's revocable or irrevocable—whether you retain the right to amend or terminate it during your lifetime. Most living trusts are revocable initially and become irrevocable upon the grantor's death. Finally, the document must include proper execution formalities—your signature, date, and any notarization or witness requirements your state imposes. Without these essential elements, your trust document may be legally deficient or so ambiguous that it fails to accomplish your purposes. This need for completeness reflects the biblical principle of thorough work. Ecclesiastes 9:10 instructs, "Whatever your hand finds to do, do it with all your might." Drafting a trust document deserves your full effort and attention to ensure all essential elements are included and properly addressed, creating a complete and effective instrument rather than a partial or deficient one.

Clarity of Purpose: Precise Language Prevents Disputes

Clarity of purpose and precise language are essential in the trust instrument. Ambiguities lead to disputes and unnecessary court involvement, transforming what should be a private estate administration into public litigation that depletes the estate and destroys family relationships. The document should state in clear, unambiguous terms how and when assets are to be managed and distributed, leaving as little room as possible for differing interpretations. For example, rather than vaguely stating that property should be distributed "when children are mature," specify exact ages: "when each child reaches age twenty-five" or "in three equal installments at ages twenty-five, thirty, and thirty-five." Instead of saying trustees may distribute funds "for beneficiary needs," define those needs precisely: "for health, education, maintenance, and support" or even more specifically, "for medical expenses not covered by insurance, tuition and books for accredited educational institutions, reasonable living expenses, and emergency needs as determined by the trustee."

Specify distribution conditions with equal precision. If you want to encourage education, state clearly what qualifies: "If beneficiary completes a bachelor's degree from an accredited four-year college or university" rather than "if beneficiary gets an education." If you're concerned about substance abuse, define your requirements: "Provided beneficiary submits to random drug testing and maintains sobriety as verified by the trustee" rather than "if beneficiary stays clean." These specific standards give trustees clear guidance and reduce the likelihood that disappointed beneficiaries will challenge distributions in court arguing the trustee misinterpreted vague instructions. Include express provisions for incapacity, specifying how successor trustees are to determine incapacity and what powers they have to manage the property during that period. You might require written certification from two licensed physicians that you're unable to manage your affairs, or allow your successor trustee to rely on their own reasonable judgment. Define what powers the successor trustee has during your incapacity—can they sell property, make gifts, amend the trust, or are they limited to basic management and maintenance?

This commitment to clarity and precision reflects wisdom praised throughout Scripture. Proverbs 21:5 teaches, "The plans of the diligent lead surely to abundance, but everyone who is hasty comes only to poverty." Precise drafting is how diligent plans are preserved—taking time to think through exactly what you mean and expressing it clearly rather than hastily using vague language that seems adequate but creates problems later. James 5:12 instructs, "Let your 'Yes' be yes, and your 'No,' no," emphasizing clear, unambiguous communication. While this verse addresses oaths, the principle applies to legal documents—say clearly what you mean without ambiguity that could be interpreted multiple ways. Your trust document should speak with clarity that minimizes misunderstanding and dispute, allowing your intentions to be carried out faithfully without requiring courts to guess what you meant.

Trustee Powers and Fiduciary Duties: Balancing Authority with Accountability

Trustee powers and fiduciary duties should be spelled out with balance: give the trustee sufficient authority to manage trust property effectively while also requiring accountability through reporting and adherence to fiduciary standards. The document should grant trustees broad powers to collect income from trust property, pay all necessary expenses including property taxes, insurance, and maintenance, maintain and repair real property to preserve its value, insure trust property against loss or damage, invest trust funds prudently to generate income and growth, engage professionals such as attorneys, accountants, and financial advisors when needed, sell property when appropriate and reinvest proceeds, distribute property to beneficiaries according to trust terms, file tax returns and pay taxes owed by the trust, and defend the trust against claims or litigation.

These powers should be stated explicitly even though many are implied under state law, as explicit statements prevent questions about trustee authority.

At the same time, the document should impose fiduciary duties that protect beneficiaries from trustee abuse: require trustees to act in beneficiaries' best interests rather than their own, mandate duty of loyalty prohibiting self-dealing or conflicts of interest, impose duty of impartiality requiring fair treatment of multiple beneficiaries, require prudent investment of trust assets according to modern portfolio theory or your state's prudent investor rule, mandate duty to inform beneficiaries about trust administration and respond to reasonable requests for information, require periodic accounting showing all receipts, disbursements, and current trust assets, and impose personal liability on trustees who breach their fiduciary duties through negligence or intentional misconduct. Consider including successor trustee succession procedures specifying who becomes trustee if your first choice is unable or unwilling to serve, and whether co-trustees must act unanimously or can act by majority vote if you name multiple trustees. Address bond requirements—whether trustees must post bonds guaranteeing faithful performance, or whether you're waiving bond requirements to save expense because you trust your chosen trustees. Specify compensation terms clearly: will trustees serve without compensation, receive reasonable compensation as determined by themselves or by independent parties, or receive specific amounts or percentages?

These measures reflect the scriptural call to faithful stewardship. First Corinthians 4:2 states, "Moreover, it is required of stewards that they be found faithful." Your trustee is a steward of property you're entrusting to their management, and faithfulness requires both adequate authority to accomplish necessary tasks and clear accountability standards ensuring they exercise authority properly. First Peter 4:10 similarly teaches, "Each of you should use whatever gift you have received to serve others, as faithful stewards of God's grace in its various forms." Just as we're called to be faithful stewards of God's grace, your trustee must be a faithful steward of the property and responsibility you've entrusted to them. The balance of powers and duties in your trust document creates the structure for this faithful stewardship to occur.

Special Protective Clauses: Shielding Beneficiaries and Preserving Flexibility

Special clauses add protection and adaptability where appropriate, allowing your trust to address unique family circumstances and protect against various threats to your beneficiaries' inheritances. Spendthrift provisions can shield beneficiary interests from creditors by stating that beneficiaries cannot voluntarily or involuntarily transfer their interests before actually receiving distributions. This prevents beneficiaries from borrowing against anticipated inheritances, and it protects trust assets from being seized by creditors, ex-spouses, or others who might have claims against beneficiaries personally. Typical spendthrift language states: "No beneficiary shall have the power to sell, transfer, assign, or encumber their interest in this trust, nor shall any such interest be subject to claims of creditors or other parties through bankruptcy, attachment, garnishment, or other legal process."

Disabled-benefits protective language (supplemental needs trust provisions) can preserve eligibility for public assistance for beneficiaries with disabilities. If you have a child or other beneficiary receiving Supplemental Security Income, Medicaid, or other needs-based government benefits, leaving them an inheritance outright could disqualify them from these essential programs. Supplemental needs trust language allows the trust to hold assets for their benefit and distribute funds for quality-of-life expenses that government benefits don't cover—education, recreation, therapy, transportation, personal care attendants—without counting as resources that disqualify them from benefits. This language typically gives the trustee complete discretion over distributions and prohibits using trust funds for basic needs like food and shelter that government benefits cover. Trustee discretion clauses allow flexible administration without court intervention by giving trustees authority to make distribution decisions based on beneficiaries' circumstances rather than rigid formulas. Pure discretionary trusts give trustees complete authority to distribute or withhold funds based on their judgment. More commonly, trusts use standards like "health, education, maintenance, and support" that give trustees guidance while allowing flexibility to adapt to changing circumstances.

If tax or creditor exposure is significant concerns, consider tailored irrevocable provisions or separate subtrusts that provide enhanced protection. Dynasty trust provisions allow property to remain in trust for multiple generations, protecting it from estate taxes and creditors at each generational transition. Qualified Personal Residence Trusts (QPRTs) can remove your home's future appreciation from your taxable estate while allowing you to continue living there. Charitable Remainder Trusts provide income to you or other beneficiaries for life while ultimately benefiting charitable organizations, offering tax deductions and avoiding capital gains on appreciated property. Remember that greater protection usually means less flexibility—irrevocable trusts cannot be modified if circumstances change, and restrictions that protect beneficiaries from creditors also limit beneficiaries' access to trust property. Your choices should balance protection with flexibility based on your family's specific circumstances and concerns.

These choices should be made with integrity and wisdom. Proverbs 28:6 teaches, "Better is a poor person who walks in his integrity than one who is crooked in his ways though he be rich." While using legal structures to protect your beneficiaries' inheritances is legitimate and wise, ensure your motivations are pure—protecting family rather than defrauding legitimate creditors or evading legal obligations. Proverbs 11:1 similarly states, "A false balance is an abomination to the Lord, but a just weight is his delight." Use protective trust provisions justly and appropriately, not to cheat others but to provide legitimate protection for your family. When implemented with integrity, these special provisions demonstrate wise stewardship that protects what God has blessed you with while respecting the legitimate rights of others.

Technical Requirements and State Law Compliance

Address technical and state-law requirements explicitly to ensure your trust is legally valid and enforceable in your jurisdiction. Include choice-of-law provisions specifying which state's laws govern trust interpretation and administration. This is particularly important if you own property in multiple states, have beneficiaries in different jurisdictions, or might relocate before death. Typically you'll choose your home state's law, but some states have more favorable trust laws than others, so discuss options with your attorney. Include powers of appointment if desired—provisions allowing beneficiaries to direct where their share goes at their death, either among a limited class of people you designate or more broadly. Powers of appointment provide flexibility and can achieve tax benefits by giving beneficiaries some control while keeping assets in trust for creditor protection and professional management.

Provide instructions about funding and recordkeeping. Specify that the trust holds "all property transferred to it by any means" and include procedures for updating trust schedules or attachments as property is added or removed. State whether the trustee must maintain detailed records and how long records must be preserved. Require the trustee to locate and preserve original documents including the trust itself, amendments, recorded deeds transferring property to the trust, and beneficiary designation forms for financial accounts. These original documents prove the trust's existence and terms if questions arise years later. Include directions for notice to beneficiaries about trust existence and terms. Some states require trustees to notify beneficiaries within certain timeframes after the grantor's death, while others leave notice to trustee discretion. Specifying notice requirements in your trust ensures beneficiaries receive information they need while protecting against claims that they weren't properly informed.

Address tax elections and administrative matters. Specify what powers the trustee has to make tax elections such as qualifying trust assets for marital deductions, allocating generation-skipping transfer tax exemption, or electing alternate valuation dates. Clarify who bears the burden of taxes—whether beneficiaries receiving distributions must also bear a proportionate share of income or estate taxes, or whether taxes are paid from principal before distributions. Include provisions about trust division after your death if you're creating separate shares for multiple children, specifying whether division occurs immediately or is delayed until certain events. Legal compliance and orderly administration echo Paul's exhortation in Romans 13:1, "Let every person be subject to the governing authorities. For there is no authority except from God, and those that exist have been instituted by God." Ensuring your trust complies with applicable state laws and includes necessary provisions for tax reporting, beneficiary notice, and administrative requirements demonstrates submission to governing authorities and creates a structure that will be recognized and enforced by courts if necessary.

This attention to technical details may seem tedious, but it's essential for creating a trust that functions properly. Second Timothy 2:15 encourages, "Do your best to present yourself to God as one approved, a worker who does not need to be ashamed and who correctly handles the word of truth." While Paul is addressing handling Scripture, the principle applies to any important work—do it carefully and correctly so you need not be ashamed of the result. A trust document drafted with attention to technical requirements is correctly handled work that will stand the test of time and scrutiny, accomplishing your purposes without shame or failure.

The Importance of Professional Legal Counsel

Finally, drafting should not be done in isolation or through do-it-yourself approaches that seem attractive because of their low cost. Engage experienced estate planning counsel and, when appropriate, tax and elder-law advisors to tailor the document to your jurisdiction and family circumstances. Estate planning attorneys understand your state's specific requirements for trust validity, the latest developments in tax law affecting estate planning strategies, how to structure trusts to protect against creditors while avoiding fraudulent transfer issues, techniques for protecting disabled beneficiaries while preserving government benefit eligibility, and countless other nuances that online forms and books cannot adequately address. Every family situation is unique, and effective trust drafting requires customization rather than one-size-fits-all templates.

Tax advisors can analyze how different trust structures affect income taxes during your life and estate taxes at death, helping you make informed choices that minimize tax burdens while accomplishing your family goals. Elder law attorneys specialize in planning for long-term care costs and Medicaid eligibility, critical concerns for many older adults. If nursing home care or Medicaid planning is a concern, these specialists can structure trusts to protect assets while complying with Medicaid's complex rules and look-back periods. The cost of professional counsel may seem significant—comprehensive trust drafting typically ranges from $1,500 to $5,000 or more depending on complexity—but this investment is modest compared to the value it provides. A poorly drafted trust can create problems costing tens of thousands in legal fees to resolve, or worse, can fail entirely to accomplish your purposes, leaving your family without the protection you intended. Professional counsel ensures your trust is properly tailored to your circumstances, legally valid in your jurisdiction, and likely to accomplish your goals effectively.

This investment in professional guidance fulfills biblical instruction. Proverbs 15:22 teaches, "Plans fail for lack of counsel, but with many advisers they succeed." Engaging experienced attorneys and other professionals to help draft your trust is exactly the kind of counsel that causes plans to succeed rather than fail. Proverbs 11:14 similarly states, "For lack of guidance a nation falls, but victory is won through many advisers." While you're not leading a nation, you are stewarding your family's future, and victory in that stewardship comes through seeking skilled advisers. Proverbs 19:20 adds, "Listen to advice and accept instruction, that you may gain wisdom in the future." The estate planning attorney's advice during trust drafting is instruction that gives you wisdom you wouldn't possess on your own, enabling you to make better decisions than you could independently. Don't let the cost of professional counsel deter you from obtaining it—this is precisely the kind of expense that represents wise investment rather than wasteful consumption.

Post-Drafting Follow-Through: Making Your Trust Effective

After execution of your trust document, your work is far from finished. Follow through by funding the trust—transferring your home and other assets into it through deeds, assignments, and beneficiary designations as discussed in other sections. An unfunded trust is merely paper that accomplishes nothing; diligent follow-through transforms your carefully drafted document into a functioning structure that protects your family. Update insurance and titles to reflect trust ownership, ensuring your homeowners insurance lists the trust as named insured and your title insurance company acknowledges the ownership change. Verify that beneficiary designations on life insurance, retirement accounts, and financial accounts coordinate with your trust's provisions. Sometimes you'll name the trust as beneficiary directly; other times you'll name individuals as beneficiaries but structure distributions to coordinate with what the trust provides.

Communicate the plan to successor trustees and key family members. Your successor trustee needs to understand that you've appointed them, where trust documents are located, who your professional advisors are, and generally what your trust provides. You needn't share every detail of your estate plan with your children or other beneficiaries if you prefer privacy, but ensuring your successor trustee understands their role and has access to necessary information is essential. Consider holding a family meeting where you explain your general estate plan, introduce your successor trustee, and answer questions. This transparency often prevents later misunderstandings and disputes, as family members understand your reasoning and intentions rather than being surprised by distributions they don't understand after your death.

Schedule periodic reviews of your trust every three to five years or after major life events—marriages, divorces, births, deaths, significant changes in asset values, or major changes in tax laws. Estate planning is not one-and-done but requires ongoing maintenance to remain effective as your life and circumstances evolve. Your attorney can review whether your trust still reflects your current wishes, whether any amendments are needed, and whether new planning strategies might benefit your situation. This ongoing attention demonstrates faithful stewardship across time. In Luke 12:42, Jesus asks, "Who then is the faithful and wise manager, whom the master puts in charge of his servants to give them their food allowance at the proper time?" The faithful manager provides oversight at proper times, not just once but continually. Similarly, faithful stewardship of your estate plan requires periodic attention and updates, ensuring it continues serving your family appropriately as circumstances change.

Seeking wise counsel and following through diligently in both initial drafting and ongoing maintenance fulfills biblical instruction. Proverbs 15:22 promises that with many advisers, plans succeed. In doing so, you create a durable legacy governed by both prudence and faith—prudence in the careful legal structures you establish, and faith expressed through the values and priorities those structures reflect. Your trust document becomes not just a legal instrument but a testimony to your love for family, your commitment to wise stewardship, and your desire to continue blessing and providing for loved ones long after you've gone to be with the Lord.

Conclusion: A Foundation Built to Last

Drafting the trust document represents perhaps the most intellectually demanding and consequential aspect of estate planning. Unlike gathering documents or recording deeds—tasks that are straightforward if time-consuming—trust drafting requires careful thought about your values, priorities, and hopes for your family's future, combined with technical legal knowledge about how to structure provisions that accomplish your goals while complying with applicable laws. The document you create becomes the controlling authority for your property after death or incapacity, speaking when you can no longer speak and directing distributions according to the wisdom you've accumulated over a lifetime. Getting this document right is therefore of paramount importance, worthy of whatever time, effort, and professional expense is required to ensure excellence.

As you embark on trust drafting, approach it prayerfully and thoughtfully, considering not just the legal and financial implications but also the spiritual and relational dimensions of what you're creating. Your trust document will shape family dynamics for years or even generations, potentially bringing family members together in gratitude and harmony or driving them apart in conflict and resentment depending on how wisely you craft its provisions. Seek God's wisdom in making these decisions, asking Him to guide you toward structures that honor Him, bless your family, and reflect the values and priorities He's taught you throughout your life. James 1:5 promises, "If any of you lacks wisdom, you should ask God, who gives generously to all without finding fault, and it will be given to you." Don't rely solely on your own understanding or even on professional counsel alone—seek divine wisdom that transcends human knowledge, praying that God would guide both your thinking and your advisors' counsel toward what is truly best for your family. With careful drafting, professional guidance, and divine wisdom, your trust document becomes a foundation built to last—a durable structure that will protect, provide for, and bless your family long after you've finished your earthly journey and entered into the joy of your Master.

***

Ensuring the Trust Is Properly Funded: Completing What You've Begun

Properly funding a trust means transferring title and ownership of the assets you intend the trust to hold so the trust can operate as written and accomplish the purposes for which you created it. This critical step transforms your trust from a theoretical document into a practical structure that will actually protect your family and avoid probate. A trust that exists only on paper but holds no assets is like a beautiful empty container—perfectly formed but serving no purpose because it contains nothing. Real property, bank and investment accounts, vehicles, business interests, and titled valuables must be re-titled or otherwise assigned to the trust to achieve probate avoidance and seamless administration. Without proper funding, all the time, effort, and expense you invested in creating your trust document and estate plan will have been wasted, as unfunded trusts accomplish nothing when you die.

Scripture underscores the need to complete the work we begin rather than leaving tasks half-finished. Jesus taught in Luke 14:28-30, "Suppose one of you wants to build a tower. Won't you first sit down and estimate the cost to see if you have enough money to complete it? For if you lay the foundation and are not able to finish it, everyone who sees it will ridicule you, saying, 'This person began to build and wasn't able to finish.'" Creating a trust document without funding it is precisely this kind of incomplete building—laying a foundation but failing to complete the structure, leaving something that appears impressive but serves no function. The funding process is the execution step that makes your planning effective, transforming good intentions and legal documents into actual protection and provision for your family. Just as a tower builder must not only design and start construction but must see the project through to completion, you must not only create your trust but must complete the funding process that makes it operational and effective.

Funding Real Property: The Foundation of Trust Assets

Begin with real property by preparing and recording the correct deed (often a quitclaim or warranty deed) that names the trust precisely as the grantee, using the exact trust name and date as it appears in the trust instrument. As discussed in previous sections, for transfers to your own revocable living trust, a quitclaim deed is typically appropriate and cost-effective. The deed must identify you as grantor exactly as your name appears on your current title, and must identify the trust as grantee with absolute precision: "[Your Full Name], Trustee of the [Exact Trust Name] dated [Month Day, Year]." Even minor variations in how the trust is identified can create title problems, so copy the trust name and date character-for-character from your trust document.

Use the full legal description from your current recorded deed rather than relying on a street address, which is legally insufficient for real estate transfers. The legal description might be lengthy and technical, involving lot and block numbers, metes and bounds measurements, or government survey references, but it must be copied exactly onto your new deed. Follow your county's notarization and recording requirements meticulously to ensure the transfer is effective and visible to third parties who might later search title records. Your signature must be notarized, and in some states witness signatures are also required. Submit the original executed deed to the county recorder's office with appropriate fees, and keep the stamped recorded copy with your trust documents as proof the transfer was completed. Don't assume the transfer is complete simply because you've signed a deed—until that deed is properly recorded with the county, the ownership change isn't fully effective against third parties and won't show up in title searches.

This careful attention to detail in real property funding mirrors the biblical call to diligence. Proverbs 21:5 teaches, "The plans of the diligent lead surely to abundance, but everyone who is hasty comes only to poverty." Diligently following proper procedures for deed preparation, execution, and recording leads to the abundance of a properly funded trust that will protect your family, while hastily skipping steps or using imprecise language leads to the poverty of title problems, family confusion, or trust failure. Real property is typically your most valuable asset, making its proper transfer into your trust absolutely essential. Don't allow carelessness or impatience in this critical step to undermine your entire estate plan. Take whatever time and care are necessary to ensure your real property is correctly transferred into your trust, and verify through county records that the transfer has been properly recorded and indexed.

Funding Financial Accounts: Banks, Investments, and Brokerage Assets

Next, address financial accounts: banks, investment custodians, and brokerage accounts. For many bank and brokerage accounts you will either re-title the account directly in the name of the trust or establish "payable on death" (POD) or "transfer on death" (TOD) designations that align with your trust plan. Re-titling means changing the account ownership from your individual name to your name as trustee of your trust. The new account title would typically be "[Your Name], Trustee of [Trust Name] dated [Date]." Most banks and investment companies have their own forms and procedures for this re-titling, requiring you to provide a copy of your trust document (or at least the relevant pages showing the trust's existence, date, trustee, and powers) along with their institution-specific forms.

Contact each financial institution where you hold accounts and inform them you'd like to transfer the account into your trust. They'll provide the necessary paperwork and guide you through their specific process. Some institutions complete the re-titling quickly, while others take several weeks, so begin this process promptly and follow up to ensure completion. Keep confirmation statements or letters from each institution showing that accounts have been successfully re-titled in your trust's name. These confirmations serve as proof of funding and help your successor trustee identify trust assets after your death. For accounts that don't need to be held in the trust during your lifetime but should pass to trust beneficiaries at death, consider using payable-on-death or transfer-on-death designations. These beneficiary designations cause accounts to transfer automatically to designated beneficiaries (which could be your trust or could be individuals) upon your death without going through probate. POD/TOD designations work well for accounts where you want simplicity during life but coordinated distribution at death.

However, ensure these beneficiary designations align with your overall trust plan rather than creating conflicts. If your trust provides that all your assets should be divided equally among your three children, but you name only one child as POD beneficiary on a large bank account, you've created an inconsistency that may cause family conflict or unintended unequal distributions. Retirement accounts and IRAs present special considerations and are not typically re-titled into revocable trusts during your lifetime. Transferring retirement accounts directly into trusts can trigger immediate income taxation of the entire account balance—a disastrous result that destroys the tax-deferred growth these accounts provide. Instead, beneficiary designations on retirement accounts should align with your trust objectives without actually transferring account ownership during life. You might name your trust as beneficiary of retirement accounts, or you might name individual beneficiaries directly but coordinate those designations with your trust's distribution plan.

Because retirement account taxation is complex and the wrong decisions can create substantial tax burdens for your beneficiaries, consult with tax counsel before finalizing retirement account beneficiary designations. The Bible encourages wise counsel in complex matters, and retirement account taxation certainly qualifies as complex. Proverbs 15:22 teaches, "Plans fail for lack of counsel, but with many advisers they succeed." Don't attempt to navigate retirement account planning alone—seek expert advice to ensure your decisions accomplish your goals without creating unnecessary tax problems. Proverbs 11:14 adds, "For lack of guidance a nation falls, but victory is won through many advisers." The victory of successfully passing retirement accounts to your family with minimal tax consequences comes through seeking skilled tax advisers who understand the intricate rules governing these accounts.

Funding Tangible Personal Property and Business Interests

Tangible personal property and business interests require clear transfer steps as well, though the specific procedures vary depending on what you're transferring. Vehicles often need title changes recorded with your state's motor vehicle department. Most states have forms for transferring vehicle titles into trusts, typically requiring you to submit the current title, a transfer form, and sometimes a copy of your trust document or a certification that the trust exists. Some states charge transfer fees or require emissions testing or safety inspections when title changes hands, so research your state's specific requirements. For valuable vehicles, boats, or recreational vehicles with formal titles, complete these title transfers to ensure they're properly owned by your trust and will pass according to trust terms rather than through probate.

Valuable personal items such as jewelry, art, collectibles, antiques, and household furnishings may be assigned to your trust through a written schedule or assignment incorporated into the trust or kept separately and referenced by the trust. Many trusts include language like "all tangible personal property of the grantor" to sweep in household items without requiring individual listing, but for particularly valuable items, creating a specific schedule listing major pieces provides clarity. This schedule might describe each item, note its approximate value, and confirm it's assigned to the trust. Update this schedule as you acquire or dispose of significant items, and keep it with your trust documents so your successor trustee knows what tangible property the trust holds. For less valuable everyday household items, detailed scheduling is usually unnecessary—general trust language covering "all personal property" suffices.

Ownership interests in closely held businesses—whether corporations, limited liability companies, partnerships, or sole proprietorships—should be transferred according to operating agreements or corporate bylaws to avoid unintended consequences. For corporations, this typically means issuing new stock certificates in the name of your trust and updating the corporate books to reflect the ownership change. For LLCs and partnerships, an assignment of membership or partnership interest must be prepared and the entity's records updated. Review operating agreements, shareholder agreements, and buy-sell agreements before transferring business interests, as these documents may restrict transfers, require consent from other owners, or trigger buyout provisions when ownership changes. Even transfers to your own trust sometimes implicate these provisions, so understand what restrictions exist and comply with any required procedures.

If your business has multiple owners or your ownership is subject to agreements with co-owners, discuss your trust planning with them and obtain any necessary consents before transferring interests. Don't inadvertently trigger buy-sell provisions or violate agreements in the process of funding your trust. Proper documentation and compliance with entity requirements protect both the trust and your business relationships, honoring your obligations to business partners. This careful attention to business agreements reflects biblical teaching about honoring commitments and dealing honestly with others. Galatians 6:5 instructs, "Each one should carry their own load," meaning each person should fulfill their own responsibilities. Part of your responsibility as a business owner is complying with agreements you've made with co-owners. Romans 13:8 similarly teaches, "Let no debt remain outstanding, except the continuing debt to love one another." While this verse addresses financial debts, the principle extends to contractual obligations—honor your business agreements by following required procedures when transferring ownership interests to your trust.

Insurance, Tax Records, and Creditor Considerations

Don't overlook insurance, tax records, and creditor considerations when funding your trust, as these administrative matters are essential for protecting trust assets and maintaining proper coverage. Notify homeowner's and umbrella liability insurers to list the trust or trustee as the named insured interest. Your homeowners insurance policy must reflect the actual property owner—which is now your trust rather than you individually—to ensure coverage remains in effect if you need to file a claim. The typical updated designation would be "[Your Name], Trustee of [Trust Name] dated [Date]." Most insurance companies make this change routinely without affecting premiums or coverage terms, but they need written notification and sometimes require documentation such as a copy of your recorded deed or relevant trust pages.

Contact your insurance agent, explain that you've transferred your home into your trust, and request that the policy be updated accordingly. Get written confirmation that the change has been made and keep this confirmation with your trust documents. Similarly, if you have umbrella liability coverage, notify that insurer as well, as umbrella policies typically follow underlying property ownership. Inform your title insurance company when appropriate, particularly if you obtained owner's title insurance when you purchased your home. As discussed in previous sections, most title insurance policies automatically continue covering property after transfer to the owner's revocable living trust, but notifying the company and obtaining written confirmation of continued coverage provides documentation and peace of mind.

Verify whether recording your deed triggers transfer taxes or property tax reassessments in your jurisdiction. Most states specifically exempt transfers to revocable living trusts from transfer taxes, recognizing these as administrative changes in ownership form rather than true sales, but rules vary by state and even by county. Similarly, most jurisdictions don't reassess property values or eliminate homestead exemptions when property is transferred to the owner's living trust, but some require filing forms to maintain exemptions. Contact your county assessor's office before or immediately after recording your deed to understand requirements and ensure you don't inadvertently lose valuable property tax benefits. If a mortgage exists on your property, review lender provisions before transfer, even though federal law (the Garn-St. Germain Act) generally permits transfers to a grantor's revocable living trust for estate planning purposes without triggering due-on-sale clauses.

Lender practices vary, and while they cannot legally accelerate your loan for transferring property to your own living trust where you remain the beneficiary and continue occupying the property, maintaining good relationships through communication reflects wisdom and integrity. Consider sending your lender a brief notification letter with a copy of the recorded deed, explaining the transfer is for estate planning purposes and confirming you remain the trustee and beneficiary. Most lenders acknowledge the letter and note the change without any action regarding your loan terms. Acting with integrity and foresight in addressing these insurance, tax, and lender matters reflects godly stewardship. Proverbs 27:12 teaches, "The prudent see danger and take refuge, but the simple keep going and pay the penalty." Addressing insurance updates, tax considerations, and lender communications before problems arise is prudent seeing of danger and taking refuge, while ignoring these matters is simplicity that later pays penalties through insurance claim denials, unexpected tax bills, or lender complications.

Creating and Maintaining Comprehensive Records

Create and maintain a funding checklist and a central trust schedule that records each asset, the method of transfer, the date completed, and the location of supporting documents. This organizational system serves multiple purposes: it helps you track funding progress and ensure no assets are overlooked, it provides documentation proving what assets the trust holds, and it creates a roadmap for your successor trustee showing what property they'll need to administer after your death. Your funding checklist might be a simple spreadsheet or document listing each asset category—real property, bank accounts, investment accounts, vehicles, business interests, life insurance, retirement accounts—with columns noting the specific asset, how it's being transferred to or coordinated with the trust, the date transfer was completed, and where supporting documentation is stored.

As you complete each transfer, check it off your list and attach confirmation documents. Keep certified copies of recorded deeds showing property transfers, account statements reflecting re-titling in your trust's name, letters from financial institutions confirming account changes, beneficiary designation forms for retirement accounts and life insurance, vehicle titles showing trust ownership, and written assignments of business interests or personal property. Store these documents in a secure file—either physical or digital or both—organized in a way that makes it easy to locate specific items. Consider using a fireproof safe for physical documents, and encrypted cloud storage or external hard drives for digital copies. Whatever storage system you use, ensure your successor trustee knows its location and has access.

Inform the successor trustee where trust funding records are stored and provide them with any necessary keys, combinations, passwords, or access instructions. Without this information, even perfectly funded trusts can create problems if successor trustees can't locate documentation proving what assets the trust holds. Some estate planners recommend creating a "successor trustee packet" containing copies of the trust document, the funding checklist and schedule, copies of key transfer documents, contact information for your attorney and financial advisors, and instructions for locating original documents and accessing online accounts. Place this packet in a secure location your successor trustee knows about, or even provide them with a copy directly if you're comfortable with them having this information during your lifetime.

This organized stewardship is a practical way to love your family by reducing confusion and conflict after your death. Proverbs 13:22 teaches, "A good person leaves an inheritance for their children's children, but a sinner's wealth is stored up for the righteous." Leaving an inheritance includes not just the assets themselves but also the organized information and clear documentation that allows your family to efficiently locate, access, and distribute those assets. An inheritance accompanied by thorough records and clear instructions is far more valuable than a larger inheritance buried in confusion and requiring expensive legal work to unravel. First Corinthians 14:40 similarly instructs, "But everything should be done in a fitting and orderly way." Creating and maintaining comprehensive funding records is exactly this kind of orderly approach that honors both your family and the God who values order and clarity in all things.

Treating Funding as an Ongoing Process

Finally, treat funding as an ongoing process rather than a one-time event that's completed and forgotten. Your financial life doesn't end when you sign your trust document and complete initial funding—you'll continue acquiring new assets, selling old ones, opening new accounts, and experiencing changes in your circumstances over the years or decades between establishing your trust and your death. New assets acquired after trust execution—inheritances you receive, real property you purchase, businesses you start, investment accounts you open, valuable items you acquire, settlements or judgments you receive—should be reviewed and, when appropriate, added to your trust promptly after acquisition. Don't allow significant assets to accumulate outside your trust simply because you established the trust years ago and haven't maintained funding discipline.

Develop a habit of asking yourself whenever you acquire a new asset: "Should this be owned by my trust?" For major assets like real property or business interests, the answer is usually yes, and you should complete transfer paperwork promptly. For financial accounts, request that new accounts be opened in your trust's name from the beginning rather than in your individual name and later transferred. For personal property, update your tangible property schedule periodically to reflect significant new acquisitions. Schedule periodic reviews with your estate planning attorney and financial adviser, especially after major life changes such as marriage, divorce, birth of children or grandchildren, death of beneficiaries, significant changes in asset values, retirement, serious illness, or major changes in tax or estate planning laws. These reviews provide opportunities to ensure the trust remains fully funded, update beneficiary designations that may have become outdated, amend trust provisions if your wishes have changed, verify that new assets have been properly added to the trust, and confirm your overall estate plan remains coordinated and effective.

Many attorneys offer periodic review services at reduced rates for existing clients, recognizing that estate plans require maintenance to remain effective over time. Take advantage of these services rather than assuming your initial funding work will remain adequate for decades without attention. Continuous care in trust administration fulfills the scriptural charge to faithful stewardship. First Corinthians 4:2 states, "Moreover, it is required of stewards that they be found faithful." Faithfulness in trust funding means not just completing initial transfers but maintaining funding discipline throughout your life, ensuring your trust continues holding the assets you want it to protect. Luke 16:10 adds, "Whoever can be trusted with very little can also be trusted with much, and whoever is dishonest with very little will also be dishonest with much." The "little" matter of maintaining trust funding over time reveals whether you'll be trusted with the much larger matter of leaving your family properly protected and provided for. Demonstrating faithfulness in ongoing trust maintenance is the mark of a wise steward who completes what they've begun.

Conclusion: Completing the Tower You've Started to Build

Ensuring your trust is properly funded represents the completion of the estate planning tower you began building when you first decided to create a trust. The foundation was laid when you gathered necessary documents, the walls were erected when you drafted your trust document, and the roof is added when you transfer assets into the trust through proper funding procedures. Without this final step, all the earlier work remains incomplete—a tower that was begun but not finished, exactly the kind of incomplete building Jesus warned about in His parable. Don't allow the estate planning tower you've invested time, money, and effort into building to remain unfinished and ineffective because you failed to complete the funding process. Take whatever steps are necessary to transfer your real property, financial accounts, business interests, and other significant assets into your trust, creating the comprehensive documentation and organizational systems that will allow your successor trustee to effectively administer the trust when their time comes.

As you work through the funding process, remember that you're not just completing legal formalities but expressing love for your family through careful provision and protection. Every deed you record, every account you re-title, every confirmation document you file away represents another layer of security you're building around your family's financial future. The time you invest in proper funding, the attention you give to detail and documentation, and the ongoing maintenance you provide through periodic reviews all demonstrate faithful stewardship of the resources God has blessed you with and loving care for the people He's placed in your life. Colossians 3:23 instructs, "Whatever you do, work at it with all your heart, as working for the Lord, not for human masters." Approach trust funding with this mindset—working diligently and thoroughly as though you're doing this work for the Lord Himself rather than merely fulfilling legal requirements. When approached with this attitude, trust funding becomes not a burden but a privilege, an opportunity to exercise faithful stewardship and provide for your family in ways that honor both God and those you love. Complete the work you've begun, finish the tower you've started building, and rest in the peace that comes from knowing your family will be protected and provided for through the trust structure you've faithfully established and funded.

Chapter 4:
Executing the Transfer

Executing the transfer of your home into a living trust is the moment when careful planning becomes effectual stewardship. Begin by confirming that the trust document is final, the trust name and date are exact, and you have the correct deed form prepared (quitclaim or warranty, as appropriate). Use the precise legal description from the recorded deed and populate the grantee language exactly as the trust states: for example, "Jane Doe, Trustee of the Jane Doe Revocable Trust dated January 1, 20XX." This attention to detail honors the scriptural call to deliberate planning: "For which of you, desiring to build a tower, does not first sit down and count the cost?" (Luke 14:28).

Arrange for proper execution: sign the deed in the presence of the required witnesses and a notary public according to your state's formalities. If someone signs by power of attorney, ensure the POA document authorizes real estate transfers and is presented with the deed. Mistakes in signatures, missing acknowledgments, or improper witness procedures can render the document ineffective or delay recording; therefore, treat the signing as a solemn and precise act. Scripture teaches that integrity and correct procedure matter: "Let all things be done decently and in order" (1 Corinthians 14:40).

Record the executed deed promptly in the county recorder or land records office where the property is located. Recording places the trust's ownership on public record, protects the priority of title, and completes the funding step that allows the trust to operate as intended. Pay any required recording fees, transfer taxes, or documentary stamps, and request a certified or stamped copy of the recorded instrument for your trust file. The simple act of recording prevents confusion and provides peace to heirs, aligning with the biblical value of prudence: "The prudent sees danger and takes refuge" (Proverbs 27:12).

After recording, notify and update all relevant parties. Inform your homeowners insurance carrier to list the trust or trustee as an insured interest and confirm coverage continues without lapse. Notify the title insurance company if applicable and provide them with a copy of the recorded deed so policy coverage is preserved or adjusted. Update HOA records, utility accounts, and property tax mailing addresses where necessary. If the property is mortgaged, review loan documents for due-on-sale clauses and consult counsel before proactively notifying the lender unless advised; many lenders permit transfers to a revocable trust, but confirming avoids surprises. Acting responsibly toward contractual obligations reflects the Scripture's call to honor agreements: "Let every person be subject to the governing authorities" (Romans 13:1).

Confirm the transfer's practical effect by updating ancillary documents and accounts. Add the property to the trust schedule, place certified copies of the recorded deed with the trust file, and make sure successor trustees know where to find these records. If rental agreements, leases, or management contracts exist, inform tenants or property managers of the trustee change in ownership and provide contact information for the trustee acting on behalf of the trust. Clear documentation and communication reduce friction and protect relationships, modeled by the biblical exhortation to walk honestly: "Whoever walks in integrity walks securely" (Proverbs 10:9).

Be aware of potential post-transfer issues and remedies. If a prior lien, encumbrance, or clerical defect is discovered after recording, work promptly with title counsel and your title insurer to clear matters; in some cases corrective deeds or affidavits may be needed. If the transfer was challenged by a lender or creditor, maintain full transparency and seek legal counsel; transfers made with fraudulent intent can be set aside, so ensure motives and timing are defensible. The Bible warns against deceptive practices and commends uprightness: "Better is a poor person who walks in his integrity than one who is crooked in speech and is a fool" (Proverbs 19:1).

Finally, complete the transfer with wise communication and end-to-end follow-through. Meet with the successor trustee to review duties, provide a copy of the trust and the recorded deed, and leave a simple, written checklist of immediate tasks for administration (insurance, taxes, utilities, emergency contacts). Schedule a brief review with your attorney or advisor within a few months to confirm all steps were properly completed and to address any new assets needing funding. Executing a transfer well is both a legal task and an act of care for those who will carry your legacy forward, fulfilling the call to faithful stewardship: "Commit your work to the Lord, and your plans will be established" (Proverbs 16:3).

***

Section 1: Naming the Trust as the Grantee

The Critical Act of Vesting Title in Your Trust

When transferring property into your revocable living trust using a quitclaim deed, one of the most critical elements is properly naming the trust as the grantee—the party receiving the property. This seemingly simple act of writing the correct name and designation on the deed is actually the precise legal mechanism that moves ownership from you as an individual into the trust structure you've created for estate planning purposes. Get this wrong, and your property may not be properly vested in the trust, potentially undermining your entire estate plan and forcing your family through the very probate process you sought to avoid. Understanding how to correctly identify the trust as grantee, what information must be included, what common mistakes to avoid, and how this designation connects to other aspects of your trust and deed is essential knowledge for anyone funding a living trust with real property.

The importance of precision and care in this naming process reflects biblical principles about attention to detail and faithful stewardship in all our endeavors. Luke 16:10 teaches, "Whoever can be trusted with very little can also be trusted with much, and whoever is dishonest with very little will also be dishonest with much." The act of correctly naming your trust as grantee may seem like a small administrative detail, but it's actually a significant act of stewardship that determines whether your carefully crafted estate plan will function as intended. This "small" detail has enormous consequences for your family's future, making it worthy of your closest attention and greatest care. By approaching this task with diligence and precision, you demonstrate faithful stewardship of the resources God has entrusted to you and ensure your planning efforts bear the fruit you intend—protection and provision for those you love.

Using the Trust's Exact Legal Name and Date

The foundation of properly naming the trust as grantee is using the trust's exact legal name as it appears in your trust document, along with the precise date of execution. Your trust has an official, legal name that appears at the beginning of the trust instrument, often on the first page or in the title. This name typically includes your full name followed by descriptive language such as "Revocable Living Trust," "Revocable Trust," "Family Trust," or similar terminology. For example, your trust might be named "The Jane Mary Doe Revocable Living Trust" or "Jane Mary Doe Living Trust" or "Doe Family Trust." Whatever name appears in your trust document is the name you must use on the quitclaim deed—exactly, without variations, abbreviations, or informal shortening.

Small discrepancies in the trust name can create administrative problems and title issues. If your trust document says "The Jane Mary Doe Revocable Living Trust" but your quitclaim deed says "Jane Doe Trust," you've created an ambiguity about whether these refer to the same trust. Future title examiners, lenders, or buyers may question whether the property is truly held in the trust named in your estate planning documents, potentially requiring corrective deeds or other documentation to clarify the matter. Similarly, you must include the trust's execution date—the date you signed the trust document—as part of the grantee designation. This date uniquely identifies your specific trust instrument, which is particularly important if you later amend your trust or create new versions. The date distinguishes your current trust from any prior trusts you may have had and from future amendments or restatements. A complete grantee designation includes both the exact trust name and the execution date: "Jane Mary Doe, Trustee of The Jane Mary Doe Revocable Living Trust dated January 1, 2024." Copy this information directly from your trust document rather than relying on memory or using variations you think are equivalent. Even differences in punctuation can create questions—if your trust document includes "The" at the beginning of the name or uses commas in particular places, match these details exactly. This precision may seem overly technical, but it prevents ambiguity and ensures perfect alignment between your deed and your trust document. The biblical emphasis on precision in important matters supports this careful approach. Luke 14:28 asks, "For which of you, desiring to build a tower, does not first sit down and count the cost, whether he has enough to complete it?" This verse emphasizes careful planning and attention to detail in significant undertakings. Transferring your home into your trust is exactly such a significant undertaking, and "counting the cost" includes ensuring every detail—including the precise trust name and date—is correct before you proceed. Carelessness with these details is like beginning to build without proper planning, risking complications and additional costs to correct mistakes later.

Identifying the Trustee Role in the Grantee Designation

Beyond naming the trust itself, your grantee designation must clearly identify who holds the trustee role—the person or entity with legal authority to hold and manage trust property. The trustee is not the trust; rather, the trustee acts on behalf of the trust, holding legal title to trust assets and managing them according to the trust's terms. For this reason, the grantee designation on your quitclaim deed must name the trustee in their capacity as trustee, not simply name the trust as an entity. The standard and clearest format is: "[Full Name], Trustee of the [Complete Trust Name] dated [Trust Date]." For example: "Jane Mary Doe, Trustee of The Jane Mary Doe Revocable Living Trust dated January 1, 2024."

This format accomplishes several important purposes. First, it identifies the specific individual who currently holds trustee authority, which is important for county recorders who need to know who has legal authority over the property. Second, it clearly connects the property to the specific trust instrument by including the trust's complete name and date. Third, it establishes the capacity in which the trustee holds the property—not as their personal property, but in their fiduciary role as trustee. This distinction is crucial because it affects how the property is treated for tax purposes, creditor protection, and estate distribution. When you eventually die and your successor trustee takes over, they can demonstrate their authority by showing the trust document that names them as successor trustee, proving they've succeeded to the role identified in the recorded deed. Some practitioners prefer adding "and his/her successors in trust" after the trustee designation to make this succession of authority even more explicit. A complete designation might read: "Jane Mary Doe, Trustee of The Jane Mary Doe Revocable Living Trust dated January 1, 2024, and her successors in trust." This addition clarifies that future successor trustees will also have authority over the property without requiring new deeds, though it's not always strictly necessary since succession is established by the trust document itself. The clarity of identifying the trustee role reflects the biblical emphasis on clearly defining responsibilities and authority. First Corinthians 4:2 teaches, "Moreover, it is required of stewards that they be found faithful." A steward must be clearly identified so everyone knows who bears responsibility and to whom faithfulness is required. Similarly, clearly identifying the trustee in the deed's grantee line ensures everyone understands who holds legal authority over the property and bears fiduciary responsibility for managing it according to the trust's terms. This clarity prevents confusion and establishes accountability.

Privacy Considerations: Recording the Deed Without the Trust

One significant advantage of using trusts for estate planning is privacy—unlike wills, which become public documents when filed with probate courts, trusts generally remain private instruments not subject to public disclosure. However, when you transfer real property into a trust, you must record the quitclaim deed with the county recorder, creating a public record of the transfer. This raises the question of whether you must also record your trust document itself or whether you can maintain its privacy while still recording the deed. In most jurisdictions, you are not required to record the trust document itself when recording a deed that transfers property into the trust. The deed alone is sufficient to establish the trust's ownership of the property, with the trust document remaining a private instrument held by you and your attorney.

This approach preserves family privacy by keeping the trust's detailed provisions, beneficiary identifications, distribution instructions, and other sensitive information out of public records where anyone could access them. The recorded deed shows that the property is held in trust and identifies the trustee, but it doesn't reveal who will inherit the property, what conditions apply to distributions, or other private family matters. If third parties later need proof of the trustee's authority—such as when you want to sell or refinance the property—most states allow you to provide a Trustee's Certification, Certificate of Trust, or Memorandum of Trust instead of the complete trust document. These abbreviated certificates include essential information like the trust's name and date, the trustee's identity and powers, and relevant provisions about real property, but they omit sensitive provisions about beneficiaries and distributions. The

Trustee's Certification is typically a short document (often just 2-3 pages) that the trustee signs and has notarized, affirming key facts about the trust and the trustee's authority. Many states have statutory forms for Trustee's Certifications that third parties must accept as proof of authority. This approach balances the need for recorded public notice of the property transfer with the legitimate interest in keeping family estate planning details private. The wisdom of maintaining appropriate privacy in family financial matters finds support in Scripture. Proverbs 27:12 counsels, "The prudent sees danger and hides himself, but the simple go on and suffer for it" (ESV). While this verse addresses physical danger, its principle applies to protecting sensitive information from public exposure. Making your trust document publicly available through recording could expose your family to dangers like predatory targeting of beneficiaries, disputes from disappointed parties who learn they weren't included, or unwanted intrusion into private family decisions. The prudent approach is to record only what's necessary (the deed) while keeping private what can remain so (the trust document's details).

Ensuring the Trust Authorizes Holding Real Property

Before naming your trust as grantee and transferring property into it, verify that your trust document actually authorizes the trustee to hold and manage real estate. While most properly drafted revocable living trusts include broad language empowering the trustee to acquire, hold, manage, and dispose of all types of property including real estate, some older or poorly drafted trusts might be silent on this point or might contain limitations on the types of property the trustee can hold. Review your trust document, particularly the sections describing trustee powers, to confirm that real estate is within the trustee's authority. Look for language granting the trustee power to "acquire, hold, manage, sell, lease, mortgage, and otherwise deal with real property" or similar broad grants of authority over real estate.

If your trust document is silent about real property or contains language that could be interpreted as limiting the trustee's authority, consult with an estate planning attorney before transferring property into the trust. You may need to amend your trust to include explicit authorization for holding real estate, or the attorney may determine that existing language is sufficient despite not being explicit. Attempting to transfer property into a trust that lacks authority to hold it creates legal ambiguity that could complicate future transactions or administration. Additionally, check whether your trust contains any unusual provisions about how real property should be held, managed, or distributed. Some trusts include specific instructions about the family home, such as allowing a surviving spouse to live there for life, or directing that it be offered to certain beneficiaries before being sold, or requiring unanimous beneficiary consent for sale. Understanding these provisions helps ensure your transfer and future management of the property align with the trust's requirements. This due diligence in confirming the trust's authority reflects the biblical principle of acting within proper bounds and with legitimate authority. Romans 13:1 teaches, "Let every person be subject to the governing authorities. For there is no authority except from God, and those that exist have been instituted by God." While this verse addresses governmental authority, it establishes a broader principle that authority matters and must be respected. Your trustee derives authority from the trust document, and the trustee can only properly hold property that the trust instrument authorizes. Confirming this authority before transferring property demonstrates respect for the proper order and legal structure you've established through your trust.

Handling Multiple Trustees and Successor Trustee Situations

If your trust has multiple trustees serving simultaneously—such as both spouses serving as co-trustees—the grantee designation on your quitclaim deed must identify all acting trustees. The format typically lists all co-trustees' names followed by the collective designation: "Jane Mary Doe and John Robert Doe, Co-Trustees of The Doe Family Trust dated January 1, 2024." This designation establishes that both individuals hold trustee authority and both have legal power over the property. In co-trustee situations, state law and your trust document govern whether both trustees must sign documents related to trust property or whether either can act independently. Most trusts require unanimous action by co-trustees for significant decisions like selling or mortgaging real property, though some allow individual action. Understanding your specific trust's requirements prevents problems when you later need to take action regarding the property.

Your trust document also identifies successor trustees—the individuals who will take over trust management when you die or become incapacitated. These successor trustees are not named in the initial quitclaim deed's grantee designation because they don't currently hold authority; they're only identified in the trust document itself, where they await the triggering event that activates their role. When that event occurs—your death or incapacity—the successor trustee steps into the role without needing a new deed because the property is held "by the trustee and his/her successors in trust." The successor trustee proves their authority by presenting the trust document showing their designation, along with proof of the event that triggered succession (such as a death certificate if you've died). If you later want to change who serves as trustee while you're alive—perhaps adding an adult child as co-trustee or resigning as trustee and appointing your successor early—you would execute a deed from yourself as trustee to the new trustee configuration. For example, if you're currently sole trustee and want to add your daughter as co-trustee, you would execute a deed from "Jane Mary Doe, Trustee of The Jane Mary Doe Revocable Living Trust dated January 1, 2024" to "Jane Mary Doe and Sarah Ann Smith, Co-Trustees of The Jane Mary Doe Revocable Living Trust dated January 1, 2024." This deed updates the public record to reflect the current trustee(s) with authority over the property. The importance of clearly identifying current authority and providing for succession reflects biblical wisdom about leadership transition and continuity. In the Old Testament, we see numerous examples of leadership succession carefully planned and executed, such as Moses appointing Joshua as his successor in Numbers 27:18-23, with clear public designation of who would assume authority. Similarly, your trust and deed documents should clearly establish current authority and provide for seamless succession when needed, ensuring continuity of management and avoiding gaps in authority.

Special Considerations for Corporate or Professional Trustees

While most people name themselves as initial trustee of their revocable living trust, some individuals use professional trustees—such as banks, trust companies, or law firms—particularly if they lack confidence in their ability to manage trust assets or have no suitable family members to serve. If a corporate or professional trustee will hold your property, the grantee designation must include the exact corporate name of the trustee entity along with the trust information. For example: "First National Bank, as Trustee of The Jane Mary Doe Revocable Living Trust dated January 1, 2024." The corporate trustee's name must match exactly how it appears in the trust document and in the corporation's official records. Don't abbreviate or use informal names—if the official name is "First National Bank and Trust Company," use that complete name rather than shortening it to "First National Bank."

When the deed is executed, a corporate trustee doesn't sign personally; instead, an authorized officer of the corporation signs on the entity's behalf. The signature block should identify both the corporate trustee and the individual signing, along with that individual's title. For example: "First National Bank and Trust Company, as Trustee of The Jane Mary Doe Revocable Living Trust dated January 1, 2024, by Robert James Anderson, Vice President." The notary public then acknowledges the signature of the corporate officer signing on behalf of the corporate trustee. Some states require additional documentation when corporate trustees sign, such as a corporate resolution authorizing the signing officer to act on the company's behalf, or a certificate of incumbency proving the person holds the title they claim. Professional trustees are familiar with these requirements and typically provide all necessary documentation. If you're transferring property from your individual name to a corporate trustee, ensure the corporate trustee has formally accepted the trusteeship before executing the deed. Most professional trustees require a signed acceptance of trusteeship document and have various account opening and administrative procedures to complete before they'll accept property. Coordinate with the corporate trustee to ensure all preliminary steps are completed before you execute the transfer deed. This attention to proper corporate authorization and procedure reflects biblical principles about acting with legitimate authority and following proper procedures. When Jesus was questioned about his authority in Matthew 21:23-27, the issue of legitimate authority was central. Similarly, when corporate trustees act, they must demonstrate they have legitimate corporate authority to do so, following proper corporate procedures and providing necessary documentation. Ensuring these requirements are met before transferring valuable property demonstrates wisdom and protects all parties.

Coordinating the Grantee Designation with Other Deed Elements

The grantee designation, while critical, is just one element of your quitclaim deed, and it must be properly coordinated with the deed's other components to create a valid, effective document. First, the grantee designation must align with the legal property description. The property you're transferring—described in detail in the legal description section of the deed—is being transferred specifically to the trustee of the trust you've named. These elements work together: "Jane Mary Doe does hereby quitclaim to Jane Mary Doe, Trustee of The Jane Mary Doe Revocable Living Trust dated January 1, 2024, the following described real property: [legal description]." Every element must be present and properly connected to create a valid transfer.

Second, the consideration statement (the statement of what's being exchanged for the property) must be appropriate for a trust transfer. Since you're not selling the property but reorganizing how you hold title, the consideration is typically nominal or stated generally. Common phrasings include "for the sum of Ten Dollars ($10.00) and other good and valuable consideration" or simply "for good and valuable consideration." Check your county's requirements, as some jurisdictions require specific consideration language or values for recording purposes. Third, ensure your notarization and witness requirements are met according to your state's law. The notary acknowledgment must identify the grantor (you, signing as an individual) properly, not the grantee (you in your capacity as trustee). The notary is witnessing your signature as the person transferring the property, verifying your identity and voluntary action. Some states require witnesses in addition to notarization, and these witnesses must sign their names and provide their addresses in the proper sections of the deed. Finally, after the deed is properly executed and recorded, update all related records to reflect the trust's ownership. Contact your homeowner's insurance company and request that the policy be updated to show the trust as the insured party. Notify your property tax assessor's office and provide any required forms to maintain homestead exemptions or other tax benefits. If you have a mortgage, notify your lender of the ownership change, though federal law protects this transfer from triggering due-on-sale clauses. Update any homeowners association records to reflect the change in ownership. This comprehensive coordination of all elements ensures the transfer is complete and effective in every respect. The principle of comprehensive attention to all related details reflects the biblical teaching about thoroughness in our work. Colossians 3:23 instructs, "Whatever you do, work at it with all your heart, as working for the Lord, not for human masters." Working at something "with all your heart" means giving it complete attention, not just focusing on one element while neglecting others. Naming the trust as grantee is essential, but it's only fully effective when coordinated with proper legal descriptions, consideration statements, execution formalities, and post-recording updates. Excellence requires attention to the complete picture, not just isolated elements.

Seeking Professional Review to Avoid Costly Mistakes

While many aspects of transferring property into a living trust are straightforward enough for informed individuals to handle, the technical legal requirements and potential for consequential errors make professional review highly advisable. Estate planning attorneys and title professionals see deed preparation as a routine matter—something they handle regularly and can complete efficiently based on extensive experience. For you, it may be your first time preparing such a document, with higher risk of errors that could create title problems, cloud your ownership, or undermine your estate plan. Common mistakes in naming the trust as grantee include using incomplete or incorrect trust names, omitting the trust date, failing to designate the trustee capacity, using inconsistent names between the deed and trust document, and improperly formatting the designation for your jurisdiction's requirements.

The modest cost of having an attorney or title company prepare your quitclaim deed—typically $150 to $500—is insignificant compared to the potential cost of correcting mistakes later. If your deed is improperly prepared and creates title problems, you may need to execute a corrective deed, obtain quiet title action through the courts, or deal with refusals from title insurance companies or lenders to accept your property as security. These corrections can cost thousands of dollars and significant time, far exceeding what you saved by preparing the deed yourself without professional review. Even if you choose to prepare the deed yourself using forms or templates, having an attorney review the completed document before you sign and record it provides valuable assurance that everything is correct. Most attorneys charge minimal fees for document review compared to full preparation, making this a cost-effective way to gain professional verification while still doing most of the work yourself. The value of seeking counsel in important matters is emphasized throughout Scripture. Proverbs 15:22 teaches, "Plans fail for lack of counsel, but with many advisers they succeed." Transferring your home into your trust is a significant plan that deserves the benefit of professional counsel to ensure its success. Proverbs 11:14 similarly observes, "Where there is no guidance, a people falls, but in an abundance of counselors there is safety." The safety and security of knowing your deed is properly prepared, your trust correctly named as grantee, and your property validly transferred into trust is well worth the modest investment in professional review. Don't let false economy or overconfidence lead you to skip this important step. The temporary savings could result in far greater costs and complications later, particularly if problems aren't discovered until after your death when correction becomes more difficult and your family must deal with the consequences.

Conclusion: Converting Intention into Effective Stewardship

Properly naming your trust as the grantee on your quitclaim deed is the critical act that transforms your estate planning intentions into legal reality. Your carefully drafted trust document is merely potential until property is actually transferred into it, and that transfer happens through the precise act of correctly identifying the trust and trustee as grantee on a properly executed and recorded deed. This technical requirement—using exact trust names, including proper dates, identifying trustee capacity, coordinating with other deed elements, and following all applicable formalities—may seem burdensome, but it's the indispensable mechanism that makes your entire estate plan operational. Without accurate grantee designation, your property remains outside the trust and subject to probate despite your planning efforts, defeating your purposes and burdening your family.

As you prepare to transfer your property into your trust, approach the grantee designation with the care and precision it deserves. Use your trust document as your reference, copying names and dates exactly. Include all necessary elements: trustee identity, capacity designation, complete trust name, and execution date. Coordinate this designation with proper legal descriptions, appropriate consideration language, and required execution formalities. After recording, update all related records so the transfer is recognized universally. And when in doubt, seek professional counsel to verify your work before proceeding. These steps demonstrate faithful stewardship of significant resources and wise planning for family protection. Proverbs 16:3 promises, "Commit your work to the Lord, and your plans will be established." When you approach property transfers and estate planning with diligence, integrity, and care, committing your efforts to honoring God and serving your family, you can trust that your plans will indeed be established. The technical precision required in naming the trust as grantee is not merely legal formality but faithful stewardship that ensures your provision reaches those you love, your plans function as intended, and your legacy honors both your family and the God who blessed you with resources to manage. Take the time to do this work with excellence, and the fruit of your careful planning will bless generations to come.

Chapter 4: Overview

This chapter provides a step-by-step guide to transferring your home into your living trust using a quitclaim deed. It's designed for homeowners who want to handle the process discreetly, without triggering lender involvement.

Step 1: Prepare Your Living Trust

Before transferring your home, ensure your trust is properly drafted and signed. Key elements include:

- **Trust name** (e.g., "The John and Jane Doe Living Trust")
- **Trustee(s)**: Who will manage the trust
- **Beneficiaries**: Who inherits the property
- **Revocability**: Most homeowners use a revocable trust for flexibility

Step 2: Obtain a Blank Quitclaim Deed Form

You can find state-specific quitclaim deed templates online or at your local county recorder's office. Make sure the form complies with your state's requirements.

Step 3: Fill Out the Quitclaim Deed

Key fields to complete:

- **Grantor**: Your name as the current owner
- **Grantee**: The name of your trust (e.g., "John Doe, Trustee of the John Doe Living Trust dated January 1, 2025")
- **Legal description**: Use the exact description from your original deed
- **Parcel number**: Optional but helpful
- **Consideration**: Typically listed as "$0" or "For no consideration"

Step 4: Sign and Notarize

- Sign the deed in front of a **notary public**

- Some states require **witnesses** — check local rules
- Do not alter the deed after notarization

Step 5: Record the Deed

- Take the signed deed to your **county recorder's office**
- Pay the **recording fee** (usually $10–$50)
- Ask for a **certified copy** for your records

Step 6: Maintain Discretion

- Do not notify your lender unless required
- Most lenders do not object to transfers into revocable trusts
- Avoid refinancing or selling immediately after the transfer to prevent scrutiny

⚠ **Legal Tip**

While transferring without lender notification is common, it may violate the **due-on-sale clause** in your mortgage. However, federal law (Garn-St. Germain Act) generally protects transfers into revocable living trusts for estate planning purposes.

***

Section 2: Signing and Notarizing the Deed

Introduction: The Solemn Act That Creates Legal Reality

The moment you sign your quitclaim deed in the presence of a notary public and required witnesses is the pivotal point when your intentions and preparations transform into legal reality. All the careful planning, document preparation, and attention to detail that preceded this moment culminate in the simple act of putting pen to paper and affixing your signature to the deed. Yet this seemingly simple act carries profound legal significance and must be executed with precision according to your state's specific requirements. A deed that is improperly signed, inadequately witnessed, or incorrectly notarized may be deemed invalid, unrecordable, or legally defective—rendering all your preparation efforts worthless and leaving your property transfer incomplete or challenged.

Understanding the formalities required for proper deed execution and why each element matters is essential for anyone transferring real property. These requirements are not arbitrary bureaucratic hurdles but carefully designed safeguards that protect property owners from fraud, coercion, and forgery while providing certainty about property ownership. The biblical principle of doing things properly and in order applies directly to this process. As 1 Corinthians 14:40 instructs, "But everything should be done in a fitting and orderly way." Executing your deed with all required formalities—proper signatures, adequate witnesses, correct notarization—is precisely this kind of orderly, fitting procedure that ensures your property transfer is legally sound and will be recognized by courts, recorders, and future parties. This comprehensive guide will walk you through every aspect of signing and notarizing your quitclaim deed, helping you execute this critical document correctly and confidently.

Understanding Signature Requirements and Matching Your Legal Name

The most fundamental requirement for executing a quitclaim deed is that the grantor—the person or entity transferring the property—must sign the document. However, the signature cannot be casual or informal; it must match the grantor's legal name exactly as it appears on the current title to the property. This requirement exists because the deed purports to transfer property from the record owner, and the signature must demonstrate that the actual record owner is executing the transfer. If your current deed shows your name as "Jane Mary Doe," you must sign the quitclaim deed as "Jane Mary Doe," not as "Jane Doe," "J.M. Doe," or "Jane M. Doe," even if you commonly use one of these shortened versions in daily life.

Review your current recorded deed—the deed by which you acquired the property—to determine exactly how your name appears. If your name includes your middle name spelled out, include it in your signature on the quitclaim deed. If it includes only a middle initial, use only the initial. If your name appears with a suffix like "Jr." or "III," include that suffix in your signature. The signature you place on the deed should be your normal, customary signature, but it should represent the complete legal name shown on the signature line. If you've legally changed your name since acquiring the property—perhaps through marriage, divorce, or court order—you may need to establish the connection between your current name and the name on title. This might require recording a name change affidavit or other documentation before executing the quitclaim deed, or it might mean signing with both names: "Jane Mary Smith, formerly known as Jane Mary Doe." Consult with a real estate attorney about the proper procedure in your jurisdiction for handling name changes in property transfers.

For married individuals, pay attention to any marital status designation in your current deed. If it shows you as "Jane Mary Doe, a married woman" or "Jane Mary Doe and John Robert Doe, husband and wife," maintain consistency with this designation in your quitclaim deed. Some states require both spouses to sign deeds even when only one spouse holds title, due to homestead rights or community property laws, so verify your state's requirements. The importance of accurate identification and using proper names has biblical precedent. Throughout Scripture, names carry significance and are used with precision. God knew Moses "by name" (Exodus 33:17), and in Revelation 2:17, believers are promised a white stone with a new name written on it that no one knows except the recipient. Names matter to God because they represent identity, and legal names matter in property transfers for the same reason—they establish who is actually conveying the property. Using your correct legal name on the deed honors this principle of accurate identification and prevents ambiguity about the transferor's identity.

Determining Who Must Sign When Multiple Owners Exist

If your property is owned by multiple people—such as spouses holding property jointly, siblings who inherited property together, or business partners who co-own real estate—all owners with an interest in the property must sign the quitclaim deed unless some have previously conveyed their interests away. This requirement exists because each owner holds a distinct legal interest that only they can transfer; no co-owner has authority to transfer another owner's interest without explicit authorization through power of attorney or other legal mechanism. When determining who must sign, review your current deed to see exactly who holds title and in what form of ownership.

Common forms of co-ownership include joint tenancy with right of survivorship (where all owners have equal undivided interests and the property passes to survivors when one dies), tenancy in common (where owners may have unequal interests that pass to their heirs rather than to co-owners when they die), tenancy by the entirety (a special form of joint ownership available only to married couples in some states), and community property (in community property states, where spouses hold equal interests in property acquired during marriage). The form of ownership affects what happens to interests when owners die, but for purposes of executing a quitclaim deed during everyone's lifetime, all current owners must sign regardless of ownership form. If you and your spouse jointly own your home and want to transfer it into your joint trust, both of you must sign the quitclaim deed as grantors. If three siblings inherited property as tenants in common, all three must sign to transfer complete ownership, though each could individually sign separate deeds transferring only their individual interests if desired.

In situations where one co-owner is deceased, that person's interest has already passed either to survivors (in joint tenancy) or to their heirs or beneficiaries (in tenancy in common), and the appropriate parties must sign. If a co-owner is incapacitated and unable to sign, their guardian or agent under power of attorney may need to sign on their behalf with proper authorization. The requirement that all owners sign protects each owner's property rights and prevents one co-owner from unilaterally transferring property without others' consent. This reflects biblical principles about respecting others' ownership and not taking what belongs to them. Exodus 20:15 commands simply, "You shall not steal," and Proverbs 22:28 warns, "Do not move an ancient boundary stone set up by your ancestors." While these verses address different contexts, they establish God's strong concern for property rights and boundaries. Requiring all owners to sign respects each person's property interest and ensures no one's ownership is stolen or moved without their consent and participation.

Handling Powers of Attorney and Agency Signing Authority

Sometimes the property owner cannot personally appear to sign the deed—perhaps due to distance, illness, incapacity, or other circumstances—and must authorize someone else to sign on their behalf. This is accomplished through a power of attorney (POA), a legal document that grants one person (the agent or attorney-in-fact) authority to act on behalf of another person (the principal). However, not just any power of attorney will suffice for real estate transactions. The POA must specifically grant authority to convey real property, as general powers of attorney may not include this authority unless explicitly stated. Review the power of attorney document carefully to confirm it includes language authorizing the agent to "convey, sell, transfer, or deed real property" or similar explicit real estate authority.

When an agent signs a deed under power of attorney, specific procedures must be followed. First, the agent must have the original power of attorney document or a certified copy to present to the notary public at signing. Many states require that powers of attorney used for real estate transactions be recorded in the same county where the property is located, either before or simultaneously with the deed being signed. Check your county recorder's requirements regarding POA recording. Second, the signature on the deed should reflect the agency relationship. The proper format is typically: "[Principal's Name] by [Agent's Name], Attorney in Fact" or "[Principal's Name] by [Agent's Name], Agent under Power of Attorney." For example: "Jane Mary Doe by Robert James Smith, Attorney in Fact." This signature format makes clear that the agent is signing on behalf of the principal, not in their personal capacity.

Third, the notarial acknowledgment must be specially formatted for power of attorney signings, acknowledging that the agent appeared and signed on behalf of the principal. Many states have specific notarial certificate language required for POA signings that differs from standard acknowledgments. The notary should see both the agent's identification and the power of attorney document, verifying the agent's identity and authority. Fourth, some jurisdictions require the power of attorney document to be attached to the deed or at least referenced in the deed's body, creating a clear record of the agent's authority. Consult with a real estate attorney about your state's specific requirements for POA deed signings, as these vary significantly and errors can invalidate the deed. The concept of acting as another's agent or representative has biblical precedent in the relationship between God and His prophets or messengers. When God sent Moses to Pharaoh in Exodus 3-4, Moses acted as God's representative with specific authority to speak and act on God's behalf. Similarly, agents under power of attorney carry specific authority to act on their principal's behalf within the bounds of the authority granted. Properly documenting and executing this agency relationship through correct POA procedures and signature formats ensures the agent's actions are recognized as valid and binding on the principal.

Corporate and Entity Signing Requirements

When the grantor is a corporate entity, limited liability company, partnership, or other business organization rather than an individual, different signing requirements apply. Entities cannot personally sign documents; they must act through authorized representatives—typically officers, managers, or partners who have authority to bind the entity. If a corporate trustee or business entity is transferring property via quitclaim deed, the deed must be signed by a person with authority to act on the entity's behalf, and that person's signature must include their title or capacity to show they're acting for the entity, not personally.

For corporations, authorized signers typically include the president, vice president, secretary, or other officers designated in corporate bylaws or by board resolution. The signature block should identify both the corporate grantor and the signing officer: "ABC Corporation by Robert James Anderson, President." Some jurisdictions require corporate seals on deeds, though this requirement has been eliminated in many states. For limited liability companies (LLCs), authorized signers are typically members or managers, depending on the LLC's management structure. The signature block might read: "XYZ Properties, LLC by Sarah Ann Wilson, Manager." For partnerships, general partners typically have authority to sign on behalf of the partnership: "Smith & Jones Partnership by John Smith, General Partner."

Beyond proper signature formatting, many states require additional documentation to prove the signatory's authority to act on behalf of the entity. This might include a certified copy of a corporate resolution authorizing the transaction and designating the signing officer, a certificate of good standing from the state where the entity is incorporated or organized, articles of incorporation or organization, or a certificate of incumbency proving the person holds the office they claim. Requirements vary by state and sometimes by county, so check with the county recorder where you'll record the deed about what supporting documentation is needed. When corporate trustees sign deeds for trust property, similar requirements apply—the corporate trustee signs through an authorized officer, and documentation proving both the corporation's authority as trustee and the officer's authority to act for the corporation may be required. This attention to proper corporate authorization and procedure reflects biblical teaching about acting with legitimate authority within established structures. Titus 1:5 speaks of appointing elders "as I directed you," showing that proper appointment and authority matter in organizational contexts. When corporate entities act, they must do so through properly authorized representatives following their governing documents and state law. Ensuring these requirements are met demonstrates respect for proper order and protects all parties by confirming the transaction is authorized.

The Critical Role of Notarization and Proper Acknowledgment

Notarization is the process by which a notary public—an official authorized by the state—verifies the identity of the person signing a document, confirms they're signing voluntarily and competently, and witnesses their signature. For real estate deeds, notarization serves as formal proof that the signature is genuine and that the signing was done freely without fraud or coercion. Most states require notarization of all deeds as a condition for recording them with the county, and even in states where it's not legally required, recorders typically won't accept unnotarized deeds. The notary's acknowledgment—the certificate the notary completes and signs on the deed—becomes a permanent part of the recorded instrument and provides future parties with assurance about the signature's authenticity.

When you appear before a notary to sign your quitclaim deed, bring valid government-issued photo identification such as a driver's license, passport, state ID card, or military ID. The notary will examine your ID to verify you are who you claim to be, matching the name on your ID to the name on the deed. You must appear before the notary in person; they cannot notarize your signature if you've already signed the document elsewhere or if you're not physically present. The notary will ask you to confirm that you understand the document and are signing it voluntarily, ensuring you're not under duress or incapacitated. After verifying your identity and voluntary intent, the notary watches you sign the deed (or acknowledges your signature if you've just signed in their presence). The notary then completes an acknowledgment certificate on the deed, which includes several key elements: the date and location of the notarization, your name as it appears on your identification, a statement that you personally appeared before the notary and acknowledged signing the document, the notary's signature, the notary's printed name, the notary's commission expiration date, and the notary's official seal or stamp.

The exact wording of the acknowledgment certificate varies by state, and it's crucial to use the correct form for your jurisdiction. Many quitclaim deed forms include acknowledgment certificates, but verify that the certificate language complies with your state's current requirements, as these sometimes change. Using outdated or incorrect acknowledgment language can cause the county recorder to reject the deed. Some states distinguish between "acknowledgments" (where you acknowledge you signed the document) and "jurats" (where you swear or affirm the document's contents are true); deeds typically require acknowledgments rather than jurats. If your deed will be used in a state other than where it's signed, you may need a different acknowledgment form or additional notarial certificates. The notary's role as impartial witness to your signature reflects the biblical principle of establishing matters through credible witnesses. Deuteronomy 19:15 teaches, "One witness is not enough to convict anyone accused of any crime or offense they may have committed. A matter must be established by the testimony of two or three witnesses." While this verse addresses criminal matters, the principle that important acts should be witnessed by credible observers applies broadly. The notary serves as that credible, impartial witness who can testify that you signed the deed voluntarily and that you are who you claim to be, providing evidence that protects against later fraud claims or disputes.

Witness Requirements Beyond Notarization

While notarization is nearly universal for deed execution, some states require additional witnesses beyond the notary public to observe the signing. These witness requirements vary significantly by state—some states require two witnesses, some require one, and many require none beyond the notary. States with witness requirements include Florida, Georgia, Louisiana, South Carolina, and others, though specific rules differ by state. Where witnesses are required, they serve an additional layer of authentication, providing extra testimony that the grantor signed the document voluntarily and appeared to be of sound mind.

Witnesses must be disinterested parties—people who have no stake in the transaction and won't benefit from the property transfer. Family members, beneficiaries of your trust, real estate agents involved in the transaction, or others with financial interest should not serve as witnesses. Ideally, witnesses should be adults who are not related to you and who have no connection to the property or transaction. They must be present when you sign the deed and must watch you sign (or hear you acknowledge your signature). After you sign, each witness signs their name on designated witness lines on the deed and typically prints their name and address below their signature. Witnesses do not need to be notaries themselves, and their signatures usually do not need to be notarized (though the notary may sign as one of the witnesses if multiple witnesses are required).

If your state requires witnesses but you execute the deed in another state (perhaps you own property in Florida but you live in Texas), you must comply with the witness requirements of the state where the property is located, not where you're signing. This may mean having witnesses present even if your current state doesn't require them, or following other formalities mandated by the property's jurisdiction. This can create logistical challenges, so consider consulting with an attorney in the property's state about acceptable procedures for out-of-state execution. The principle of multiple witnesses providing confirmation of important events appears throughout Scripture. John 8:17-18 records Jesus saying, "In your own Law it is written that the testimony of two witnesses is true. I am one who testifies for myself; my other witness is the Father, who sent me." The presence of multiple witnesses establishes truth and protects against false claims. When your deed is witnessed by multiple parties who can testify they saw you sign voluntarily, it provides strong evidence against anyone who might later claim the signature was forged or that you were coerced. This protection benefits you, your family, and future owners of the property by ensuring the transfer's validity cannot easily be challenged.

Proper Execution Sequence and Avoiding Common Mistakes

The sequence and timing of signing and notarization matter significantly, and several common mistakes can invalidate deeds or create problems at recording. First, never sign the deed before appearing before the notary. The notary must watch you sign or hear you acknowledge that the signature is yours, and if you sign beforehand at home or elsewhere, the notary cannot properly certify they witnessed your signature. If you accidentally sign early, either execute a new deed or appear before the notary, draw a line through your premature signature, initial the strikethrough, and then sign again properly in the notary's presence. Second, do not leave blanks in the deed that will be filled in later after signing and notarization. All material information—grantor, grantee, property description, consideration—must be complete before you sign. Filling in blanks after notarization creates questions about whether you agreed to those terms and whether the document has been altered after execution.

Third, ensure all pages of the deed are present when you sign and that you initial each page if your form includes signature or initial lines on multiple pages. Some deeds require the grantor to initial the bottom of each page to prove all pages were part of the document when signed. If pages could be removed or substituted after signing, the document's integrity is compromised. Fourth, make sure dates are correct and consistent throughout the deed. The execution date (when you sign) should match the date in the acknowledgment certificate. Don't date the deed far in advance; date it the day you actually sign. Fifth, do not make handwritten changes or corrections after the deed is signed and notarized. If you discover an error after execution, prepare and execute a corrected deed rather than making changes to the signed original. Handwritten alterations raise questions about whether changes were made without your knowledge or consent, potentially invalidating the deed or causing recording rejection.

Sixth, ensure everyone who needs to sign does so at the same time in front of the same notary when possible, particularly if witnesses are required. Having co-owners sign at different times or in different locations can create complications with witness and notarial requirements. If simultaneous signing isn't possible, each person's signature may need separate notarization with separate acknowledgment certificates on the deed. These execution details may seem overly technical, but they protect the document's integrity and prevent challenges to its validity. The biblical principle of being thorough and careful in important undertakings supports this meticulous approach. Proverbs 21:5 teaches, "The plans of the diligent lead to profit as surely as haste leads to poverty." Taking time to execute your deed carefully, following proper sequence, avoiding blanks and alterations, and ensuring all parties sign properly reflects the diligence that leads to profit—in this case, a valid deed that accomplishes your purposes. Haste or carelessness in execution can lead to poverty—potentially an invalid deed that fails to transfer your property and requires expensive corrective action.

Preserving Copies and Preparing for Recording

After your quitclaim deed is fully executed with all required signatures, witnesses, and notarization, but before taking it to the county recorder, make multiple copies for your records. The original deed will be given to the county recorder and will become part of the permanent public records; you'll receive it back after recording with the recorder's stamp showing when and where it was recorded, but that original should then be kept in safe, permanent storage. Before submitting the original for recording, make at least three copies: one for your personal files, one for your trust file (if you're transferring property into a trust), and one for your successor trustee or other key person who should have this information.

Some people also provide copies to their attorney, financial advisor, or family members who need to know about the transfer. These copies serve as evidence of the property transfer and can be referenced if questions arise later. Make copies of the complete deed including all pages, signatures, and notarial certificates, ensuring every element is clearly legible. If your deed includes exhibits (such as an attached legal description or power of attorney), copy those as well. Once you have your copies, review the original deed one final time before submitting it for recording. Check that all blanks are filled, all required signatures are present, all witnesses have signed if required, and the notarial certificate is complete with the notary's signature and seal clearly visible. Review the property description for accuracy, verify grantee and grantor information is correct, and confirm the execution date and consideration are properly stated.

Along with the deed itself, determine what additional documents your county recorder requires. Some counties want a completed cover sheet or transmittal form that provides indexing information about the document. Many counties require a separate documentary transfer tax declaration (even if no tax is due, you may need to file a declaration claiming an exemption for trust transfers). Some jurisdictions require that powers of attorney be recorded with or before deeds signed under POA authority. Others may want a trustee's certification or certificate of trust when property is being transferred into a trust. Contact your county recorder's office before submitting documents to learn what's required and what fees will be charged. Having all required supporting documents assembled with the deed prevents delays or rejection at recording. This careful preservation of copies and preparation for recording reflects the biblical principle of maintaining good records and being prepared. Luke 14:31 asks, "Or suppose a king is about to go to war against another king. Won't he first sit down and consider whether he is able with ten thousand men to oppose the one coming against him with twenty thousand?" This consideration and preparation before acting is exactly what you do by making copies, reviewing the deed, and assembling all required documents before attempting to record. The prepared person succeeds where the unprepared fail.

The Recording Process and What Happens Next

With your fully executed deed and all supporting documents assembled, you're ready for the final step: recording. Take your documents to the county recorder's office (also called register of deeds or clerk's office in some jurisdictions) in the county where the property is located during regular business hours. Most recorders have drop-off windows or counters where you submit documents for recording. Some counties now offer mail-in recording (where you send documents with payment and return envelope) or electronic recording through approved title companies or online portals. Check your county's website for available options and instructions.

When you submit your deed for recording, a clerk will review it to ensure it meets local requirements. They'll check that it's properly signed and notarized, that it includes all required information, and that any supporting documents are present. If the deed is acceptable, the clerk will stamp it with recording information—the date and time of recording, the document number or instrument number assigned to it, and the book and page number where it's recorded (in jurisdictions still using book-and-page indexing) or simply the document number (in jurisdictions using document numbering systems). This recording stamp creates an official record of when the deed was filed, which is crucial for establishing priority if multiple claims to the property exist. You'll pay recording fees at this time, which vary by county but typically range from $15 to $200 depending on the number of pages and local fee schedules. Some counties charge per page, while others charge a flat fee per document.

After recording, the deed becomes part of the public record accessible to anyone who wants to search property records. The transfer of ownership from you individually to you as trustee (or whoever the grantee is) is now officially documented and publicly noticed. The recorder will either return the original deed to you immediately with the recording stamp affixed, or will mail it to you within a few days if you used mail-in recording. When you receive the recorded deed back, store it safely with your other important estate planning documents. File one copy with your trust documents, keep another in your safe deposit box or fireproof safe, and provide copies to appropriate parties like your successor trustee or attorney. The public recording of property transfers has biblical precedent in the public nature of land transactions in ancient Israel. Ruth 4:9-11 describes Boaz's purchase of property: "Then Boaz announced to the elders and all the people, 'Today you are witnesses that I have bought from Naomi all the property of Elimelek, Kileab and Mahlon. I have also acquired Ruth the Moabite, Mahlon's widow, as my wife, in order to maintain the name of the dead with his property, so that his name will not disappear from among his family or from his hometown. Today you are witnesses!' Then the elders and all the people at the gate said, 'We are witnesses.'" This public declaration before witnesses created a clear record of the property transfer that could not be disputed. Your recorded deed serves the same purpose—it creates public notice of the ownership change that protects your interests and provides certainty about who owns the property.

Post-Recording Updates and Notifications

After your deed is successfully recorded and you've received the original back with recording information, several important tasks remain to complete the property transfer process fully. These post-recording steps ensure that all parties and entities that need to know about the ownership change are properly informed and that coverage and protections continue uninterrupted. First and most important, contact your homeowner's insurance company to update your policy. Provide them with a copy of the recorded deed and request that the policy be updated to show the trust as the insured party rather than you individually. The insured designation should typically read: "Jane Mary Doe, Trustee of The Jane Mary Doe Revocable Living Trust dated January 1, 2024" or similar language matching your deed's grantee designation.

Most insurance companies will make this change at no charge since you're still the beneficial owner through your revocable trust. However, failing to update your insurance policy could create problems if you have a claim—the policy might not pay if the insured name doesn't match the property owner. Some insurance companies may also request a copy of relevant pages from your trust document to verify the trust's existence and your role as trustee. Second, notify your mortgage lender if your property has a mortgage. While federal law protects transfers to revocable living trusts from triggering due-on-sale clauses (meaning the lender cannot demand full loan payment just because you transferred the property to your trust), it's still good practice to inform them of the ownership change. Send them a letter with a copy of the recorded deed explaining that you've transferred the property into your revocable living trust for estate planning purposes and that you remain both the trustee and beneficiary.

Third, contact your county property tax assessor's office to ensure your property tax records are updated and any homestead exemptions or other tax benefits are maintained. Many states specifically protect homestead exemptions when property is transferred to the owner's revocable living trust, but you may need to file a form or provide documentation to maintain the exemption. Ask the assessor's office what's required in your jurisdiction and complete any necessary paperwork promptly. Fourth, if your property is part of a homeowners association (HOA), notify the association of the ownership change and provide them with updated contact information if needed. HOA documents and communications may need to be addressed to you as trustee rather than as an individual. Fifth, update utility accounts, property tax payment arrangements, and any other accounts or services associated with the property to reflect the new ownership structure if required by the service providers. Sixth, update your trust's schedule of assets—the document that lists all property held in the trust. Add your property to this schedule with the recording information and date, creating a clear record that the asset is now held in trust. This comprehensive follow-through after recording ensures the property transfer is recognized by all relevant parties and that no coverage gaps or administrative problems arise from the ownership change. The faithfulness of completing every step of a process reflects biblical teaching about finishing what we start. In 2 Timothy 4:7, Paul writes, "I have fought the good fight, I have finished the race, I have kept the faith." This perseverance to completion—not stopping partway through but seeing the task fully accomplished—is what you demonstrate by completing all post-recording updates and notifications. Don't let your property transfer remain partly incomplete by neglecting these final steps; finish the work by ensuring everyone who needs to know about the change is properly informed.

Conclusion: The Completion of Faithful Stewardship

Properly signing and notarizing your quitclaim deed, following all required formalities, recording it with the county, and completing all post-recording tasks transforms your estate planning intentions into accomplished reality. This careful execution process, with its many technical requirements and procedural steps, may seem burdensome, but it serves essential purposes: protecting property rights, preventing fraud, establishing clear ownership records, and ensuring smooth property transfers that benefit your family. When you approach deed execution with diligence, attention to detail, and respect for legal formalities, you demonstrate faithful stewardship of significant resources and wise planning that honors both your family and God.

The commitment to excellence in completing these administrative tasks reflects the biblical call to do all work as unto the Lord. Colossians 3:23-24 instructs, "Whatever you do, work at it with all your heart, as working for the Lord, not for human masters, since you know that you will receive an inheritance from the Lord as a reward. It is the Lord Christ you are serving." When you carefully sign your deed with the correct name, ensure proper notarization, include required witnesses, record promptly, and update all related records, you're working with your whole heart—giving the task the attention and care it deserves because you recognize its significance. This isn't merely paperwork; it's stewardship of resources God has blessed you with and provision for people you love. Proverbs 16:3 promises, "Commit to the Lord whatever you do, and he will establish your plans." As you commit your property transfer to the Lord, doing it with integrity, care, and thoroughness, trust that your plans will indeed be established—your property will be properly transferred, your trust will be effectively funded, and your family will be protected through the structures you've created. The solemn act of signing and notarizing your deed is the culmination of faithful planning, and when done with excellence, it ensures your stewardship continues blessing those you love long after you're gone.

***

Section 3: Recording the Deed with the County

Recording the deed with the county is the final public step that converts a private transaction into a matter of public record and protects the trust's ownership against subsequent claims. Deliver the original, fully executed and notarized deed to the county recorder or clerk in the county where the property lies, pay the required recording fees and any transfer taxes, and request a stamped or certified copy for your trust file. Recording gives constructive notice to the world that the trust holds title, secures priority against later conveyances or liens, and completes the funding process so the trust can operate as intended. The Scripture calls us to prudent preparation and protection: "The prudent sees danger and takes refuge" (Proverbs 27:12).

Before recording, confirm you have the correct county form requirements and any supporting documents the recorder may ask for, such as a trustee's certification, county transfer declaration, or payoff statement when a mortgage exists. Some counties require additional information for tax assessment or documentary transfer tax calculations; others accept nominal consideration language. Verify the precise legal description, parcel number, and exact trust name and date on the deed to avoid clerical rejection or the need for corrective filings. Doing this carefully honors the biblical command to plan deliberately: "For which of you, desiring to build a tower, does not first sit down and count the cost?" (Luke 14:28).

Recording promptly reduces the risk of intervening claims or clerical confusion. Once recorded, obtain a certified or stamped copy and place it with the trust documents; provide notice to your successor trustee and store one additional copy in a secure but accessible location. Recording also triggers practical follow-up tasks: update homeowner's insurance to reflect trust ownership, notify the title insurer if applicable, and confirm property tax records and HOA accounts show the trust or trustee as the owner of record. These steps preserve the protections that recording provides and reflect faithful stewardship of family assets: "A good person leaves an inheritance for their children's children" (Proverbs 13:22).

Be prepared to address problems if the recorder finds defects or if post-recording issues surface, such as prior liens, incorrect legal descriptions, or missing signatures. Work quickly with title counsel or your title insurance carrier to obtain corrective deeds, affidavits, or re-recording when necessary; in many cases a simple corrective deed or affidavit of scrivener's error will resolve clerical mistakes. If a creditor or lender raises concerns after recording, respond transparently and consult counsel—transfers made to defraud creditors can be set aside, so righteous motive and proper timing matter. The Bible warns against deceit and commends upright conduct: "Whoever walks in integrity walks securely" (Proverbs 10:9).

Finally, view recording as both a legal act and an act of care for those who will follow. Recording turns private intention into public protection, simplifies administration for your successors, and clarifies title for future buyers or lenders. After recording, schedule a brief review with your attorney or advisor to confirm the deed was recorded as intended and that all post-recording updates were completed. Completing the record-keeping and communication faithfully fulfills the call to stewardship and loving provision: "Commit your work to the Lord, and your plans will be established" (Proverbs 16:3).

***

Section 4: Recording the Deed with the County

The Public Act That Completes the Transfer

Recording your quitclaim deed with the county recorder's office is the final and essential step that transforms your property transfer from a private transaction between parties into an official public record that protects your interests and provides notice to the world of the ownership change. Until a deed is recorded, it exists only as a private agreement between grantor and grantee—legally valid between those parties but potentially vulnerable to competing claims and lacking the full protection that recording provides. The act of recording creates "constructive notice," meaning that everyone is legally presumed to know about the transfer whether they actually reviewed the public records or not. This notice protects the new owner (in this case, your trust) from subsequent claims, liens, or transfers by establishing priority and documenting the chain of title in official county records.

Understanding the recording process, why it matters, what can go wrong, and what follow-up steps are necessary ensures you complete your property transfer properly and secure all the protections recording provides. The importance of completing and documenting significant transactions in public records has biblical precedent. In Jeremiah 32:9-14, the prophet Jeremiah purchases a field and carefully documents the transaction: "I bought the field at Anathoth from my cousin Hanamel and weighed out for him seventeen shekels of silver. I signed and sealed the deed, had it witnessed, and weighed out the silver on the scales. I took the deed of purchase—the sealed copy containing the terms and conditions, as well as the unsealed copy—and I gave this deed to Baruch...in the presence of my cousin Hanamel and of the witnesses who had signed the deed and of all the Jews sitting in the courtyard of the guard. In their presence I gave Baruch these instructions: 'This is what the Lord Almighty, the God of Israel, says: Take these documents, both the sealed and unsealed copies of the deed of purchase, and put them in a clay jar so they will last a long time.'" This detailed documentation and preservation of property records demonstrates the importance of creating permanent, accessible records of property transfers—exactly what modern recording accomplishes through county records systems.

Understanding the Recording System and Its Purpose

County recording systems exist in every jurisdiction to maintain organized, chronological records of all documents affecting real property ownership within the county. These records create a comprehensive history of each property's ownership, known as the "chain of title," showing every transfer from the original grant of land to the current owner. When you record your quitclaim deed transferring property from yourself individually to yourself as trustee of your trust, you're adding a link to this chain, documenting the ownership change in the official public record. The recording system serves multiple critical functions that protect property owners and facilitate real estate transactions.

First, recording provides constructive notice to all persons that the ownership change has occurred. This means potential buyers, lenders, creditors, or anyone else interested in the property is legally presumed to have knowledge of your recorded deed, whether they actually searched the records or not. If someone later claims they didn't know your trust owned the property, the law responds that they should have searched the public records where your deed was available for inspection. Second, recording establishes priority among competing claims to the same property based on the principle "first in time, first in right." If multiple deeds or liens affect the same property, they're generally given priority in the order they were recorded. By recording your deed promptly after execution, you protect your trust's interest from being subordinated to later-recorded claims. Third, recording creates an official, permanent record that can be referenced decades or even centuries later, providing evidence of ownership that survives loss or destruction of original documents.

Fourth, recorded deeds are typically admissible as evidence in court without additional authentication, making it easier to prove ownership if disputes arise. Fifth, recording protects subsequent purchasers and lenders who rely on the public record when deciding to buy property or make loans secured by it. The organized, public nature of recording systems reflects biblical principles about order, transparency, and creating reliable records.

In Nehemiah 7:5, we read: "So my God put it into my heart to assemble the nobles, the officials and the common people for registration by families. I found the genealogical record of those who had been the first to return." This careful record-keeping and public registration ensured accurate information was available and protected people's rights and identities. County recording systems serve similar purposes—maintaining accurate records that protect rights and provide reliable information for all who need it.

Preparing to Record: Verifying Requirements and Gathering Documents

Before taking your quitclaim deed to the county recorder for filing, careful preparation helps ensure smooth processing and avoids rejection or delay. Start by contacting the county recorder's office (sometimes called the register of deeds, county clerk, or similar title depending on your state) or visiting their website to understand their specific requirements, accepted filing methods, and applicable fees. Most recorder offices provide detailed information about document formatting requirements, what supporting documents are needed, how to calculate fees, and whether they accept mail-in or electronic recording in addition to in-person filing. Pay particular attention to any county-specific forms or cover sheets required with your deed. Many counties require a completed recording cover sheet or transmittal form that provides indexing information—grantor and grantee names, property address, assessor's parcel number, document type, and other details that help the recorder properly index the document in their system.

Next, verify you have all supporting documents the county may require along with the deed itself. Common supporting documents include documentary transfer tax declarations (forms declaring the value of the transfer and calculating any transfer taxes due, or claiming an exemption from such taxes), preliminary change of ownership reports (forms providing information for property tax reassessment purposes, though transfers to revocable trusts are typically exempt from reassessment), trustee's certifications or certificates of trust (abbreviated documents proving the trust's existence and the trustee's authority, required by some counties when property is transferred into a trust), and powers of attorney (if someone signed the deed under POA authority, the POA may need to be recorded along with or before the deed). Not all counties require all these documents, and requirements vary significantly by jurisdiction, so verify what your specific county needs. If your deed includes a legal description attached as an exhibit, ensure the exhibit is properly attached and labeled. Review your deed one final time before submitting it, checking that all required signatures are present, notarization is complete and proper, witness signatures are included if required, all blanks are filled with no missing information, dates are correct and consistent, the legal property description is accurate and complete, and grantor and grantee designations exactly match your intentions. Confirm the exact trust name and date appear correctly if you're transferring into a trust. Verify the property's assessor parcel number (APN) if included on the deed, as errors can cause indexing problems. This thorough preparation before recording reflects the biblical principle of counting the cost and preparing properly before undertaking important work. Luke 14:28-30 asks, "Suppose one of you wants to build a tower. Won't you first sit down and estimate the cost to see if you have enough money to complete it? For if you lay the foundation and are not able to finish it, everyone who sees it will ridicule you, saying, 'This person began to build and wasn't able to finish.'" Preparing thoroughly before recording—gathering required documents, verifying information, understanding fees and procedures—is exactly this kind of cost-counting that enables you to finish what you start without embarrassment or complications.

The Recording Process: Submission, Review, and Acceptance

With your deed and all supporting documents prepared and verified, you're ready to submit them for recording. Most counties offer multiple submission methods. In-person recording involves taking your documents to the recorder's office during business hours, typically to a counter or window designated for document submissions. A clerk will review your documents on the spot, identify any immediate problems, accept the documents if they comply with requirements, collect fees, and provide a receipt. Many recorders can return the recorded original to you the same day or within a few days, stamped with recording information. Mail-in recording involves mailing your documents to the recorder with appropriate fees (often requiring a check or money order) and a self-addressed stamped envelope for return of the recorded originals. Include a cover letter explaining what you're submitting and requesting return of the originals. Processing times for mail-in recording vary but typically take one to three weeks. Electronic recording (e-recording) is increasingly available, where approved title companies, attorneys, or online services submit documents electronically through secure systems. E-recording typically processes faster than mail-in but may require using specific service providers approved by your county.

When you submit your documents, the recorder's clerk will review them for compliance with county requirements. They'll check that documents are properly executed with required signatures and notarization, that any required supporting documents are included, that formatting meets county standards (some counties have requirements about paper size, margins, font sizes, or ink colors), that grantor and grantee names are clearly stated, and that legal descriptions are complete. If problems are identified, the clerk may either reject the documents entirely (returning them to you for correction and resubmission) or accept them conditionally (recording them but noting the defects, which may require corrective documentation later). If the documents are acceptable, the clerk will accept them for recording, assign them a document number or instrument number for tracking, calculate and collect applicable fees, and provide a receipt showing what was submitted and when.

The recording fees you'll pay typically include a base recording fee charged per document (often $15 to $50 for the first page and a few dollars per additional page), transfer taxes or documentary stamps if applicable (though most jurisdictions exempt transfers to revocable living trusts from these taxes when no consideration is paid), and special fees for certain services like expedited processing or extra copies. After accepting your documents and collecting fees, the recorder will process them for recording—entering information into indexing systems, microfilming or scanning the documents for digital preservation, stamping the original with recording information, and filing the documents in the official records. The recording stamp includes the date and time the document was recorded (which establishes priority), the document or instrument number assigned to it, and often the book and page number where it's filed (in jurisdictions still using book-and-page systems) or simply the document number (in modern electronic systems). This stamped original will be returned to you either immediately, mailed to you, or made available for pickup depending on the submission method used and the county's procedures. The thoroughness of the recorder's review and the official nature of the recording process reflect biblical principles about careful examination and official authentication of important matters. In 1 Thessalonians 5:21, Paul instructs, "Test everything; hold fast what is good" (ESV). The recorder's review is exactly this kind of testing—examining documents to ensure they meet legal requirements before entering them into official records. The recording stamp then officially authenticates the document as properly filed in public records, giving it legal force and protection.

Understanding Priority and the Importance of Prompt Recording

One of the most critical reasons for recording your quitclaim deed promptly after execution is to establish and protect your priority against other potential claims to the property. Recording systems generally follow the principle of "first in time, first in right," meaning that between competing recorded interests in the same property, the one recorded first usually takes priority. If you delay recording your deed after signing it, you create a dangerous window during which someone else could record a competing claim that might take priority over yours. While this risk may seem theoretical when you're simply transferring property into your own trust, understanding how priority works helps appreciate why immediate recording is important.

Consider this scenario: You execute a quitclaim deed transferring your home into your trust but don't immediately record it, intending to get around to it eventually. During the recording delay, you're sued and a judgment is entered against you personally. The judgment creditor records their judgment lien against your property. When you finally record your deed weeks or months later, the question arises: which came first, the judgment lien or the transfer to your trust? If the lien was recorded before your deed, the creditor may argue their lien attached to the property before you transferred it, giving them a claim against the property even though it's now in your trust. Prompt recording immediately after execution would have established your trust's ownership before the lien was recorded, protecting the property.

Another scenario involves fraud or mistake. Suppose someone fraudulently claims an interest in your property and records a forged deed or lien. If your legitimate deed is already recorded, the fraudulent document won't gain priority over yours. But if yours isn't yet recorded when the fraudulent document is filed, sorting out the mess becomes more complicated, even though your legitimate claim should ultimately prevail. The lesson is clear: record your deed as soon as possible after execution—ideally the same day or within a few days at most—to establish and protect your priority. Don't delay recording while you attend to other matters or because you don't think it's urgent. The time and modest cost required to record immediately is insignificant compared to the protection it provides. This principle of acting promptly to secure what's important reflects biblical wisdom about not delaying in significant matters. Proverbs 3:27-28 instructs, "Do not withhold good from those to whom it is due, when it is in your power to act. Do not say to your neighbor, 'Come back tomorrow and I'll give it to you'—when you already have it with you." When you have the power to secure your property transfer by recording, do it immediately rather than saying "I'll do it tomorrow" and creating unnecessary risks through delay. The good you can do for your family by establishing clear, protected ownership should not be withheld when you have the power to accomplish it today.

Obtaining and Preserving Recorded Copies

After your deed is successfully recorded, the county recorder returns the original document to you with the recording stamp affixed, creating a "recorded original" that serves as proof of both the transfer and its recording. This recorded original is valuable and should be preserved carefully. When you receive it, immediately make several copies before filing the original away in secure storage. Create at least three to five copies: one for your permanent personal files, one to be filed with your trust documents (stored wherever you keep your trust instrument and related estate planning documents), one for your successor trustee or other key person who should have this information, one for your estate planning attorney if they maintain files for you, and one additional copy for backup purposes or to provide to third parties who may need evidence of the transfer.

These copies should be clear, complete reproductions showing the entire deed including all pages, signatures, notarial certificates, and most importantly, the recorder's stamp with recording information. The recorder's stamp proves the deed was officially filed and shows when it was recorded, which is crucial information for establishing priority and confirming the transfer. Store the recorded original in secure but accessible storage—a home safe, safety deposit box, or fireproof document storage container. Don't store it in a location where it could be lost, damaged by fire or flood, or inaccessible to those who might need it. If you use a safety deposit box, consider whether your successor trustee or spouse can access it if needed, as some banks restrict access to safety deposit boxes after the owner's death. Ensure at least one copy is stored separately from the original so that if one location is compromised, you still have documentation of the recorded deed.

Some people create a dedicated binder or folder for trust-related documents where they file the recorded deed, the trust instrument, trustee certifications, trust asset schedules, and other related documents, making it easy for successors to find everything in one place. Consider also scanning the recorded deed and saving digital copies in multiple locations—your computer, cloud storage, and external backup drives. Digital copies make it easy to provide documentation to insurance companies, lenders, or others who need evidence of the transfer without giving away one of your physical copies. However, always retain the physical original and at least one physical copy, as some parties may require original or certified documents rather than accepting digital versions. The diligence in obtaining, copying, and preserving these recorded documents reflects biblical teaching about being prepared and maintaining good records. Proverbs 24:27 advises, "Put your outdoor work in order and get your fields ready; after that, build your house." This verse emphasizes preparation and having affairs in order before moving forward, and properly preserving your recorded deed is exactly this kind of preparation. You're putting your legal affairs in order, making sure your successor trustees and family members will be able to find and access the documentation they need to administer your trust and manage your property after you're gone.

Post-Recording Notifications and Updates

Recording your deed completes the legal transfer of property into your trust, but several important practical steps remain to ensure the transfer is recognized by all relevant parties and that coverage and protections continue uninterrupted. First and most critical, update your homeowner's insurance policy to reflect the trust's ownership. Contact your insurance company or agent, provide them with a copy of the recorded deed, and request that the policy be amended to show the trust as the insured party. The proper insured designation typically matches the grantee designation on your deed: "Jane Mary Doe, Trustee of The Jane Mary Doe Revocable Living Trust dated January 1, 2024." Most insurers make this change at no cost since you're still the beneficial owner through your revocable trust. However, they may request a copy of relevant pages from your trust document to verify its existence and your authority. Failing to update your insurance could create claim problems if a loss occurs and the insured name doesn't match the property owner.

Second, notify your owner's title insurance company if you purchased an owner's title policy when you acquired the property. While most title policies automatically cover transfers to the insured person's revocable living trust, it's good practice to notify the title company of the transfer and verify coverage continues. Some companies issue an endorsement confirming coverage for the trust; others simply note the transfer in their records. Either way, having written confirmation that your title insurance remains in effect provides valuable peace of mind. Third, contact your county property tax assessor's office to update property tax records and ensure homestead exemptions or other tax benefits continue. Most states exempt transfers to revocable living trusts from property tax reassessment and allow homestead exemptions to continue, but you may need to file a form or provide documentation. Ask the assessor's office what's required and complete any necessary paperwork promptly to avoid losing valuable tax benefits. Provide them with a copy of the recorded deed and any required exemption claim forms.

Fourth, if your property has a mortgage, notify your lender of the ownership change. While federal law (the Garn-St. Germain Act) protects transfers to revocable living trusts from triggering due-on-sale clauses, and lenders cannot demand full loan payment, they should still be informed of the ownership change for their records. Send them a letter with a copy of the recorded deed explaining that you've transferred the property into your revocable living trust for estate planning purposes and that you remain both trustee and beneficiary. Most lenders simply note this in their files, though some may request documentation proving the trust is revocable and you're the beneficiary. Fifth, if your property is part of a homeowners association, notify the HOA of the ownership change and provide them with updated trustee contact information if needed. Some HOAs require updated documents or forms when ownership changes. Sixth, update any automatic payment arrangements for property taxes, HOA dues, or utilities if the payee name needs to change from your individual name to your trustee designation, though many times this isn't necessary. These thorough post-recording notifications ensure everyone who interacts with your property recognizes the trust's ownership and that all protections and benefits continue seamlessly. The faithfulness in completing these follow-up tasks reflects biblical teaching about finishing the work we begin. Second Timothy 4:7 records Paul saying, "I have fought the good fight, I have finished the race, I have kept the faith." This perseverance to completion—not stopping when the primary task is done but following through on all related tasks—is what you demonstrate by completing these post-recording notifications. The recording itself is crucial, but these follow-up steps ensure the transfer is fully effective in every practical way.

Addressing Recording Problems and Defects

Despite careful preparation, sometimes county recorders identify problems with submitted deeds that result in rejection or conditional recording with noted defects. Common reasons for rejection include incomplete or improper notarization (missing notary seal, expired commission, incorrect acknowledgment wording), missing required signatures (co-owners who didn't sign, missing witness signatures), incomplete information (missing property descriptions, blank consideration statements, missing parcel numbers), formatting problems (margins too narrow, fonts too small, poor print quality), or missing supporting documents (required tax declarations, trustee certifications). If your deed is rejected, the recorder will typically provide a written explanation of the deficiency, allowing you to correct the problem and resubmit.

Address rejection issues promptly to minimize the time your deed remains unrecorded. If the problem is simple—such as a missing supporting form—obtain and complete the required document and resubmit everything together. If the problem is with the deed itself—such as improper notarization or a missing signature—you may need to execute a new deed or obtain corrective documentation. For notarization problems, you might need to re-execute the deed before a notary who completes the acknowledgment correctly. For missing co-owner signatures, the missing owner must sign a corrective deed or the original deed must be re-executed. For incorrect legal descriptions or other substantive errors in the deed's content, prepare and execute a corrective deed that references the defective deed and corrects the error. Work with your real estate attorney or title company to determine the appropriate corrective action for your specific problem.

Even after a deed is successfully recorded, problems sometimes surface later—perhaps someone discovers the legal description was incorrect, or an old lien that should have been released still appears in the records, or a signature was questioned. Address these post-recording issues promptly by working with title counsel or your title insurance company. Common solutions include recording corrective deeds that reference the original recorded deed and correct specific errors, affidavits of scrivener's error (sworn statements by the person who prepared the deed explaining that a clerical error occurred and stating what the correct information should be), reconveyances or lien releases (documents from creditors releasing old liens or clarifying that debts were paid), or quiet title actions (court proceedings that clear title defects and confirm ownership). Your title insurance may cover costs of correcting certain title defects, so contact your title insurer about problems rather than assuming you must bear all correction costs yourself. The willingness to address problems promptly and transparently rather than ignoring them reflects biblical principles about integrity and making things right. Proverbs 10:9 teaches, "Whoever walks in integrity walks securely, but whoever takes crooked paths will be found out." When defects or errors are discovered in your recorded deed, walk in integrity by addressing them honestly and promptly rather than hoping they go unnoticed. Taking crooked paths by ignoring problems or attempting to conceal errors will eventually be found out and create worse complications. The secure path is honest acknowledgment and prompt correction of any defects, ensuring your property transfer is fully effective and clear of problems.

Understanding Fraudulent Transfer Concerns

When recording a deed that transfers property, particularly when transferring assets into a trust, it's important to be aware of fraudulent transfer laws that exist to protect creditors from debtors who attempt to hide assets to avoid paying legitimate obligations. Fraudulent transfer statutes allow courts to set aside property transfers made with intent to defraud, delay, or hinder creditors, or made for inadequate consideration when the transferor was insolvent or became insolvent as a result of the transfer. While transferring your home into your own revocable living trust for estate planning purposes is entirely legitimate and legal, the timing and circumstances matter if you have significant debts or pending claims against you.

If you're transferring property into your trust while facing lawsuits, large debts, or financial distress, creditors might later challenge the transfer as fraudulent, arguing you were attempting to shield assets from legitimate claims. Several factors courts consider include your intent when making the transfer (were you motivated by estate planning or by desire to avoid creditors?), whether you received adequate value in exchange for the property (in revocable trust transfers you retain full control and beneficial ownership, which courts generally view as adequate value to yourself), your solvency before and after the transfer (did the transfer make you unable to pay debts?), the timing relative to creditor claims (did you transfer property right before being sued or after judgment?), and whether you retained benefits from the property (in revocable trusts you do retain full benefit, which is less suspicious than transfers where you give up all benefit).

To avoid any appearance of fraudulent transfer, consider timing your trust funding when you're not facing immediate creditor problems, and ensure your motivation is legitimate estate planning rather than creditor avoidance. If you have significant debts, consult with an attorney before transferring property into trusts to ensure you're not creating fraudulent transfer problems. Document your legitimate estate planning purposes for the transfer. And remember that revocable living trusts generally don't protect assets from your creditors during your lifetime anyway (since you control the trust and can revoke it), so they're not effective creditor protection vehicles. If creditor protection is your goal, discuss other strategies with an attorney. The biblical principle of paying what we owe and dealing honestly with creditors is paramount. Romans 13:7-8 commands, "Give to everyone what you owe them: If you owe taxes, pay taxes; if revenue, then revenue; if respect, then respect; if honor, then honor. Let no debt remain outstanding, except the continuing debt to love one another." Attempting to shield assets from legitimate creditors through transfers violates this principle of paying what we owe. Make sure your property transfers are motivated by legitimate estate planning purposes and not by desire to avoid paying rightful obligations. God values honesty in financial dealings, and courts will set aside transfers made in bad faith to defraud creditors.

Recording as an Act of Stewardship and Care

Beyond its legal functions, recording your deed represents an act of care and stewardship toward those who will come after you—your successor trustees who will manage your trust when you no longer can, your beneficiaries who will inherit your property, and even future owners who will eventually purchase the property from your trust or heirs. By recording your deed and creating clear public documentation of the trust's ownership, you simplify administration for your successors and provide clarity for everyone who may interact with the property in the future. When your successor trustee needs to act—perhaps selling the property after your death or managing it during your incapacity—the recorded deed provides immediate proof of their authority to act on behalf of the trust.

Without a recorded deed, your successor would need to explain that the property was supposed to be in the trust but wasn't properly transferred, creating complications, delays, and potential costs. For your beneficiaries who will eventually inherit the property, a clearly recorded chain of title makes their inheritance smoother and more certain, allowing them to sell or refinance without title problems. For future buyers or lenders who may interact with the property, the recorded deed provides clear documentation of ownership history, making transactions easier and title insurance more readily available. This forward-thinking care for those who follow you reflects biblical teaching about providing for future generations and leaving clear, ordered affairs. Proverbs 13:22 states, "A good person leaves an inheritance for their children's children, but a sinner's wealth is stored up for the righteous."

Leaving an inheritance isn't just about accumulating wealth; it's about organizing and documenting that wealth so it actually reaches your descendants in usable form. A valuable property with unclear title or improper transfer documentation may be difficult or impossible for your heirs to use or sell, diminishing its value despite your good intentions. By recording your deed and creating clear documentation, you ensure your inheritance is not just valuable but also accessible and usable for those who receive it. This care extends even to strangers—future buyers or lenders who will rely on the recorded chain of title when they interact with the property. Your recorded deed becomes part of that chain, and its clarity and correctness affect not just your family but everyone who deals with the property in perpetuity. This comprehensive view of recording as stewardship toward both family and future strangers reflects the biblical call to love and serve not just those close to us but everyone whose lives our actions touch. In Luke 6:31, Jesus teaches, "Do to others as you would have them do to you." Recording your deed carefully, correctly, and promptly is exactly this kind of considerate action—creating clear records that serve others just as you would want others to create clear records that serve you.

Final Review and Confirmation of Completion

After recording your deed and completing all post-recording notifications, schedule a brief final review to confirm everything was completed correctly and all necessary parties have been informed. This review might be a meeting with your estate planning attorney, a phone call with your financial advisor, or simply a personal checklist you work through to verify completion. Confirm that the deed was recorded successfully by checking online property records (most counties now provide online access to recorded documents) or reviewing the recorded original you received back from the recorder. Verify the recording information is correct—date, document number, and any indexing information that appears in the recorder's stamp.

Check that the deed shows the correct grantor, grantee, property description, and all required signatures and notarizations. Confirm you've received back the recorded original and have made adequate copies stored in multiple secure locations. Verify you've updated your homeowner's insurance policy and received confirmation from the insurer that the trust is now the named insured. Check that you've notified your mortgage lender and received any acknowledgment they provide. Confirm you've contacted your property tax assessor and completed any required forms to maintain tax exemptions. Verify you've notified your title insurance company if applicable and any homeowners association if relevant. Update your trust's asset schedule to show the property is now held in trust, including recording information for reference.

Provide copies of the recorded deed to your successor trustee, adult children, or others who should have this information for future reference. Consider preparing a simple memo or letter to your successor explaining where the recorded deed and other important documents are stored and what steps they should take when they need to act as trustee. This final review ensures nothing was overlooked and that your property transfer is fully complete in every respect. The discipline of reviewing completed work to confirm thoroughness reflects biblical wisdom about finishing well and paying attention to details. In Nehemiah 6:15-16, we read: "So the wall was completed on the twenty-fifth of Elul, in fifty-two days. When all our enemies heard about this, all the surrounding nations were afraid and lost their self-confidence, because they realized that this work had been done with the help of our God." The completion of the wall was noted, recorded, and recognized, providing assurance that the work was truly finished. Similarly, confirming your deed recording is complete and all follow-up tasks are accomplished provides assurance that your property transfer is truly finished and effective. Don't assume everything was done correctly; take time to verify completion so you know with certainty that your stewardship responsibilities have been faithfully fulfilled.

Conclusion: The Public Record as Lasting Testament

Recording your quitclaim deed with the county completes the property transfer process and transforms your private estate planning efforts into public, protected reality. This final step—delivering your executed deed to the county recorder, paying modest fees, and obtaining the stamped recorded original—takes only minutes of your time but provides lasting benefits that extend far beyond your lifetime. The recorded deed protects your trust's ownership against competing claims, provides constructive notice to the world, establishes priority, simplifies administration for your successors, clarifies title for future transactions, and creates a permanent public record that serves everyone who interacts with the property in the years and decades to come.

As you complete this recording process and the follow-up tasks that ensure its full effect, remember that you're engaging in faithful stewardship of significant resources God has blessed you with. Proverbs 16:3 promises, "Commit to the Lord whatever you do, and he will establish your plans." By committing your property transfer to the Lord—doing it with integrity, thoroughness, and care—you can trust that your plans will be established. Your property will be properly transferred into your trust, your estate plan will function as intended, and your family will benefit from the protections and provisions you've created. The recorded deed stands as lasting testament to your faithful stewardship, providing clear documentation that serves your loved ones and honors the God who entrusted these resources to your care. Take time to record your deed promptly and properly, complete all follow-up tasks diligently, and preserve the recorded documentation carefully. These final steps complete the good work you've begun and ensure your estate planning efforts bear lasting fruit for generations to come.

Chapter 5:
Privacy and Discretion

Privacy in estate planning is a sacred practical aim: a well-crafted trust can keep family affairs out of public probate files, protect sensitive financial details, and preserve dignity for surviving loved ones. Unlike wills, which become public when probated, a living trust typically allows the disposition of real property and personal assets to occur without court scrutiny, maintaining confidentiality over beneficiaries, distributions, and the size of the estate. This respect for privacy honors the scriptural call to discretion and modesty in handling our affairs: "A prudent man conceals knowledge, but the heart of fools proclaims folly" (Proverbs 12:23).

Discretion begins with limiting what is recorded. Record only the deed necessary to show the trust as owner and avoid filing the entire trust instrument unless a third party specifically requires it; instead use a trustee certification or limited affidavit to prove authority when needed. By doing so you balance the legal need to show title with the desire to shield details of beneficiaries and distribution provisions. Prudence in disclosure reflects the biblical wisdom to guard what is entrusted to us: "Keep your heart with all vigilance, for from it flow the springs of life" (Proverbs 4:23).

Be mindful of who holds copies and who has authority to view trust contents. Provide the successor trustee and key advisors with secure access to the trust documents while limiting wide circulation of originals or full trust copies to reduce risk of loss, fraud, or misunderstanding. For many families a short, plain-language memorandum for heirs—explaining where documents are kept and whom to contact—serves better than circulating the full legal text. Responsible custody and selective sharing mirror the scriptural counsel to steward resources faithfully: "Moreover, it is required of stewards that they be found faithful" (1 Corinthians 4:2).

Privacy must not be used to conceal wrongdoing, avoid legitimate creditor claims, or frustrate legal obligations. Transfers timed or structured solely to evade known creditors can be set aside by courts and carry moral as well as legal consequences; honesty in dealing with obligations honors

God and neighbor. The Scriptures warn against deceptive gain and call us to uprightness in our dealings: “Better is a poor man who walks in his integrity than a rich man who is crooked in his ways” (Proverbs 28:6).

Consider professional tools that enhance discretion: trustee certification forms, nominee deeds where appropriate, and the use of corporate or professional trustees to receive notices and shield family members from direct public listings. When privacy concerns intersect with tax reporting, Medicaid planning, or lending relationships, coordinate with counsel so legal compliance and confidentiality goals align. Seeking wise counsel reflects the biblical injunction to obtain good advice: “Plans fail for lack of counsel, but with many advisers they succeed” (Proverbs 15:22).

Finally, cultivate family communication alongside discretion. Privacy should not become secrecy that breeds suspicion; a measured discussion with beneficiaries and the successor trustee about the existence of the trust, its purpose, and where to find documents provides peace and prevents conflict after death or incapacity. This blend of prudent confidentiality and loving transparency fulfills both practical stewardship and the biblical command to live peaceably with others: “If possible, so far as it depends on you, live peaceably with all” (Romans 12:18).

***

Section 1: Why Some Homeowners Prefer Not to Notify Their Bank

The Question of Lender Notification

When homeowners transfer their primary residence into a revocable living trust for estate planning purposes, a practical question arises: Should they notify their mortgage lender about the transfer? This question generates varying opinions among attorneys, financial advisors, and homeowners themselves, with some advocating for proactive notification and others recommending discretion and silence. Many homeowners, after consulting with their estate planning attorneys or conducting their own research, choose not to notify their lender about the trust transfer, particularly when the transfer meets specific legal protections that prevent the lender from calling the loan due. This decision is not made carelessly or with intent to deceive, but rather reflects a thoughtful assessment of legal rights, practical considerations, privacy concerns, and the desire to avoid unnecessary complications in what should be a straightforward estate planning transaction.

Understanding why homeowners make this choice, the legal foundation supporting it, the practical benefits it provides, and the important boundaries that must be observed helps clarify when non-notification is appropriate and when communication with the lender becomes necessary or advisable. The biblical principle of prudent discretion—knowing when to speak and when to remain silent, when disclosure serves a purpose and when it creates unnecessary problems—guides this decision. Proverbs 10:19 teaches, "Sin is not ended by multiplying words, but the prudent hold their tongues." Sometimes prudence means not initiating conversations that serve no necessary purpose and could create complications where none need exist. However, this discretion must always be balanced with integrity and honesty, never crossing into deception or violation of legitimate obligations. As we explore the reasons homeowners often choose not to notify lenders about trust transfers, we'll examine both the legitimate basis for this approach and the important ethical boundaries that must be respected.

Federal Law Protection: The Garn-St. Germain Act

The primary legal foundation for homeowners' decision not to notify lenders when transferring property into revocable living trusts is the Garn-St. Germain Depository Institutions Act of 1982, a federal law that specifically protects certain property transfers from triggering due-on-sale clauses in mortgages. Most mortgage agreements contain due-on-sale clauses (also called acceleration clauses) that give lenders the right to demand immediate payment of the entire loan balance if the property is sold or transferred to a new owner. These clauses protect lenders from having their loans assumed by unknown parties with different credit profiles without the lender's consent. However, the Garn-St. Germain Act recognizes that certain property transfers don't actually change the economic substance of the lending relationship and therefore shouldn't trigger these clauses.

Section 1701j-3(d) of the Act specifically exempts from due-on-sale enforcement "a transfer into an inter vivos trust in which the borrower is and remains a beneficiary and which does not relate to a transfer of rights of occupancy in the property." In plain language, this means lenders cannot call a loan due simply because the borrower transfers their property into a living trust, as long as the borrower remains a beneficiary of the trust and continues living in the property. This federal protection applies to all mortgages on residential property containing fewer than five dwelling units, covering virtually all single-family homes, condominiums, and small multi-family properties. The law doesn't require the borrower to notify the lender or obtain the lender's permission for such transfers—it simply prohibits lenders from enforcing due-on-sale clauses in these specific circumstances.

This federal protection gives homeowners confidence that transferring their primary residence into their revocable living trust is legally protected and doesn't constitute a default under their mortgage, regardless of whether they notify the lender. Since the law protects the transfer and the lender has no right to object or take adverse action, many homeowners and their attorneys conclude that notification serves no necessary purpose. The lender cannot legally do anything about the transfer anyway, so why invite potential confusion, bureaucratic complications, or misunderstanding by notifying them? This reasoning is legally sound: when you have a protected right under federal law, you're not obligated to seek permission or provide notice to exercise that right. The biblical principle of understanding and exercising legitimate rights appears in Scripture, most notably when the Apostle Paul invoked his Roman citizenship to protect himself from unjust treatment in Acts 22:25-29. When Paul was about to be flogged, he asked, "Is it legal for you to flog a Roman citizen who hasn't even been found guilty?" His exercise of legal rights without asking permission reflects the principle that we may appropriately use lawful protections available to us. Similarly, homeowners may appropriately rely on the Garn-St. Germain Act's protection without seeking lender permission for transfers the law explicitly protects.

Avoiding Unnecessary Administrative Complications

Beyond the legal protection itself, homeowners often choose not to notify lenders because doing so can trigger unnecessary administrative complications, bureaucratic procedures, or confusion among lender personnel who may not fully understand the legal protections for trust transfers. Many mortgage servicers—the companies that handle day-to-day loan administration—have limited experience with estate planning trusts and may not properly recognize the Garn-St. Germain Act's protections. When notified of a trust transfer, some servicers mistakenly treat it as a sale or ownership change requiring full underwriting review, borrower qualification, and possibly loan acceleration or refinancing. This misunderstanding can create significant problems: the lender might send threatening letters demanding loan payoff, they might initiate foreclosure proceedings based on mistaken belief the transfer violated the loan terms, or they might require extensive documentation and review before "approving" a transfer they actually have no right to prohibit.

Dealing with these complications wastes homeowners' time and energy, creates stress and anxiety about potentially losing their home or facing loan acceleration, requires engaging attorneys to communicate with lenders about legal protections, and may result in damage to credit if lenders erroneously report the loan as in default. Even when these issues are eventually resolved—usually with the lender acknowledging their error once properly educated about the Garn-St. Germain Act—the process can take weeks or months and cause significant disruption. Many homeowners and attorneys, aware of these potential complications from past experiences, conclude that the simplest and safest approach is not to notify the lender in the first place. If the lender doesn't know about the transfer, they can't mistakenly treat it as a problem. The loan continues being paid as always, the homeowner continues living in the property, and the relationship proceeds undisturbed.

This approach of avoiding unnecessary complications by not volunteering information that could be misunderstood reflects practical wisdom about when communication serves useful purposes and when it creates needless problems. The biblical principle of choosing peace and avoiding unnecessary conflict supports this approach when done with integrity. Romans 12:18 counsels, "If it is possible, as far as it depends on you, live at peace with everyone." Choosing not to notify a lender about a legally protected trust transfer, thereby avoiding potential administrative confusion and conflict that would serve no useful purpose, is exactly the kind of peace-making that depends on you. You're not creating conflict where none need exist; you're preserving peaceful continuation of the mortgage relationship by not introducing information that might be misunderstood or mishandled. However, this principle applies only when you're exercising legitimate rights and not concealing violations or obligations. If the mortgage actually required notification, avoiding conflict by concealing violation would not be righteous peace-making but deceptive conflict-avoidance, which Scripture condemns.

Protecting Family Privacy and Sensitive Information

Another significant reason homeowners prefer not to notify lenders about trust transfers is the desire to protect family privacy and avoid disclosing sensitive information contained in trust documents. When lenders are notified of property transfers into trusts, they typically request copies of the trust document to verify that the transfer qualifies for Garn-St. Germain Act protection—specifically, that the borrower remains a trust beneficiary and continues occupying the property. While homeowners can provide trustee certifications rather than complete trust documents, some lenders unfamiliar with these alternatives insist on seeing the full trust, or at least substantial portions of it. This disclosure requirement exposes sensitive family information that homeowners prefer to keep private: the identities and addresses of beneficiaries who will inherit the property, the identities of successor trustees who will manage affairs after death or incapacity, specific distribution provisions and any unequal distributions among children, provisions for disinherited family members or estranged relatives, charitable giving plans, and special needs provisions for disabled beneficiaries.

This information is deeply personal and, in some cases, sensitive enough that disclosure could create family conflict, expose vulnerable beneficiaries to targeting or exploitation, or reveal private matters the homeowner legitimately wishes to keep confidential. Lenders have no legitimate business need for this information—the only relevant facts for Garn-St. Germain protection are that the trust is revocable and the borrower remains a beneficiary, which can be established through brief trustee certifications without disclosing complete trust terms. Yet some lenders, acting out of excessive caution or lack of knowledge about alternatives, demand more information than they need. Homeowners who wish to avoid this intrusion into family privacy may reasonably choose not to notify lenders, thereby avoiding any request for trust document disclosure. Since the transfer is legally protected regardless of notification, avoiding notification preserves privacy without sacrificing any legal rights or protections.

The biblical principle of guarding what is sacred and not casting pearls before those who have no need or right to receive them supports this privacy protection. Matthew 7:6 warns, "Do not give dogs what is sacred; do not throw your pearls before pigs. If you do, they may trample them under their feet, and turn and tear you to pieces." While this verse addresses spiritual truths, its principle applies to valuable or sacred information generally: we're not obligated to share everything with everyone, particularly when sharing serves no useful purpose and could result in harm. Your family's estate planning details, beneficiary information, and distribution provisions are "pearls"—valuable private information that should be shared only with those who have legitimate need to know. Mortgage servicers reviewing routine payment processing have no such need, so withholding this information by not notifying them about trust transfers protects appropriate privacy. However, this principle doesn't excuse withholding information when there's legitimate need or legal requirement for disclosure. If your mortgage terms explicitly require notification of any title transfer, that creates a different situation where the lender does have contractual right to notice, even if they don't have right to object to the substance of the transfer.

Maintaining Continuity in Mortgage Administration

Homeowners who don't notify lenders about trust transfers often appreciate the administrative continuity this provides—the mortgage relationship continues exactly as before with no disruptions, no changes to account numbers or payment processing, no new paperwork or documentation requirements, and no risk of servicer errors during transition. When property ownership changes, even when the change is protected by law, lenders typically update their records, issue new account statements showing the trust as borrower, and potentially make various administrative adjustments. Each of these changes creates opportunities for errors: payments might be misapplied during transition, automatic payment arrangements might be disrupted, escrow accounts for taxes and insurance might require reconfiguration, or communication about the loan might be misdirected.

While these errors should be correctable, dealing with them requires time and effort from homeowners who might struggle to reach competent customer service representatives, might face delays in correcting problems that affect credit or payment status, and might experience stress about whether everything is being handled properly. For homeowners whose mortgage payments have been processing smoothly for years, the prospect of introducing changes that could disrupt this smooth operation is unappealing, particularly when notification serves no necessary purpose given federal law protection. By not notifying the lender, homeowners ensure the mortgage relationship continues unchanged: payments process as always, escrow accounts continue functioning, statements arrive as expected, and nothing disrupts the established rhythm. If and when the lender eventually discovers the trust transfer—perhaps when the property is refinanced, sold, or passes through trust administration after the homeowner's death—the transfer will be recognized as having been legally protected all along, and no harm will have resulted from the lack of earlier notification.

This preference for continuity and avoiding unnecessary disruption reflects biblical wisdom about not disturbing what's functioning well without good reason. Ecclesiastes 7:10 warns, "Do not say, 'Why were the old days better than these?' For it is not wise to ask such questions." While this verse addresses longing for the past, its underlying principle—that we shouldn't disrupt functioning systems without wisdom and purpose—applies to maintaining continuity in administrative relationships. If your mortgage is being serviced properly and payments are processing correctly, introducing changes by notifying the lender about a trust transfer that's legally protected regardless of notification lacks wisdom. The "old" (pre-notification) system works fine; the "new" (post-notification) system might introduce problems without providing benefits. Wisdom counsels maintaining what works rather than creating change for its own sake. However, this preference for continuity must be balanced against legitimate obligations—if your mortgage contract requires notification, maintaining continuity by violating contractual terms would not be wise but deceptive.

Understanding When Notification Becomes Necessary or Advisable

While many homeowners legitimately choose not to notify lenders about trust transfers, certain circumstances make notification necessary, advisable, or even required. First and most importantly, if your mortgage documents explicitly state that borrowers must notify the lender of any ownership changes or title transfers, including transfers to trusts, you're contractually obligated to provide that notification regardless of whether the transfer itself is protected from acceleration. The Garn-St. Germain Act protects you from loan acceleration but doesn't eliminate contractual notification requirements if they exist. Read your mortgage agreement carefully, looking for provisions about notifying the lender of ownership changes, title transfers, or trust placements. If such notification requirements exist, honor them even though the lender cannot accelerate your loan. Provide written notice with a brief explanation that you've transferred the property to your revocable living trust for estate planning purposes and that you remain both trustee and beneficiary.

Second, if you plan to refinance your mortgage in the near future, consider notifying the lender about the trust transfer or transferring the property back to your individual name before refinancing. Many refinance lenders prefer property to be in borrowers' individual names during the refinancing process, though you can transfer it back into trust after closing. Notification or temporary transfer out of the trust avoids complications during refinancing underwriting. Third, if you're planning to sell the property soon, the title company conducting the sale will discover the trust ownership when they examine title, so there's no point in avoiding lender notification if a sale is imminent anyway. Fourth, if you're no longer occupying the property as your primary residence—perhaps you've moved elsewhere or converted it to a rental—the Garn-St. Germain protection may not apply (as it requires the borrower to remain in occupancy), and you should notify the lender and potentially seek their approval for the change in use.

Fifth, if your financial situation has changed significantly—you've lost income, fallen behind on payments, or face potential foreclosure—attempting to transfer property into a trust without notifying the lender could be viewed as attempted fraud or hiding assets, which would not be protected behavior. In financial distress, communicate openly with your lender about your situation rather than making quiet transfers that might appear suspicious. Finally, if you simply prefer transparency and have no concerns about the administrative complications notification might create, there's nothing wrong with proactively notifying your lender. Some people feel more comfortable with full disclosure and would rather address any questions upfront than wonder whether problems might arise later. The biblical principle guiding these situations is honoring our commitments and being truthful in our dealings. Psalm 15:4 describes the righteous person as one who "keeps an oath even when it hurts, and does not change their mind." If your mortgage contract requires notification, keep that commitment even though it might create administrative inconvenience. Proverbs 12:22 teaches, "The Lord detests lying lips, but he delights in people who are trustworthy." Trustworthiness means honoring our agreements, including notification provisions in contracts, even when we might prefer to avoid the obligation. Let your practice be guided by both your legal rights under the Garn-St. Germain Act and your contractual obligations under your specific mortgage agreement, seeking to honor both in appropriate balance.

The Ethical Boundaries: When Non-Notification Becomes Problematic

While choosing not to notify lenders about legally protected trust transfers is generally appropriate, certain situations cross ethical boundaries and make non-notification problematic or even fraudulent. First, if you're transferring property into a trust specifically to hide it from the lender because you're in default, facing foreclosure, or attempting to make the property harder for the lender to reach, this is not legitimate estate planning but attempted fraud. The Garn-St. Germain Act protects estate planning transfers, not asset hiding during financial distress. If your motive is avoiding legitimate lender claims rather than planning for family succession, you're misusing trust structures. Second, if the trust you're creating doesn't qualify for Garn-St. Germain protection—perhaps it's an irrevocable trust, or you're not a beneficiary, or you're not maintaining occupancy—the transfer isn't protected and you're actually triggering the due-on-sale clause. Not notifying the lender in this situation isn't exercising protected rights but concealing a loan violation.

Third, if your mortgage explicitly requires notification and you're deliberately ignoring this requirement, you're breaching your contract even if the transfer itself is protected. The distinction is crucial: the lender can't accelerate your loan because of the transfer, but they might have other remedies for your failure to notify as required, such as charging fees, reporting the contract breach, or taking other actions short of acceleration. Fourth, if you're not actually continuing to pay the mortgage as required, or if the trust transfer is part of a broader scheme to avoid legitimate obligations, non-notification becomes part of fraudulent conduct. Fifth, if asked directly by your lender whether ownership has changed, lying or providing false information would be fraud regardless of whether the underlying transfer was protected. There's a significant difference between not volunteering information (which may be appropriate when exercising protected rights) and affirmatively lying when asked (which is never appropriate).

These ethical boundaries reflect biblical teaching about honesty and integrity in all dealings. Proverbs 20:17 warns, "Food gained by fraud tastes sweet, but one ends up with a mouth full of gravel." The temporary benefit of fraud—perhaps keeping a home you can't afford by concealing transfers from lenders, or avoiding administrative hassles by deliberately violating notification requirements—may seem sweet initially, but ultimately becomes gravel that destroys you. Proverbs 11:3 teaches, "The integrity of the upright guides them, but the unfaithful are destroyed by their duplicity." Let integrity guide your decisions about lender notification: if you're exercising legitimate, legally protected rights to transfer property into a trust for estate planning while continuing to occupy and pay as required, non-notification is likely appropriate. But if you're concealing violations, hiding from legitimate claims, or deliberately breaching contractual notification requirements, your duplicity will ultimately destroy you regardless of temporary advantages it provides. The test is simple: could you explain your actions honestly and openly to your lender, your family, and God without shame? If not, reconsider your approach.

Practical Guidance for Making the Notification Decision

Given the competing considerations—legal protection under Garn-St. Germain, desire for privacy and continuity, potential for administrative complications, and obligation to honor contractual requirements—how should homeowners decide whether to notify their lender about trust transfers? Here's practical guidance for making this decision wisely. First, carefully review your mortgage documents to determine whether they contain any notification requirements. Look for provisions requiring you to notify the lender of ownership changes, title transfers, or property being placed in trust. If such requirements exist, lean toward providing notification to honor your contractual commitment, though you can still explain that the transfer is protected under federal law. If no notification requirement exists, you have greater freedom to choose non-notification based on other factors.

Second, consult with your estate planning attorney about their standard practice and recommendation. Attorneys with extensive experience in trust funding have seen how various lenders respond to notifications and can advise whether notification in your specific situation is likely to create problems or proceed smoothly. They can also help you understand what your mortgage requires. Third, consider your personal comfort level with disclosure versus privacy. If you're someone who prefers transparency and would feel uncomfortable not notifying the lender, go ahead and notify them—the administrative complications you might face may be worth the peace of mind. If you strongly value privacy and avoiding bureaucratic hassle, and your mortgage doesn't require notification, choosing silence is reasonable. Fourth, assess your near-term plans for the property. If you plan to sell or refinance within the next few years, the trust transfer will come to light anyway, so avoiding notification provides only temporary benefit. If you plan to remain in the home long-term, non-notification may provide lasting benefit by avoiding complications.

Fifth, if you decide not to notify the lender, be prepared to address the issue if it arises later. Keep copies of the Garn-St. Germain Act provisions, your trust transfer documents, and information about your estate planning attorney in case you need to educate lender personnel about legal protections. If the lender discovers the transfer and contacts you with concerns, respond promptly and clearly, explaining the transfer's estate planning purpose and federal law protection. Don't ignore lender communications or become defensive; engage constructively to resolve any misunderstandings. The biblical principle of seeking wise counsel applies directly to this decision. Proverbs 11:14 teaches, "For lack of guidance a nation falls, but victory is won through many advisers." Deciding whether to notify your lender about a trust transfer may seem simple, but it involves legal, practical, and ethical considerations that benefit from professional guidance. Don't make this decision based solely on online articles or friends' experiences; consult with your attorney who understands both general principles and your specific situation. The modest cost of professional advice is insignificant compared to the potential cost of making wrong decisions about lender notification that could complicate your estate planning or create mortgage problems.

Alternative Approaches: Proactive Communication Without Full Disclosure

For homeowners who feel uncomfortable with complete non-notification but also want to avoid administrative complications or extensive disclosure of trust details, middle-ground approaches exist that provide some communication with the lender without full disclosure. One option is sending a brief informational letter to the lender explaining that you've transferred your property into a revocable living trust for estate planning purposes, that you remain both the trustee and beneficiary, that you continue occupying the property as your primary residence, and that the transfer is protected under the Garn-St. Germain Act. Attach a simple trustee certification (not the full trust document) showing the trust name, your role as trustee and beneficiary, and language about your continued occupancy. This letter provides notice without requesting permission or approval, making clear you're informing them of a protected transfer rather than seeking consent.

Another approach is contacting the lender's legal or compliance department (rather than customer service) if you anticipate potential confusion, asking to speak with someone knowledgeable about Garn-St. Germain Act protections before notifying them about your transfer. This conversation can help you gauge whether the lender's personnel understand these protections and will handle notification smoothly, or whether they're likely to create problems. If the conversation reveals significant confusion or concerning attitudes, you might choose not to formally notify after all. A third approach is waiting to notify until you have a specific need for the lender to recognize the trust ownership—perhaps when updating insurance, dealing with an insurance claim, or making changes to escrow accounts. At that point, notification serves a practical purpose beyond mere disclosure, potentially reducing administrative resistance.

These middle-ground approaches recognize that the choice between notification and non-notification isn't strictly binary—various levels and types of communication exist, and you can tailor your approach to your specific situation and comfort level. The principle of wise communication—sharing what serves useful purposes in appropriate ways—guides these alternatives. Proverbs 15:23 observes, "A person finds joy in giving an apt reply—and how good is a timely word!" An apt and timely communication with your lender—perhaps a brief informational notice when you transfer property, rather than either complete silence or extensive disclosure—may be the wisdom approach for your situation. The "timely word" is information shared at the right time, in the right amount, for the right purposes. Consider what communication approach best serves your legitimate needs for privacy and smooth mortgage administration while honoring any contractual obligations and maintaining integrity in your lender relationship.

Conclusion: Exercising Rights While Honoring Obligations

The decision whether to notify mortgage lenders about property transfers into revocable living trusts involves balancing legitimate rights under federal law, practical considerations about administrative complications and privacy, contractual obligations that may require notification, and ethical commitments to honesty and integrity in all dealings. Many homeowners appropriately choose not to notify lenders when transferring property into trusts, relying on Garn-St. Germain Act protections that make such transfers legally permissible regardless of lender approval. This choice reflects prudent discretion—not volunteering information that could create unnecessary complications when exercising protected legal rights. It preserves privacy over sensitive family estate planning details, maintains continuity in mortgage administration, and avoids potential confusion among lender personnel unfamiliar with trust law.

However, this discretion must always be bounded by integrity. If your mortgage requires notification, provide it even if inconvenient. If you're transferring property to hide from legitimate claims rather than for estate planning, recognize this as fraud not protected conduct. If asked directly about ownership changes, answer honestly rather than concealing the truth. The biblical principles are clear: we may exercise legitimate rights without asking permission, we may maintain appropriate privacy over family matters, but we must honor our commitments and deal honestly in all things. Proverbs 14:8 teaches, "The wisdom of the prudent is to give thought to their ways, but the folly of fools is deception." Give thought to your way in deciding about lender notification—consider your legal rights, your contractual obligations, your privacy needs, and your commitment to integrity. Choose the path that honors all these considerations, consulting with qualified attorneys to ensure your decision is both legally sound and ethically appropriate. When done thoughtfully and honestly, choosing not to notify your lender about a protected trust transfer is not deception but prudent exercise of legal rights that serves your family's legitimate estate planning needs while maintaining the mortgage relationship's peace and continuity.

***

Section 2: Risks of Transferring Without Lender Notification

Understanding the Full Picture

While the previous chapter explored why many homeowners choose not to notify their mortgage lenders when transferring property into revocable living trusts, wisdom requires examining the other side of this decision—the potential risks and complications that can arise from non-notification. Even when federal law protects trust transfers from loan acceleration, and even when non-notification may be technically permissible under mortgage terms, the decision to proceed without informing the lender is not without potential consequences. Understanding these risks empowers homeowners to make fully informed decisions, weighing both the benefits of discretion and the potential costs of complications that might arise. A wise decision-maker considers not just what's legally permissible but what's practically prudent, anticipating potential problems and preparing to address them if they occur.

The biblical principle of prudent forethought before action applies directly to this decision. Proverbs 14:15 teaches, "The simple believe anything, but the prudent give thought to their steps." A simple approach to trust transfers might assume that federal law protection means nothing can go wrong with non-notification, while a prudent approach carefully considers what complications might arise despite legal protections and whether those risks are worth taking in your specific situation. Proverbs 22:3 similarly counsels, "The prudent see danger and take refuge, but the simple keep going and pay the penalty." Examining the risks of non-notification before deciding whether to notify your lender is exactly this kind of prudent danger-recognition that helps you avoid penalties. This chapter explores the various risks homeowners face when transferring property into trusts without lender notification, helping you see potential dangers clearly so you can decide whether to take refuge in proactive notification or proceed confidently with discretion, fully aware of what complications might arise and how to address them.

Risk of Lender Misunderstanding and Loan Acceleration Threats

Perhaps the most significant and immediate risk of not notifying your lender when transferring property into a trust is that if the lender later discovers the transfer through other means, they may misunderstand its nature and mistakenly threaten or attempt loan acceleration. Despite the clear protections of the Garn-St. Germain Act, not all mortgage servicers and their personnel are familiar with these protections or properly trained to recognize them. When a lender's system flags an ownership change—perhaps discovered through title monitoring services, property tax records updates, insurance policy changes, or routine title checks—frontline personnel may automatically treat it as a violation of the due-on-sale clause without investigating whether the transfer qualifies for an exception.

This misunderstanding can lead to the lender sending acceleration demand letters requiring immediate payment of the entire loan balance, threatening foreclosure if the loan isn't paid within a short timeframe (often 30 days), freezing or restricting the mortgage account and online access, refusing to accept regular monthly payments or applying them incorrectly, reporting the loan as in default to credit bureaus, and initiating formal foreclosure proceedings. These actions, even though ultimately improper when the transfer is legally protected, create immediate and serious problems for homeowners. You must respond quickly to prevent actual foreclosure, often requiring hiring a real estate attorney to communicate with the lender and educate them about Garn-St. Germain protections. The stress, time, expense, and potential credit damage caused by lender misunderstanding can be substantial, even when you ultimately prevail in proving the transfer was protected.

The particular risk is that mortgage servicing—the day-to-day administration of loans—is often handled by companies separate from the original lenders, and these servicers frequently employ less experienced personnel working from standardized procedures that may not account for legal nuances like Garn-St. Germain exceptions. When their system flags an ownership change, they may automatically apply standard procedures for unauthorized transfers without recognizing that your specific transfer is legally protected. Correcting their misunderstanding requires getting through to knowledgeable supervisors or legal departments, providing documentation proving the transfer's protected status, and potentially dealing with multiple representatives who each misunderstand the situation before finding someone competent to resolve it. This administrative nightmare, while ultimately resolvable, is exhausting and stressful for homeowners who may feel their home is threatened and their credit at risk. The biblical warning about not assuming things will go smoothly applies here. Proverbs 27:12 cautions, "The prudent see danger and take refuge, but the simple keep going and suffer for it." The danger of lender misunderstanding is real and foreseeable based on numerous homeowners' experiences with servicer confusion. The prudent response is either taking refuge in proactive notification (explaining the transfer upfront to prevent misunderstanding) or proceeding without notification but prepared with documentation, attorney contact information, and knowledge about how to respond if misunderstanding occurs. The simple approach—assuming the lender will never discover the transfer or will automatically understand it's protected—may lead to suffering when reality doesn't match these optimistic assumptions.

Administrative Disruptions and Account Management Problems

Even when lenders don't threaten acceleration, discovering undisclosed trust transfers can create various administrative disruptions that complicate account management and future transactions. Many mortgage servicers operate with rigid computer systems and standardized procedures that struggle to handle situations outside normal parameters, and an undisclosed ownership change discovered after the fact often triggers administrative complications. Common disruptions include freezing or restricting online account access until the ownership change is documented and verified, requiring extensive documentation about the trust, your authority as trustee, and the transfer's legitimacy before restoring normal account access, disrupting or canceling automatic payment arrangements, requiring new authorizations and setup under the trust's name, potentially causing missed payments if the transition isn't handled smoothly, changing account numbers or payment addresses, creating confusion about where to send payments and requiring updates to any automatic payments from your bank, delaying or complicating refinancing applications if you're in the middle of that process when the transfer is discovered, and creating holds on escrow accounts for property taxes and insurance pending verification of ownership and insurance coverage.

These disruptions, while temporary and ultimately resolvable, create hassle, stress, and risk of payment problems during the transition. If automatic payments are disrupted without your knowledge, you might inadvertently miss a payment, incurring late fees and potentially credit damage before you discover the problem. If your account is frozen during a refinance application, the process may be delayed or complicated, potentially causing you to lose a favorable interest rate or miss closing deadlines. If escrow account changes aren't handled properly, property tax or insurance payments might be missed, exposing you to tax penalties or insurance lapses. Each of these problems can be fixed, but fixing them requires your time, attention, and effort dealing with customer service representatives, submitting documentation repeatedly, and monitoring your accounts carefully to ensure corrections are properly applied.

The risk of administrative disruption increases when you need to interact with the lender for any reason—applying for refinance, requesting loan modifications, adding or removing co-borrowers, or dealing with escrow issues. At these touchpoints, the lender's discovery of the undisclosed trust transfer adds complication to what might otherwise be straightforward transactions. By contrast, if you had notified the lender when you initially made the transfer, their records would already reflect the trust ownership, and future transactions would proceed smoothly without surprise discoveries triggering reviews. The biblical principle of avoiding unnecessary troubles through foresight supports considering these potential disruptions. Proverbs 14:16 teaches, "The wise fear and depart from evil, but a fool rages and is self-confident." While "evil" in this verse refers to moral wrong, the principle applies to foolish versus wise approaches generally: wisdom involves fearing (respecting and considering) potential negative consequences and adjusting behavior to avoid them, while foolishness involves self-confident presumption that problems won't arise. Self-confidently assuming administrative disruptions won't occur if you don't notify your lender is the fool's approach; wisely considering that disruptions could occur and deciding whether that risk is acceptable is the wise approach.

Insurance and Escrow Complications

Transferring your home into a trust without notifying your lender creates specific risks related to homeowner's insurance and escrow account management, areas where lender knowledge of proper ownership is important for protecting their collateral and ensuring required coverage remains in force. Most mortgage agreements require borrowers to maintain adequate homeowner's insurance naming the lender as loss payee (meaning insurance proceeds from covered losses must pay off the mortgage first). When you transfer property into a trust, best practice is updating your insurance policy to show the trust as the insured party while maintaining the lender as loss payee. However, if the lender doesn't know about the trust transfer, several complications can arise.

First, when you request your insurance company to update the policy showing the trust as insured, they typically notify the lender of this change as part of standard insurance verification procedures. If the lender's records still show you as individual owner but they receive insurance verification showing the trust as insured, this mismatch triggers questions and potential problems. The lender may reject or refuse to accept the updated insurance policy, insisting that insurance must be in the name matching their ownership records (your individual name). This puts you in an impossible position: you've transferred the property to the trust and need insurance to reflect this, but the lender won't accept insurance that doesn't match their outdated records. Resolving this requires you to then notify the lender about the trust transfer anyway, explain the legal protections, provide documentation, and potentially go through the administrative review process you were trying to avoid.

Second, if you don't update your insurance to reflect the trust ownership, you may have coverage gaps or issues if you need to file a claim. Insurance companies might question whether they're obligated to pay claims on property not owned by the named insured, potentially denying coverage or delaying payment while they investigate ownership. Third, if your mortgage includes an escrow account from which the lender pays property insurance premiums, the lender's payment on outdated insurance (in your individual name rather than trust name) might be rejected by the insurance company if they've already updated their records to show trust ownership, or the insurance company might issue refunds that create confusion in the escrow account. Fourth, the lender might place "force-placed insurance"—expensive lender-purchased coverage that protects only the lender's interest—if they believe you lack adequate insurance, charging you high premiums through the escrow account for coverage you don't need because you actually have proper insurance they're not aware of. These insurance and escrow complications often force disclosure of the trust transfer anyway, negating any benefit from initial non-notification, and they create administrative hassles and potential coverage gaps during the sorting-out process. The biblical principle of faithful stewardship of property includes maintaining proper insurance and not creating unnecessary risks. Proverbs 27:23-24 counsels, "Know well the condition of your flocks, and give attention to your herds, for riches do not last forever; and does a crown endure to all generations?" (ESV). This verse emphasizes carefully monitoring and protecting your assets, recognizing their vulnerability. Proper insurance aligned with proper ownership records is exactly this kind of careful monitoring, while allowing ownership records and insurance to become misaligned creates vulnerability. Don't let non-notification of your lender create insurance complications that could leave your most valuable asset inadequately protected.

Risks in Financial Distress or Foreclosure Situations

While most trust transfers are straightforward estate planning moves by homeowners in good standing with their mortgages, a particularly serious risk of non-notification arises when homeowners transfer property into trusts while facing financial distress, default, or potential foreclosure. In these situations, even legally protected trust transfers can be viewed with suspicion and subject to challenge, and non-notification compounds these problems significantly. If you're behind on mortgage payments, facing foreclosure, involved in bankruptcy proceedings, or dealing with other significant financial problems, transferring your home into a trust without notifying the lender can be interpreted as an attempt to hide assets, frustrate the lender's remedies, or engage in fraudulent conveyance.

Courts and lenders may question whether your trust transfer was genuinely for estate planning purposes or was actually an attempt to make foreclosure more difficult by obscuring ownership, delay foreclosure proceedings by creating confusion about who owns the property, shield equity from creditors by moving the property into trust structures, or retain occupancy and control while avoiding direct legal exposure. Even if your trust transfer technically qualifies for Garn-St. Germain protection (because you remain trustee and beneficiary), courts may view the transfer more skeptically when it occurs during financial distress, potentially finding that you engaged in fraudulent conveyance if the transfer was intended to hinder creditors. The fact that you didn't notify the lender about the transfer strengthens their argument that you were acting secretively and with improper motives rather than transparently for legitimate estate planning purposes.

Additionally, some of the Garn-St. Germain Act's protections arguably require ongoing compliance with loan terms, including payment requirements. If you're in default when you make the transfer or you default afterward, the lender might argue that the protection no longer applies because you're not fulfilling your loan obligations. While this argument is legally questionable, the practical reality is that lenders facing foreclosure on delinquent borrowers will pursue every available angle, and undisclosed trust transfers provide them additional grounds for attacking your actions. The biblical warning against deceptive financial dealings is particularly relevant here. Proverbs 20:17 teaches, "Bread gained by deceit is sweet to a man, but afterward his mouth will be full of gravel." If you're transferring property into a trust during financial distress without notifying your lender, examine your motives honestly: Are you engaging in legitimate estate planning that happens to occur during difficult times, or are you attempting to hide assets or make foreclosure more difficult? If the latter, you're gaining "bread" (temporary advantage) by deceit, but your mouth will ultimately be full of gravel when courts unwind the transfer and impose additional penalties for fraudulent conduct. The ethical approach when facing financial distress is transparency with your lender, not secretive transfers of property, even when those transfers might technically be legally permitted.

Impact on Future Refinancing and Loan Modifications

An often-overlooked risk of not notifying your lender about trust transfers is the complication it creates for future refinancing or loan modification applications. When you apply to refinance your mortgage or request a loan modification (perhaps to obtain better terms or address payment difficulties), the new lender or your existing lender conducting the refinance will perform title searches and require documentation showing current ownership. If their title search reveals your property is held in a trust but their records show individual ownership, this discrepancy must be addressed before the refinance or modification can proceed.

Common complications include delays while you explain the trust transfer and provide documentation about when and why it occurred, additional underwriting requirements to verify the trust structure and your authority to refinance as trustee, potential requirements that you temporarily transfer the property back out of the trust into your individual name for refinancing purposes, then back into the trust after closing, suspicion about why the transfer wasn't disclosed earlier, potentially causing underwriters to scrutinize your application more carefully for other undisclosed issues, and in some cases, denial of refinancing or modification if the lender decides they can't properly document the transaction or verify ownership to their satisfaction. These complications can cost you favorable interest rates if they cause delays that make you miss rate locks, add expense through additional title work, legal fees, or extra transfer deeds, create stress and frustration during what should be a straightforward process, and in worst cases, prevent you from refinancing at all, leaving you stuck with less favorable loan terms.

The irony is that the administrative headache you avoided when initially not notifying the lender about the transfer may come back multiplied when you seek to refinance, because now you're dealing with underwriters and new lender policies rather than routine account servicing, and the undisclosed transfer raises questions about your disclosure practices generally. If you had simply notified your original lender when you made the transfer, their records would be correct and refinancing would proceed without these complications. The biblical principle about short-term gains creating long-term problems applies here. Proverbs 21:5 teaches, "The plans of the diligent lead surely to abundance, but everyone who is hasty comes only to poverty." The "hasty" approach—quickly transferring property into a trust without notifying the lender to avoid immediate administrative hassle—may lead to "poverty" (or at least problems) when you need to refinance and the undisclosed transfer creates complications. The "diligent" approach—taking time to notify the lender properly when you make the transfer, even if it requires some extra effort—leads to "abundance" (or at least smooth processing) when you later seek to refinance because all records are correct and no surprises exist.

Credit Reporting and Documentation Challenges

When lenders discover undisclosed trust transfers and respond inappropriately—perhaps threatening acceleration, reporting the loan as in default, or placing the account in limbo pending review—these actions can impact your credit and create documentation challenges that persist even after the immediate situation is resolved. Credit bureaus receive regular updates from mortgage servicers about loan status, and if a servicer mistakenly reports your loan as in default or under review due to an unauthorized ownership transfer, this negative information appears on your credit report and damages your credit score. Even though the report is incorrect and based on the servicer's misunderstanding of Garn-St. Germain protections, the damage occurs immediately and can take significant time to repair.

Correcting credit report errors requires submitting disputes to credit bureaus, providing documentation proving the negative report was erroneous, following up repeatedly to ensure corrections are made, and potentially dealing with multiple credit bureaus if the error was reported to all three major agencies. During the correction period—which can take months—your damaged credit score may prevent you from obtaining other credit, cause you to be denied for credit cards or other loans, result in higher interest rates on approved credit due to lower credit scores, and create problems if you're applying to rent property, changing jobs, or engaging in other activities where credit checks are performed. Even after corrections are made, the time period when your credit was damaged represents lost opportunity if you needed to access credit during that time. Additionally, the documentation challenges extend beyond credit reports. If you've been through a complicated situation with your lender regarding an undisclosed trust transfer—even if ultimately resolved in your favor—you may need to explain this history when applying for future mortgages, refinancing, or other credit. Lenders may ask about previous mortgage issues, and disclosing the situation may raise questions that complicate underwriting, even though you were legally in the right. The administrative record of the dispute remains in the lender's files and may come up in future dealings.

The biblical teaching about our reputation and the importance of maintaining good standing applies to credit reports and financial documentation. Proverbs 22:1 teaches, "A good name is more desirable than great riches; to be esteemed is better than silver or gold." Your credit report and financial reputation are your "good name" in modern economic life, and damage to this name—even damage that's unjustified and ultimately corrected—affects your ability to function effectively in financial matters. While you shouldn't make decisions solely to avoid any possible credit risk, neither should you dismiss the potential credit and documentation complications that can arise from lender misunderstanding of undisclosed trust transfers. These are real consequences that affect your good name in the financial marketplace, and wisdom considers them when deciding whether to notify your lender or proceed with discretion.

State Law Variations and Ambiguities

While the Garn-St. Germain Act is federal law that applies nationally, state laws also govern various aspects of trusts, property transfers, and mortgage requirements, creating potential complications when federal and state provisions interact. Some states have additional protections or requirements beyond federal law, while others have ambiguities in how trust transfers are treated. These state law variations create risks of uncertainty about whether your specific transfer in your specific state is as clearly protected as you believe. Some states have statutes explicitly confirming that revocable trust transfers don't trigger due-on-sale clauses, reinforcing federal protections, while other states are silent on the issue, leaving only federal law as protection. Some states have mortgage regulations requiring specific notification procedures or disclosures when ownership changes, even for protected transfers, and violating these state requirements could create separate problems beyond federal due-on-sale issues.

In a few states, court decisions have created nuances or limitations on trust transfer protections that don't exist elsewhere, such as requiring certain trust provisions to qualify for protection or imposing additional requirements beyond what federal law specifies. These state-specific variations mean that blanket advice about trust transfers and lender notification may not account for particular requirements or risks in your state. Additionally, some states have stronger fraudulent conveyance laws or creditor protection statutes that affect trust transfers made in certain circumstances, particularly during financial distress. What's clearly protected in one state might be more questionable in another based on state law variations. The existence of these state law complexities creates risk for homeowners who rely solely on general information about federal Garn-St. Germain protections without verifying how their specific state treats trust transfers and what additional requirements might exist. If your state has notification requirements that apply even to federally protected transfers, not notifying your lender violates state law regardless of federal protection from acceleration. If your state has particular trust or conveyance requirements you didn't meet, your transfer might not qualify for the protections you're assuming apply.

The biblical principle of not presuming you know everything when local conditions may vary applies here. In Acts 15, the early church held a council to determine what requirements applied to Gentile believers in various locations, recognizing that blanket rules might not fit all situations and that local circumstances mattered. Similarly, understanding how trust transfers work in your specific state and under your specific mortgage terms requires research and professional guidance rather than assuming generic information applies perfectly to your situation. Consult with a real estate attorney licensed in your state who understands local law, not just federal protections, to ensure your trust transfer is structured correctly and you understand all notification requirements that might apply in your jurisdiction.

The Practical Reality: When Theory Meets Practice

Finally, an overarching risk of not notifying lenders about trust transfers is the gap between legal theory (federal law protects these transfers) and practical reality (lenders sometimes don't respond as theory predicts). In theory, your legally protected trust transfer shouldn't create any problems whether you notify the lender or not, because the Garn-St. Germain Act prohibits them from accelerating the loan. In practice, you're dealing with bureaucratic institutions staffed by human beings working from procedures that may not perfectly account for all legal nuances, and the practical reality sometimes diverges from what theory predicts should happen. Lenders theoretically should recognize Garn-St. Germain protections immediately and process trust transfers smoothly. In practice, many servicers create complications, send threatening letters, and require extensive education before acknowledging these protections.

In theory, if problems arise from an undisclosed transfer, you can simply cite federal law and the servicer will immediately correct their error. In practice, getting through to knowledgeable personnel who understand the law and have authority to correct problems often requires persistence, documentation, and sometimes attorney assistance. In theory, your legal rights protect you from any serious harm. In practice, dealing with lender confusion, administrative complications, and potential credit impacts creates real stress, expense, and hardship even if you ultimately prevail. This theory-practice gap means that even when you're legally right and your transfer is clearly protected, the practical experience of dealing with lender discovery of the transfer may be significantly more complicated and problematic than legal theory suggests it should be. Risk assessment requires considering not just whether you're legally protected but whether practical complications might arise despite that protection, and whether you're prepared to deal with those complications if they occur.

The biblical teaching about the difference between how things should be and how they actually are in a fallen world applies here. Jesus acknowledged this gap when he taught his disciples to be "as shrewd as snakes and as innocent as doves" (Matthew 10:16). Innocence (being legally in the right) isn't always sufficient protection in a world where shrewd awareness of practical realities is also necessary. You can be innocent—completely legally protected under Garn-St. Germain—and still suffer practical harm from lender confusion or administrative problems. Shrewdness means anticipating this possibility and deciding whether to take steps (like proactive notification) that might prevent practical problems even though you're theoretically protected without them. The truly wise approach combines innocence (operating within legal rights) with shrewdness (anticipating practical complications and preparing to address them).

Conclusion: Making Informed Decisions with Eyes Wide Open

The risks of transferring property into trusts without notifying mortgage lenders are real and varied, ranging from administrative inconveniences to serious complications that can threaten your home, damage your credit, or create expensive legal problems requiring professional assistance to resolve. Understanding these risks doesn't necessarily mean you must notify your lender—the benefits of discretion discussed in the previous chapter remain valid for many homeowners in many situations. Rather, understanding risks empowers you to make informed decisions with eyes wide open to potential complications, prepared to address them if they arise, and realistic about what you're choosing when you decide whether to notify or not.

The biblical principle of wise decision-making requires considering both benefits and risks, not just focusing on one side of the equation. Proverbs 14:8 teaches, "The wisdom of the prudent is to give thought to their ways, but the folly of fools is deception." Give thought to your way—consider both the benefits of discretion (privacy, avoiding administrative hassle, continuity) and the risks (lender misunderstanding, administrative disruptions, insurance complications, future transaction problems). Don't deceive yourself by considering only the benefits and assuming risks won't materialize. A prudent decision about lender notification weighs all factors: your mortgage terms, your state's laws, your future plans for the property, your lender's track record and sophistication, your comfort with potential complications, and your access to professional help if problems arise. Consult with estate planning and real estate attorneys, review your specific mortgage documents, understand your state's particular requirements, and make a decision appropriate for your circumstances. Whether you choose to notify your lender or proceed with discretion, do so with full awareness of both the benefits you're gaining and the risks you're accepting, prepared to respond wisely if complications arise. Proverbs 16:3 promises, "Commit to the Lord whatever you do, and he will establish your plans." Commit your decision about lender notification to the Lord—make it prayerfully, ethically, and with wise counsel—and trust that your plans for protecting your family through trust-based estate planning will be established, whether through proactive notification or prudent discretion, as long as your approach honors both your legal rights and your commitment to integrity in all dealings.

***

Section 3: Due-on-Sale Clause and Its Implications

Understanding Lender Protection Mechanisms

The due-on-sale clause, also called an acceleration clause or alienation clause, is one of the most important yet commonly misunderstood provisions in modern mortgage agreements. This contractual provision appears in virtually all residential mortgages originated since the 1970s and gives lenders significant power to protect their interests when property ownership changes. At its core, the due-on-sale clause allows the lender to declare the entire loan balance immediately due and payable—to "accelerate" the loan—if the borrower transfers the property to someone else without the lender's consent. For homeowners planning to transfer property into living trusts or engaging in other estate planning transfers, understanding what due-on-sale clauses are, how they work, when they apply, and critically, when federal law prohibits their enforcement is essential for making informed decisions that protect both your estate planning goals and your mortgage relationship.

The confusion and concern many homeowners feel about due-on-sale clauses is understandable. The language in mortgage documents describing these clauses can sound threatening, stating that any transfer of the property or any interest in it may trigger the lender's right to demand full payment. For homeowners with significant mortgage balances who couldn't possibly pay the full amount immediately if demanded, this sounds terrifying—as though any change in how they hold title could result in losing their home to foreclosure. However, the reality is more nuanced, particularly for estate planning transfers into revocable living trusts, which federal law specifically protects from due-on-sale enforcement. The biblical principle of understanding before acting applies powerfully here. Proverbs 4:7 teaches, "The beginning of wisdom is this: Get wisdom. Though it cost all you have, get understanding." Before transferring property into a trust, or before refraining from such transfer due to fear of due-on-sale consequences, get understanding about what these clauses actually mean, when they apply, when they don't apply, and how to navigate them properly. This understanding enables wise decisions rather than decisions based on fear or misunderstanding.

The Purpose and Function of Due-on-Sale Clauses

To understand due-on-sale clauses properly, we must first understand why they exist and what legitimate purposes they serve for lenders. When a bank or mortgage company lends money secured by real estate, they make the loan based on evaluation of the borrower's creditworthiness, the property's value, and the loan-to-value ratio. The lender knows who the borrower is, has reviewed their credit history, verified their income, assessed their ability to repay, and has determined that lending to this particular person at this particular interest rate on this particular property is an acceptable risk. The property serves as collateral—if the borrower defaults, the lender can foreclose and sell the property to recover their money. This entire risk assessment is specific to the original borrower and the specific loan terms negotiated.

Without a due-on-sale clause, the borrower could sell or transfer the property to someone else, and that new owner would essentially assume the existing mortgage at its current interest rate and terms without the lender's involvement or approval. The new owner might have terrible credit, insufficient income, or might be a much higher risk borrower than the lender would ever approve for a loan. Additionally, if interest rates have risen since the original loan was made, the original loan's lower rate represents below-market financing that the lender would prefer to replace with a new loan at current higher rates. The due-on-sale clause protects lenders from these scenarios by giving them the right to demand full payment when ownership changes, effectively preventing informal loan assumptions and ensuring that when property changes hands, the new owner must either pay cash or obtain their own financing at current market terms based on their own creditworthiness.

This protection is legitimate and reasonable from the lender's perspective. They contracted with a specific borrower to lend money at specific terms based on that borrower's qualifications. Allowing that loan to be informally transferred to unknown new owners without the lender's consent would fundamentally change the lending relationship the lender agreed to. The biblical principle of honoring agreements and protecting legitimate interests supports the basic concept of due-on-sale clauses. When two parties enter a contract, both have rights and both should honor the agreement's terms. Proverbs 11:1 teaches, "The Lord detests dishonest scales, but accurate weights find favor with him." A loan agreement is exactly this kind of scale or weight—a measurement of obligations between parties. For borrowers to transfer property in ways that fundamentally change the lender's risk without their consent would be like using dishonest scales, changing the balance of the agreement unfairly. Due-on-sale clauses keep the scales honest by ensuring ownership changes are handled properly with lender involvement when appropriate.

Federal Law Exception: The Garn-St. Germain Act

While due-on-sale clauses serve legitimate purposes in protecting lenders from unauthorized loan assumptions and ownership changes to unknown new owners, federal law recognizes that certain property transfers don't actually change the economic substance of the lending relationship and therefore shouldn't trigger lender rights to accelerate loans. The Garn-St. Germain Depository Institutions Act of 1982, codified at 12 U.S.C. § 1701j-3, specifically prohibits lenders from enforcing due-on-sale clauses in several enumerated situations where transfers don't meaningfully change the lender's risk position. The most relevant exception for estate planning purposes appears in Section 1701j-3(d)(8), which states that lenders may not exercise their due-on-sale option in the case of "a transfer into an inter vivos trust in which the borrower is and remains a beneficiary and which does not relate to a transfer of rights of occupancy in the property."

Breaking down this language, "inter vivos trust" means a trust created during the borrower's lifetime (as opposed to a testamentary trust created by will at death), which includes revocable living trusts. "In which the borrower is and remains a beneficiary" means the person who borrowed the money must continue to benefit from the trust—they can't transfer the property into a trust for someone else's benefit only. "Which does not relate to a transfer of rights of occupancy" means the borrower must continue living in the property; they can't transfer it into a trust and then rent it out or leave it vacant while transferring occupancy rights to someone else. When all these conditions are met—the property is transferred into a living trust created during the borrower's lifetime, the borrower remains a beneficiary of that trust, and the borrower continues occupying the property as before—federal law prohibits the lender from enforcing the due-on-sale clause. The loan must continue at its existing terms regardless of the trust transfer.

This federal protection is powerful and explicit. Lenders are not permitted to demand full payment, are not permitted to call the loan due, are not permitted to foreclose based on the trust transfer, and are not permitted to change loan terms or interest rates because of the transfer. The law doesn't give lenders discretion to approve or disapprove estate planning trust transfers that meet these criteria; it flatly prohibits enforcement of due-on-sale clauses in these circumstances. This protection applies to all residential mortgages on property containing fewer than five dwelling units (covering virtually all single-family homes, condos, and small multi-family properties) and applies uniformly across all states, as federal law preempts any conflicting state laws or mortgage contract provisions. The biblical principle of legitimate authority establishing protective rules for vulnerable people applies here. God established laws throughout Scripture to protect people from oppression and unfair treatment. Similarly, Congress established the Garn-St. Germain Act to protect homeowners engaging in legitimate estate planning from being oppressed by lenders who might otherwise use due-on-sale clauses to force unnecessary refinancing or loan payoff when no meaningful change in lending risk has occurred. Romans 13:1 teaches that governing authorities are established by God, and in this case, the governing authority has established protection for estate planning trust transfers. This protection is both legal right and God's provision for homeowners seeking to plan responsibly for their families.

Critical Distinctions: When Protection Applies and When It Doesn't

Understanding the Garn-St. Germain Act's protection requires careful attention to its requirements and limitations. The protection is not blanket coverage for all trust transfers but specifically applies only when certain conditions are met. First, the trust must be revocable during the borrower's lifetime. If you transfer property into an irrevocable trust, where you give up all control and cannot change or revoke the trust, this likely doesn't qualify for the Garn-St. Germain exception because you've fundamentally changed the ownership structure in a way that does affect the lender's interest. Irrevocable trusts may trigger the due-on-sale clause, giving the lender right to demand payment.

Second, you must remain a beneficiary of the trust. If you transfer your property into a trust solely for your children's benefit with no provisions benefiting you, this doesn't qualify for protection because you're no longer a beneficiary. The typical revocable living trust structure—where you are both the trustee and the primary beneficiary during your lifetime, with property passing to your children or other beneficiaries only after your death—clearly satisfies this requirement. But trust structures where you give away all beneficial interest to others during your lifetime may not be protected. Third, you must continue occupying the property as your residence. If you transfer your primary residence into a trust but then move out, convert the property to a rental, or otherwise transfer occupancy rights to someone else, you've violated this requirement and the lender may be able to enforce the due-on-sale clause. The protection is specifically for homeowners transferring their primary residence into trust while continuing to live there, not for transferring rental properties or properties you're moving away from.

Fourth, the protection applies specifically to transfers into trusts, not to other types of transfers. If you deed your property directly to your children, this is not protected and does trigger the due-on-sale clause. If you transfer property to a business entity, this is generally not protected. If you transfer property as part of a sale to another person, this obviously triggers due-on-sale provisions. The Garn-St. Germain Act enumerates specific exceptions; transfers not listed are not protected. Fifth, while the federal statute protects the trust transfer itself, it doesn't protect violations of other mortgage terms. If you stop making payments, violate property maintenance requirements, or breach other loan conditions, the lender can still pursue remedies including foreclosure—they just can't use the trust transfer itself as the reason for acceleration. These distinctions are critical because operating outside the protected categories exposes you to potential loan acceleration, while operating within them provides ironclad federal protection. The biblical principle of careful obedience to the details of law, not just its general spirit, applies here. God gave Israel detailed laws with specific requirements, and obedience required following those details, not just approximating them. Leviticus repeatedly emphasizes doing things "just as the Lord commanded Moses." Similarly, to receive the Garn-St. Germain Act's protection, you must ensure your trust transfer fits within the specific requirements Congress established. Approximating them isn't sufficient; precise compliance is necessary.

How Lenders May Respond: Theory Versus Reality

In theory, when homeowners transfer property into qualifying revocable living trusts protected by the Garn-St. Germain Act, lenders should recognize the federal protection, accept the transfer without objection, update their records accordingly, and continue servicing the loan normally at existing terms. In practice, as discussed in previous chapters, lender responses vary widely based on factors including the sophistication and training of mortgage servicer personnel, whether the lender discovers the transfer and how they discover it, the lender's internal policies and procedures regarding trust transfers, and whether the homeowner proactively notified the lender or the lender discovered the transfer through other means.

Some lenders and servicers handle trust transfers smoothly, particularly when proactively notified by borrowers. They may have streamlined procedures for documenting trust ownership, require only basic information like a trustee certification showing the borrower remains trustee and beneficiary, update their records to show the trust as owner while maintaining the same loan number and terms, and continue servicing the loan without disruption. These best-case scenarios occur most commonly with sophisticated lenders familiar with estate planning and federal protections, when borrowers provide clear documentation upfront, and when transfers are obviously for estate planning (not during foreclosure or financial distress). However, other lenders and servicers respond poorly, particularly when they discover transfers they weren't notified about or when frontline personnel lack training about Garn-St. Germain protections. Poor responses include sending acceleration demand letters threatening to call the loan due, initiating foreclosure proceedings based on supposed due-on-sale violations, freezing accounts and refusing to accept payments pending "review," requiring extensive documentation and treating the transfer as requiring lender "approval," and creating administrative complications that delay resolution even when they ultimately acknowledge the transfer is protected.

These problematic responses, while legally improper when the transfer qualifies for federal protection, create real stress and expense for homeowners who must then educate the lender about the law, provide documentation proving the transfer meets protection requirements, potentially hire attorneys to communicate with lenders on their behalf, and deal with credit impacts if lenders erroneously report loans as in default. The gap between theory (federal law clearly protects these transfers) and reality (some lenders still create problems) reflects the biblical reality that we live in an imperfect world where rules aren't always followed perfectly and where human error and ignorance create complications. Jesus acknowledged this imperfection when he taught his disciples to be "shrewd as serpents and innocent as doves" (Matthew 10:16). Innocence—being legally right and protected—doesn't always prevent problems caused by others' errors or ignorance. Shrewdness means anticipating potential complications despite being right, preparing to address them, and making choices that minimize risk even when you're legally protected. A shrewd approach to trust transfers considers not just federal law protection but also how your specific lender likely will respond, whether you should notify proactively to prevent misunderstandings, and whether you're prepared to deal with complications if they arise.

Examining Your Mortgage Documents

While the Garn-St. Germain Act provides federal protection for qualifying trust transfers regardless of what your mortgage says, examining your actual mortgage documents remains important for several reasons. First, understanding what your specific mortgage says about due-on-sale provisions helps you recognize when the lender might raise concerns and what language they might cite. Most mortgages contain due-on-sale language in a section about transfers of the property or assumption of the loan. This section typically states that if the borrower transfers the property or any interest in it without the lender's prior written consent, the lender may require immediate payment of all sums secured by the mortgage. Some mortgages explicitly list exceptions—transfers that don't trigger the due-on-sale clause—and may or may not specifically mention trust transfers. Even if your mortgage doesn't explicitly list the trust transfer exception, the federal Garn-St. Germain Act still applies because federal law preempts contrary contract provisions.

Second, your mortgage may contain notification requirements separate from acceleration rights. Some mortgages state that borrowers must notify the lender of any ownership changes or transfers even if those transfers are otherwise permitted. This notification requirement is separate from whether the lender can call the loan due; it's a contractual obligation to inform the lender of changes. If your mortgage contains such language, you're technically obligated to provide notification even though the lender cannot accelerate the loan. Violating notification requirements could potentially be considered a default under other mortgage provisions, though this is rarely enforced for trust transfers that don't otherwise change the lending relationship. Third, examining your mortgage documents helps you understand any other relevant provisions about property maintenance, insurance requirements, payment obligations, or other terms that continue applying after you transfer property to your trust. The trust transfer doesn't change your obligation to maintain the property, keep it insured, pay property taxes, and make mortgage payments; understanding these continuing obligations helps ensure you remain in compliance.

To examine your mortgage documents, locate the mortgage or deed of trust you signed when you purchased the property or most recently refinanced. This is separate from the promissory note (which states how much you owe and payment terms); the mortgage or deed of trust is the security instrument that gives the lender rights in the property itself. Look for sections titled "Transfer of the Property or a Beneficial Interest in Borrower," "Due-on-Sale," "Assumption," or similar headings. Read this section carefully, noting what transfers the mortgage says require lender consent and whether it lists any exceptions. Look also for sections about notifying the lender of changes. If the language is confusing or you're uncertain about its implications, consult with a real estate attorney who can interpret your specific mortgage in light of federal protections. The principle of diligent examination of important documents appears throughout Scripture. In Acts 17:11, the Bereans were commended because "they received the message with great eagerness and examined the Scriptures every day to see if what Paul said was true." Similarly, examine your mortgage documents carefully to see what they actually say rather than relying on assumptions or general information. This examination, combined with understanding of federal law, gives you complete picture of your rights and obligations regarding trust transfers.

Strategic Timing and Circumstances of Transfer

While Garn-St. Germain Act protection applies whenever the technical requirements are met, the timing and circumstances of your trust transfer can significantly affect how lenders and courts view the transaction, particularly if complications arise. Transfers made during normal circumstances for obvious estate planning purposes receive the least scrutiny and strongest presumption of legitimacy. If you're current on your mortgage, financially stable, working with an estate planning attorney, and transferring property into a trust as part of comprehensive estate planning while continuing to live in the home and make payments, this clearly falls within the Garn-St. Germain protection's intended scope. Even if your lender raises questions, the circumstances make clear this is legitimate estate planning, not an attempt to avoid obligations or manipulate ownership for improper purposes.

By contrast, transfers made in suspicious circumstances invite greater scrutiny even if technically protected. Circumstances that raise red flags include transferring property into a trust immediately after being served with foreclosure papers, making the transfer while significantly behind on mortgage payments, transferring during bankruptcy proceedings or other financial distress, transferring while facing lawsuits or significant debts, or transferring after the lender has already raised concerns about the loan. While these transfers may still technically qualify for Garn-St. Germain protection if you remain trustee, beneficiary, and occupant, the circumstances suggest possible improper motives—attempting to hinder foreclosure, hide assets from creditors, or complicate legal proceedings—rather than pure estate planning purposes. Courts and lenders will scrutinize such transfers more carefully, potentially finding that they constitute fraudulent conveyances or don't qualify for protection because they're not made for the statute's intended estate planning purposes.

The safest timing for trust transfers is when your financial house is in order: you're current on all mortgage payments, you have no pending legal actions or financial distress, you're working openly with estate planning professionals, and the transfer is clearly part of broader estate planning including a properly drafted trust, updated beneficiary designations, and related planning steps. This timing establishes that your motive is legitimate planning for family succession, not avoiding current obligations or hiding from creditors. If you're already facing financial problems or legal issues, consult with both an estate planning attorney and possibly a bankruptcy or creditors' rights attorney before transferring property, to ensure the transfer won't be challenged as fraudulent and to determine whether alternative approaches might better serve your situation. The biblical principle of acting with pure motives and timing our actions appropriately appears throughout Scripture. Ecclesiastes 3:1 teaches, "There is a time for everything, and a season for every activity under the heavens." There's an appropriate season for transferring property into trusts—a time when your circumstances make clear this is about planning for the future, not avoiding the present. Choose your timing accordingly, ensuring your actions can withstand examination of your motives and circumstances.

Dealing with Lender Inquiries and Challenges

If your lender discovers your trust transfer and raises questions or concerns, how you respond significantly affects the outcome. First, respond promptly to any lender communications. Ignoring acceleration demand letters, foreclosure warnings, or requests for information makes situations worse and may cause lenders to proceed with adverse actions they might otherwise have reconsidered. Second, respond in writing with clear documentation. Prepare a letter explaining that you transferred your property into your revocable living trust for estate planning purposes, you remain the trustee and beneficiary of the trust, you continue to occupy the property as your primary residence, and therefore the transfer is protected by the Garn-St. Germain Depository Institutions Act of 1982, 12 U.S.C. § 1701j-3(d)(8). Attach a trustee certification or relevant pages of your trust document proving you remain trustee and beneficiary. Include a copy of the recorded deed showing the transfer. Consider attaching the actual text of the Garn-St. Germain Act provision for reference.

Third, direct your communication to the appropriate department—often the lender's legal department or compliance department rather than general customer service, as these departments are more likely to understand federal law protections. Fourth, keep copies of all communications with dates and delivery confirmations, creating a paper trail if issues escalate. Fifth, if the lender continues asserting the transfer violates the due-on-sale clause despite your explanation, consider having your real estate attorney send a letter on your behalf. Attorney correspondence often receives more serious attention and demonstrates you're prepared to defend your rights. Sixth, if the lender threatens or initiates foreclosure based on the trust transfer, immediately consult with an attorney about obtaining a temporary restraining order or preliminary injunction to prevent wrongful foreclosure. Courts will typically enjoin foreclosures based on due-on-sale violations when the homeowner establishes the transfer is federally protected. Seventh, document any damages you suffer from the lender's improper threats or actions—credit damage, attorney fees, emotional distress—as you may have claims against the lender for violating federal law if their actions were egregious.

Most situations resolve once you educate the lender about federal protections and provide basic documentation, though getting to the right person with authority and understanding may take persistence. The biblical teaching about responding to challenges with wisdom and preparation applies here. First Peter 3:15 instructs, "Always be prepared to give an answer to everyone who asks you to give the reason for the hope that you have. But do this with gentleness and respect." When lenders question your trust transfer, be prepared with answers—documentation, legal citations, clear explanations—delivered with professionalism and respect. Don't become defensive or hostile; simply educate them about the law and prove your transfer qualifies for protection. This prepared, respectful response typically achieves better results than emotional reactions or refusal to engage with lender concerns.

Long-Term Implications and Future Transactions

Understanding due-on-sale implications extends beyond the initial trust transfer to considering how the trust ownership affects future transactions involving the property. When property is held in a trust, certain future transactions require special attention to ensure they don't inadvertently trigger due-on-sale concerns or complicate processes. Refinancing typically requires either transferring property back out of the trust temporarily into your individual name for the refinancing, then back into trust after closing, or finding a lender willing to refinance property held in trust, which some do routinely while others prefer individual ownership. The process is manageable but requires coordination.

Selling the property from the trust is straightforward—your successor trustee or you as trustee can execute the sale deed, and title companies routinely handle sales from trusts. The buyer will obtain new financing in their own name, paying off your existing mortgage as part of the sale, so due-on-sale is appropriately triggered but satisfied through the payoff. Taking out a second mortgage or home equity line of credit on trust-held property may require the same temporary transfer out of trust as refinancing, or finding a lender willing to work with trust ownership. Adding or removing co-trustees generally doesn't trigger due-on-sale concerns as long as you remain a trustee and beneficiary, though you may need to provide updated information to the lender. Changing the trust from revocable to irrevocable (which happens automatically at your death in most trust structures) may raise lender concerns, though by that point your successor trustee is typically administering the estate and will either pay off the mortgage from estate funds, sell the property and pay it off with proceeds, or distribute the property to beneficiaries who will refinance in their own names.

Understanding these implications helps you plan appropriately and avoid surprises. The biblical principle of considering long-term consequences before acting appears in Jesus's teaching about counting the cost before building. Luke 14:28-30 asks, "Suppose one of you wants to build a tower. Won't you first sit down and estimate the cost to see if you have enough money to complete it? For if you lay the foundation and are not able to finish it, everyone who sees it will ridicule you, saying, 'This person began to build and wasn't able to finish.'" Before transferring property into a trust, consider the long-term implications—how will this affect refinancing if you want to access better rates? How will it affect selling if you decide to move? How will it work when you die and the trust becomes irrevocable? Counting these costs ensures you can finish what you start without complications that could have been anticipated and planned for.

Conclusion: Navigating Due-on-Sale Clauses with Confidence

Due-on-sale clauses, while potentially intimidating in their language and implications, need not prevent homeowners from transferring property into revocable living trusts for legitimate estate planning purposes. The Garn-St. Germain Depository Institutions Act provides clear, strong federal protection for these transfers when borrowers remain trustees and beneficiaries and continue occupying their homes. This protection is not discretionary or subject to lender approval; it's a federal prohibition on lenders enforcing due-on-sale clauses in these specific circumstances. Understanding this protection empowers homeowners to proceed with confidence in their estate planning while recognizing that practical complications may arise from lender misunderstanding or administrative confusion, even though the transfers are legally protected.

The wise approach to navigating due-on-sale implications combines several elements: thorough understanding of federal protection and its requirements, careful examination of your specific mortgage terms, strategic timing of transfers when circumstances clearly establish estate planning purposes, thoughtful decision-making about whether to notify your lender proactively, preparation to respond effectively if lender challenges arise, and consultation with qualified estate planning and real estate attorneys who can guide your specific situation. This comprehensive approach ensures you exercise your legitimate rights while minimizing practical complications and maintaining integrity in your financial dealings. Proverbs 16:3 promises, "Commit to the Lord whatever you do, and he will establish your plans." Commit your estate planning to the Lord by doing it properly, legally, and ethically—understanding due-on-sale implications, structuring your trust appropriately, ensuring you meet federal protection requirements, and handling the process with wisdom and integrity. When you approach your planning this way, you can trust that your plans will be established—your property will be properly transferred into your trust, your mortgage will continue on its terms despite the transfer, and your family will receive the protection and provision you intend, all while honoring God through faithful stewardship and honest dealings. Walk forward confidently, knowing that federal law protects your right to engage in responsible estate planning without unjustified interference from lenders who might otherwise use due-on-sale clauses to frustrate legitimate planning goals.

***

Section 4: Strategies for Minimizing Attention

The Wisdom of Quiet Diligence

In an era of increasing transparency, data sharing, and public accessibility of information, the desire to conduct personal affairs with appropriate discretion has become both more challenging and more valuable. When transferring property into a living trust, homeowners face a tension between necessary legal compliance—which requires recording deeds and maintaining proper documentation—and legitimate preferences for privacy and minimal attention to family estate planning matters. The goal is not concealment of wrongdoing or evasion of legitimate obligations, but rather the quiet, dignified execution of lawful estate planning without inviting unnecessary scrutiny, bureaucratic complications, or unwanted attention to private family matters. This approach reflects both practical wisdom and biblical principles about conducting our affairs with appropriate discretion.

The concept of minimizing attention must be clearly distinguished from hiding or deception. Hiding involves concealing information that should be disclosed, avoiding obligations we owe, or operating in darkness because our actions won't withstand light. Minimizing attention, by contrast, involves exercising legitimate rights to privacy, not volunteering information beyond what's required, and conducting lawful business quietly without fanfare. The biblical distinction appears in Jesus's teaching about doing good works. In Matthew 6:1-4, Jesus warns against practicing righteousness before others to be seen by them, instructing that when giving to the needy, "do not let your left hand know what your right hand is doing, so that your giving may be in secret." Yet Jesus also taught in Matthew 5:16, "Let your light shine before others, that they may see your good deeds and glorify your Father in heaven." The difference is motive and appropriateness: some actions should be public to glorify God and serve others; other actions should be private to avoid self-glorification and maintain appropriate boundaries. Similarly, estate planning requires appropriate public actions (recording deeds) while maintaining appropriate privacy over details (keeping trust terms confidential). The balance is conducting required public acts quietly and professionally while protecting legitimately private family information from unnecessary disclosure.

Using Simple, Straightforward Deed Language

One of the most effective strategies for minimizing attention when transferring property into a trust is using simple, straightforward language in the quitclaim deed itself, avoiding terms or descriptions that might trigger unnecessary scrutiny or misunderstanding by county recorders, lenders, or others who might review the recorded document. The deed should contain all legally required elements—grantor, grantee, property description, consideration, signatures, and notarization—but presented in the most straightforward manner possible without embellishment or language that invites questions. For the consideration statement, which describes what's being exchanged for the property, use simple language like "for good and valuable consideration" or "for the sum of Ten Dollars ($10.00) and other good and valuable consideration." These phrases satisfy the legal requirement for consideration statements while avoiding specific dollar amounts that might trigger property tax reassessments or suggest a commercial sale requiring transfer taxes.

Avoid language like "in consideration of love and affection" which, while legally sufficient, can sound unusual and invite questions about the nature of the transaction. Avoid stating the property's actual market value as consideration, as this definitely triggers tax assessment attention even though no sale occurred. The conveyance language should use standard quitclaim terminology: "does hereby remise, release, and quitclaim" or simply "does hereby quitclaim." Avoid adding unnecessary explanatory language about why you're making the transfer, your estate planning goals, or other commentary. The deed itself doesn't need to explain your motives; it simply needs to accomplish the legal transfer. The grantee designation should identify the trustee and trust precisely but without unnecessary detail: "Jane Mary Doe, Trustee of The Jane Mary Doe Revocable Living Trust dated January 1, 2024" is sufficient. You don't need to add language like "for estate planning purposes" or "to avoid probate" or other explanatory phrases that, while accurate, add nothing legally necessary and potentially invite questions.

The property description should be copied exactly from your current deed without modification or embellishment. Don't add descriptive language about the property's features, value, or characteristics; simply provide the legal description as required. This straightforward approach accomplishes the legal transfer efficiently while minimizing any language that might trigger questions, suggest commercial activity, or invite review beyond what's routinely applied to recorded deeds. County recorders process hundreds or thousands of documents daily, and most routine quitclaim deeds receive only cursory review if they contain all required elements in standard format. Using simple, professional language helps your deed blend into this routine flow rather than standing out as unusual or requiring special attention. The biblical principle of using plain, honest language without unnecessary embellishment appears throughout Scripture. Jesus taught in Matthew 5:37, "All you need to say is simply 'Yes' or 'No'; anything beyond this comes from the evil one." While legal documents require more than yes or no, the principle of simple, direct communication without unnecessary elaboration applies. Your deed should say what's legally necessary, clearly and directly, without adding commentary or explanation that serves no legal purpose and potentially invites attention you prefer to avoid.

Recording Only Required Documents

Another key strategy for minimizing attention is recording only those documents that are legally required to be recorded, while keeping other estate planning documents private. For property transfers into living trusts, the only document that must be recorded is the deed transferring ownership from you individually to you as trustee of your trust. This deed becomes part of the public record and is accessible to anyone who searches property records. However, your trust document itself—which contains your complete estate plan including beneficiaries, distribution provisions, trustee powers, and private family instructions—does not need to be recorded and should not be recorded. Recording your complete trust would make all these private details publicly accessible, defeating one of the primary privacy benefits of trust-based estate planning.

Instead of recording your trust, keep the original trust document in secure private storage and provide copies only to those who have legitimate need to see it (your attorney, your successor trustee, and potentially certain beneficiaries or advisors). When third parties like banks, title companies, or others need verification of the trust's existence and your authority as trustee, provide them with a trustee certification or certificate of trust rather than the complete trust document. As discussed in previous chapters, a trustee certification is a short document (typically 2-5 pages) that contains essential information—trust name and date, trustee identity and powers, relevant provisions about property management—without disclosing beneficiaries or distribution provisions. Many states have statutory trustee certification forms that third parties are required to accept, and most institutions routinely accept these certifications without demanding complete trust documents.

If you've executed your quitclaim deed under power of attorney rather than signing personally, some counties require that the power of attorney document be recorded along with or before the deed to establish the agent's authority. In this situation, record the power of attorney as required, but otherwise avoid recording documents beyond what's legally necessary. Don't record trust amendments unless they specifically relate to real property provisions that need to be part of the public record (which is rare). Don't record internal trust administration documents, trustee certifications (unless specifically required by your county), or correspondence about the trust. Each additional document you record adds to the public record and potentially invites scrutiny or questions. The principle of appropriate boundaries and not disclosing more than necessary has biblical support in the concept of wisdom about what to share and what to keep private. Proverbs 11:13 teaches, "A gossip betrays a confidence, but a trustworthy person keeps a secret." Estate planning details—who your beneficiaries are, how you're distributing assets, private family arrangements—are confidential matters that trustworthy people keep appropriately private rather than unnecessarily disclosing. Recording only legally required documents demonstrates this trustworthy discretion, maintaining appropriate boundaries around private family matters while fully complying with legal recording requirements.

Strategic Timing of the Transfer

The timing of when you transfer property into your trust can significantly affect the amount of attention the transfer receives and how it's perceived by lenders, tax authorities, and others who might become aware of it. Strategic timing means choosing a moment when the transfer is least likely to trigger questions, complications, or administrative reviews. The ideal time to transfer property into a trust is during stable periods when you're current on all mortgage payments, not facing any financial difficulties or legal actions, not in the process of refinancing or applying for new loans, not involved in divorce proceedings or significant family disputes, several years before you might need to apply for Medicaid or other needs-based benefits (to avoid look-back period issues), and working with an estate planning attorney as part of comprehensive planning that includes proper trust drafting and execution.

Transfers made during these stable circumstances are clearly for estate planning purposes and unlikely to invite suspicion or extra scrutiny. By contrast, timing your transfer during or immediately before problematic circumstances creates risks: transferring right before or during foreclosure proceedings suggests attempting to hide assets or complicate the lender's remedies, transferring while significantly delinquent on payments raises questions about trying to shield property from creditors, transferring during divorce suggests attempting to hide marital assets from your spouse, transferring immediately before applying for Medicaid raises questions about trying to qualify for benefits by artificially reducing countable assets, and transferring while facing lawsuits or significant debts suggests fraudulent conveyance to avoid paying legitimate obligations. Even if your transfer technically qualifies for legal protections, the timing affects how others perceive it and whether they'll challenge or scrutinize it.

Additionally, consider timing relative to property tax assessment cycles. In many jurisdictions, property transfers trigger automatic reassessment of property value for tax purposes, though most states exempt transfers to revocable living trusts from reassessment when the beneficial ownership doesn't actually change. Timing your transfer shortly after your property's regular assessment (rather than shortly before) means any administrative review of the transfer occurs when reassessment isn't scheduled anyway, reducing likelihood of triggering unintended tax increases. Similarly, if you know you'll need to refinance or sell the property within the next few months, consider whether transferring to your trust now creates complications you'll have to undo shortly. Sometimes the strategic choice is delaying the transfer until after completing other transactions, then transferring when you have a longer stable period ahead. The biblical teaching about appropriate timing appears in Ecclesiastes 3:1-8, which describes seasons for every activity: "There is a time for everything, and a season for every activity under the heavens...a time to scatter stones and a time to gather them." Transferring property into a trust has its appropriate season—ideally a time of stability and clear estate planning purpose, not a time of crisis or questionable circumstances. Choosing your timing wisely minimizes attention and complications while ensuring your transfer achieves its intended purposes.

Quiet Communication with Financial Institutions

How you communicate (or don't communicate) with financial institutions about your trust transfer significantly affects the attention and scrutiny you receive. The strategic approach balances legal requirements, contractual obligations, and practical considerations to accomplish necessary communication while minimizing unnecessary attention. As discussed in previous chapters, federal law protects transfers to revocable living trusts from mortgage due-on-sale enforcement when you remain a beneficiary and occupant, and this protection exists regardless of whether you notify your lender. However, some mortgage agreements contain notification requirements separate from acceleration rights, and honoring these contractual provisions matters even when the lender can't accelerate your loan.

If your mortgage requires notification but doesn't specify format or timing, you have flexibility in how you communicate. Rather than proactively calling the lender and creating a lengthy phone discussion that might involve uninformed representatives and generate administrative confusion, consider a brief written notice sent after the transfer is complete. A simple letter stating: "Please be advised that I have transferred my property located at [address] into my revocable living trust for estate planning purposes. I remain the trustee and beneficiary of the trust and continue to occupy the property as my primary residence. This transfer is protected under the Garn-St. Germain Depository Institutions Act, 12 U.S.C. § 1701j-3(d)(8), and does not affect my obligations under the mortgage or give rise to any right of acceleration. Enclosed is a trustee certification providing information about the trust. I will continue making all mortgage payments as required." This letter provides required notification without requesting permission or approval, states the legal protection, and establishes that nothing about your obligations changes.

For bank accounts and investment accounts held in your name that you want to transfer into your trust, the approach differs. Most financial institutions have specific procedures for re-titling accounts into trust names, and you'll need to work with them directly to accomplish these transfers. However, you can minimize scrutiny by preparing thoroughly before contacting them. Have your trustee certification ready (not your complete trust), know your account numbers and be prepared to provide identification, choose a time to visit or call when you can speak with knowledgeable personnel (often trust officers or private bankers understand trusts better than frontline tellers), and frame the request as routine estate planning rather than a response to crisis or problems. Simply state: "I'd like to retitle these accounts into my revocable living trust. Here's my trustee certification showing my authority." Most institutions have processed hundreds or thousands of similar requests and will handle yours routinely if you present it as routine.

For property insurance, notify your insurance company or agent that you've transferred your property into your trust and request that the policy be updated to show the trust as the insured party. Provide a copy of the recorded deed and, if requested, your trustee certification. Frame this as a routine policy update to reflect proper ownership, not as a crisis or problem requiring extensive review. The principle of quiet, professional communication without unnecessary drama or elaboration reflects biblical teaching about conducting business with integrity and simplicity. Colossians 4:6 instructs, "Let your conversation be always full of grace, seasoned with salt, so that you may know how to answer everyone." When communicating with financial institutions about your trust transfer, let your conversation be graceful (professional, respectful, clear) and seasoned with salt (preserving truth, avoiding decay through dishonesty), providing the information needed to answer their questions without unnecessary elaboration that invites scrutiny or complications.

Limiting Family Disclosures During Your Lifetime

While family communication about your estate plan is important (as discussed in the privacy chapter), the timing and extent of that communication requires wisdom, and minimizing unnecessary attention includes being strategic about what you share with whom and when. During your lifetime, while you retain full control over your trust and can amend it at any time, you're generally not required to share trust details with beneficiaries. Some families benefit from open discussion of estate plans, managing expectations and preventing surprises, while other families experience conflict, pressure, or manipulation when beneficiaries know too much about their potential inheritances. The strategic approach considers your specific family dynamics and shares information on a need-to-know basis.

Your successor trustee—the person who will manage your trust when you die or become incapacitated—needs certain information during your lifetime: They need to know they've been appointed and have accepted this responsibility, they need to know where your trust document and other important papers are located and how to access them, they need to understand their general responsibilities and whom to contact for help (your attorney, financial advisor), and they need enough information about your assets and affairs to step in effectively when needed. However, even your successor trustee doesn't necessarily need complete details about beneficiaries and distributions during your lifetime if you might still modify these provisions. Consider providing a general overview: "I've named you as successor trustee. The trust provides for my spouse during her lifetime, then distributes assets among our children according to specific provisions I've outlined. Here's where the documents are stored, and here's my attorney's contact information."

For beneficiaries who will inherit from your trust, consider whether disclosure during your lifetime serves useful purposes or creates problems. Disclosing everything immediately after creating your trust means beneficiaries develop expectations that might be disappointed if you later amend the trust in response to changed circumstances or relationships. It also potentially creates pressure on you to maintain provisions beneficiaries know about, even if you later believe changes are appropriate. Not disclosing anything might create surprise and potential conflict after your death, particularly if distributions are unequal or exclude someone who expected to inherit. A middle approach might involve general discussions: "I've established a trust that will provide for all of you after I'm gone. I've tried to be fair while accounting for different circumstances and needs. The details will become clear after my death when the successor trustee shares the relevant provisions." This provides assurance without creating specific expectations that might prevent you from making appropriate future changes.

The biblical principle of appropriate discretion about family matters appears in various contexts. In Proverbs 31:10-31, the virtuous woman manages household affairs competently, and verse 27 notes "she watches over the affairs of her household and does not eat the bread of idleness." This watching over affairs includes making decisions about what information is shared, with whom, and when, exercising wisdom about household management. Similarly, as you watch over your family's estate planning affairs, exercise wisdom about what information family members need during your lifetime versus what can wait until your death when the successor trustee must inform beneficiaries of relevant provisions. The goal is minimizing unnecessary attention, conflict, and pressure during your lifetime while ensuring those who need information have it and those who will eventually inherit understand your care for them even if they don't know all details immediately.

Avoiding Patterns That Trigger Automatic Reviews

Modern financial institutions, tax authorities, and government agencies increasingly use automated systems that flag certain transactions or patterns for review based on algorithms designed to detect fraud, money laundering, tax evasion, or other problematic activity. While your legitimate trust transfer shouldn't trigger these systems, certain patterns or characteristics can increase the likelihood of automatic flagging and subsequent attention. Understanding what triggers these reviews helps you structure your transfer to minimize this risk. Automated property tax reassessment systems in many counties flag ownership changes for review. However, transfers to revocable living trusts typically qualify for reassessment exemptions when beneficial ownership hasn't changed. To minimize triggering these reviews, use consideration language that clearly indicates this isn't a sale ("for good and valuable consideration" rather than stating a purchase price), ensure your quitclaim deed uses clear language identifying the transfer as going to a revocable trust with you as trustee and beneficiary, and promptly file any reassessment exemption forms required by your county to claim the exemption rather than waiting for the assessor to question the transfer.

Mortgage servicing systems may flag changes in property ownership discovered through title monitoring services. While you have federal law protection, you can minimize the likelihood of these systems triggering reviews by maintaining absolutely current status on all mortgage payments (even one late payment can increase scrutiny when ownership changes are detected), ensuring your insurance remains current and properly reflects ownership (mismatches between property owner and insurance insured party trigger flags), and avoiding any other mortgage account irregularities (disputes about escrow, requests for modifications, etc.) around the time of your transfer. Financial institution fraud detection systems flag unusual account activity or patterns that might indicate identity theft, money laundering, or other crimes. When transferring financial accounts into your trust, minimize triggering these systems by making changes during normal business hours through normal channels (not online at 2 AM), visiting branches in person with proper identification when possible rather than attempting everything by phone or online, changing account titling before making any unusual transactions on those accounts, and avoiding transferring accounts into trust while simultaneously conducting unusual financial activity (large withdrawals, transfers to foreign accounts, etc.) that combined with ownership changes might appear suspicious.

IRS systems flag certain transactions for potential audit or review. While properly structured trust transfers shouldn't create tax liabilities, you can minimize attention by ensuring any gift tax returns required for trust funding are filed timely and accurately (if you transfer assets exceeding annual exclusion amounts), avoiding transfers of property to trusts in the same tax year you're claiming significant casualty losses, large charitable deductions, or other items that might already increase audit risk, and maintaining clear documentation of all transfers and their estate planning purposes in case questions arise. The principle of avoiding unnecessary attention extends to not creating patterns or combinations that trigger automated review systems, even when your individual actions are entirely legitimate. This reflects biblical wisdom about avoiding situations that might be misunderstood or create unnecessary trouble. First Thessalonians 5:22 instructs, "Abstain from every form of evil" or in some translations, "Avoid every kind of evil" or "Abstain from all appearance of evil." While your trust transfer isn't evil, structuring it to avoid appearing suspicious or unusual to automated systems helps you abstain from even the appearance of problematic activity, minimizing unwanted attention and reviews.

Documentation That Supports Quiet Transfer

Ironically, maintaining excellent private documentation about your transfer can help minimize public attention by enabling you to respond quickly and effectively if questions arise, preventing situations from escalating into larger problems that draw more attention. Immediately after executing and recording your quitclaim deed, assemble a comprehensive documentation file that includes the original or certified copy of your recorded quitclaim deed showing the transfer, the complete original trust document and all amendments, trustee certifications or certificates of trust prepared for use when needed, copies of any communications with your mortgage lender about the transfer, proof that you've updated homeowner's insurance to reflect trust ownership, proof that you've notified your property tax assessor if required and claimed reassessment exemptions, a simple memo documenting why you made the transfer and when (estate planning purposes, date of transfer), and contact information for your estate planning attorney and any other professionals involved.

Store this documentation file in a secure, organized location where you or your successor trustee can quickly access it if questions arise from a lender, tax authority, or anyone else. If your lender discovers the transfer and questions it, you can immediately provide documentation proving the transfer qualifies for Garn-St. Germain protection—recorded deed, trustee certification, occupancy confirmation—often resolving the issue before it escalates. If the property tax assessor questions why the transfer shouldn't trigger reassessment, you can immediately provide proof of exemption qualification and statute citations, preventing the matter from going to formal hearing. If you need to refinance and the new lender questions the trust ownership, you have everything they need to verify the legitimate estate planning nature of the transfer. This comprehensive private documentation enables quiet, efficient resolution of any questions without the matter escalating into prolonged disputes that draw attention and create complications.

Additionally, prepare your successor trustee by ensuring they know where this documentation is located and understand its importance. Create a simple cover memo: "This file contains documentation of the transfer of our home into the family trust. If questions ever arise from lenders, tax authorities, or during estate administration, this file provides everything needed to establish that the transfer was proper, legal, and for estate planning purposes. Our attorney's contact information is included." This preparation means questions can be resolved quickly even if they arise after your death or incapacity when you're no longer available to explain the transfer. The biblical principle of careful record-keeping and documentation appears throughout Scripture. In Ezra 2, detailed records of families returning from exile were essential for establishing identities and entitlements. Nehemiah 7 contains similar careful genealogical records. Luke 2:1-5 describes the census requiring everyone to register, creating official records. These examples show God's people maintained careful documentation of important matters, and this documentation served them well when proof or verification was needed. Similarly, maintaining excellent private documentation of your trust transfer serves you well if verification is ever needed, enabling quiet resolution of questions without escalation into disputes that draw unwanted attention.

When Minimizing Attention Crosses Into Problematic Concealment

Throughout this discussion of strategies for minimizing attention, a critical boundary must be maintained: there's a clear line between legitimate discretion and problematic concealment, between appropriate privacy and fraudulent hiding. Understanding this boundary ensures your strategies for minimizing attention remain ethical, legal, and honoring to God. Legitimate discretion that minimizes attention includes not volunteering information beyond what's legally required, using simple professional language in required documents rather than elaborate explanations, keeping private estate planning documents (like complete trusts) confidential rather than filing them publicly, timing transfers during stable periods rather than crises, and conducting necessary communications professionally and briefly without unnecessary elaboration. These strategies are appropriate because they involve exercising legitimate privacy rights while fully complying with all legal requirements.

Problematic concealment that crosses ethical and legal lines includes failing to disclose information when legally required (such as on loan applications, benefit applications, or court filings), making transfers specifically to hide assets from creditors, spouses, or authorities entitled to them, lying or providing false information when asked direct questions about ownership or transfers, timing transfers specifically to defeat known creditors or pending legal judgments, and using trusts or other structures primarily to evade taxes, avoid legitimate obligations, or frustrate legal processes. These actions aren't about privacy but about dishonesty, and they violate both legal and moral standards. The test is whether your actions would withstand honest examination. Could you explain what you did and why to a judge, your lender, or God without shame? If so, you're likely on the legitimate side of the line. If you'd need to conceal, minimize, or misrepresent your actions and motives when explaining them, you've likely crossed into problematic concealment.

Another test is whether you're exercising legal rights or violating legal obligations. Declining to volunteer information you're not required to disclose is exercising privacy rights. Concealing information you're legally obligated to disclose is violating legal obligations. The biblical standard is absolute honesty in all our dealings while maintaining appropriate boundaries. Ephesians 4:25 commands, "Therefore each of you must put off falsehood and speak truthfully to your neighbor, for we are all members of one body." Speaking truthfully doesn't mean volunteering every detail of your life to everyone, but it absolutely means never lying, concealing when disclosure is required, or misrepresenting situations. Proverbs 28:13 warns,

"Whoever conceals their sins does not prosper, but the one who confesses and renounces them finds mercy." While this verse addresses sin specifically, its principle applies to concealment generally: hiding what should be revealed prevents prospering, while honest acknowledgment brings mercy and blessing. Let your strategies for minimizing attention always operate within the boundaries of honesty, legal compliance, and integrity, never crossing into concealment of what should be disclosed or misrepresentation of your actions and motives.

Conclusion: Quiet Confidence Through Proper Planning

The strategies for minimizing attention when transferring property into living trusts reflect wise stewardship that honors both legal requirements and legitimate privacy interests. By using simple deed language, recording only required documents, timing transfers strategically, communicating professionally with institutions, maintaining excellent private documentation, and observing ethical boundaries, homeowners can accomplish their estate planning goals efficiently while minimizing bureaucratic complications, unwanted scrutiny, and unnecessary attention to private family matters. This approach combines full legal compliance with appropriate discretion—the balance that characterizes wise, mature stewardship.

The confidence to proceed quietly comes from knowing your actions are entirely legal, appropriate, and able to withstand any scrutiny. You're not hiding because your actions won't bear examination; you're being appropriately private because your actions are legitimate and don't require public announcement or invitation of unnecessary attention. This quiet confidence reflects the biblical character of those who live with integrity, having nothing to hide but maintaining appropriate boundaries. Proverbs 10:9 teaches, "Whoever walks in integrity walks securely, but whoever takes crooked paths will be found out." When your estate planning is done with integrity—legally, honestly, and with pure motives—you can walk securely, conducting it quietly without fear that anything problematic will be found out. The security comes from integrity, not from successfully concealing wrongdoing. First Thessalonians 4:11-12 captures the spirit of this approach: "Make it your ambition to lead a quiet life: You should mind your own business and work with your hands, just as we told you, so that your daily life may win the respect of outsiders and so that you will not be dependent on anybody." Leading a quiet life while minding your own business and working diligently describes exactly the approach to estate planning we've discussed—quietly handling your affairs competently, without unnecessary drama or attention, in ways that win respect precisely because they're done properly and professionally. As you implement these strategies for minimizing attention, commit your planning to the Lord, ensuring everything is done with integrity, and proceed with confidence that your quiet diligence honors both God and your family while accomplishing your legitimate estate planning goals.

Chapter 6:

Navigating Mortgage and Title Issues

Introduction: The Intersection of Property, Finance, and Trust Law

Transferring property into a living trust requires navigating the complex intersection of property law, mortgage finance, title requirements, and trust administration—areas that each carry their own technical requirements, terminology, and potential pitfalls. For homeowners who have worked years to build equity in their property and who carry significant mortgages representing major financial obligations, understanding how these elements interact when transferring property into a trust is essential for avoiding complications that could jeopardize either their estate planning goals or their mortgage relationship. The stakes are high: errors in title work can cloud ownership and create expensive correction requirements; mishandling mortgage issues can trigger acceleration demands or foreclosure threats; and failures to update insurance or tax records can leave property inadequately protected or subject to penalties.

Yet despite these complexities, millions of homeowners successfully transfer mortgaged properties into living trusts every year, accomplishing their estate planning objectives while maintaining their existing mortgage terms and avoiding problems. The key is understanding what issues can arise, knowing how to address them properly, and approaching the process with the diligence and attention to detail that major financial transactions require. This chapter explores the mortgage and title issues homeowners face when funding trusts with real property, providing guidance for navigating these challenges successfully while maintaining both legal compliance and the integrity that honors God. The biblical principle of careful attention to important matters provides our foundation. Proverbs 27:23-24 counsels, "Be sure you know the condition of your flocks, give careful attention to your herds; for riches do not endure forever, and a crown is not secure for all generations." While most modern homeowners don't tend flocks and herds, we do have properties and mortgages that require our careful attention and knowledge. Understanding their condition—the state of your title, the terms of your mortgage, the requirements for proper transfer—is exactly the kind of careful attention this passage commends. This attention ensures that the riches (property and equity) you've accumulated through years of mortgage payments can endure for future generations through proper estate planning.

Understanding Your Current Title and Its Implications

Before transferring property into a trust, the essential first step is understanding exactly how you currently hold title and what implications that current ownership structure has for the transfer process. The way property title is held affects who must sign the transfer deed, what legal descriptions must be used, whether special requirements apply, and what recordings might already exist that you need to be aware of. To understand your current title, locate the most recent recorded deed showing you as the grantee (the person receiving the property)—this is typically the deed you received when you purchased the property or when you last refinanced if the refinancing involved recording a new deed. Review this deed carefully, noting several key elements.

First, identify exactly how your name appears as grantee. Does it show your name alone, or are others listed? Is your middle name spelled out or abbreviated? Is any marital status shown? The name format on this current deed determines how you must be identified as grantor on your quitclaim deed transferring to your trust—the names must match exactly. Second, note the form of ownership if you hold title with others. Common forms include "John Smith and Mary Smith, husband and wife" (indicating joint ownership with survivorship rights in most states), "John Smith and Mary Smith, as joint tenants with right of survivorship" (explicitly stating survivorship rights), "John Smith and Mary Smith, as tenants in common" (indicating separate interests without survivorship), or "John Smith, a married man, as his sole and separate property" (in community property states, showing separate property ownership). The ownership form affects whether all owners must sign the transfer deed and how interests pass at death.

Third, examine the legal description of your property. This description might use metes and bounds (describing boundaries by directions and distances), lot and block numbers (in platted subdivisions), or government survey descriptions (using townships, ranges, and sections). Whatever format your current deed uses, you must copy this description exactly onto your quitclaim deed—any variations could create title problems. Fourth, check for any encumbrances or conditions noted in your deed. Some deeds include references to easements, covenants, or restrictions affecting the property. Understanding these helps you know what burdens transfer with the property into your trust. Fifth, verify the property's legal owner matches who you think owns it. Sometimes homeowners are surprised to discover that property they assumed was in both spouses' names is actually in only one name, or that a previous deed inadvertently left off a co-owner, or that old estate settlements after a parent's death weren't properly completed. Discovering these issues before attempting to transfer property into a trust allows you to correct them first.

The importance of understanding your starting point before making changes reflects biblical wisdom about knowing where you are before determining where you're going. In Luke 14:28-30, Jesus asks, "Suppose one of you wants to build a tower. Won't you first sit down and estimate the cost to see if you have enough money to complete it? For if you lay the foundation and are not able to finish it, everyone who sees it will ridicule you, saying, 'This person began to build and wasn't able to finish.'" Before building your estate plan by transferring property to a trust, first sit down and examine your current title to understand what you're working with. This examination is the foundation that enables you to complete the transfer properly without discovering partway through that you can't finish because of title issues you didn't know existed.

Addressing Title Defects Before Transfer

Sometimes examination of your current title reveals defects or issues that should be corrected before transferring property into your trust. While some minor title issues might not prevent the trust transfer itself, correcting them first creates cleaner title and prevents complications for your successor trustee when they later need to sell property or distribute it to beneficiaries. Common title defects include: names spelled incorrectly in previous deeds, creating inconsistency in the chain of title; previous owners' names remaining on title when they should have been removed years ago; unreleased liens or mortgages from loans that were paid off but never formally released of record; old judgments or tax liens that were satisfied but never cleared from title; breaks in the chain of title where a deed appears to be missing or improperly recorded; and boundary disputes or encroachment issues that haven't been formally resolved.

If you discover significant title defects, consult with a real estate attorney or title company about the best approach for clearing them. Common solutions include: recording corrective deeds that fix name spellings or other errors in previous deeds; obtaining releases of old liens from creditors or using title company services to clear ancient liens; recording affidavits of death for deceased former owners whose interests need to be formally cleared; obtaining quiet title judgments through court proceedings when informal correction isn't possible; and securing boundary agreements or surveys to resolve property line disputes. Some title defects are minor and can be noted as exceptions in title insurance without correction, while others are significant enough that they should be addressed before transferring property, especially if they'd make the property difficult to sell or finance in the future. Title insurance plays a crucial role in identifying and protecting against title defects. If you have owner's title insurance from when you purchased the property, that policy insures you against title defects that existed at the time of purchase.

However, it doesn't cover defects that arose afterward, and it might not transfer when you place property in trust (though most policies do cover this transfer automatically). Consider obtaining an updated title report or title commitment before transferring to your trust, showing the current state of title and identifying any issues. This report, typically available from title companies for modest cost, provides professional examination of your title and identifies problems you should address. If significant defects are found, correcting them before the trust transfer means your trust takes clean title rather than inheriting problems that might complicate future administration. The principle of addressing problems promptly rather than passing them forward appears in Jesus's teaching about reconciliation. Matthew 5:23-24 instructs, "Therefore, if you are offering your gift at the altar and there remember that your brother or sister has something against you, leave your gift there in front of the altar. First go and be reconciled to them; then come and offer your gift." The parallel to title defects is clear: if you discover problems with your title, address them first before proceeding with the trust transfer (your "offering" of property into the trust structure). Don't transfer problematic title forward, requiring your successor trustee to deal with messes you could have cleaned up. Reconcile title issues first, then proceed with the transfer, giving your trust the gift of clean, unencumbered ownership.

Mortgage Due-on-Sale Provisions and Federal Protections

As discussed extensively in previous chapters, the interaction between mortgage due-on-sale clauses and trust transfers is one of homeowners' primary concerns when considering placing mortgaged property into living trusts. To review briefly: virtually all modern mortgages contain due-on-sale clauses (also called acceleration clauses or alienation clauses) that give lenders the right to demand immediate payment of the entire loan balance if the borrower transfers the property without the lender's consent. These clauses protect lenders from having their loans informally assumed by unknown new owners with potentially poor credit, and they allow lenders to replace below-market rate loans with new loans at current rates when property changes hands. However, the Garn-St. Germain Depository Institutions Act of 1982 (12 U.S.C. § 1701j-3) specifically prohibits lenders from enforcing due-on-sale clauses when property is transferred "into an inter vivos trust in which the borrower is and remains a beneficiary and which does not relate to a transfer of rights of occupancy in the property."

This federal protection means that when you transfer your primary residence into your revocable living trust, where you are the trustee and a beneficiary and you continue living in the home, the lender cannot accelerate your loan, cannot demand immediate payment, cannot change your loan terms or interest rate, and cannot foreclose based on the transfer. This protection is absolute—it's not discretionary or subject to lender approval—and it applies uniformly across all states. However, several important qualifications affect how this protection applies in practice. First, the protection is specifically for revocable living trusts where you remain a beneficiary. If you transfer property into an irrevocable trust where you're not a beneficiary, or into a trust for someone else's sole benefit, the protection may not apply. Second, you must continue occupying the property as your residence. If you transfer your primary home into a trust but then move out, rent it out, or otherwise transfer occupancy rights, you violate this requirement and risk triggering the due-on-sale clause.

Third, the Garn-St. Germain Act protects the transfer itself but doesn't protect violations of other mortgage terms. If you stop making payments, fail to maintain property insurance, don't pay property taxes, or breach other loan conditions, the lender can still pursue remedies including foreclosure. The trust transfer protection only means the transfer itself can't be the basis for acceleration. Fourth, while federal law prohibits lenders from enforcing due-on-sale clauses for protected transfers, some mortgage agreements contain notification requirements separate from acceleration rights. If your mortgage requires you to notify the lender of ownership changes, you may be contractually obligated to provide that notice even though the lender can't do anything about the transfer. Understanding these protections and qualifications is essential for confidently proceeding with your trust transfer. The biblical principle of understanding the law before relying on it appears throughout Scripture. In Ezra 7:25-26, King Artaxerxes commands Ezra, "And you, Ezra, in accordance with the wisdom of your God, which you possess, appoint magistrates and judges to administer justice...to all who know the laws of your God. And you are to teach any who do not know them. Whoever does not obey the law of your God and the law of the king must surely be punished." Understanding both God's law and the king's law was essential for faithful living. Similarly, understanding both the law (Garn-St. Germain federal protection) and your mortgage agreement (the contractual "king's law" between you and your lender) is essential for proceeding properly with your trust transfer.

Working with Lenders: Practical Strategies

Given the federal protection for trust transfers, the practical question becomes how to work with lenders to minimize complications despite this protection. Lenders theoretically should recognize Garn-St. Germain protections and process trust transfers smoothly, but practical reality often diverges from theory due to servicer training inadequacies, automated systems that flag ownership changes without distinguishing protected transfers, and bureaucratic procedures that create complications even when transfers are legally protected. Several practical strategies help navigate lender relationships successfully.

First, decide whether to notify your lender proactively or proceed without notification, as discussed in previous chapters. This decision should be based on your mortgage terms (do they require notification?), your lender's reputation and sophistication, your comfort level with discretion versus transparency, your plans for the property (will you need lender cooperation soon for refinancing or modification?), and advice from your estate planning attorney based on their experience with similar transfers. If you decide to notify your lender, prepare documentation in advance including a brief notification letter explaining the estate planning transfer and citing Garn-St. Germain protection, a trustee certification showing you remain trustee and beneficiary, a copy of the recorded quitclaim deed, and possibly the relevant Garn-St. Germain Act statute text for reference. Direct your communication to the lender's legal or compliance department rather than general customer service, as these departments better understand federal protections. Frame your communication as informational notice rather than requesting permission: "This letter informs you that I have transferred my property into my revocable living trust for estate planning purposes, a transfer protected under federal law. I continue to occupy the property and remain fully obligated under the mortgage terms."

Second, if your lender raises concerns or questions despite your explanation, respond promptly and professionally with additional documentation and explanation. Many concerns result from initial reviewer's lack of knowledge and resolve once you reach knowledgeable personnel. Third, if your lender threatens or initiates improper acceleration or foreclosure despite the protected nature of your transfer, immediately consult with a real estate attorney about responding legally. Possible responses include demand letters from your attorney explaining the federal protection and demanding the lender cease improper actions, complaints to regulatory agencies (state banking departments, Consumer Financial Protection Bureau) about the lender's failure to comply with federal law, and in extreme cases, seeking temporary restraining orders or preliminary injunctions preventing wrongful foreclosure. Fourth, document all communications with your lender, keeping copies of letters, notes from phone conversations with dates and names of representatives, and records of any negative actions they take. This documentation provides evidence if you need to pursue legal remedies or regulatory complaints.

Fifth, consider timing your trust transfer when you don't have immediate need for lender cooperation. If you're planning to refinance within months, consider whether to delay the trust transfer until after refinancing or to transfer property out of trust temporarily for the refinance, then back in afterward. If you need a loan modification or other lender assistance, complicated mortgage relationships with trust transfer disputes might hinder cooperation. The principle of shrewd navigation of worldly systems while maintaining integrity appears in Jesus's teaching. Luke 16:8-9 records Jesus commending the shrewd manager: "The master commended the dishonest manager because he had acted shrewdly. For the people of this world are more shrewd in dealing with their own kind than are the people of the light. I tell you, use worldly wealth to gain friends for yourselves." While we must never be dishonest like this manager was, we can learn from his shrewdness in navigating systems. Work shrewdly with lenders—understanding their concerns, communicating strategically, timing actions wisely, escalating to knowledgeable personnel when needed—while maintaining absolute integrity and honesty in all dealings. This combination of shrewdness and integrity enables you to protect your legitimate rights while working effectively within financial systems.

Title Insurance Considerations and Continuity

Title insurance is a crucial protection that most homeowners obtain when purchasing property but may not fully understand, particularly regarding how it interacts with trust transfers. Unlike other insurance that protects against future events, title insurance protects against defects in title that existed in the past but might not have been discovered during the title search before purchase. Your owner's title insurance policy (distinct from the lender's title insurance, which only protects the lender) insures that you have good title to the property and protects you financially if title defects are discovered that impair your ownership. Common title problems that owner's title insurance covers include: unknown liens or mortgages from previous owners that surface after your purchase, forged deeds in the chain of title that could void your ownership, errors in public records that create ownership questions, unknown heirs of previous owners who claim ownership interests, and boundary disputes or survey errors that challenge your property's extent.

When you transfer property into your revocable living trust, an important question is whether your existing owner's title insurance continues protecting the property or whether the transfer voids coverage. The good news is that most owner's title insurance policies automatically continue covering property transferred into the insured person's revocable living trust without requiring endorsements or additional premiums. This is because you remain the beneficial owner—you just hold the property through your trust rather than individually—and the trust is revocable, meaning you can take the property back out at any time. The transfer doesn't change the underlying ownership in a way that increases risk to the title insurer. However, despite this general rule, best practice is notifying your title insurance company about the trust transfer and requesting written confirmation that coverage continues. Contact the title company that issued your policy (their information is on the policy document), provide them with a copy of the recorded quitclaim deed and a trustee certification, and request an endorsement or letter confirming that your title insurance remains in effect with the property now held in trust.

Most title companies will provide this confirmation at no charge or for a minimal fee, giving you documentary evidence that your title protection continues. If you're transferring property into a newly purchased policy soon after establishing your trust, consider whether to take title directly in the trust name rather than in your individual name first. Many title companies will issue owner's title insurance directly to you as trustee of your trust when you purchase property, avoiding the need for a subsequent transfer and re-verification of coverage. Some title companies charge slightly higher premiums for policies issued to trusts, while others charge the same rate. This approach is particularly useful if you're purchasing property specifically to hold in your trust for estate planning purposes. Finally, understand that title insurance is a one-time premium that provides lifetime coverage for issues that existed when the policy was issued. It doesn't cover title defects that arise after the policy date. If your trust owns property for many years and title issues develop during that time, the title insurance protects against issues that existed when you purchased the property but not against new issues. This is one reason maintaining good records and addressing title issues promptly remains important even with title insurance protection.

The biblical principle of maintaining protection and not presuming that past coverage extends automatically to new circumstances appears in various contexts. In Joshua 9, the Israelites made a covenant with the Gibeonites without inquiring of the Lord, assuming the Gibeonites were who they claimed to be. This presumption led to a covenant they regretted but had to honor. The lesson: don't presume; verify and confirm. Similarly, don't presume your title insurance automatically covers your property after transferring to a trust without verifying this with the title company. Take the time to confirm coverage continues, ensuring your protection remains in place in the new ownership structure.

Homeowner's Insurance Updates and Requirements

Updating your homeowner's insurance to reflect trust ownership is one of the most important and often overlooked steps when transferring property into a living trust. Your mortgage lender requires you to maintain adequate hazard insurance on the property as a condition of the loan, and they require that the insurance policy names them as loss payee or mortgagee (meaning insurance proceeds from covered losses must be used to pay off or repair the property securing the loan). When you transfer the property into your trust, the property owner changes from you individually to you as trustee of your trust. If your insurance policy still lists you individually as the insured while the property is actually owned by your trust, a technical mismatch exists that could create problems if you need to file a claim.

Insurance companies might question whether they're obligated to pay claims on property owned by an entity different from the named insured, potentially denying coverage or delaying payment while they investigate the ownership discrepancy. Additionally, if your lender discovers the property is in a trust but the insurance doesn't reflect this, they might consider this a violation of mortgage terms requiring proper insurance, potentially placing expensive force-placed insurance on the property at your expense.

To update your homeowner's insurance properly, contact your insurance company or agent promptly after recording your quitclaim deed, inform them that you've transferred your property into your revocable living trust for estate planning purposes, provide them with a copy of the recorded deed and a trustee certification if requested, and request that the policy be updated to show the trust or trustee as the named insured. The updated insured designation typically should match your deed's grantee designation: "Jane Mary Doe, Trustee of The Jane Mary Doe Revocable Living Trust dated January 1, 2024."

Some insurance companies prefer slightly different formats, and they'll tell you their requirement. Ensure the lender remains named as loss payee or mortgagee—this doesn't change just because the insured name changes. The lender still holds a mortgage on the property and must remain protected. Most insurance companies make this change at no charge and without affecting your premium, as you're the same person and the same risk, just holding property in a different form. Some might request to see portions of your trust document to verify the trust's existence and your role as trustee, though most accept trustee certifications without demanding complete trust documents. After the insurance company processes the change, they typically send you a new declaration page or endorsement showing the updated insured name and send a copy to your mortgage lender confirming insurance remains in force. Keep a copy of this updated insurance documentation with your trust records. If you ever refinance or sell the property, having current insurance documentation showing proper ownership helps transactions proceed smoothly.

The biblical principle of maintaining proper protections and not allowing coverage gaps appears in Proverbs 22:3: "The prudent see danger and take refuge, but the simple keep going and pay the penalty." Maintaining proper homeowner's insurance with correct ownership designation is exactly this kind of prudent refuge-taking that protects against the danger of uncovered losses. Don't be simple by keeping going with outdated insurance that might not provide coverage when needed. Be prudent by updating insurance to reflect current ownership, ensuring your refuge (insurance protection) actually covers the danger (property losses) when it occurs. The modest effort required to update insurance is insignificant compared to the penalty (denied claims, coverage gaps) that could result from neglecting this important step.

Property Tax and Assessment Considerations

Transferring property into a living trust raises questions about property tax reassessment and maintaining property tax benefits like homestead exemptions. Understanding how your jurisdiction treats trust transfers for property tax purposes helps you avoid unnecessary tax increases and preserve valuable exemptions. Property taxes are assessed based on property value, and most jurisdictions periodically reassess property to adjust taxes when values change. Additionally, ownership changes often trigger reassessments under the theory that the sale price in ownership changes reflects current market value. However, transferring property into your revocable living trust doesn't represent a true sale or change in beneficial ownership—you still own and occupy the property, just through a trust structure rather than individually.

Recognizing this, most states have laws or administrative policies that exempt transfers to revocable living trusts from property tax reassessment when the beneficial ownership doesn't actually change. The specific rules vary by state and sometimes by county, but common approaches include: statutory exemptions explicitly stating that transfers to grantor's revocable trusts don't trigger reassessment, administrative policies where assessors have discretion to exempt estate planning trust transfers, and requirements to file specific forms claiming reassessment exemptions after the transfer. To preserve your property tax assessment and rates when transferring to your trust, research your state and county's specific rules about trust transfers and property tax reassessment. Contact your county property tax assessor's office or visit their website to learn what documentation or forms are required. Complete and file any required forms promptly after recording your quitclaim deed, typically including a copy of the recorded deed and possibly a trustee certification. Common forms include change of ownership statements that explain the nature of the transfer and claim applicable exemptions, affidavits of transfer between parties that don't constitute changes in ownership for assessment purposes, or homestead exemption continuation forms if you have homestead protection.

Beyond avoiding reassessment, homeowners must ensure that any property tax exemptions or reductions they currently enjoy continue after transferring property to a trust. Homestead exemptions, available in most states, reduce the assessed value of owner-occupied primary residences by a certain amount (often $25,000 to $50,000 or more), significantly lowering property taxes. To qualify, property must typically be owned and occupied by the person claiming the exemption. When property is transferred to a trust, some jurisdictions automatically continue homestead exemptions recognizing that occupancy hasn't changed, while others require filing updated applications or certifications to maintain the exemption. Similarly, senior citizen property tax reductions, disabled veteran exemptions, agricultural use valuations, and other special assessment programs may have specific rules about whether they continue when property is transferred to trusts. Don't assume these benefits automatically continue; verify requirements and complete necessary filings to preserve valuable tax benefits. The cost of losing a homestead exemption could be hundreds or thousands of dollars annually in increased property taxes, making a few minutes' effort to maintain the exemption extremely worthwhile.

The biblical principle of not losing valuable benefits through neglect appears in Jesus's parable of the talents in Matthew 25:14-30. The servant who buried his talent and didn't use it productively was condemned for unfaithfulness to his master. While this parable primarily teaches about using our God-given abilities and resources, it also illustrates the principle that we must actively maintain and protect what's been entrusted to us. Property tax exemptions and benefits are resources that have been entrusted to you (granted by law based on your qualifying circumstances), and maintaining them after transferring property to your trust is part of faithful stewardship. Don't bury these benefits through neglect of required filings; actively maintain them by complying with your jurisdiction's requirements for preserving exemptions when property is transferred to trusts.

Escrow Account Management and Payment Continuity

Many mortgages include escrow accounts (also called impound accounts) where the borrower makes monthly payments that include not just principal and interest but also amounts for property taxes and insurance. The lender holds these additional amounts in escrow and pays the property taxes and insurance premiums when due on the borrower's behalf. Escrow accounts benefit both borrowers (who don't have to budget for large lump-sum tax and insurance payments) and lenders (who ensure taxes and insurance are paid, protecting their collateral). When you transfer property into your trust, ensuring continuity of escrow account management and preventing disruptions requires attention.

Several potential complications can arise if escrow accounts aren't properly updated after trust transfers. First, if property tax records aren't updated to show the trust as owner, tax bills might still be issued in your individual name. Your lender's escrow account pays these bills, but if the name mismatch creates confusion, payments might be delayed or misdirected. Second, if insurance isn't updated to show the trust as insured, the lender's escrow payment of insurance premiums might be rejected by the insurance company or paid on an outdated policy that no longer properly covers the property. Third, if the lender discovers the property is in a trust but their escrow records still show individual ownership, they might freeze the escrow account pending documentation updates, potentially causing gaps in tax or insurance payments. To prevent these complications, take proactive steps after transferring property to your trust: Ensure property tax records are updated to reflect trust ownership, as discussed above. Confirm updated tax bills will be sent to your lender at their escrow payment address or that the lender knows where to remit payment.

Update homeowner's insurance to show the trust as insured and confirm updated insurance bills are sent to your lender's escrow payment address. If you notified your lender about the trust transfer, provide them with updated tax and insurance information so their escrow records reflect the current ownership structure. If you didn't notify your lender but they discover the transfer, be prepared to quickly provide documentation that property taxes and insurance have been properly updated and the lender can continue paying them through escrow. Monitor your escrow account statements to ensure tax and insurance payments are being made timely and correctly. If you notice gaps or problems, contact the lender's escrow department immediately to address issues before they cause penalties, late fees, or coverage lapses. Most escrow account management continues smoothly after trust transfers because the practical substance hasn't changed—the same person living in the same property making the same mortgage payments for the same taxes and insurance. However, administrative mismatches in names between various systems (tax assessor, insurance company, lender's escrow account) can create temporary confusion that you should monitor and address promptly.

The biblical principle of faithful attention to ongoing responsibilities appears in the parable of the faithful steward. Luke 12:42-44 describes the manager whom the master puts in charge of household servants to give them their food allowance at proper times. Jesus commends the servant who faithfully discharges this ongoing responsibility. Managing your escrow account, ensuring taxes and insurance are properly paid through it, and addressing any administrative issues that arise from your trust transfer is exactly this kind of faithful stewardship of ongoing responsibilities. Don't assume everything will automatically work perfectly; pay attention to ensure your "household" (property) continues receiving what it needs (tax and insurance payments) at proper times despite the ownership change.

Joint Ownership and Co-Trustee Situations

When property is owned jointly by multiple people—most commonly married couples but sometimes siblings, business partners, or other co-owners—transferring that property into a trust requires additional considerations beyond individual ownership situations. The most important principle is that all current owners must participate in the transfer unless their interest has already been conveyed or terminated. You cannot unilaterally transfer co-owned property into your individual trust without the other owners' consent and participation. For married couples who jointly own their primary residence, the typical approach is establishing either a joint revocable living trust (one trust created together by both spouses) or separate revocable living trusts for each spouse, then transferring the jointly owned property accordingly.

If you establish a joint trust, both spouses sign the quitclaim deed as grantors, transferring from "John Smith and Mary Smith, husband and wife" to "John Smith and Mary Smith, as Trustees of the Smith Family Trust dated January 1, 2024." This transfers both spouses' interests into the one joint trust where both serve as co-trustees. If you establish separate trusts, you have options: transfer the entire property into one spouse's trust (requiring both spouses to sign the transfer deed), with the trust provisions addressing how the property is handled after the first spouse's death, or transfer each spouse's interest into their respective trust, creating co-ownership between the two trusts (requiring separate deeds from each spouse transferring their individual interest). The best approach depends on your overall estate planning goals, state law regarding community property versus separate property, tax considerations, and advice from your estate planning attorney.

In community property states (Arizona, California, Idaho, Louisiana, Nevada, New Mexico, Texas, Washington, Wisconsin), special attention is required to maintain the property's community property character when transferring to trusts. Community property has valuable tax benefits, particularly the "double step-up in basis" when one spouse dies, where both halves of the property receive stepped-up basis to fair market value at death, not just the deceased spouse's half. To preserve this benefit, the deed transferring community property into a trust should include language explicitly stating the property is being transferred as community property: "John Smith and Mary Smith, as Trustees of the Smith Family Trust dated January 1, 2024, as community property." Without this language, the property might be treated as losing its community property character, sacrificing valuable tax benefits. If co-owners are not spouses—perhaps siblings who inherited property together—each owner can only transfer their individual interest unless all agree to transfer the entire property into one trust. Typically, each sibling would establish their own trust and transfer their fractional interest into it, creating co-ownership between multiple trusts. This works but creates complexity when the property is eventually sold or one co-owner dies.

The biblical principle of respecting multiple parties' interests and not acting unilaterally appears throughout Scripture's teachings about relationships and community. Philippians 2:3-4 instructs, "Do nothing out of selfish ambition or vain conceit. Rather, in humility value others above yourselves, not looking to your own interests but each of you to the interests of the others." When property is co-owned, all owners have legitimate interests that must be respected. You cannot transfer co-owned property into your trust for your benefit without considering and honoring your co-owners' interests and obtaining their participation. This humble, others-focused approach ensures estate planning doesn't become a source of conflict but rather reflects consideration for all parties with legitimate stakes in the property.

Conclusion: Diligence in the Details

Navigating mortgage and title issues when transferring property into living trusts requires careful attention to numerous details, from understanding your current title and addressing defects, to working with lenders regarding due-on-sale concerns, maintaining title and homeowner's insurance protection, preserving property tax benefits, managing escrow accounts, and addressing joint ownership complexities. While the breadth of these issues might seem overwhelming, millions of homeowners successfully navigate them every year by approaching the process methodically, seeking professional guidance when needed, and maintaining diligence in addressing each element properly. The reward for this careful work is enormous: property properly transferred into your trust, ready to pass smoothly to your beneficiaries without probate, while your mortgage continues on its existing terms, your insurance and tax benefits are preserved, and all administrative matters are properly handled.

The biblical principle that undergirds all these technical details is faithful stewardship of what God has entrusted to us. First Corinthians 4:2 teaches, "Moreover, it is required of stewards that they be found faithful." Faithfulness in stewardship includes both big-picture planning (establishing trusts to provide for family) and detailed execution (properly recording deeds, updating insurance, maintaining tax benefits). Both matter equally because details improperly handled can undermine even the best high-level plans. As you work through mortgage and title issues in your trust funding, approach each requirement as an opportunity to demonstrate faithful stewardship, giving careful attention to details because you're managing resources God has blessed you with for purposes that extend beyond your lifetime. Colossians 3:23 reminds us, "Whatever you do, work at it with all your heart, as working for the Lord, not for human masters." Updating insurance policies, filing property tax forms, communicating with lenders, and recording deeds properly might seem like mundane administrative tasks, but when done as unto the Lord, they become acts of worship—faithful execution of stewardship responsibilities that honor God and serve your family. Commit these details to the Lord, work through them diligently, and trust that your careful attention to properly navigating mortgage and title issues will establish your estate plans on firm foundations that serve your family for generations to come.

***

Section 1: What Happens If Your Home Has a Mortgage

Understanding the Mortgage-Trust Relationship

For the vast majority of American homeowners, their residence is not owned free and clear but is encumbered by a mortgage—a loan secured by the property itself that represents both a significant financial obligation and a valuable tool that enabled home purchase. When these homeowners consider transferring their mortgaged property into a living trust for estate planning purposes, a critical question arises: What happens to the mortgage? Does the trust transfer affect the loan? Will the lender demand immediate payment? Does the borrower's personal responsibility for the debt change? Understanding the relationship between mortgages and trust transfers is essential for the millions of homeowners who want to accomplish estate planning goals without jeopardizing their mortgage relationships or triggering unwanted financial consequences.

The fundamental principle to understand is this: transferring property into a living trust changes the legal ownership of the property (who holds title) but does not change the debt secured by that property or the borrower's personal liability for that debt. The mortgage remains attached to the property regardless of who holds legal title, and the person who signed the promissory note (the debt instrument) remains personally obligated to repay the loan according to its terms. The trust doesn't assume the debt, doesn't become responsible for payments, and doesn't relieve the original borrower of their obligation. What changes is simply that the property securing the debt is now titled in the trust's name rather than the borrower's individual name. This distinction between ownership of property and responsibility for debt is crucial for understanding how mortgaged property can be successfully transferred into trusts.

The biblical principle of honoring our debts and obligations regardless of changes in other circumstances provides our foundation. Romans 13:8 commands, "Let no debt remain outstanding, except the continuing debt to love one another." When you transfer your mortgaged home into a trust, this command continues applying—the mortgage debt remains outstanding (secured by the property) and you remain obligated to pay it. The trust transfer doesn't diminish, alter, or excuse this obligation. Similarly, Psalm 37:21 observes, "The wicked borrow and do not repay, but the righteous give generously." Righteousness in financial matters includes faithfully repaying what we've borrowed, and this faithfulness continues after transferring property into trusts. Understanding how mortgages and trusts interact enables homeowners to accomplish legitimate estate planning while maintaining their righteous commitment to honoring debt obligations fully.

The Continuing Nature of Mortgage Obligations

When you transfer your home into a living trust, the first and most important reality to understand is that your mortgage obligation continues exactly as before—same payment amount, same interest rate, same payment schedule, same total debt, and same personal liability. The quitclaim deed that transfers legal title to your property from you individually to you as trustee of your trust has no effect whatsoever on the promissory note you signed when you borrowed money from the lender. That promissory note is a separate legal instrument from the deed, and it creates your personal promise to repay the borrowed funds. This personal obligation survives the deed transfer and continues binding you regardless of how property title is held.

Similarly, the mortgage or deed of trust (the security instrument that gives the lender rights in your property) remains in full force and effect after the trust transfer. This security interest doesn't disappear or diminish just because legal title has changed hands. The lender's right to foreclose on the property if you default on loan payments continues, and all other mortgage terms remain enforceable. From a practical standpoint, this means several things. First, you must continue making all mortgage payments exactly as before—same amount, same due date, same payment method. The trust transfer gives you no payment holiday, reduction, or modification. Second, you remain personally liable if payments aren't made. If the trust hypothetically failed to make payments (though since you're the trustee, this would only happen if you failed to make them), the lender could pursue you personally for the debt, not just foreclose on the property. Your personal credit remains at risk if mortgage obligations aren't met.

Third, all other mortgage terms remain in effect, including requirements to maintain property insurance, pay property taxes, maintain the property in good condition, and comply with any other covenants in the mortgage agreement.

The trust transfer changes none of these obligations; it simply changes who holds legal title to the property serving as collateral. This continuing obligation reality is actually protective for homeowners because it means the trust transfer itself doesn't create any new obligations, payment changes, or complications with the loan—everything continues as it was. The biblical principle of continuing faithfulness to commitments we've made, regardless of changing circumstances, appears throughout Scripture. In Numbers 30:2, God commands, "When a man makes a vow to the Lord or takes an oath to obligate himself by a pledge, he must not break his word but must do everything he said." The promissory note you signed when you took out your mortgage is exactly this kind of pledge—you obligated yourself to repay the borrowed funds, and you must do everything you said (make all payments as promised) regardless of subsequent life changes, including transferring property into a trust. God values this kind of faithfulness to commitments, and honoring your mortgage obligation after transferring property into a trust demonstrates this faithful commitment-keeping.

Federal Protection: The Garn-St. Germain Act Revisited

While your mortgage obligation continues after transferring property into a trust, federal law provides crucial protection ensuring that the trust transfer itself cannot be used by lenders as a reason to accelerate your loan or change its terms. As discussed extensively in previous chapters, the Garn-St. Germain Depository Institutions Act of 1982 (12 U.S.C. § 1701j-3) specifically prohibits lenders from enforcing due-on-sale clauses when property is transferred "into an inter vivos trust in which the borrower is and remains a beneficiary and which does not relate to a transfer of rights of occupancy in the property." This federal protection means that despite language in your mortgage agreement giving the lender rights to accelerate the loan if property is transferred, the lender cannot exercise those rights when you transfer your property into your revocable living trust if you remain a beneficiary and continue living in the home.

To review the practical implications: The lender cannot demand immediate payment of your entire loan balance simply because you transferred the property to your trust. The lender cannot increase your interest rate or change other loan terms because of the transfer. The lender cannot refuse to accept your regular monthly payments or claim you're in default based solely on the transfer. The lender cannot initiate foreclosure proceedings based on the transfer itself (though they can still foreclose if you default on payments or violate other mortgage terms). This protection is absolute and mandatory—it's not subject to lender discretion or approval, and it applies uniformly across all states regardless of what your specific mortgage agreement says. The protection exists as a matter of federal law that preempts contrary mortgage provisions.

However, this protection comes with important qualifications that homeowners must understand to ensure they remain protected. First, the trust must be revocable during your lifetime. If you transfer property into an irrevocable trust where you surrender all control and rights, the Garn-St. Germain protection may not apply and the lender might be able to enforce the due-on-sale clause. Second, you must remain a beneficiary of the trust. If you transfer property into a trust for someone else's sole benefit with no provisions benefiting you, the protection doesn't apply. The typical revocable living trust structure—where you are both the trustee managing the trust and the primary beneficiary receiving benefits during your lifetime—clearly satisfies this requirement. Third, you must continue occupying the property. The protection is specifically for homeowners transferring their primary residence while continuing to live there. If you transfer rental property, vacation homes you don't occupy as primary residence, or if you transfer your home but then move out, the protection may not apply. Fourth, the Garn-St. Germain protection shields you from loan acceleration based on the transfer but doesn't protect you from consequences of violating other mortgage terms. If you stop making payments, let property insurance lapse, fail to pay property taxes, or breach other mortgage obligations, the lender can still pursue all available remedies including foreclosure.

The biblical principle of legitimate authority establishing protective laws for the benefit of the people appears throughout Scripture. In

Deuteronomy, God established numerous laws protecting vulnerable people from oppression and ensuring justice. Similarly, Congress established the Garn-St. Germain Act to protect homeowners from lenders who might otherwise use due-on-sale clauses oppressively to force refinancing or loan payoff when no meaningful change in lending risk has occurred. Romans 13:3-4 teaches, "For rulers hold no terror for those who do right, but for those who do wrong...For the one in authority is God's servant for your good." The Garn-St. Germain Act is exactly this kind of governmental servant for your good—it protects homeowners engaging in legitimate estate planning from terror (loan acceleration) they don't deserve, ensuring lenders don't use technical property transfers as excuses to disrupt stable mortgage relationships. Understanding and relying on this protection allows you to proceed confidently with trust-based estate planning despite having mortgaged property.

Practical Lender Responses: What to Expect

While federal law clearly protects trust transfers from loan acceleration, homeowners with mortgages must still navigate the practical realities of how lenders and mortgage servicers actually respond when they discover trust transfers. The theoretical legal protection doesn't always translate into smooth, problem-free experiences because of variations in lender sophistication, servicer training, automated systems that flag ownership changes, and bureaucratic procedures that sometimes create complications despite legal protections. Understanding what responses you might encounter helps you prepare appropriately and respond effectively if issues arise.

Best-case scenarios occur when lenders handle trust transfers routinely and professionally. Sophisticated lenders familiar with estate planning recognize Garn-St. Germain protections immediately. They may have streamlined procedures for documenting trust ownership, requiring only basic information like trustee certification showing you remain trustee and beneficiary. They update their records to show the trust as property owner while maintaining the same account, loan number, and payment requirements. They continue servicing the loan without disruption, treating the ownership change as an administrative update rather than a significant event. These smooth experiences most commonly occur with large national lenders who process thousands of trust transfers annually, when borrowers proactively notify lenders with clear documentation upfront, when transfers are obviously for estate planning and the borrower is in good standing on the loan, and when borrowers can quickly reach knowledgeable personnel (legal departments, compliance officers) rather than frontline customer service.

However, problematic scenarios also occur with regularity, particularly when servicers are poorly trained, automated systems flag transfers inappropriately, or borrowers encounter uninformed personnel. Common problems include acceleration demand letters threatening to call the loan due if you don't immediately provide documentation or transfer property back, initiation of foreclosure proceedings based on supposed due-on-sale violations, freezing of online mortgage account access pending "review" of the ownership change, disruption of automatic payment arrangements requiring reconfiguration, demands for extensive documentation treating the transfer as requiring lender "approval," and escrow account complications if the servicer becomes confused about property ownership for tax and insurance payment purposes. These problems, while ultimately resolvable through education about federal protections, create stress, waste time and money, and potentially affect credit if servicers erroneously report loans as in default or begin foreclosure proceedings.

The gap between legal theory (you're protected) and practical reality (some lenders still create problems) means homeowners must prepare for both possibilities. Have documentation ready to prove your transfer qualifies for protection—recorded deed, trustee certification, occupancy confirmation, and Garn-St. Germain statute citation. Know your rights under federal law so you can confidently explain them if your lender questions the transfer. Have your estate planning attorney's contact information readily available so they can intervene if necessary. Be prepared to escalate to supervisors, legal departments, or regulatory agencies if initial contacts don't resolve issues. Monitor your loan account, credit reports, and escrow accounts carefully after transferring property to catch and address any problems quickly. The biblical teaching about being prepared for both favorable and unfavorable responses to right action appears in Jesus's instructions to his disciples. Matthew 10:16-17 warns, "I am sending you out like sheep among wolves. Therefore be shrewd as snakes and as innocent as doves. Be on your guard." Even though your trust transfer is innocent (legally protected and proper), you must be shrewd (aware that some lenders might respond like wolves) and on your guard (prepared to defend your rights and respond to problems). This combination of innocence and shrewdness enables you to proceed with legitimate estate planning while being prepared to address any complications that might arise from lender confusion or resistance.

Administrative Updates and Account Management

Beyond the fundamental question of whether lenders can accelerate loans (they can't for protected transfers), homeowners transferring mortgaged property into trusts must address various administrative and account management matters to ensure smooth continuation of the mortgage relationship. These practical administrative steps, while often overlooked, are important for preventing complications and maintaining good standing with your lender. First, consider whether and how to notify your lender about the trust transfer, as discussed extensively in previous chapters. If your mortgage explicitly requires notification of ownership changes, provide that notice even though the lender can't accelerate the loan. If notification isn't required but you prefer transparency, send a brief informational letter with supporting documentation. If you choose not to notify proactively, be prepared to respond if the lender discovers the transfer through other means.

Second, update your contact information with the lender if necessary. If you want mortgage correspondence sent to you as trustee rather than as an individual, or if you want statements addressed to the trust, provide this information to your servicer. However, many borrowers find it simpler to maintain existing contact arrangements, receiving correspondence in their individual names even though property is technically held in trust, since they're the same person either way. Third, ensure automatic payment arrangements continue functioning properly. If you have automatic mortgage payments set up from your bank account, the trust transfer shouldn't affect these since you're making payments from the same account. However, if your bank requires account names to match exactly, you might need to update payment instructions to reference the trust. Monitor the first few payments after transferring to ensure they process correctly.

Fourth, address escrow account management as discussed in the previous section. Ensure property tax records are updated so tax bills go to the right place for lender payment. Update homeowner's insurance to reflect trust ownership so insurance payments from escrow are accepted by the insurance company. Verify that escrow account statements continue showing proper credits and debits for taxes and insurance. If you notice discrepancies or problems, contact your servicer's escrow department promptly. Fifth, if you're planning to refinance, sell, or otherwise transact regarding the property in the near future, consider how the trust ownership affects these plans. Some refinance lenders prefer property to be in borrowers' individual names during refinancing; if so, you may need to temporarily transfer property out of trust for the refinance, then back in afterward. Coordinate with your mortgage broker or refinance lender about their requirements and timing.

Sixth, keep records of all communications with your lender about the trust transfer and all updated documentation showing proper insurance, escrow management, and payment processing. This paper trail proves you've maintained the mortgage properly and addressed all obligations despite the ownership change. The biblical principle of faithful management of ongoing administrative responsibilities appears in various parables about stewards. Luke 16:10 teaches, "Whoever can be trusted with very little can also be trusted with much, and whoever is dishonest with very little will also be dishonest with much." The administrative details of mortgage account management—maintaining payment arrangements, updating contact information, managing escrow accounts—are "very little" compared to the larger estate planning goals you're accomplishing. But being trustworthy with these little things demonstrates the faithful stewardship that qualifies you to be trusted with much. Don't neglect small administrative matters assuming they'll take care of themselves. Give them the attention they deserve, ensuring your mortgage relationship continues smoothly throughout the trust ownership period.

Insurance Coordination: Homeowner's and Title Coverage

Proper insurance coordination is one of the most critical yet frequently overlooked aspects of transferring mortgaged property into trusts. Two types of insurance require attention: homeowner's hazard insurance (protecting against property damage from fire, storms, theft, etc.) and owner's title insurance (protecting against title defects and ownership challenges). Both forms of coverage are important for protecting your investment and meeting mortgage requirements, and both require updates after transferring property to a trust. Regarding homeowner's insurance, your mortgage agreement requires you to maintain adequate hazard coverage with the lender named as mortgagee or loss payee, ensuring insurance proceeds from covered losses pay off the mortgage before you receive any funds. When you transfer property into your trust, the insured party changes from you individually to you as trustee of your trust, creating a technical mismatch if the policy isn't updated.

To maintain proper coverage, contact your insurance company or agent immediately after recording your quitclaim deed. Explain that you've transferred your property into your revocable living trust for estate planning purposes and need the policy updated to reflect this. Provide a copy of the recorded deed and a trustee certification if requested. Request that the insured party designation be changed to match your trust ownership, typically formatted as: "Jane Mary Doe, Trustee of The Jane Mary Doe Revocable Living Trust dated January 1, 2024." Ensure the lender remains listed as mortgagee or loss payee—this doesn't change despite the insured party change. Most insurance companies process this update at no charge and without premium changes, recognizing you're the same insured just holding property differently. After the update, the insurance company typically sends you an updated declarations page and sends a copy to your lender confirming continued coverage. Keep this documentation with your trust records. Failure to update homeowner's insurance creates several risks: insurance companies might deny claims or delay payment when they discover the insured party doesn't match the property owner; lenders might place expensive force-placed insurance when they discover property isn't properly insured or property owner doesn't match insured party; and coverage gaps might exist if the insurance company determines they have no obligation to cover property owned by an entity different from the named insured.

Regarding owner's title insurance, this coverage protects you against title defects that existed when you purchased the property but weren't discovered during the title search. As discussed in the previous section, most owner's title insurance policies automatically continue covering property transferred into the insured's revocable living trust without requiring endorsements or additional premiums. However, best practice is confirming this with your title insurance company. Contact the title company that issued your policy (information is on the policy document), provide them with a copy of the recorded deed and trustee certification, and request written confirmation that coverage continues with property held in trust. Most title companies provide this confirmation at no charge, giving you peace of mind that your title protection continues. If you're purchasing property specifically to hold in your trust, consider taking title directly in the trust name initially rather than in your individual name first, avoiding the need for subsequent transfer and confirmation of continued coverage. The biblical principle of maintaining proper protections for valuable assets appears in Proverbs 27:23-24: "Be sure you know the condition of your flocks, give careful attention to your herds; for riches do not endure forever, and a crown is not secure for all generations." Knowing the condition of your property's insurance coverage—verifying that both hazard insurance and title insurance properly protect property held in your trust—is exactly this kind of careful attention that ensures your riches (home equity and property) endure and remain secure. Don't assume coverage continues automatically; verify and confirm, ensuring your protections remain in place through the ownership change.

Addressing Financial Distress and Creditor Concerns

The discussion thus far has assumed homeowners transferring property into trusts are current on mortgage payments, financially stable, and transferring purely for estate planning purposes. However, some homeowners consider trust transfers while facing financial difficulties, delinquent payments, pending foreclosure, or significant debt problems. Understanding how these circumstances affect the appropriateness and legality of trust transfers is crucial for avoiding serious legal problems.

The fundamental principle is this: transferring property into a trust while facing financial distress or creditor claims, though technically permitted by Garn-St. Germain Act for revocable trusts, can be scrutinized as potential fraudulent conveyance if the transfer's purpose is hiding assets from creditors rather than legitimate estate planning.

Fraudulent conveyance laws, which exist in all states, allow courts to set aside property transfers made with intent to hinder, delay, or defraud creditors, or made for inadequate consideration when the transferor was insolvent or became insolvent as a result. If you transfer your home into a trust while significantly behind on mortgage payments, facing foreclosure, or dealing with other major debts, creditors and courts may question whether your motive was estate planning or asset hiding. Several factors affect how such transfers are viewed: Timing relative to financial problems—transferring property into a trust years before any financial difficulties arise, as part of general estate planning, is clearly legitimate. Transferring right before or during foreclosure proceedings, immediately after being sued, or while actively negotiating with creditors about debt settlement raises serious questions about motive.

Your actual intent—if you genuinely established the trust for estate planning purposes (avoiding probate, providing for family, ensuring smooth succession) and financial problems arose coincidentally, this differs from establishing the trust primarily to shield assets from known creditors. The effect on creditors—revocable living trusts generally don't protect assets from your creditors during your lifetime because you retain control and can revoke the trust at any time. If creditors can still reach the assets, the transfer arguably doesn't hinder them. However, the transfer might make foreclosure or collection more complicated administratively, which could be viewed as hindering creditors. Your honesty and transparency—attempting to hide the transfer, lying about motives, or failing to disclose the trust when required (such as on loan modification applications or bankruptcy filings) strongly suggests fraudulent intent. Being transparent about the trust and its estate planning purposes suggests legitimate motives.

If you're facing financial distress and considering transferring property into a trust, consult with both a bankruptcy attorney or creditors' rights attorney and an estate planning attorney before proceeding. They can advise whether the transfer is appropriate in your circumstances or whether it could be challenged as fraudulent. In some cases, alternative approaches might better serve your situation—such as addressing financial problems first, then establishing trusts after stabilizing your finances. The biblical standard for financial dealings, even during difficult times, is absolute honesty and integrity. Proverbs 28:6 teaches, "Better the poor whose walk is blameless than the rich whose ways are perverse." If you're facing financial hardship, it's better to address it honestly—working with creditors, considering bankruptcy if appropriate, being transparent about your situation—than to attempt using trusts or other structures to hide assets or avoid legitimate obligations. Such perverse ways might seem to protect wealth temporarily, but they violate both legal and moral standards. Psalm 37:21 observes, "The wicked borrow and do not repay, but the righteous give generously." Righteousness in financial difficulties means continuing to honor obligations to the extent possible, not using legal structures to avoid repaying what you've borrowed. If you can't fully repay debts, address this honestly through legal processes like bankruptcy or debt settlement, not through transfers designed to shield assets from legitimate creditors.

Refinancing and Future Mortgage Transactions

An important consideration when transferring mortgaged property into a trust is how the trust ownership affects future mortgage transactions you might want to conduct. While the current mortgage continues on its existing terms after the transfer (protected by Garn-St. Germain), future transactions involving the property may require coordination between the trust ownership and lender requirements. The most common future transaction is refinancing—replacing your existing mortgage with a new loan, typically to obtain a lower interest rate, change loan terms, or access equity through cash-out refinancing. When you're ready to refinance and your property is held in a trust, lenders typically handle this one of two ways.

Many refinance lenders prefer property to be in the borrower's individual name during the refinancing process. If so, you would execute a quitclaim deed temporarily transferring property from your trust back into your individual name, complete the refinance with property in individual ownership, then execute another quitclaim deed transferring property back into your trust after the refinance closes. This approach adds two deeds and recording fees to the process but satisfies lenders who are more comfortable with traditional individual ownership. Some refinance lenders, particularly those with extensive experience in estate planning, are comfortable refinancing property held in trusts. They'll lend to you as trustee of your trust, taking a mortgage against the trust-held property. This approach avoids the back-and-forth transfers but requires finding a lender willing to work with trust-owned property. When refinancing approaches, discuss with your mortgage broker or lender whether they require property to be in individual name or will work with trust ownership.

Other future mortgage transactions that might arise include obtaining a home equity loan or line of credit secured by your property, adding or removing co-borrowers to an existing loan (typically requiring refinancing), and selling the property (which isn't technically a mortgage transaction but involves paying off the mortgage with sale proceeds). For home equity borrowing, similar considerations apply as for refinancing—some lenders require individual ownership while others work with trust-held property. For sales, your successor trustee or you as trustee can execute the sale deed transferring property from the trust to the buyer, and the buyer's purchase money pays off your mortgage as part of the transaction. Title companies routinely handle sales of trust-held property and ensure mortgages are properly satisfied from proceeds.

The key is planning ahead and coordinating with lenders about their requirements. Don't assume all lenders handle trust-held property the same way; ask upfront about requirements and adjust your approach accordingly. The biblical principle of planning ahead and counting the cost before proceeding appears in Luke 14:28: "Suppose one of you wants to build a tower. Won't you first sit down and estimate the cost to see if you have enough money to complete it?" Before transferring property into a trust, count the costs—including potential future complications with refinancing or other transactions—and ensure you can complete what you start. This doesn't mean avoiding trust transfers because of potential future refinancing complications; it means being aware of these considerations and prepared to address them when the time comes. The modest inconvenience of temporarily transferring property out of and back into your trust for refinancing is small compared to the estate planning benefits trusts provide. Just be aware of this potential need and plan accordingly rather than being surprised when your refinance lender raises it as a requirement.

Working with Professionals: Title Companies and Attorneys

Successfully navigating the mortgage and title issues involved in transferring property into trusts often requires professional assistance from title companies, real estate attorneys, and estate planning attorneys who understand both the technical requirements and the practical realities of these transactions. Understanding when to seek professional help and how to work effectively with these professionals ensures your transfer is done correctly while avoiding unnecessary expense. Title companies provide several valuable services related to trust transfers. They can conduct title searches revealing any defects or encumbrances that should be addressed before transferring to your trust. They can prepare quitclaim deeds with proper legal descriptions, grantee designations, and all required elements for recording. They can coordinate recordings with county offices, ensuring proper filing and obtaining recorded originals for your records.

They can verify that your owner's title insurance continues protecting property after the transfer or provide endorsements confirming coverage. Many title companies offer trust funding services as packages, handling all deed preparation and recording for flat fees, typically ranging from a few hundred to several hundred dollars depending on complexity and location. Working with title companies provides professional expertise in deed preparation and recording procedures, reducing risk of errors that could create title problems. Real estate attorneys provide different services focused on legal issues and problem-solving. They can review your existing title and mortgage documents, advising whether any issues require attention before transferring to your trust. They can explain how your specific mortgage language interacts with Garn-St. Germain protections. They can communicate with lenders on your behalf if questions or problems arise about the trust transfer, often resolving issues more quickly than homeowners could alone. They can prepare quitclaim deeds and other legal documents needed for the transfer.

They can provide opinion letters to lenders or other parties confirming the legality and protected nature of trust transfers. When problems arise—lenders threaten improper acceleration, title defects surface, or other complications develop—real estate attorneys can pursue legal remedies on your behalf. Estate planning attorneys, who draft your trust document, often coordinate trust funding including real property transfers as part of their services. They understand how property ownership interacts with overall estate planning goals and can ensure transfers are structured consistently with your plan. They can advise about coordinating property transfers with other trust funding (financial accounts, business interests, etc.). They can prepare trustee certifications and other documents needed when dealing with lenders or institutions. Many estate planning attorneys either prepare quitclaim deeds themselves or coordinate with title companies for this work, ensuring all trust funding aspects are properly completed.

The decision about which professionals to engage depends on your situation's complexity, your comfort level with handling technical matters, and your budget. For straightforward situations—simple property title, no mortgage complications, cooperative lender—working with a title company for deed preparation and recording might suffice, particularly if your estate planning attorney coordinates the process. For complex situations—title defects, difficult lenders, joint ownership complications—engaging a real estate attorney provides additional legal expertise and advocacy. The biblical teaching about seeking multiple counselors in important matters supports consulting professionals. Proverbs 11:14 teaches, "For lack of guidance a nation falls, but victory is won through many advisers." Proverbs 15:22 similarly states, "Plans fail for lack of counsel, but with many advisers they succeed." Transferring mortgaged property into trusts involves sufficient complexity and potential for problems that seeking professional guidance—from title companies, real estate attorneys, estate planning attorneys—is wise stewardship, not unnecessary expense. The cost of professional help is modest compared to the value of your property and the potential cost of fixing mistakes or addressing problems that proper professional guidance would have prevented.

Conclusion: Confidence in Proper Planning and Execution

Homeowners with mortgaged properties can confidently transfer their homes into revocable living trusts for estate planning purposes, knowing that federal law protects these transfers from loan acceleration, that mortgage obligations continue normally, and that with proper attention to administrative details, the process can proceed smoothly without jeopardizing mortgage relationships. The key elements for success include understanding that mortgage obligations continue unchanged after the transfer, relying on Garn-St. Germain Act protection against improper loan acceleration, being prepared to address practical lender responses ranging from smooth cooperation to temporary confusion, maintaining proper homeowner's and title insurance coverage through the ownership change, coordinating escrow account management and payment processing, addressing any financial distress or creditor concerns honestly and transparently, planning ahead for potential future refinancing or other mortgage transactions, and engaging appropriate professional assistance from title companies and attorneys when needed.

By approaching these mortgage and title issues systematically and thoroughly, you can accomplish your estate planning goals—avoiding probate, providing for smooth asset management during incapacity, ensuring family succession—while maintaining your existing mortgage on its current terms and preserving good standing with your lender. The biblical principle that undergirds all these technical considerations is faithful stewardship that honors both our estate planning responsibilities to our families and our debt obligations to our lenders. Proverbs 16:3 promises, "Commit to the Lord whatever you do, and he will establish your plans." Commit your trust-based estate planning to the Lord, approaching it with integrity, diligence, and faithful attention to both legal requirements and moral obligations. Handle mortgage issues honestly, maintain insurance properly, keep payment obligations current, and address all administrative details thoroughly. When you commit this work to the Lord and execute it with excellence, you can trust that your plans will be established—your property will be properly transferred into your trust, your mortgage will continue on existing terms, your estate planning goals will be accomplished, and your family will benefit from the protection and provision you've created. Walk forward confidently, knowing that with proper planning and execution, mortgaged property can be successfully incorporated into trust-based estate plans that honor both God and family while maintaining integrity in all financial obligations and relationships.

***

Section 2: How Lenders View Trust Transfers

Understanding the Lender's Perspective

To navigate trust transfers successfully when your home has a mortgage, it's valuable to understand not just your own rights and goals but also how lenders view these transactions and what concerns drive their responses. Mortgage lenders and servicers are businesses with fiduciary responsibilities to investors who own the loans they service, regulatory obligations to government agencies that oversee lending practices, and contractual rights established in mortgage agreements. When they discover or are notified that a borrower has transferred mortgaged property into a trust, they evaluate the situation through lenses of risk management, contractual compliance, and operational efficiency. Understanding these institutional perspectives—even when they sometimes conflict with homeowners' interests or reflect incomplete understanding of legal protections—helps homeowners anticipate lender responses and address concerns proactively.

The lender's fundamental concern in any ownership change is ensuring their security interest in the property remains enforceable and that their ability to collect debt and foreclose if necessary hasn't been impaired. When property is transferred from a borrower's individual name to a trust, lenders want to know: Does the trust transfer violate the mortgage's due-on-sale clause? Can they still foreclose on the property if the borrower defaults? Is the property still adequately insured with the lender properly named as loss payee? Will tax and insurance escrow arrangements continue functioning properly? Can they contact and communicate with the responsible party about the loan? These concerns are legitimate from the lender's perspective—they have a security interest in the property worth potentially hundreds of thousands of dollars, and changes in legal ownership could theoretically affect that interest. However, these concerns must be balanced against borrowers' rights under federal law to transfer property into revocable living trusts without loan acceleration, borrowers' legitimate privacy interests in not disclosing complete trust details, and the practical reality that properly structured trust transfers don't actually impair lender interests in any meaningful way.

The biblical principle of understanding others' perspectives before judging their actions appears in Proverbs 18:13: "To answer before listening—that is folly and shame." Before condemning lenders for asking questions or creating complications when you transfer property to a trust, listen to and understand their perspective—they're trying to protect their interests and fulfill their responsibilities, even if their methods sometimes seem burdensome or reflect misunderstanding of legal protections. This understanding doesn't mean accepting improper lender actions (such as threatening acceleration for protected transfers), but it does mean approaching lender relationships with empathy and recognition that their concerns, while sometimes misguided in application, often stem from legitimate business responsibilities. This empathetic understanding enables more productive communication and problem-solving when lender concerns arise.

The Routine Processing of Standard Trust Transfers

When lenders function properly and their personnel are adequately trained about estate planning trust transfers and federal protections, the discovery or notification of a trust transfer can be processed as a routine administrative matter requiring minimal documentation and creating no disruption to the mortgage relationship. Many large national mortgage servicers, banks, and lending institutions have standardized procedures for handling transfers of mortgaged property into revocable living trusts, recognizing that these transfers are common, legally protected, and don't meaningfully affect lending risk. These lenders' routine processing typically involves several standard steps.

First, when notified of or discovering a trust transfer, the servicer's system generates a review task assigned to personnel trained in ownership change processing. These reviewers examine the transfer to determine whether it falls within protected categories under Garn-St. Germain Act, specifically looking for confirmation that the transfer is to a revocable trust, the borrower remains a beneficiary, and the borrower continues occupying the property as primary residence. Second, the servicer requests documentation proving the transfer qualifies for protection. Typically, this means requesting a trustee certification or certificate of trust showing the trust's name and date, confirming the trust is revocable, identifying the borrower as trustee and beneficiary, and establishing the borrower's continued occupancy. The servicer may also request a copy of the recorded deed showing the transfer from individual to trust ownership, confirmation of continued hazard insurance with the trust or trustee listed as insured party and the lender listed as mortgagee, and verification that property taxes continue being paid through escrow or directly.

Third, once the servicer receives and reviews this documentation, confirming the transfer is protected, they update their internal systems and records to reflect the trust ownership. This update includes changing ownership records to show the trust or trustee as property owner, updating mailing addresses if necessary for correspondence to be directed to the trustee, noting the trust's existence in servicing notes and documentation, and confirming with tax and insurance payees that payments through escrow continue processing correctly. Fourth, after updating records, the servicer continues servicing the loan exactly as before—same account number, same payment terms, same online access, same escrow arrangements. From the borrower's perspective, nothing changes except that servicing records correctly reflect trust ownership. This entire routine process typically takes a few weeks and creates minimal disruption, particularly when borrowers proactively provide all requested documentation promptly.

Lenders who handle trust transfers routinely in this professional manner are operating consistently with both legal requirements and sound business practices. They're verifying that transfers qualify for federal protection (which is reasonable diligence), obtaining documentation that would be needed if the borrower defaults and foreclosure becomes necessary (prudent record-keeping), and ensuring insurance and tax arrangements continue protecting their collateral (protecting their security interest). None of these reasonable steps violates borrowers' rights or creates undue burden. The biblical principle of legitimate authority exercising reasonable oversight appears in various contexts in Scripture. In Luke 3:12-14, tax collectors and soldiers ask John the Baptist what they should do, and he doesn't tell them to abandon their roles but to execute them justly—tax collectors should collect only proper amounts, soldiers should not extort or falsely accuse. Similarly, when lenders reasonably verify and document protected trust transfers, they're executing their oversight role properly. Homeowners can cooperate with these reasonable requests without feeling their rights are being violated, understanding that lenders have legitimate interests in maintaining accurate records and ensuring their security interests remain protected.

Variation in Lender Sophistication and Training

While routine professional processing represents best practices, the reality is that lender sophistication and training regarding trust transfers varies enormously across institutions and even within different departments of the same institution. This variation in knowledge and competence creates inconsistent experiences for homeowners, with some encountering smooth processing while others face significant complications despite having identical factual situations. Several factors contribute to this variation in lender sophistication.

First, institutional size and focus affect expertise. Large national banks and mortgage servicers that handle millions of loans see trust transfers constantly and develop expertise and systems for handling them. Smaller regional or local lenders may encounter trust transfers less frequently and lack specialized knowledge. Similarly, lenders focused on sophisticated estate planning clientele (private banks, wealth management divisions) understand trusts better than lenders primarily serving first-time homebuyers with simpler financial situations. Second, personnel training and turnover affect consistency. Well-trained personnel who understand Garn-St. Germain protections and estate planning concepts process trust transfers smoothly. Poorly trained or new personnel with minimal knowledge may respond incorrectly, threatening acceleration or demanding unnecessary documentation. High turnover in mortgage servicing industries means borrowers often deal with different representatives on successive contacts, and each may have different knowledge levels.

Third, automated systems versus human review affects outcomes. Some lenders' systems automatically flag any ownership change for manual review without distinguishing between sales (which properly trigger due-on-sale) and protected trust transfers. If the manual reviewers who examine these flags lack training, they may improperly treat protected transfers as violations. Other lenders have more sophisticated systems that recognize common trust transfer patterns and auto-approve them without extensive review. Fourth, organizational structure affects coordination. Lenders with well-coordinated communication between servicing departments, legal departments, and escrow departments handle trust transfers more smoothly because all parts of the organization understand the transaction. Lenders with siloed departments where servicing doesn't communicate well with legal or escrow may create complications because different departments respond inconsistently.

Fifth, risk tolerance and legal conservatism affect approach. Some lenders take expansive views of their rights and conservative interpretations of borrowers' protections, demanding extensive documentation and treating trust transfers suspiciously. Other lenders take more reasonable, balanced approaches that respect borrowers' federal protections while protecting legitimate lender interests. This variation in sophistication means homeowners' experiences with trust transfers can range from completely smooth to highly problematic based largely on which lender they're dealing with and which personnel they happen to reach. The biblical principle of not assuming universal competence or consistency appears in Jesus's parable of the talents in Matthew 25:14-30, where three servants given responsibilities handle them with dramatically different competence and faithfulness. Similarly, different lenders and servicers handle the responsibility of processing trust transfers with dramatically different competence. Recognizing this variation helps homeowners understand that problems they encounter may reflect their lender's limitations rather than issues with their transfer, and that persistence in reaching knowledgeable personnel or escalating to supervisors and legal departments often resolves initial incorrect responses from untrained frontline staff.

Triggers for Enhanced Scrutiny and Review

While many trust transfers are processed routinely, certain circumstances trigger enhanced scrutiny and more intensive review by lenders concerned about potential problems. Understanding what raises red flags helps homeowners either avoid these situations when possible or be prepared to address lenders' heightened concerns when circumstances necessitate transfers during sensitive periods. Common triggers for enhanced scrutiny include delinquency or default status on the loan. If you're behind on mortgage payments when you transfer property to a trust, lenders immediately question whether the transfer is an attempt to complicate foreclosure, hide assets, or frustrate collection efforts. They may scrutinize the transfer as potential fraudulent conveyance even though technically protected by Garn-St. Germain.

Pending or active foreclosure proceedings also trigger intense scrutiny. Transferring property after receiving foreclosure notices or during foreclosure litigation suggests attempts to interfere with the foreclosure process, and lenders will examine whether the transfer should be challenged. Loan modification applications or active loss mitigation raise concerns. If you're negotiating with the lender about modifying loan terms, reducing payments, or other assistance due to financial hardship, then transferring property to a trust may appear inconsistent with the financial distress you're claiming and could suggest asset hiding. Concurrent bankruptcy filings or recent bankruptcy discharge also raise flags. Transferring property while in bankruptcy or shortly after discharge may be viewed as attempt to shield assets from bankruptcy estate or from creditors. Significant equity in the property combined with transfer during financial distress suggests possible fraudulent conveyance—using the trust to protect substantial home equity from creditors while remaining in financial difficulty.

Non-occupancy or change in property use triggers concerns. If lenders discover you're no longer occupying the property as primary residence after transferring to a trust, Garn-St. Germain protection may not apply and they may have legitimate acceleration rights. Transfers to irrevocable trusts or trusts where you're not a beneficiary also raise concerns, as these may not qualify for Garn-St. Germain protection. Corporate or non-individual trustees trigger additional documentation requirements. Lenders want to verify corporate trustees' authority, proper officer signatures, and organizational legitimacy. Timing coinciding with significant life events like divorce, business failure, or lawsuits may trigger questions about whether the trust transfer is asset protection maneuvering rather than pure estate planning. Complex ownership structures involving multiple trusts, entities, or parties also invite enhanced review to understand the arrangement and ensure lender interests remain protected.

When any of these triggers are present, lenders typically conduct more intensive review including requesting extensive documentation about the trust, your financial situation, and the transfer's purpose; potentially involving their legal departments in evaluating the transfer's propriety; considering whether to challenge the transfer as fraudulent conveyance or as violating mortgage terms beyond Garn-St. Germain protection; placing holds on servicing or escrow accounts pending resolution; and possibly threatening or initiating foreclosure if they conclude the transfer violates their rights. The biblical principle of expecting greater scrutiny when circumstances appear questionable appears in various contexts. In 1 Thessalonians 5:22, Paul advises, "Abstain from all appearance of evil" or in other translations, "Avoid every kind of evil" or "Stay away from every kind of evil." While transferring property to a trust isn't evil, doing so during circumstances that create appearance of asset hiding or creditor avoidance invites scrutiny. The wise approach is either avoiding trust transfers during these sensitive periods or being transparently prepared to prove legitimate estate planning motives and address lender concerns forthrightly if circumstances require transferring during difficult times.

Insurance Verification and Escrow Management Concerns

Among lenders' most concrete and legitimate concerns when property is transferred to a trust are ensuring that hazard insurance and title insurance remain adequate and properly structured, and that escrow account management continues functioning correctly. These concerns directly affect lenders' security interests and their ability to protect collateral, making them reasonable areas for lender attention even in protected trust transfers. Regarding hazard insurance, lenders' mortgage agreements require borrowers to maintain insurance covering the property against fire, storms, and other hazards, with the lender named as mortgagee or loss payee. This ensures that if the property is damaged or destroyed, insurance proceeds go toward either repairing the property (maintaining collateral value) or paying off the mortgage (satisfying the debt secured by now-damaged collateral).

When property ownership changes from individual to trust, lenders want verification that insurance has been updated to reflect trust ownership while maintaining the lender as loss payee. Without this verification, lenders worry that insurance companies might deny claims based on ownership mismatches (insured party doesn't match property owner), leaving the property uninsured or underinsured and the lender's collateral exposed to loss. To address this concern, lenders typically request updated insurance declarations pages showing the trust or trustee as named insured and the lender listed as mortgagee/loss payee, confirmation from the insurance company that coverage continues at adequate levels, and verification that premiums remain current and are being paid either through escrow or directly. If borrowers don't promptly provide this verification, lenders may take protective actions including placing expensive force-placed insurance on the property at the borrower's expense, creating holds on escrow accounts until insurance is verified, or in extreme cases, declaring the loan in default for failure to maintain adequate insurance as required by the mortgage.

Regarding escrow accounts, lenders that collect monthly escrow payments for property taxes and insurance must ensure these systems continue functioning after trust transfers. They need confirmation that property tax bills will be issued correctly and paid timely (by the lender from escrow), and that insurance invoices will be sent to appropriate parties for payment. When ownership changes from individual to trust but escrow arrangements continue, administrative mismatches can occur—tax assessors might send bills to the individual even though the property is now trust-owned, or insurance companies might send invoices to trustees at different addresses than the lender's escrow department expects. These mismatches can cause missed payments, penalties, or coverage lapses if not addressed. To prevent these problems, lenders request verification that tax assessors have been notified of the trust ownership and will continue sending bills to appropriate parties, that insurance companies have updated their records and will send invoices correctly, and that escrow account calculations remain accurate for the coverage and taxes being paid.

The biblical principle of ensuring protection remains in place appears in various contexts about maintaining walls, boundaries, and defenses. Nehemiah 4:17-18 describes rebuilding Jerusalem's walls: "Those who carried materials did their work with one hand and held a weapon in the other, and each of the builders wore his sword at his side as he worked." This continuous attention to protection while working reflects what lenders seek regarding insurance and escrow—continuous protection (adequate insurance) while the work (servicing the loan) proceeds, even through administrative changes like trust transfers. Homeowners should share lenders' concern that protection remains in place and should promptly provide requested verification of insurance and escrow continuity. These aren't unreasonable or burdensome requests but prudent verification that protections remain adequate despite ownership changes.

Corporate and Professional Trustee Considerations

When homeowners use corporate trustees (banks, trust companies) or professional trustees (attorneys, professional fiduciaries) rather than serving as their own trustees, lenders face additional considerations and typically require additional documentation beyond what individual trustees need to provide. These enhanced requirements reflect lenders' needs to verify that corporate entities claiming trustee authority actually have that authority and that officers signing on behalf of corporate trustees have proper authorization to bind the corporation. Common additional documentation requested when corporate or professional trustees are involved includes corporate organizational documents such as articles of incorporation or certificates of formation proving the trustee entity legally exists, corporate resolutions or board minutes authorizing the specific trustee to accept the trusteeship and conduct transactions on behalf of the trust including managing mortgaged property, certificates of incumbency or authority certifying that the officer signing documents on behalf of the corporate trustee holds the position they claim and has authority to execute those documents, certificates of good standing from the state where the corporate trustee is organized proving the entity is current on all filings and legally able to conduct business, and trust acceptance documents where the corporate trustee formally accepts the trusteeship and acknowledges duties and responsibilities.

Additionally, lenders may require signature authorizations or officer acknowledgments with specific notarization language verifying that officers signing on the corporate trustee's behalf are properly authorized and that signatures bind the corporation. These requirements arise because corporate entities can only act through human agents, and lenders must verify those agents actually have authority to act on the entity's behalf. For homeowners using corporate trustees primarily for privacy, asset management expertise, or continuity reasons, gathering this additional documentation may seem burdensome, but it's reasonable diligence by lenders ensuring the party claiming trustee authority actually has it. The complexity of corporate trustee documentation is one reason many homeowners choose to serve as their own trustees during their lifetimes, naming corporate or professional successor trustees to take over only after death or incapacity. This approach avoids corporate documentation requirements during the homeowner's life while still providing professional management when needed later.

The biblical principle of proper authority and authorization appears throughout Scripture's teaching about leadership and representation. In Matthew 8:9, the centurion explaining his understanding of authority says, "For I myself am a man under authority, with soldiers under me. I tell this one, 'Go,' and he goes; and that one, 'Come,' and he comes." This centurion understood that authority flows through proper chains of command and authorization. Similarly, when corporate trustees act, they must show they're operating under proper authority granted by their organizations. Lenders requesting documentation of this authority aren't being unreasonable but are ensuring that the parties claiming to act on the trust's behalf actually have the authority they claim. Homeowners working with corporate trustees should anticipate these documentation requirements and work with the corporate trustee to gather needed materials, understanding that this verification serves legitimate purposes even though it adds administrative burden.

Communication and Documentation Best Practices

Given lenders' legitimate concerns and the variation in their sophistication and processing capabilities, homeowners can significantly smooth the trust transfer experience by following communication and documentation best practices when dealing with lenders. These practices minimize misunderstandings, address concerns proactively, and create paper trails proving compliance if questions arise later. First, decide your communication strategy before the transfer. Will you notify your lender proactively, wait to respond if they discover the transfer, or proceed without communication unless problems arise? This decision should be based on your mortgage terms (notification requirements), your lender's reputation (sophisticated or problematic with trust transfers), your personal preference (transparency versus privacy), and advice from your estate planning attorney. Each approach has benefits and risks as discussed in previous chapters.

Second, if notifying your lender, prepare comprehensive documentation in advance. Don't just call with verbal notification; send written communication with supporting documents attached. Include a clear notification letter explaining the estate planning purpose and citing federal protection, a trustee certification showing you remain trustee and beneficiary, a copy of the recorded quitclaim deed, verification of updated homeowner's insurance showing trust as insured and lender as mortgagee, confirmation of continued occupancy of the property as your primary residence, and your contact information for any questions. Third, direct communication to appropriate departments. Don't contact general customer service for complex trust transfer issues; instead, direct correspondence to the lender's legal department, compliance department, or specialized loan servicing units that handle ownership changes. These departments are more likely to have knowledgeable personnel who understand federal protections and can process your transfer appropriately.

Fourth, maintain written records of all communications. Keep copies of letters sent, note dates and names of representatives you speak with by phone, document what was said in phone conversations, save emails and online messages, and retain receipts showing mail delivery or file upload confirmations. This paper trail proves you communicated appropriately and can refute lender claims that you failed to notify them or provide requested documentation. Fifth, respond promptly to lender requests. If your lender requests additional documentation or information, provide it quickly rather than delaying. Prompt response demonstrates good faith cooperation and prevents lenders from escalating concerns due to your non-responsiveness. Sixth, escalate problems appropriately. If initial contacts with frontline personnel create problems or you receive incorrect information about loan acceleration, don't accept these responses as final. Escalate to supervisors, ask to speak with legal or compliance departments, and if necessary, have your attorney contact the lender on your behalf. Many incorrect initial responses are corrected through escalation to more knowledgeable personnel.

Seventh, be prepared to educate lenders about federal protections. Bring copies of Garn-St. Germain Act text and be ready to explain that your transfer is federally protected and the lender cannot accelerate your loan. Many lender problems stem from lack of knowledge, and borrowers who can clearly explain their protections often resolve issues that seemed serious initially. The biblical principle of wise communication appears in Proverbs 15:23: "A person finds joy in giving an apt reply—and how good is a timely word!" Timely, apt communication with lenders—providing needed documentation promptly, directing inquiries to appropriate departments, responding professionally to questions—is exactly this kind of good word that prevents problems and brings joy (resolution) rather than conflict. Poor communication—ignoring lender inquiries, providing incomplete information, being defensive or hostile—creates the opposite effect, escalating concerns that might have been resolved through patient, thorough communication.

Conclusion: Working Successfully with Lenders Through Understanding

Understanding how lenders view trust transfers—through lenses of risk management, contractual compliance, and operational efficiency—enables homeowners to anticipate lender responses, address concerns proactively, and navigate what can be a complex institutional landscape with varying levels of sophistication. While frustrations with lender confusion, bureaucratic complications, and sometimes incorrect responses are understandable, approaching lender relationships with empathy for their legitimate concerns, patience with their limitations, and readiness to provide appropriate documentation serves homeowners' interests better than adversarial approaches. Most lender concerns about trust transfers are reasonable when understood in context: they want to ensure their security interests remain protected, their ability to collect debt and foreclose if necessary hasn't been impaired, and adequate insurance and tax payment systems continue functioning. Meeting these reasonable concerns through appropriate documentation while firmly standing on your federal rights when lenders overreach creates the best path forward.

The biblical principle that guides successful navigation of lender relationships is the balance between asserting legitimate rights and honoring legitimate obligations, between standing firm on protections while being respectful and professional in communication, and between understanding others' perspectives while not accepting improper treatment. Romans 12:18 counsels, "If it is possible, as far as it depends on you, live at peace with everyone." Living at peace with your lender after transferring property to a trust depends significantly on you—your communication approach, your documentation preparation, your patience with their processes, and your willingness to address reasonable concerns. However, living at peace has limits—"if it is possible, as far as it depends on you"—and when lenders violate your federal rights or act improperly despite your good faith efforts, standing firm and pursuing legal remedies becomes necessary. The balance is giving peace every reasonable opportunity while not accepting treatment that violates your legal protections.

As you work with your lender regarding trust transfers, commit the relationship to the Lord, approaching it with integrity, patience, and wisdom. Proverbs 16:7 promises, "When the Lord takes pleasure in anyone's way, he causes their enemies to make peace with them." When your way (your trust transfer and how you handle it) pleases the Lord—done with honest motives, proper documentation, respectful communication, and faithful attention to both your rights and obligations—even potentially adversarial lender relationships often result in peace and smooth resolution. Trust this promise as you navigate what can sometimes be challenging institutional responses to legitimate estate planning, knowing that faithful, wise handling of lender relationships honors God and serves your family's long-term interests in preserving both estate planning benefits and mortgage relationships.

***

Section 3: Title Insurance Considerations

The Shield Against Hidden Title Defects

Title insurance represents one of the most important yet commonly misunderstood protections homeowners possess, providing financial safeguards against title defects that could challenge or impair property ownership. Unlike other forms of insurance that protect against future events—homeowner's insurance guards against future fires or storms, health insurance covers future medical needs—title insurance protects against problems that already exist but haven't been discovered. It insures that your ownership is valid, that no undisclosed liens or claims threaten your title, and that the property's legal description and boundaries are accurate as represented. When transferring property into a living trust, understanding how title insurance interacts with the ownership change, what steps are necessary to maintain coverage, and what additional protections might be needed ensures this valuable shield remains in place protecting both you during your lifetime and your beneficiaries after your death.

The fundamental concept of title insurance is providing peace of mind that the title you received when you purchased property is actually good title—free from defects, liens, encumbrances, or competing claims that would impair your ownership or make the property less valuable than you believed. Title defects come in numerous forms: forged deeds in the chain of title, unknown heirs of previous owners who claim interests, unreleased mortgages or liens from decades ago, errors in public records or legal descriptions, boundary disputes or survey mistakes, and undisclosed easements or restrictions affecting property use. Any of these defects could emerge years after purchase, potentially costing tens or hundreds of thousands of dollars to resolve through litigation or settlements. Title insurance protects you financially against these historical defects, paying for legal defense if your title is challenged and compensating you for losses if defects are found that the title search before purchase should have discovered but didn't.

When you transfer property into your living trust, the critical question becomes: Does your existing title insurance continue protecting the property under its new ownership structure, or does the transfer somehow void coverage? Understanding this question and taking appropriate steps to maintain protection reflects the biblical principle of wise stewardship and preparation for unknown dangers. Proverbs 22:3 teaches, "The prudent see danger and take refuge, but the simple keep going and pay the penalty." Title defects represent potential dangers—unknown, hidden problems that could surface at any time. Your title insurance is the refuge you've taken against these dangers. When transferring property to a trust, being prudent means ensuring this refuge remains in place rather than simply assuming it does. The simple person might transfer property without thinking about title insurance implications, potentially discovering too late that coverage was lost and they must now pay penalties (legal costs, settlement payments) for title defects without insurance protection.

Understanding Your Existing Owner's Title Insurance

Before addressing how trust transfers affect title insurance, homeowners must understand what title insurance they currently have and what it covers. When you purchased your property, you likely obtained two separate title insurance policies as part of the closing process, though you may not have realized they were distinct coverages. The lender's title insurance policy (also called a loan policy) protects your mortgage lender against title defects that might impair their security interest in the property. This policy's coverage amount equals the loan amount and decreases as you pay down the mortgage. Importantly, this policy protects only the lender, not you as the property owner. If a title defect is discovered, the lender's policy ensures the lender is compensated, but you as the homeowner receive no protection from this policy.

The owner's title insurance policy (also called an owner's policy) protects you as the property owner against title defects that impair your ownership. This policy's coverage amount typically equals the purchase price of the property, and importantly, it remains in effect for as long as you or your heirs have an interest in the property, even after any mortgage is paid off. Unlike the lender's policy that protects only mortgage amounts and expires when the loan is satisfied, your owner's policy continues protecting your ownership interest indefinitely. When you transfer property into your trust, the owner's title insurance is what matters—this is the policy that potentially continues protecting you and your trust, and this is what you need to verify remains in effect after the transfer.

To understand your existing owner's title insurance, locate your title insurance policy documents. These were provided at closing when you purchased the property, typically in a large package of closing documents. If you can't find your original policy, contact the title company that issued it (their information should be on closing documents or recorded documents from your purchase) and request a copy. Review the policy's key elements including the policy number and issuance date, the coverage amount (typically your purchase price), the description of the insured property (should match your property's legal description), the schedule of exceptions (title defects, liens, easements, or restrictions that existed at purchase and aren't covered), and the policy's effective date (usually your purchase date). Understanding what you currently have enables you to determine what protection might continue after transferring to your trust and what additional steps might be needed.

The biblical principle of knowing what you possess before determining how to manage it appears in Jesus's parable about the king going to war. Luke 14:31 asks, "Or suppose a king is about to go to war against another king. Won't he first sit down and consider whether he is able with ten thousand men to oppose the one coming against him with twenty thousand?" Before engaging in the "war" of estate planning through trust transfers, sit down and consider what resources you have—including what title insurance protection currently exists. This assessment enables wise decisions about how to proceed, what additional protections might be needed, and what steps will maintain the protections you already possess.

How Trust Transfers Affect Title Insurance Coverage

The central question for homeowners transferring property into living trusts is whether their existing owner's title insurance continues providing coverage after the transfer or whether the ownership change somehow voids or impairs protection. The good news is that most owner's title insurance policies issued by reputable title companies automatically continue covering property transferred into the insured person's revocable living trust without requiring policy amendments, endorsements, or additional premiums. This automatic continuation exists because the title insurance industry generally recognizes that transfers to revocable living trusts don't meaningfully change beneficial ownership or increase risk to the title insurer.

The reasoning is straightforward: when you transfer your property from individual ownership to ownership as trustee of your revocable trust, you remain the beneficial owner with complete control over the property. You can revoke the trust at any time and take the property back into individual ownership. The trust transfer doesn't introduce new parties with competing claims, doesn't represent a sale to someone else who might have different title issues, and doesn't increase the likelihood that historical title defects will emerge. From the title insurer's perspective, they're still insuring the same person's ownership of the same property with the same historical title chain. The only change is the legal form in which that ownership is held—individual versus trust—and this form change doesn't affect the existence or likelihood of discovering historical title defects.

However, despite this general principle of automatic continuation, three important qualifications apply. First, while most policies continue automatically, not all do. Some older policies, policies issued by smaller regional title companies, or policies with unusual terms might not automatically extend to trust ownership. The only way to know with certainty is reviewing your specific policy's terms or contacting your title insurer for confirmation. Second, even policies that continue automatically often require notification of the ownership change. While coverage continues regardless of notification, the title insurer needs to update their records to show the current ownership structure. Failure to notify them doesn't void coverage but can create administrative complications if you ever need to make a claim or if questions arise about who the policy currently protects. Third, automatic continuation applies specifically to revocable living trusts where you remain the beneficial owner and can revoke the trust. If you transfer property into an irrevocable trust, where you surrender control and beneficial ownership, the title insurance analysis becomes more complex and you may need to obtain title insurer approval or new coverage.

The biblical principle of not presuming ongoing protection without verification appears in various contexts. In Joshua 9, the Israelites made a covenant with the Gibeonites without inquiring of the Lord or properly investigating, assuming the Gibeonites' story was true. This presumption led to consequences they later regretted. Similarly, presuming your title insurance automatically continues after transferring to a trust without verifying this with your insurer risks discovering too late that coverage was lost or impaired. The prudent approach is verification: contact your title insurer, provide information about your trust transfer, and obtain written confirmation that coverage continues. This simple step eliminates uncertainty and ensures your protection remains firmly in place.

Steps to Maintain Title Insurance Protection

To ensure your owner's title insurance continues protecting your property after transferring it into your living trust, follow several straightforward steps that verify coverage continuation and update insurer records appropriately. First, locate your title insurance policy documents and confirm which company issued the policy. This information typically appears on the policy's first page or declaration page. If you've moved or changed title companies since purchase, note both the original issuing company and any successor companies that may have acquired them, as title insurance companies frequently merge or are acquired by larger insurers. Second, contact the title insurance company to inform them of the trust transfer and request confirmation that coverage continues. You can typically find contact information on the policy document or through online searches for the company's customer service department.

When contacting the title insurer, explain that you've transferred your property into your revocable living trust for estate planning purposes and want to verify that your owner's title insurance policy continues providing coverage. Provide them with your policy number, the property address, and basic information about when you purchased the property. Be prepared to provide documentation including a copy of the recorded quitclaim deed showing the transfer from you individually to you as trustee of your trust, and a trustee certification or relevant pages of your trust document showing the trust is revocable, you're the trustee, and you remain a beneficiary. Most title companies don't need to see your complete trust document but just enough information to verify the transfer meets criteria for automatic coverage continuation.

Third, request that the title company provide written confirmation that your policy remains in effect with the property now held in trust. This confirmation might take the form of an endorsement to the policy explicitly stating coverage continues with trust ownership, a letter from the title company confirming continued coverage, or updated policy documents showing the trust or trustee as the insured party. Whatever form it takes, obtain this confirmation in writing and keep it with your trust documents and title insurance policy. Written confirmation eliminates any future question about whether coverage continued after the transfer. Fourth, update the title company's contact information for you if necessary. If you want correspondence about the policy sent to you as trustee with a specific address, provide this information. However, many people find it simpler to maintain existing contact arrangements since they're the same person whether contacted individually or as trustee.

Fifth, if the title company indicates any concerns about coverage continuation or suggests the transfer might not be automatically covered, ask to speak with a supervisor or legal department. Often, initial customer service representatives lack knowledge about trust transfers and coverage continuation, but more experienced personnel or legal staff understand the standard practice of automatic continuation for revocable trusts. If necessary, have your estate planning attorney contact the title company to explain the transfer and confirm coverage should continue. Sixth, if for any reason your existing title insurance company won't confirm coverage continuation (rare but possible with unusual policies or small insurers), consider obtaining a new owner's title insurance policy from a different, more sophisticated title company. The cost of a new policy (typically several hundred to over a thousand dollars depending on property value) may be worthwhile for the protection it provides, particularly if your property has substantial equity or if title issues could seriously impair value.

The biblical principle of taking reasonable steps to maintain protection appears in Nehemiah's account of rebuilding Jerusalem's walls. Nehemiah 4:9 records, "But we prayed to our God and posted a guard day and night to meet this threat." Prayer alone wasn't sufficient; practical protective measures (posting guards) were also necessary. Similarly, trusting that your title insurance continues isn't sufficient; taking practical steps to verify and confirm continuation provides the active protection your property deserves. These steps aren't burdensome—a phone call, some documentation, obtaining written confirmation—but they provide enormous value in ensuring your title insurance shield remains firmly in place.

Considerations When Purchasing New Properties or Refinancing

While most of this discussion has focused on maintaining existing title insurance after transferring property you already own into a trust, different considerations apply when purchasing new property or refinancing existing property. In these situations, you have opportunities to structure title insurance coverage from the beginning to accommodate trust ownership, avoiding any question about coverage continuation. When purchasing new property that you intend to hold in your living trust, you have two primary options for how to take title and structure title insurance.

Option one is taking title directly in your trust name and obtaining title insurance in that name from the start. At closing, the deed from the seller transfers property directly to you as trustee of your trust rather than to you individually. The title insurance company issues your owner's policy listing the insured party as "Jane Mary Doe, Trustee of The Jane Mary Doe Revocable Living Trust dated January 1, 2024" (or whatever your trust name is). This approach is clean and straightforward—property goes directly into trust ownership from the beginning, and title insurance is issued for trust ownership with no questions about whether coverage continues after subsequent transfers. Many title companies routinely issue policies for trust-owned property at standard premium rates. However, some title companies charge slightly higher premiums (perhaps 10-20% more) for policies issued to trusts, and some are less familiar with trusts and prefer issuing to individuals.

Option two is taking title initially in your individual name, obtaining title insurance in your name, then immediately transferring property into your trust after closing via quitclaim deed. This approach accommodates title companies that prefer issuing policies to individuals and avoids any premium surcharges some companies assess for trust policies. After closing and recording the deed to you individually, you execute and record a quitclaim deed transferring the property to yourself as trustee of your trust. Then follow the steps outlined in the previous section to notify the title company and confirm coverage continues. The practical difference between these approaches is modest—option one is slightly simpler because you don't need a second deed and title insurance notification, but option two may save premium costs if your title company charges more for trust policies. Discuss with your title company or real estate attorney which approach they recommend for your specific situation.

When refinancing existing property that's held in your trust, similar options exist. Some refinance lenders and title companies are comfortable refinancing trust-owned property, taking a new mortgage against property held by the trust and issuing new lender's title insurance for that mortgage. If you're refinancing property currently held in trust and your lender is comfortable with this, new lender's title insurance will be issued for the trust-owned property, and you can request that your owner's policy be updated or reissued to reflect current values if appropriate. Other refinance lenders, as discussed in previous chapters, prefer property to be in borrowers' individual names during refinancing. If so, you would temporarily transfer property from trust to individual ownership via quitclaim deed, complete the refinance with property in individual ownership, then transfer property back into trust via another quitclaim deed after closing. In this scenario, your title insurance likely goes through a cycle: continuing to cover the property when it's temporarily out of trust, then continuing again when you transfer it back in.

The biblical principle of thoughtful planning at the beginning of undertakings appears in Jesus's teaching about building towers and kings going to war. Luke 14:28-30 emphasizes sitting down first to count costs and plan before beginning construction. Similarly, when purchasing new property or refinancing, taking time to plan how title will be held and how title insurance will be structured from the beginning avoids later complications. Discussing trust ownership and title insurance with your title company, real estate attorney, and closing agent before closing day ensures everyone understands the plan and can execute it properly, rather than discovering conflicts or problems during closing when it's too late to easily adjust.

Special Endorsements and Enhanced Coverage

Beyond basic owner's title insurance that continues protecting property after trust transfers, homeowners may want to consider special endorsements or enhanced coverage options that provide additional protection specifically relevant to trust ownership and estate planning situations. Title insurance endorsements are amendments to the basic policy that add specific coverages, expand protections, or address particular concerns not covered by the standard policy. Several endorsements may be particularly valuable in trust ownership contexts.

A trust endorsement (sometimes called an ALTA 12 endorsement or successor trustee endorsement) explicitly confirms that the policy covers the trust, the trustee, and importantly, successor trustees who take over after the original trustee's death or incapacity. This endorsement provides clarity that when your successor trustee needs to act—perhaps selling the property after your death—they're protected by the title insurance policy just as you were. Without this endorsement, technical questions could arise about whether successors are covered. Many title companies include successor trustee coverage in their standard policies for trusts, but obtaining an explicit endorsement eliminates any ambiguity.

An ALTA 9 endorsement (restrictions, encumbrances, minerals endorsement) provides enhanced coverage for certain types of restrictions, easements, and mineral rights that might affect the property. While standard policies exclude these from coverage or cover them only limitedly, this endorsement expands protection. For properties with complex easement situations, oil and gas rights, or restrictive covenants that might be challenged, this endorsement provides valuable additional coverage. A boundary endorsement or survey endorsement provides enhanced coverage for boundary disputes, encroachments, and survey errors beyond what standard policies cover. If your property has complicated boundaries, is in an area where boundary disputes are common, or has structures near property lines, this endorsement adds protection. Enhanced access endorsements confirm and insure that the property has legal access to public roads, an issue that sometimes creates problems particularly with rural properties. Standard policies may not insure access, but this endorsement does.

Inflation endorsements or increased value endorsements provide that the policy's coverage amount will increase over time to reflect property appreciation, ensuring that as your property becomes more valuable, your title insurance protection keeps pace rather than remaining fixed at the original purchase price coverage amount. Some title companies offer automatic inflation adjustments while others require specific endorsements. When purchasing title insurance for trust-owned property or updating coverage after trust transfers, ask your title company what endorsements are available and appropriate for your situation. The cost of endorsements is typically modest (often $25 to $100 per endorsement) compared to the additional protection they provide, making them worthwhile investments for comprehensive coverage.

The biblical principle of not settling for minimum protection when additional protection is available and affordable appears in various contexts. In the Old Testament, when cities of refuge were established to protect those who accidentally killed someone, Deuteronomy 19:8-9 provides for additional cities of refuge to be designated if needed to ensure adequate protection: "If the Lord your God enlarges your territory...you are to set aside three more cities." The principle is that when protection can be enhanced to better serve its purpose, such enhancement should be pursued. Similarly, when title insurance endorsements can enhance protection for modest cost, pursuing these endorsements demonstrates wise stewardship that maximizes protection for yourself and your beneficiaries.

Addressing Title Defects Discovered After Trust Transfer

While the focus thus far has been on maintaining title insurance coverage through trust transfers, another important consideration is what happens if title defects are discovered after property has been transferred into a trust. If your title insurance coverage has been properly maintained through the transfer, the policy should protect you even if defects are discovered after the ownership change. However, understanding how claims work and what your rights and responsibilities are helps ensure you receive full protection if problems arise.

Title defects can be discovered in various ways after property is in a trust: during routine title searches when you attempt to refinance or sell property, through surveys conducted for other purposes that reveal boundary issues, when previous owners' heirs or creditors surface claiming interests, when local governments discover easement or restriction violations, or through curative work examining old records that reveals historical deed problems. When a potential title defect is discovered, the first step is immediately notifying your title insurance company. Most policies require prompt notice of any claims or potential claims against title, and delays in notification can potentially jeopardize coverage. Provide your title insurer with all information about the discovered defect including documentation of the issue, correspondence from parties claiming interests, survey results showing boundary problems, or whatever evidence exists.

The title insurance company will assign a claims examiner to investigate the issue, determining whether the discovered problem is actually a title defect, whether it's covered by your policy (not excluded or outside the policy's protection), how the defect affects your ownership, and what remedy is appropriate. If the defect is covered, the title company will typically take one of several approaches: defending your title if someone challenges it in court (the insurer pays for attorneys and litigation costs), curing the defect if possible (the insurer pays for corrective work such as obtaining releases, recording corrective deeds, or purchasing competing interests), or compensating you for loss if the defect can't be cured and genuinely impairs your ownership (the insurer pays you up to the policy's coverage amount for the diminished value of your property). Throughout the claims process, cooperate fully with the title insurance company providing requested information, allowing their attorneys to defend you if litigation is necessary, not settling claims or agreeing to anything without the insurer's approval, and following the policy's procedures for claims handling.

One particular concern in trust situations is ensuring that your successor trustee knows about the title insurance and can make claims if defects are discovered after your death. When your successor takes over, they need to know where the title insurance policy is located, how to contact the title insurer if problems arise, and what their rights are under the policy. Including information about title insurance in your trust administration instructions and keeping policy documents with other important estate planning papers ensures this protection remains available when needed. The biblical teaching about faithful stewardship of protections we've received appears in Jesus's parable of the talents. Matthew 25:21 records the master saying, "Well done, good and faithful servant! You have been faithful with a few things; I will put you in charge of many things." Being faithful with your title insurance—maintaining coverage, understanding how claims work, ensuring successors know about it—demonstrates the faithful servant's character. This faithfulness ensures that the protection (the "few things" you've been given) remains available and effective, enabling it to protect the "many things" (your property's full value and your beneficiaries' inheritance) entrusted to your care.

Coordination with Estate Planning and Trust Administration

Title insurance doesn't exist in isolation but is part of the broader context of estate planning and trust administration, and coordinating title insurance with these other elements ensures comprehensive protection. Several coordination considerations are important. First, ensure your estate planning attorney knows about your title insurance and its coverage. When they're preparing your trust, drafting successor trustee instructions, or advising about property transfers, they should know what title protection exists so they can factor this into planning and instructions. If your attorney doesn't ask about title insurance, proactively inform them about your coverage.

Second, include information about title insurance in your successor trustee's instructions and documentation. Create a section in your trust administration manual or letter to successor that explains where title insurance policies are located, provides contact information for the title insurance company, and explains that the policy protects the trust property even after your death. Include copies of title insurance policies in your trust documents file, clearly labeled and accessible to your successor. Third, review title insurance during major trust amendments or modifications. If you significantly revise your trust, change its name, change from revocable to irrevocable structure, or make other major changes, verify with your title insurer that coverage continues under the modified trust structure. Most changes won't affect coverage, but verification prevents surprises.

Fourth, coordinate title insurance with property tax and insurance records. When updating property tax assessor records and homeowner's insurance after trust transfers, also update title insurance in the same timeframe, ensuring all property-related records and protections reflect current ownership consistently. This coordination prevents administrative confusion where different entities have inconsistent information about ownership. Fifth, consider title insurance in property distribution planning. When planning how property will eventually be distributed from your trust to beneficiaries, consider whether title insurance will transfer with the property to protect beneficiaries or whether they'll need to obtain new coverage. Generally, owner's title insurance continues protecting property as it passes to heirs, but specific policy terms govern this, and some policies may require notification when property passes to beneficiaries.

The principle of coordinating multiple elements of a comprehensive system appears in Paul's teaching about the body of Christ. First Corinthians 12:12-27 describes how the body's many parts must function together, each contributing its role while coordinating with others. Verse 25 states, "There should be no division in the body, but...its parts should have equal concern for each other." Your estate planning system—trust, property ownership, title insurance, homeowner's insurance, property tax management—is like a body with multiple parts that must coordinate and work together. Title insurance is one part, but it must be integrated with the others rather than operating in isolation. This integration ensures the whole system functions effectively to protect your property and provide for your beneficiaries.

Documentation and Record-Keeping Best Practices

Proper documentation and record-keeping regarding title insurance might seem mundane compared to other estate planning considerations, but these administrative practices ensure protection remains accessible and effective when needed, potentially years or decades after policies are issued. Several best practices help maintain proper title insurance records. First, maintain a comprehensive property file for each real property you own that includes the original owner's title insurance policy and all endorsements, copies of all recorded deeds including the most recent deed showing current trust ownership, survey documents and property descriptions, closing documents from when you purchased the property, correspondence with the title insurance company including confirmation of coverage continuation after trust transfers, contact information for the title insurance company including phone numbers, policy numbers, and claims procedures, and notes about any title issues or concerns that have arisen over the years.

Second, store these documents securely but accessibly. Use fireproof home safes, safety deposit boxes with your successor trustee having access, or attorney's offices that maintain client files. Don't store everything in one location—consider keeping originals in one secure location and copies in a second location so that if one location is compromised (fire, theft, natural disaster), you still have access to essential documents. Third, create an inventory list of all insurance policies including title insurance. This master list, kept with your trust documents and shared with your successor trustee, should identify all properties you own, where title insurance policies for each property are located, policy numbers and coverage amounts, title insurance company contact information, and any special endorsements or coverage features. This inventory enables your successor to quickly identify what protection exists for each property without needing to search through files.

Fourth, update documentation when changes occur. If you amend your trust, transfer additional properties into it, purchase new properties, or refinance, update your property files and inventory lists to reflect these changes and ensure title insurance information remains current. Don't allow documentation to become outdated and confusing. Fifth, include instructions in your successor trustee letter or manual about title insurance and where documentation is located. A simple paragraph explaining that title insurance policies are kept in the property file at a specific location and providing guidance about verifying coverage when the successor takes over helps ensure this protection isn't overlooked when it might be needed most.

The biblical principle of careful record-keeping appears throughout Scripture in contexts ranging from genealogies to temple treasures. Nehemiah 7:5 describes finding genealogical records: "So my God put it into my heart to assemble the nobles, the officials and the common people for registration by families. I found the genealogical record of those who had been the first to return." These careful records served essential purposes when needed. Similarly, your title insurance records—properly maintained, securely stored, and accessible to successors—serve essential purposes by enabling protection to be accessed when needed, sometimes many years after policies were issued. First Chronicles 9:22 notes, "All these...were enrolled by genealogies...David and Samuel the seer had appointed them to their positions of trust." The phrase "positions of trust" is appropriate—maintaining records is itself a position of trust, a stewardship responsibility that serves future generations by preserving information they'll need. Fulfill this trust faithfully by maintaining excellent title insurance documentation.

Conclusion: Preserving the Shield of Protection

Title insurance represents a crucial shield protecting property ownership against historical defects, unknown claims, and title impairments that could threaten your investment and your family's inheritance. When transferring property into living trusts, maintaining this shield requires understanding how transfers affect coverage, taking appropriate steps to verify continuation, coordinating with title insurance companies, and maintaining proper documentation that ensures protection remains accessible when needed. The great majority of trust transfers proceed smoothly from a title insurance perspective, with coverage continuing automatically when properly maintained, but taking proactive steps to confirm continuation and document coverage eliminates uncertainty and ensures protection remains firmly in place.

The biblical principle underlying all title insurance considerations is wise stewardship that takes reasonable precautions against known risks. While we cannot eliminate all dangers, we can take refuge against those we can anticipate and protect against. Proverbs 27:12 teaches, "The prudent see danger and take refuge, but the simple keep going and suffer for it." Title defects are potential dangers—hidden problems that could surface decades after property purchase. Title insurance is the refuge prudent people take against these dangers. Maintaining this refuge through trust transfers, ensuring it continues protecting property under new ownership structures, and preserving documentation so successors can access protection when needed reflects the prudent foresight that honors God and serves family.

As you transfer property into your living trust or plan future property acquisitions that will be trust-owned, commit your title insurance considerations to the Lord along with all other estate planning elements. Proverbs 16:3 promises, "Commit to the Lord whatever you do, and he will establish your plans." When you approach title insurance with diligence—verifying coverage, maintaining documentation, coordinating with your estate planning, ensuring successors have necessary information—you demonstrate faithful stewardship that God delights in. Trust that this faithful attention to seemingly mundane administrative details is part of the comprehensive stewardship that ensures your estate planning accomplishes its purposes and your property protection remains in place through all ownership changes and transitions, serving both you during your lifetime and your beneficiaries who will eventually inherit the fruit of your faithful planning and careful preparation.

***

Section 4: When Banks Typically Get Involved

Banks typically get involved in property transfers when there is a change in title that could affect their security interest in the home. This is especially true when a mortgage is attached to the property, and the lender wants to ensure that the borrower remains responsible for repayment and that the collateral remains intact. If the transfer appears to violate the terms of the loan—such as triggering a due-on-sale clause—the bank may initiate a review, request documentation, or even threaten acceleration of the loan. Scripture reminds us to honor our agreements and walk in integrity: "The wicked borrows but does not pay back, but the righteous is generous and gives" (Psalm 37:21).

In estate planning, banks often become involved when the homeowner transfers the property into a trust. While federal law protects transfers into revocable living trusts when the borrower remains a beneficiary and occupant, some banks still request notification or documentation to update their records. This involvement is usually administrative, not punitive, but it can delay refinancing, escrow adjustments, or online account access. The Bible encourages us to act with foresight and wisdom: "The prudent sees danger and hides himself, but the simple go on and suffer for it" (Proverbs 22:3).

Banks may also get involved when insurance policies are updated to reflect the trust or trustee as the new insured party. If the lender is not informed or if the insurance company fails to list the trust correctly, the bank may reject the policy or place its own coverage, often at a higher cost. This underscores the importance of clear communication and diligent follow-through. Scripture calls us to be faithful stewards: "Be diligent to know the state of your flocks, and attend to your herds" (Proverbs 27:23).

In cases of financial hardship, delinquency, or legal disputes, banks may scrutinize trust transfers more closely. If they suspect the transfer was made to avoid creditors or conceal assets, they may challenge the transaction or seek legal remedies. Acting with transparency and righteousness is essential in these moments. The Word of God warns against deceit and exalts integrity: “Better is a poor man who walks in his integrity than a rich man who is crooked in his ways” (Proverbs 28:6).

Ultimately, banks get involved when their interests are affected or when legal compliance requires it. Homeowners can minimize disruption by reviewing their mortgage terms, consulting legal counsel, and providing documentation when appropriate. This proactive approach honors both legal obligations and spiritual principles: “Commit your work to the Lord, and your plans will be established” (Proverbs 16:3). By navigating these interactions with wisdom and grace, you protect your legacy and maintain peace with all parties involved.

Chapter 7:
After the Transfer

The Beginning of Faithful Trust Administration

The moment your quitclaim deed transferring property into your living trust is recorded with the county represents a significant milestone in your estate planning journey—legal ownership of your property has changed hands from you as an individual to you as trustee of your trust. However, this recording represents not an ending but a beginning. While the legal transfer is complete, the practical work of ensuring your trust functions effectively, that all related systems and institutions recognize the ownership change, and that your property continues being properly managed and protected has only just begun. The post-transfer phase requires diligent attention to numerous administrative details, each seemingly small but collectively essential for ensuring your estate planning accomplishes its intended purposes. Neglecting these follow-through tasks can undermine even the most carefully prepared trust and property transfer, while faithful attention to them ensures your planning efforts bear full fruit.

The biblical principle that faithful stewardship extends beyond initial actions to include ongoing maintenance and follow-through appears throughout Scripture. Jesus's parable of the talents in Matthew 25:14-30 commends servants who actively managed what was entrusted to them, not those who simply took initial action and then neglected ongoing responsibilities. The servants who were commended didn't just receive the talents and set them aside; they worked with them, managed them, and ensured they produced results. Similarly, your estate planning doesn't end with signing documents and recording deeds; these initial actions must be followed by ongoing management—updating insurance, coordinating with institutions, maintaining records, and ensuring all systems function together to protect your property and provide for your family. This chapter explores the essential post-transfer tasks and ongoing administration responsibilities that transform your legal trust structure from paper documents into living, effective estate planning that serves its purposes throughout your lifetime and beyond.

The urgency of completing post-transfer tasks promptly rather than procrastinating cannot be overstated. Proverbs 3:27-28 teaches, "Do not withhold good from those to whom it is due, when it is in your power to act. Do not say to your neighbor, 'Come back tomorrow and I'll give it to you'—when you already have it with you." When you've recorded your deed but haven't yet updated insurance, notified necessary parties, or organized documentation, you have the power to complete these tasks and you shouldn't withhold this "good" (proper administration) by delaying. The work needs to be done, you're capable of doing it, and postponing serves no purpose while creating risks. This chapter provides systematic guidance for completing all necessary post-transfer tasks, ensuring nothing is overlooked and your trust administration begins with the thoroughness and attention to detail that faithful stewardship requires.

Updating Homeowner's Insurance: Immediate Priority

Among all post-transfer administrative tasks, updating your homeowner's insurance to reflect trust ownership stands as the highest immediate priority. Your mortgage lender requires you to maintain adequate hazard insurance as a loan condition, and failure to maintain proper coverage could be considered a default under your mortgage terms. Additionally, if you experience a loss—fire, storm damage, theft—and your insurance doesn't properly reflect current ownership, you risk claim denial, payment delays, or reduced settlements while the insurance company investigates ownership discrepancies. Updating insurance immediately after recording your deed eliminates these risks and ensures continuous, proper coverage.

To update your homeowner's insurance, contact your insurance company or agent within days of recording your quitclaim deed. Many insurance agents recommend notifying them before recording the deed so the insurance update can be processed concurrently with the property transfer, ensuring no gap exists between when ownership changes and when insurance reflects the change. However, if you've already recorded the deed without first updating insurance, contact your insurer immediately—don't delay. Explain that you've transferred your property into your revocable living trust for estate planning purposes and need the policy updated to reflect this ownership change. Be prepared to provide several pieces of information and documentation: a copy of the recorded quitclaim deed showing the transfer to you as trustee, a trustee certification or relevant pages of your trust document proving the trust's existence, your role as trustee, and that the trust is revocable, your policy number and property address for the insurance company to locate your account, and confirmation that you continue occupying the property as your primary residence (important for maintaining residential coverage rather than being reclassified as vacant or rental property).

Most insurance companies have standard procedures for processing trust ownership updates. They will update your policy declarations page to show the insured party as: "Jane Mary Doe, Trustee of The Jane Mary Doe Revocable Living Trust dated January 1, 2024" (or whatever your specific trustee and trust designation is). This change typically occurs at no additional cost and without premium increases, as you're the same insured person with the same property and same risk profile, just holding property in a different legal form. However, the insurance company will want to verify that your mortgage lender remains properly protected. Ensure the insurance company maintains your lender as the mortgagee or loss payee on the policy—this designation means insurance proceeds from covered losses must be used to repair the property or pay off the mortgage, protecting the lender's interest. The lender should remain as mortgagee regardless of the insured party change.

After the insurance company processes the update, they will send you an updated declarations page or endorsement showing the new insured designation and typically will send a copy to your mortgage lender confirming that insurance remains in force with proper coverage levels and the lender properly named. Review this updated documentation carefully to ensure all information is correct: the trust name and date match your trust exactly, you as trustee are properly listed, coverage amounts remain adequate, the lender is still listed as mortgagee, and the property address and other details are accurate. Keep a copy of the updated insurance documentation with your trust records and property files. If you discover any errors in the updated policy, contact the insurance company immediately for corrections—don't wait, as errors in insurance documentation can create problems if claims arise.

The biblical principle of ensuring protection remains in place through transitions appears in various contexts about maintaining walls, guards, and defenses. In Nehemiah 7:1-3, after Jerusalem's walls were rebuilt, Nehemiah didn't consider the work complete simply because walls stood. He appointed gatekeepers, singers, and Levites, gave his brother and a commander charge over Jerusalem, and gave instructions about when gates should be opened and closed. The physical walls were only effective because of this ongoing administration and attention. Similarly, your trust structure and property transfer (the "walls") are only effective if you maintain ongoing administration including proper insurance coverage (the "gatekeepers" protecting your property). Don't consider the work complete when the deed is recorded; complete it by ensuring insurance protection continues properly through the ownership change.

Property Tax Assessment and Exemption Preservation

Immediately after updating homeowner's insurance, turn attention to property tax matters, ensuring your property tax assessment isn't inappropriately increased due to the trust transfer and that any property tax exemptions you currently enjoy—such as homestead exemptions, senior citizen reductions, or other tax benefits—continue without interruption. While most states and counties have laws or policies exempting transfers to revocable living trusts from property tax reassessment when beneficial ownership hasn't changed, you typically must take action to claim these exemptions and ensure tax authorities properly recognize the ownership change as non-reassessable.

Research your specific state and county's rules about trust transfers and property tax. Contact your county property tax assessor's office or visit their website to learn what forms or notifications are required after transferring property to a trust. Common requirements include filing a change of ownership statement or property transfer declaration that explains the nature of the transfer and claims applicable reassessment exemptions, providing a copy of the recorded quitclaim deed showing the transfer, sometimes providing a trustee certification or excerpts from the trust document proving it's a revocable trust with you as trustee and beneficiary, and completing specific exemption continuation forms if you have homestead or other exemptions.

Many counties have specific forms titled "Claim for Reassessment Exclusion for Transfer Between Original Co-Owners" or "Preliminary Change of Ownership Report" or similar names that must be filed within a certain timeframe (often 45 days to 6 months) after recording the deed. These forms typically ask about the nature of the transfer, relationship between grantor and grantee (in this case, you're both), whether consideration was paid (typically "no" or nominal for trust transfers), whether the property remains your primary residence, and whether the trust is revocable with you as beneficiary. Filing these forms promptly and completely provides the assessor with information needed to recognize that your transfer qualifies for reassessment exemption.

In addition to avoiding reassessment, ensure any existing property tax exemptions continue. If you have a homestead exemption reducing your assessed value, verify with the assessor that this exemption continues after the trust transfer and complete any required forms to maintain it. Many jurisdictions require updated homestead exemption applications or certifications after ownership changes, even though the exemption should continue. If you have senior citizen, disabled veteran, agricultural, or other special property tax benefits, verify each continues and complete necessary filings. Don't assume exemptions automatically continue; affirmatively verify and document continuation. If the assessor's office indicates the transfer might trigger reassessment or that exemptions might be lost, don't accept this initial response without question. Research your state's laws (most protect revocable trust transfers from reassessment) and if necessary, have your estate planning or real estate attorney contact the assessor to explain that the transfer qualifies for protection under state law.

After filing all required forms and completing communications with the assessor, monitor your next property tax bill to verify that assessed value hasn't increased inappropriately and that exemptions appear correctly. If problems arise—unexpected value increases or lost exemptions—contact the assessor immediately and be prepared to appeal if necessary, providing documentation that the transfer qualified for exemption and that state law protects such transfers. Most property tax issues related to trust transfers resolve quickly once assessors understand the transfer's nature, but you must be proactive in providing information and following up to ensure proper treatment. The biblical principle of ensuring you receive what law provides and not paying more than required appears in Jesus's teaching about rendering to Caesar what is Caesar's. Matthew 22:21 records Jesus saying, "Give back to Caesar what is Caesar's." This implies giving Caesar what is owed—no more, no less. When your transfer qualifies for property tax protection under state law, claiming that protection isn't tax evasion but legitimate use of legal provisions designed precisely for your situation. Don't pay more property tax than the law requires; take the steps necessary to claim exemptions and protections the law provides for estate planning trust transfers.

Mortgage Lender and Escrow Account Coordination

If your transferred property has a mortgage with an escrow account for taxes and insurance, coordinating with your lender about the trust transfer and ensuring escrow arrangements continue functioning properly ranks among your important post-transfer tasks. As discussed extensively in previous chapters, federal law protects transfers to revocable living trusts from mortgage acceleration, so your lender cannot call your loan due based on the transfer. However, administrative coordination ensures your mortgage relationship proceeds smoothly and prevents complications with payment processing or escrow management.

Whether you proactively notified your lender before or immediately after the transfer, or whether you chose not to notify and will address any questions only if the lender discovers the transfer through other channels, certain escrow-related tasks are important regardless. First, ensure your property tax records are updated properly so tax bills continue going to the appropriate place for payment. If your lender pays taxes from escrow, they need to receive tax bills or need to know where to remit payment. If the tax assessor sends bills to different addresses after the ownership change, this could disrupt payment processing. Verify with the assessor that tax bills will continue going to your lender's escrow payment address or that your lender knows the correct payment information.

Second, confirm your updated homeowner's insurance information is provided to your lender. When your insurance company updates your policy to show the trust as insured, they typically send a copy to your lender confirming coverage. However, verify this occurs and if you're uncertain, provide your lender with a copy of the updated insurance declarations page yourself. Lenders must verify that adequate insurance exists with them named as mortgagee, and if they don't receive updated insurance information, they may place expensive force-placed insurance on the property. Third, monitor your escrow account statements after the transfer to ensure property tax and insurance payments continue processing correctly. Your escrow statement should show payments being made to tax authorities and insurance companies on schedule. If you notice discrepancies, gaps in payments, or unusual activity, contact your lender's escrow department immediately to address issues before they result in penalties, late fees, or coverage lapses.

Fourth, ensure your mortgage payment processing continues smoothly. If you have automatic payments set up from your bank account, verify these continue processing correctly after the transfer. While the trust transfer shouldn't affect payment processing (you're making payments from the same account), occasionally administrative changes in lender systems can disrupt automatic payments. Monitor the first few post-transfer payments to confirm they're processed correctly. If you pay online through your lender's website, verify your login and account access continue functioning. Some lenders freeze online access when they discover ownership changes pending verification; if this happens, contact the lender to provide documentation and restore access. Fifth, if you notified your lender about the transfer, follow up to confirm they've completed their processing. Request confirmation that they've updated their ownership records, continue recognizing the loan as current and in good standing, maintain the same account number and payment terms, and don't anticipate any changes or additional requirements.

The biblical principle of attention to ongoing administrative systems appears in Jesus's parable of the wise and foolish builders. Matthew 7:24-27 describes two builders—one who built on rock (representing hearing Jesus's words and acting on them) and one who built on sand (hearing but not acting). The difference appeared when storms came—the house on rock stood firm while the house on sand collapsed. Your estate planning structure (the house) is only as solid as the administrative foundation (rock or sand) you've created. Monitoring escrow accounts, verifying payments process correctly, and maintaining coordination with your lender creates the rock-solid administrative foundation that ensures your trust "house" withstands the storms of administrative complexity, lender confusion, or system glitches. Don't build your trust on sand by recording your deed and assuming everything else will work automatically; build on rock by actively monitoring and maintaining proper coordination among all systems and parties involved in your property's administration.

Trust Schedule and Asset Documentation Updates

Your living trust document typically includes or refers to a schedule of trust assets—a list or attachment showing what property and assets are held in the trust. This schedule serves multiple important functions: it provides a clear record of trust property for your reference and organization, it helps your successor trustee identify all trust assets when they take over administration after your death or incapacity, it documents the funding of your trust for tax purposes and to show the trust actually holds assets, and it creates a comprehensive inventory useful for estate administration, asset distribution, and accounting purposes. After transferring your home into your trust, updating this trust schedule to reflect the newly transferred property is an essential administrative task.

To update your trust schedule, locate the current schedule in your trust documents or create one if your trust doesn't yet have a schedule. Add a new entry for your home including several key pieces of information: the property's full legal description as it appears on the recorded quitclaim deed (copy this exactly to ensure precision), the property's street address for easy identification, the assessor's parcel number (APN) for county tax records reference, the date you executed and recorded the quitclaim deed transferring the property, the deed recording information (document number, book and page, recording date), the current approximate value of the property (for inventory and estate planning purposes), and a note indicating this is your primary residence (if applicable) and whether it has a mortgage. Additionally, attach a copy of the recorded quitclaim deed to the trust schedule or file it with your trust documents with a clear reference in the schedule such as "See Exhibit A for recorded deed."

This detailed documentation provides your successor trustee with everything needed to understand what property is in the trust, locate the deed proving trust ownership, and administer the property appropriately when the time comes. Beyond the trust schedule, create or update a comprehensive property file for the home that includes all documents related to the property: the recorded quitclaim deed transferring property to the trust, all previous deeds showing how you acquired the property, the original purchase contract and closing documents, survey and title documents, homeowner's insurance policies (current and historical), property tax records and exemption documentation, mortgage documents if applicable, title insurance policies, warranties or disclosures from when you purchased, and records of significant improvements or repairs. Organize these documents logically—chronologically or by category—and store them in a labeled file folder or binder. Keep this property file with your other trust documents or in a secure, accessible location where your successor trustee can find it.

Create a simple index or table of contents for the property file, listing what documents it contains and where key information can be found. This index might be as simple as a one-page list: "Property File Contents for 123 Main Street: Tab 1 - Recorded quitclaim deed to trust (2024); Tab 2 - Original purchase deed (2015); Tab 3 - Purchase contract and closing documents (2015); Tab 4 - Current homeowner's insurance policy; Tab 5 - Title insurance policy..." This organized documentation enables anyone who needs to administer the property—you in five years, your successor trustee after your death, your beneficiaries after inheritance—to quickly locate essential information without searching through disorganized piles of papers. The biblical principle of orderly record-keeping and organization appears throughout Scripture in contexts from temple treasures to genealogies. First Chronicles 28:11-13 describes David giving Solomon plans for the temple including "all that the Spirit had put in his mind for the courts of the temple of the Lord and all the surrounding rooms, for the treasuries of the temple of God and for the treasuries for the dedicated things." This detailed, organized planning and documentation ensured smooth transition and effective administration. Similarly, your detailed, organized trust schedule and property documentation ensures smooth transitions when your successor takes over and effective administration of the property you've placed in trust. Honor God through this kind of careful organization that reflects respect for the resources He's blessed you with and serves those who will eventually inherit them.

Communication with Successor Trustees and Family

After completing technical administrative tasks related to the property transfer, turn attention to human communication—informing appropriate people about the transfer and ensuring they have information they'll need to effectively fulfill their roles when the time comes. This communication balance requires wisdom: sharing sufficient information with those who need to know while maintaining appropriate privacy about details that don't need to be broadly disclosed. Your successor trustee—the person you've named to take over trust management when you die or become incapacitated—needs several types of information about the property transfer and ongoing trust administration.

First, ensure your successor trustee knows they've been appointed to this role and understands generally what responsibilities they'll have. While detailed training can wait until they actually need to serve, they should at least know they're named, understand this is a significant responsibility requiring time and attention, know they can decline if unwilling to serve, and understand whom to contact (your estate planning attorney, financial advisor) for guidance when the time comes to act. Second, inform your successor trustee that your home has been transferred into the trust and generally what this means. Explain that the transfer allows the property to pass to beneficiaries without probate, that the successor trustee will have authority to manage and eventually distribute the property, and that detailed instructions are provided in the trust document and supporting materials. You don't need to share every detail of the trust provisions or beneficiary distributions, but the successor should know the home is a trust asset they'll be responsible for administering.

Third, provide your successor trustee with information about where important documents are located. Create a letter or instruction sheet listing where you keep the original trust document, the trust schedule showing trust assets including the home, the property file with recorded deeds and insurance documents, contact information for your estate planning attorney, your financial advisor, and your accountant, information about any safe deposit boxes and how to access them, and login information or instructions for important online accounts (if appropriate to share). This location information enables the successor to immediately access what they'll need when they begin serving. Some people provide this information in a sealed envelope given to the successor with instructions to open only when the need arises, while others share it openly. Choose an approach appropriate for your relationship and trust level with your successor.

Regarding broader family communication, consider what information other family members—adult children, siblings, or others who will eventually inherit or who have interest in your affairs—need to know about the trust transfer. You're generally not obligated to share detailed trust information with beneficiaries during your lifetime, particularly since you retain the right to amend provisions and change beneficiaries at any time. However, some general communication can prevent future misunderstandings and demonstrate that you've planned responsibly. Consider sharing general information with adult children or other key family members: you've established a living trust for estate planning purposes; your home has been transferred into the trust; this planning ensures smooth administration of your estate and avoids probate; you've appointed [name] as successor trustee and [name] as alternate; while you're not sharing all details now, everything is documented and will be clear when the time comes for administration; and you welcome questions, though some matters must remain private until after your death.

This level of communication provides assurance that planning is complete and professional, manages expectations that you've addressed estate planning thoughtfully, prevents surprise or confusion after your death, and opens doors for questions without requiring premature disclosure of sensitive distribution details. The level of detail you share depends on your family dynamics—some families benefit from extensive openness while others function better with more privacy. Use wisdom in determining what serves your specific family best. The biblical principle of appropriate, wise communication that builds peace appears in Ephesians 4:29: "Do not let any unwholesome talk come out of your mouths, but only what is helpful for building others up according to their needs, that it may benefit those who listen." Communication about your trust transfer should be "helpful for building others up"—it should benefit those who hear it by providing assurance, clarity, and peace rather than creating confusion, anxiety, or conflict. Speak according to others' needs—sharing what they need to know while maintaining appropriate privacy over what they don't need to know yet. This balanced communication builds others up and promotes peace in family relationships rather than creating division through either excessive secrecy or premature disclosure of sensitive details.

Establishing Ongoing Review and Maintenance Schedules

Estate planning isn't a one-time event but an ongoing process requiring periodic review and updates as life circumstances change, laws evolve, and assets are acquired or disposed of. After completing the immediate post-transfer tasks, establish systems for ongoing review and maintenance of your trust and property ownership to ensure your estate plan remains current and effective throughout your life. Create a schedule for regular trust and property reviews, perhaps annually or biannually. During these reviews, verify that all properties and major assets remain properly titled in the trust, review the trust provisions to ensure they still reflect your wishes and family circumstances, update contact information for successor trustees, advisors, and beneficiaries if changes have occurred, verify that insurance coverage on all trust property remains adequate and current, and confirm that all financial accounts, business interests, and other assets that should be in the trust are properly titled.

Life events that should trigger immediate trust reviews and potential updates include marriage or divorce (requiring review of how property is held, who serves as trustee, and how assets distribute), birth or adoption of children or grandchildren (potentially requiring addition of new beneficiaries), death of a beneficiary, trustee, or other person named in the trust, significant changes in financial circumstances (large inheritance, business sale, major losses), changes in health that affect capacity or life expectancy, changes in relationships with beneficiaries that might warrant distribution changes, acquisition of new real property or major assets, moving to a different state (possibly requiring trust updates for new state laws), and changes in estate tax laws or other regulations affecting estate planning. When any of these events occur, consult with your estate planning attorney to review whether trust amendments are needed.

Beyond reviewing the trust document itself, establish systems for maintaining property-related records and documentation. Annually review your property file to ensure it contains current insurance policies, recent property tax bills showing proper ownership and exemptions, current mortgage statements if applicable, and updated values for properties (useful for estate planning and insurance purposes). Update your trust schedule any time assets are added to or removed from the trust. Maintain a simple log or journal recording significant events affecting the trust or trust property—when property was transferred, when insurance was updated, when you spoke with the mortgage lender, when trust amendments were executed. This log provides a chronological record of trust administration useful for your own reference and eventually for your successor trustee's understanding of the trust's history.

The biblical principle of ongoing, faithful attention to stewardship responsibilities rather than one-time action appears in Jesus's parable of the faithful servant. Luke 12:42-44 asks, "Who then is the faithful and wise manager, whom the master puts in charge of his servants to give them their food allowance at the proper time? It will be good for that servant whom the master finds doing so when he returns. Truly I tell you, he will put him in charge of all his possessions." The faithful servant isn't praised for acting once but for continuous, ongoing faithfulness in providing what's needed at proper times. Your estate planning stewardship similarly requires not just initial action (creating the trust, transferring property) but ongoing attention (regular reviews, updates when needed, maintenance of records). This continuous faithfulness positions you to be found "doing so" when the Master returns—when you face death or incapacity and your planning must function as intended. The reward for this faithful, ongoing stewardship is that the Master puts you "in charge of all his possessions"—in estate planning terms, your faithful stewardship now positions your successor to faithfully steward the distribution of all you've accumulated to benefit those you love.

Digital Records and Modern Documentation Systems

In our increasingly digital world, consider how technology can enhance your trust documentation and administration while also recognizing the continued importance of maintaining physical records. Many people find hybrid systems combining digital convenience with physical security work best for estate planning documentation. Consider creating digital copies of all important trust-related documents including the trust document and all amendments, recorded property deeds, trustee certifications, insurance policies, property tax records, mortgage documentation, title insurance policies, and correspondence with attorneys, lenders, and others. Scan these documents to PDF format and store them in organized digital folders, perhaps structured like "Estate Planning/Living Trust/Property Documents/123 Main Street/Recorded Deeds."

Store digital documents in multiple secure locations: on your computer's hard drive in encrypted folders, on external hard drives or thumb drives kept in secure locations separate from your computer, in cloud storage services (Dropbox, Google Drive, iCloud) that you can access from anywhere, and on your estate planning attorney's secure servers if they provide this service. This redundancy ensures documents remain accessible even if individual storage locations are compromised. However, don't rely solely on digital storage. Maintain physical originals of critical documents including the original signed trust document, recorded original deeds showing trust ownership, original title insurance policies, original insurance policies, and original mortgage documents. Store these physical originals in fireproof home safes, safety deposit boxes (ensuring your successor trustee has access), or with your attorney's office if they maintain physical document storage.

For digital security, use password managers to maintain complex, secure passwords for all estate planning related accounts and cloud storage, create a master document listing where digital files are stored and how to access them, consider providing your successor trustee with sealed instructions for accessing digital records (to be opened when needed), and regularly verify that digital files remain accessible and storage services continue functioning. Remember that digital storage, while convenient, carries risks—files can be accidentally deleted, services can be discontinued, and passwords can be forgotten. Physical originals and multiple backup locations mitigate these risks. The biblical principle of wise use of available tools while not over-relying on them appears in various contexts. When David faced Goliath in 1 Samuel 17, he had access to Saul's armor but chose not to use it, relying instead on tools he knew—his sling and stones. However, he didn't reject all tools; he selected five smooth stones. The principle is using what works for you while not being overly dependent on any single approach. Digital documentation is a valuable tool for estate planning, but don't become so dependent on digital storage that you neglect physical originals and redundant backup systems. Use digital tools wisely as part of a comprehensive system, but don't rely on them exclusively.

Planning for Incapacity: Ensuring Successor Access

While much of estate planning focuses on what happens after death, planning for potential incapacity is equally important and often more immediately relevant since people frequently experience periods of incapacity before death. After transferring your property into your trust, ensure your successor trustee can actually access what they need and take necessary actions if you become incapacitated and unable to manage your affairs. Your trust document should clearly define what constitutes incapacity and how it's determined—typically through written certification by one or more physicians that you're unable to manage financial affairs. Ensure these provisions are clear and don't create barriers that prevent timely action if you become incapacitated. Some trusts require certification by multiple physicians, creating delays if quick action is needed. Discuss with your attorney whether your incapacity provisions strike the right balance between preventing premature findings of incapacity and enabling timely transition when genuinely needed.

Verify that your successor trustee knows what authority they'll have during your incapacity. Typically, successor trustees can manage trust property, pay bills, handle investments, and do whatever is necessary to preserve trust assets and provide for your care. However, specific trust language governs, so ensure your successor understands their powers and limitations. Provide your successor with practical information they'll need if you become incapacitated including contact information for all your healthcare providers, information about your health insurance and

Medicare/Medicaid, details about any long-term care insurance you have, contact information for family members who should be notified, instructions about your preferences for care (where you want to live, what quality of care you expect), and information about financial resources available in the trust for paying care costs.

Consider creating a separate letter or instruction document specifically for incapacity scenarios, stored with your trust documents and accessible to your successor. This letter might include different information than your letter about what to do when you die, focusing on immediate practical matters about your care and ongoing bill payment. Additionally, coordinate your trust-based estate planning with healthcare documents including healthcare power of attorney or healthcare proxy (naming someone to make medical decisions if you can't), living will or advance directive (stating preferences about end-of-life care), and HIPAA authorizations (allowing healthcare providers to share medical information with people you designate). These healthcare documents work together with your trust—the trust addresses financial and property management during incapacity while healthcare documents address medical decision-making. Ensure your successor trustee and your healthcare agent (who may be the same person or different people) know about each other and understand how their roles coordinate.

The biblical principle of preparing for uncertain timing appears in Jesus's parable of the ten virgins in Matthew 25:1-13. Five wise virgins brought oil for their lamps while five foolish virgins didn't. When the bridegroom came at an unexpected hour, only the prepared were ready. Verse 13 concludes, "Therefore keep watch, because you do not know the day or the hour." Incapacity, like the bridegroom's arrival, comes at unknown times—a stroke, accident, or cognitive decline can occur suddenly without warning. The wise person prepares for this uncertain timing by ensuring successors can immediately access what they need and act effectively. The foolish person assumes they'll have time to prepare later or that incapacity won't happen to them. Be among the wise who prepare thoroughly for possibilities that might arrive at unexpected hours, ensuring your successors are equipped to act effectively whenever the need arises.

Conclusion: From Transaction to Living Administration

The recording of your quitclaim deed represents a significant legal transaction—property ownership has changed from individual to trust. However, this transaction is only the beginning of what should become living, ongoing trust administration where the legal structure you've created actually functions as intended to protect property, provide for management during incapacity, and ensure smooth distribution to beneficiaries after death. The difference between a trust that works effectively and one that fails despite being technically valid often comes down to the thoroughness of post-transfer administration and the faithfulness of ongoing maintenance. Completing all the tasks outlined in this chapter—updating insurance, coordinating with tax authorities, managing lender relationships, organizing documentation, communicating with successors, establishing review schedules—transforms your trust from static documents into dynamic, living estate planning that serves its purposes throughout your life and beyond.

The biblical principle that faithful stewardship requires both initial action and ongoing attention appears in Paul's exhortation to Timothy. Second Timothy 4:5 instructs, "But you, keep your head in all situations, endure hardship, do the work of an evangelist, discharge all the duties of your ministry." Paul doesn't just tell Timothy to start ministry but to "discharge all the duties"—to fulfill completely all that ministry requires, both the exciting initial calling and the ongoing, sometimes tedious daily responsibilities. Your estate planning similarly requires discharging all duties—not just the exciting initial creation of the trust and transfer of property, but also the ongoing duties of updating insurance, maintaining records, reviewing documents, and ensuring everything continues functioning properly. This complete discharge of duties ensures your ministry of stewardship (providing for your family through estate planning) is fully effective rather than partially completed.

As you move forward from property transfer into ongoing trust administration, commit this stewardship to the Lord, approaching it with diligence and faithfulness. Proverbs 16:3 promises, "Commit to the Lord whatever you do, and he will establish your plans." When you commit your trust administration to the Lord—completing post-transfer tasks thoroughly, maintaining records carefully, reviewing regularly, and ensuring successors are prepared—you can trust that your plans will be established. Your property will be properly protected, your administration systems will function effectively, your successors will be equipped to serve faithfully, and your estate planning will accomplish its purposes of avoiding probate, providing for incapacity management, and ensuring your legacy serves those you love. Walk forward confidently in this ongoing stewardship, knowing that faithful attention to both the inspiring initial planning and the mundane ongoing administration honors God and serves your family for generations to come.

***

Section 1: Updating Insurance Policies

Introduction: Maintaining the Shield of Protection Through Ownership Changes

Insurance represents one of the most critical protections homeowners possess, providing financial safeguards against losses that could devastate families financially—catastrophic property damage from fires, storms, or disasters; title defects that challenge ownership and require expensive litigation; and liability claims from injuries occurring on the property. When you transfer your home into a living trust, these insurance protections don't automatically adjust to the new ownership structure. Without proactive updates to insurance policies reflecting trust ownership, gaps in coverage can emerge that leave property inadequately protected, expose trustees to personal liability, or result in claim denials precisely when coverage is most needed. Understanding what insurance updates are necessary, how to accomplish them properly, and why these updates matter so critically ensures that the protective shield insurance provides continues functioning effectively through the ownership transition from individual to trust.

The fundamental principle is straightforward: insurance policies protect specific named insured parties for specific property or interests. When property ownership changes—even when the beneficial owner (you) remains the same but the legal ownership form changes (from individual to trust)—the named insured on insurance policies should be updated to reflect current legal ownership. This update isn't merely a technicality but ensures legal alignment between who owns the property (the trust/trustee) and who the insurance company has contracted to protect (the named insured). Misalignment creates risks—insurance companies might question whether they're obligated to pay claims on property owned by entities different from the named insured, or whether trustees acting in their fiduciary capacity are protected when policies name only individuals. Eliminating these misalignments and questions through proper insurance updates provides peace of mind that coverage will respond as expected when losses occur.

The biblical principle of maintaining protection and not allowing shields to deteriorate appears in various military contexts in Scripture. In 2 Samuel 1:21, David laments Saul and Jonathan's deaths, mentioning "the shield of the mighty is vilely cast away, the shield of Saul, as though he had not been anointed with oil" (KJV). The imagery of a shield cast away or fallen into disrepair represents loss of protection and vulnerability to enemies. Your insurance policies are shields protecting against financial enemies—devastating losses that could destroy wealth you've accumulated and property you've maintained. When ownership changes but insurance isn't updated, these shields are effectively cast away or fallen into disrepair, no longer providing the protection they should. The diligent steward ensures shields remain in good repair, properly positioned, and ready to provide protection when needed. Updating insurance policies after trust transfers is exactly this kind of shield maintenance that ensures protection continues effectively through ownership transitions.

Homeowner's Hazard Insurance: The Primary Coverage Update

Homeowner's insurance (also called hazard insurance or property insurance) protects your home and possessions against damage from fires, storms, theft, vandalism, and numerous other perils, and it provides liability coverage if someone is injured on your property. This insurance is typically required by mortgage lenders as a condition of the loan and is one of the most important protections homeowners maintain. When you transfer your home into your trust, updating homeowner's insurance to reflect trust ownership stands as the highest priority among all insurance updates because this coverage protects against the most common and potentially catastrophic losses.

To update homeowner's insurance, contact your insurance company or agent immediately after recording your quitclaim deed—ideally within days of the recording. Many insurance professionals recommend updating insurance before or concurrent with recording the deed to ensure no gap exists between when ownership changes and when insurance reflects the change. When contacting your insurer, provide several key pieces of information: your policy number and property address so they can locate your account, notification that you've transferred the property into your revocable living trust for estate planning purposes, the exact legal name of the trust and your designation as trustee as it appears in the trust document and on the recorded deed, a copy of the recorded quitclaim deed showing the transfer, and a trustee certification if the insurance company requests it (most don't require complete trust documents but may want basic verification of the trust's existence).

The insurance company will process an update to your policy, changing the named insured from your individual name to you as trustee of your trust. The updated designation typically reads: "Jane Mary Doe, Trustee of The Jane Mary Doe Revocable Living Trust dated January 1, 2024" or similar language matching your specific trustee and trust names. Most insurance companies make this change at no additional cost and without increasing premiums, recognizing that you're the same insured individual with the same property and risk profile, just holding ownership in a different legal form. The physical property hasn't changed, you still live there, the risks are identical, so premium rates shouldn't change. However, insurance companies will verify several things before processing the update.

First, they'll confirm the trust is revocable and you remain the beneficial owner with full control. If you transferred property into an irrevocable trust or trust for others' benefit, the insurance company might view this as more significantly changed circumstances requiring underwriting review. Revocable trusts where you're trustee and beneficiary are typically processed as routine updates. Second, they'll verify you continue occupying the property as your primary residence. Homeowner's insurance rates are based on owner-occupied residential property; if you've moved out or converted the property to rental or other use, different insurance (and typically higher premiums) would be required. Third, if you have a mortgage, they'll ensure your lender remains listed as mortgagee or loss payee on the policy. This designation protects the lender's interest by requiring insurance proceeds from covered losses to be used for property repair or mortgage payoff. The lender must remain as mortgagee regardless of the named insured change.

After the insurance company processes the update, they will send you an updated declarations page or policy endorsement showing the revised named insured designation. They typically also send a copy to your mortgage lender confirming continued coverage. Review this updated documentation carefully to verify all information is correct: trust name and date match exactly, you as trustee are properly listed, coverage amounts remain adequate for your property's value, deductibles and policy limits are as expected, the property address is correct, your mortgage lender is still listed as mortgagee (if applicable), and effective dates and premium amounts are appropriate. If you discover any errors in the updated policy, contact your insurance company immediately for corrections. Don't delay, as errors could create claim problems if losses occur before corrections are made.

Keep a copy of the updated insurance declarations page with your trust documents and provide a copy to your mortgage lender if they didn't receive one automatically. Update your property file to include current insurance documentation, removing outdated policies that no longer reflect correct ownership. The biblical principle of ensuring protection remains in place and doesn't lapse appears in various contexts about vigilance and watchfulness. First Peter 5:8 warns, "Be alert and of sober mind. Your enemy the devil prowls around like a roaring lion looking for an enemy to devour." While this verse addresses spiritual warfare, its principle of alertness and readiness against threats applies to property protection. Property losses—fires, storms, theft—prowl around looking for opportunities to devour your wealth and destroy what you've built. Homeowner's insurance is your defense against these prowling threats, and maintaining this defense properly (keeping coverage current and aligned with ownership) reflects the alert, sober-minded vigilance Scripture commends. Don't allow your defense to lapse or become ineffective through neglect of necessary updates; maintain it alertly so it's ready to protect when threats materialize.

Title Insurance Verification and Endorsements

While homeowner's insurance protects against future property damage and liability, title insurance protects against historical title defects that could challenge your ownership. As discussed extensively in the previous chapter, most owner's title insurance policies automatically continue covering property transferred into the insured person's revocable living trust. However, verification of this continued coverage and consideration of endorsements that explicitly address trust ownership and successor trustees provides additional certainty and protection. After recording your quitclaim deed, contact your title insurance company to verify coverage continuation. Provide them with your policy number, a copy of the recorded deed showing the transfer to trust, and a trustee certification if requested. Specifically ask whether your existing policy continues covering the property with trust ownership or whether any additional documentation or endorsements are needed.

Most title companies will confirm that coverage continues automatically for revocable trust transfers and will update their records to show current ownership. However, request this confirmation in writing—either an endorsement to your existing policy, a letter from the title company, or some form of documentation stating that your policy remains in effect with the property held in trust. This written confirmation eliminates any future question about coverage continuation and provides documentary evidence if claims arise. Several specific title insurance endorsements may be valuable in trust ownership contexts. An ALTA 12 or successor trustee endorsement explicitly confirms that the policy covers not only you as current trustee but also successor trustees who take over after your death or incapacity. This endorsement provides clarity that when your successor needs to act—perhaps selling property or defending against title challenges—they're protected by the title insurance policy. While many title companies include successor coverage in standard policies, an explicit endorsement eliminates ambiguity.

A trust endorsement or ALTA endorsement specifically for trust-owned property may be available from some title companies, providing explicit coverage for property held in trust with language addressing trustee changes, trust amendments, and other trust-specific scenarios. An extended coverage endorsement or comprehensive endorsement provides enhanced protection beyond standard coverage, insuring against additional title risks. If your title company offers this, consider whether the additional cost is worthwhile for more comprehensive protection. A survey endorsement or boundary endorsement provides enhanced coverage for boundary disputes and encroachments, useful if your property has complicated boundaries or is in areas where boundary disputes are common. Ask your title company what endorsements they offer and recommend for trust-owned property. The cost of endorsements is typically modest—often $25 to $150 per endorsement—compared to the property values they protect, making them worthwhile investments for enhanced, explicit coverage.

If your title insurance company indicates they won't automatically continue coverage or expresses concerns about the trust transfer (rare but possible with smaller or less sophisticated insurers), consider obtaining new owner's title insurance from a different, more knowledgeable company. The one-time premium for a new policy (typically several hundred to over a thousand dollars depending on property value) provides complete, unquestioned coverage for the trust-owned property going forward. Finally, keep all title insurance documentation—the original policy, any endorsements, and confirmation letters about coverage continuation—in a secure location with your trust documents. Provide your successor trustee with information about where these documents are stored and how to contact the title insurance company if issues arise. Title insurance protection can extend for decades, so ensure documentation is preserved and accessible throughout this time. The biblical principle of preserving important protective documents appears in Jeremiah 32:9-14, where Jeremiah purchases a field and God instructs him: "Take these documents, both the sealed and unsealed copies of the deed of purchase, and put them in a clay jar so they will last a long time." This careful preservation of property documents for long-term access is exactly what's needed for title insurance policies and endorsements. These documents may not be needed for years or decades, but when title challenges arise, they're crucial. Preserve them carefully so they remain accessible whenever needed, whether that's next year or fifty years from now when your grandchildren inherit the property and face title questions.

Umbrella and Excess Liability Coverage Considerations

Beyond standard homeowner's insurance, many homeowners carry umbrella or excess liability policies that provide additional liability coverage above homeowner's policy limits. These policies protect against large liability claims—perhaps a serious injury on your property resulting in a million-dollar lawsuit—that would exceed your homeowner's policy's liability coverage. If you have umbrella or excess liability insurance, you must also ensure these policies are updated to reflect trust ownership and to coordinate properly with your updated homeowner's coverage. Umbrella policies are typically structured to provide excess coverage above underlying policies (homeowner's and auto insurance). For umbrella coverage to respond to claims, the underlying policies must be in force with minimum liability limits, and the umbrella policy must list all underlying policies correctly.

When you update your homeowner's insurance to show trust ownership, your umbrella carrier needs to be notified so they can update their records about the underlying policy. Contact your umbrella insurance carrier and inform them of the trust transfer and homeowner's policy update. Provide them with a copy of the updated homeowner's declarations page showing the trust as named insured, information about the trust and your role as trustee, and verification that you continue occupying the property. The umbrella carrier will typically update their records to reflect the trust ownership and ensure coordination with the underlying homeowner's policy. They may also update the umbrella policy itself to name the trust or trustee as an additional insured, providing explicit coverage for liability arising from trust-owned property.

Review the updated umbrella policy to ensure it properly coordinates with your homeowner's coverage, maintains adequate liability limits for your situation (commonly $1-5 million or more), lists all underlying policies correctly including the updated homeowner's policy, and names the trust or trustee as insured for trust-owned properties. Additionally, discuss with your insurance agent whether your current umbrella limits remain appropriate given your overall asset picture. If transferring property into a trust is part of broader estate planning that reveals substantial assets, you may want to increase umbrella coverage to better protect against large liability claims that could threaten your estate. The cost of umbrella insurance is relatively modest (often $150-300 annually per million dollars of coverage), making it cost-effective protection for high-net-worth individuals. The biblical principle of taking refuge and not being exposed to dangers unnecessarily appears in Proverbs 22:3: "The prudent see danger and take refuge, but the simple keep going and pay the penalty." Umbrella insurance is exactly this kind of refuge from danger—protection against catastrophic liability claims that could devastate your estate. Ensuring this refuge properly covers trust-owned property and coordinates with underlying insurance maintains the comprehensive protection prudent stewards establish for themselves and their families.

Coordination with Mortgage Lender Requirements

If your transferred property has a mortgage, your lender requires you to maintain adequate homeowner's insurance with them named as mortgagee or loss payee as a condition of the loan. After updating your homeowner's insurance to reflect trust ownership, ensuring your lender is properly notified and their requirements continue being met prevents complications that could arise from lender confusion about insurance coverage. Most insurance companies automatically notify mortgage lenders when policies are updated, sending a copy of the revised declarations page showing the trust as named insured while confirming the lender remains listed as mortgagee. However, don't assume this notification automatically occurs; verify that it happens or provide the notification yourself.

Contact your mortgage servicer (the company that collects your payments and manages your loan) and inform them that you've updated your homeowner's insurance to reflect the trust ownership of the property. Provide them with a copy of the updated insurance declarations page showing the trust as named insured, the lender listed as mortgagee, adequate coverage amounts meeting loan requirements, and current policy status with premiums paid. The lender needs this information to verify adequate insurance exists protecting their collateral. If they don't receive updated insurance information, they may place expensive force-placed insurance on the property—lender-purchased coverage that protects only the lender's interest and for which they charge you significantly higher premiums than standard homeowner's insurance.

If your mortgage includes an escrow account from which the lender pays insurance premiums, coordination is particularly important. The lender pays premiums from your escrow account to the insurance company, so they need accurate information about the policy, premium amounts, and payment schedule. When the insured name on the policy changes to show the trust, the lender's escrow department must update their records so premium payments are processed correctly. Verify with your lender's escrow department that they've received updated insurance information, they understand premium amounts and due dates haven't changed (just the insured name), and they'll continue paying premiums from escrow without interruption. Monitor your next escrow account statement after the insurance update to confirm premium payments are being made correctly. If you notice any discrepancies or problems, contact the lender's escrow department immediately to address issues before they result in coverage lapses or force-placed insurance.

The biblical principle of ensuring systems continue functioning properly through transitions appears in various contexts about leadership succession and organizational management. When Moses prepared to transfer leadership to Joshua, Numbers 27:18-20 records specific instructions: "The Lord said to Moses, 'Take Joshua son of Elijah, a man in whom is the spirit of leadership, and lay your hand on him...Give him some of your authority so the whole Israelite community will obey him.'" This careful transition ensured systems would continue functioning under new leadership. Similarly, when property ownership transitions from individual to trust, verifying that mortgage and escrow systems continue functioning properly—premiums are being paid, lenders are satisfied with insurance coverage, no disruptions occur—ensures these important financial systems operate smoothly through the transition. Don't assume systems will automatically adjust; actively verify and coordinate to ensure smooth continued functioning.

Flood, Earthquake, and Other Specialized Coverage

Standard homeowner's insurance policies exclude certain perils such as floods and earthquakes, requiring separate specialized policies for coverage against these risks. If you have flood insurance (through the National Flood Insurance Program or private carriers), earthquake insurance, or other specialized property coverage, these policies must also be updated to reflect trust ownership. The update process for specialized policies is similar to homeowner's insurance updates. Contact each insurance carrier, inform them of the trust transfer, provide documentation (recorded deed, trustee certification), and request that policies be updated to show the trust or trustee as named insured.

However, some specialized policies have unique considerations. Federal flood insurance through the National Flood Insurance Program (NFIP) has specific rules about policy transfers and ownership changes. Generally, flood policies continue covering property transferred to trusts, but you must notify the servicing carrier and may need to complete specific forms to update the policy. The NFIP has standardized procedures for trust ownership, and most agents familiar with federal flood insurance can process these updates routinely. Ensure the updated flood policy lists the trust or trustee as named insured, maintains the same coverage amounts and deductibles, continues showing your mortgage lender as loss payee if required, and doesn't have gaps in coverage during the update process.

Earthquake insurance and other specialized coverage from private carriers typically follows similar update procedures as standard homeowner's insurance. However, because these policies are often separate from the main homeowner's policy, they require separate contact and updating. Don't assume that updating your homeowner's policy automatically updates your earthquake or other specialized coverage; contact each carrier separately and request specific updates for each policy. After updating all specialized coverage, ensure your complete insurance package—homeowner's, flood, earthquake, umbrella, and any other policies—is coordinated with all policies showing consistent named insured designations (the trust/trustee), all policies listing the mortgage lender if required, and all coverage working together to provide comprehensive protection. Create a simple insurance summary document listing all policies you have, their coverage amounts, policy numbers, carrier contact information, and annual premium amounts. Keep this summary with your trust documents and update it whenever policies change.

The biblical principle of comprehensive protection against various threats appears in Ephesians 6:11-17, which describes the full armor of God including belt, breastplate, shield, helmet, and sword. Verse 13 instructs, "Therefore put on the full armor of God, so that when the day of evil comes, you may be able to stand your ground." Just as spiritual protection requires full armor—not just one piece but comprehensive coverage—property protection requires comprehensive insurance covering various perils. Homeowner's insurance alone isn't sufficient if you're in a flood zone and lack flood coverage, or in an earthquake area without earthquake insurance. Ensure you have the full armor of property insurance appropriate for your risks, and ensure all pieces of this armor are properly updated to reflect trust ownership so every protection is in place and functioning when "the day of evil comes" in the form of property losses.

Life Insurance and Beneficiary Designation Coordination

While property insurance protects your home, life insurance protects your family by providing financial resources after your death. Life insurance doesn't directly relate to property ownership and doesn't need updating just because you've transferred your home into a trust. However, reviewing life insurance beneficiary designations as part of comprehensive post-trust-transfer administration ensures your complete estate plan—both property passing through the trust and life insurance passing through beneficiary designations—works together coherently to accomplish your goals.

Life insurance proceeds pass directly to named beneficiaries without going through probate (unless the estate is named as beneficiary). This probate avoidance benefit is similar to how trusts avoid probate for property. However, life insurance beneficiary designations and trust provisions must be coordinated to ensure they work together rather than creating conflicting plans. For example, if your trust provides for equal distribution among your children but your life insurance names only one child as beneficiary, you've created unequal treatment that might not reflect your intentions. Similarly, if your trust makes special provision for a child with disabilities through a special needs trust but your life insurance pays directly to that child, the inheritance could disqualify them from government benefits, defeating the trust's purpose.

Review your life insurance beneficiary designations after establishing your trust and consider whether changes are appropriate. Common approaches include naming your trust as life insurance beneficiary so proceeds flow into the trust and are distributed according to trust provisions, coordinating equal treatment of beneficiaries between insurance and trust assets, naming individual beneficiaries directly for insurance while using the trust for property distributions if this serves your goals, or establishing separate insurance trusts (ILITs) for life insurance if estate tax planning requires this. Discuss with your estate planning attorney and financial advisor how life insurance and your trust should coordinate, then update beneficiary designations as needed to implement the coordinated plan. After making any changes, provide copies of updated beneficiary designation forms to the insurance company and keep copies with your trust documents. Update your estate planning summary to show how life insurance and trust provisions work together.

The biblical principle of coordinating multiple elements of provision appears in Joseph's wisdom in Genesis 41. When Pharaoh's dreams revealed coming famine, Joseph didn't just plan for storing grain; he organized a comprehensive system involving collection during good years, storage facilities, distribution networks, and economic policies. This comprehensive, coordinated approach saved Egypt and surrounding nations. Similarly, comprehensive estate planning requires coordination among multiple elements—trusts, life insurance, beneficiary designations, retirement accounts, and other assets. Don't just establish a trust without considering how other estate elements coordinate with it. Review the complete picture and ensure all pieces work together toward your goals rather than working at cross-purposes because of inadequate coordination.

Documentation, Organization, and Successor Access

After updating all insurance policies following your trust transfer, organizing and preserving this documentation for future reference and successor trustee access represents the final essential step ensuring your insurance protections remain effective and accessible when needed. Create a comprehensive insurance file or section within your trust documents binder that includes current declarations pages for all insurance policies (homeowner's, title, umbrella, flood, earthquake, etc.), copies of any insurance endorsements or riders, contact information for each insurance carrier and your agents, policy numbers and coverage amounts for easy reference, premium payment information and due dates, copies of recent premium bills or payment receipts, correspondence with insurance companies about trust ownership updates, and a simple summary sheet listing all policies, their coverage, and key information.

Organize this documentation logically—perhaps by policy type with current information at the front of each section—and label everything clearly so anyone accessing the file can quickly understand what insurance exists and how to contact carriers if needed. Store this insurance documentation with your other trust documents in a secure but accessible location. Keep physical copies in fireproof safes or filing cabinets, and consider creating digital copies stored in cloud services or on external drives as backup. However, ensure originals of critical documents are preserved, as some situations may require original policy documents rather than copies. Create a simple letter or memo to your successor trustee explaining where insurance documentation is located and providing an overview of what coverage exists. Include in this letter guidance about what the successor should do regarding insurance when they take over after your death or incapacity: Immediately notify all insurance carriers of your death/incapacity; verify coverage continues for the transition period; update policies to reflect successor trustee's name if required; maintain all coverage without lapses during estate administration; and consult with insurance agents about whether any coverage changes are needed during administration or before property distributions to beneficiaries.

This guidance helps your successor navigate insurance matters confidently rather than being uncertain about what to do. Additionally, provide your successor with contact information for your insurance agent or broker who knows your coverage and can assist during the transition. Finally, schedule periodic reviews (perhaps annually) where you update insurance documentation, verify all policies remain current with adequate coverage, ensure premium payments are being made, check that policy declarations still show correct trust ownership information, and update your successor trustee's letter if changes occur. These regular reviews keep documentation current and catch any problems before they create coverage issues. The biblical principle of maintaining protection through careful attention and regular maintenance appears in Nehemiah's account of rebuilding Jerusalem's walls. Nehemiah 4:9 records, "But we prayed to our God and posted a guard day and night to meet this threat." Protection wasn't established once and forgotten but maintained continuously through ongoing vigilance. Your insurance protection similarly requires ongoing attention—not just initial updates when transferring to the trust but periodic verification that protection remains in place, coverage remains adequate, and documentation remains organized and accessible. This ongoing vigilance ensures the insurance shields protecting your property remain strong, properly positioned, and ready to defend against threats whenever they materialize.

Conclusion: The Faithful Steward's Shield Maintenance

Updating insurance policies after transferring property into living trusts represents far more than administrative busywork or legal formality. These updates are essential shield maintenance that ensures the financial protections you've established—homeowner's coverage against property damage, title insurance against ownership challenges, umbrella coverage against liability claims—continue functioning effectively through ownership transitions. The modest effort required to update policies, verify coverage, and organize documentation is insignificant compared to the potential costs of claim denials, coverage gaps, or inadequate protection resulting from neglected updates. The faithful steward recognizes that establishing protection (purchasing insurance) is only half the responsibility; maintaining that protection through life changes and ownership transitions completes the stewardship duty.

The biblical principle that faithful stewardship includes both establishing and maintaining protections appears in Jesus's teaching about building houses. Matthew 7:24-27 describes two builders—one who built on rock and one who built on sand. The difference wasn't in their initial building but in the foundations they established and maintained. When storms came, "the rain came down, the streams rose, and the winds blew and beat against that house; yet it did not fall, because it had its foundation on the rock." Your insurance policies are foundations protecting your property against the storms of fire, liability, title disputes, and other perils. These foundations must not only be established initially but maintained properly so that when storms come—and they will come—your property remains standing rather than falling because foundations (insurance) weren't properly maintained.

As you complete insurance updates following your trust transfer, commit this protective work to the Lord, recognizing that faithful attention to these practical details honors God and serves your family. Proverbs 16:3 promises, "Commit to the Lord whatever you do, and he will establish your plans." When you commit your insurance planning to the Lord—updating policies diligently, organizing documentation carefully, ensuring successors have access to needed information—you can trust that your plans for protecting property and providing for family will be established. Your insurance protections will remain in force, your coverage will respond when claims arise, and your family will be shielded from financial devastation that could occur without proper, maintained insurance coverage. Walk forward confidently, knowing that faithful attention to insurance updates and maintenance, combined with commitment to God, establishes the protective shields your family needs both now and for generations to come.

***

Section 2: Managing Property Taxes

Introduction: The Ongoing Obligation of Property Ownership

Property taxes represent one of the most significant ongoing financial obligations homeowners face, typically amounting to thousands of dollars annually and funding essential local government services including schools, police, fire departments, and infrastructure. These taxes are assessed based on property value and legal ownership, and they continue regardless of how property ownership is structured. When you transfer your home into a living trust, the obligation to pay property taxes doesn't change or diminish, but the administrative aspects of property tax management require attention to ensure bills are received properly, payments are made timely, valuable exemptions and reductions are preserved, and your successor trustee can continue managing these obligations seamlessly when they take over trust administration. Understanding how trust transfers affect property tax matters and taking appropriate steps to maintain proper administration prevents complications that could result in lost exemptions, increased assessments, payment problems, or penalties.

The fundamental principle is that property taxes follow property ownership. When legal ownership changes from you individually to you as trustee of your trust, county property tax systems must be updated to reflect this ownership change. While you remain the same person with the same property and the same tax obligations, the county's records need to show current ownership for billing purposes, exemption tracking, and other administrative functions. Additionally, most states recognize that transfers to revocable living trusts where the original owner remains trustee and beneficiary don't represent true changes in beneficial ownership that should trigger property tax reassessment or loss of exemptions. However, claiming these protections typically requires affirmative action—filing forms, providing documentation, and ensuring county assessors understand the transfer's nature. Neglecting these administrative steps can result in unnecessary tax increases or lost benefits, while faithful attention to them preserves the favorable tax treatment you currently enjoy.

The biblical principle of faithful payment of required taxes combined with diligent preservation of legitimate tax benefits appears in Jesus's teaching about taxes. In Matthew 22:21, Jesus instructs, "Give back to Caesar what is Caesar's and to God what is God's." This teaching establishes the principle of paying required taxes—what legitimately belongs to Caesar (government) should be rendered to Caesar. However, it doesn't require paying more than what's legitimately owed. When tax laws provide exemptions, reductions, or protections for estate planning trust transfers, claiming these benefits isn't tax evasion but legitimate use of provisions the law provides. Romans 13:7 similarly instructs, "Give to everyone what you owe them: If you owe taxes, pay taxes." The obligation is to pay what you owe—not more, not less—and proper property tax administration after trust transfers ensures you continue paying what's owed while preserving legitimate benefits the law allows you to keep.

Understanding Property Tax Reassessment Rules

One of the primary concerns when transferring property into trusts is whether the transfer will trigger property tax reassessment based on current market value, potentially significantly increasing annual tax bills. Property tax systems generally tax property based on assessed value, which in many jurisdictions is kept artificially low compared to market value to provide tax relief for long-term homeowners. When property changes hands through sale, most jurisdictions reassess at market value, which for homeowners who've owned property for many years can result in dramatic tax increases. However, recognizing that transfers to revocable living trusts don't represent true changes in beneficial ownership, most states have laws or administrative policies that exclude these transfers from reassessment triggers, allowing assessed values to remain unchanged when property moves into estate planning trusts.

The specific rules governing whether trust transfers trigger reassessment vary by state. California's Proposition 13, for example, strictly limits property tax increases to 2% annually and only allows reassessment at market value when ownership changes. However, California law specifically excludes transfers to revocable living trusts from constituting "changes in ownership" for reassessment purposes when the transferor is a present beneficiary and the property remains principal residence. Florida similarly excludes transfers to revocable trusts from triggering reassessment when homestead protection applies. Many other states have comparable exclusions or administrative policies recognizing that revocable trust transfers shouldn't trigger reassessment. However, the details—what types of trusts qualify, what documentation is required, what timeframes apply for claiming exemptions—vary significantly by jurisdiction.

To determine whether your specific state and county protect trust transfers from reassessment, research your state's property tax laws or contact your county property tax assessor's office. Key questions to ask include: Does state law exclude transfers to revocable living trusts from triggering reassessment? What specific requirements must be met for the exclusion to apply (must the trust be revocable, must the original owner remain beneficiary, must occupancy continue)? What forms or documentation must be filed to claim the exclusion? What timeframes apply for filing (often 45 days to 6 months after transfer)? Are there any circumstances where trust transfers would trigger reassessment despite general exclusions? Understanding these rules before transferring property—or immediately after if you've already transferred—enables you to take necessary steps to preserve current assessed values and avoid unwanted tax increases.

In rare cases where your jurisdiction doesn't protect trust transfers from reassessment, you must weigh the estate planning benefits of the trust against potential property tax increases. However, even in these jurisdictions, the increase may be modest if current assessed values are close to market value, or you might find administrative approaches that minimize increases. Additionally, the probate cost savings, incapacity protections, and family benefits trusts provide usually far exceed any property tax increases that might result. The biblical principle of counting costs before undertaking significant actions appears in Luke 14:28-30: "Suppose one of you wants to build a tower. Won't you first sit down and estimate the cost to see if you have enough money to complete it? For if you lay the foundation and are not able to finish it, everyone who sees it will ridicule you, saying, 'This person began to build and wasn't able to finish.'" Understanding property tax implications before transferring property is exactly this kind of cost-counting that ensures you can finish what you start.

Research reassessment rules, understand potential tax implications, and factor these into your decision about whether, when, and how to transfer property into your trust. This counting of costs prevents unpleasant surprises and ensures you make fully informed estate planning decisions.

Preserving Homestead and Other Property Tax Exemptions

Beyond the question of whether transfers trigger reassessment at higher values, homeowners must also address whether valuable property tax exemptions continue after transferring property into trusts. Homestead exemptions, available in most states, reduce the assessed value of owner-occupied primary residences by specified amounts—often $25,000 to $75,000 or more—significantly lowering annual property tax bills. To qualify, homeowners typically must own and occupy the property as their primary residence as of a specific date (often January 1st of the tax year). When property is transferred from individual to trust ownership, questions arise about whether homestead exemptions continue or must be reestablished under trust ownership.

Most states that offer homestead exemptions have laws or policies allowing exemptions to continue when property is transferred to the owner's revocable living trust, recognizing that occupancy and beneficial ownership haven't actually changed. However, counties often require filing specific forms or providing documentation to maintain exemptions after ownership changes. Common requirements include completing and filing homestead exemption continuation applications or certifications, providing copies of the recorded deed showing trust transfer, submitting trustee certifications proving the trust is revocable and you remain trustee and beneficiary, affirming continued occupancy of the property as primary residence, and sometimes providing copies of trust documents or excerpts proving trust structure. These filings typically must be completed within certain timeframes after the ownership change—often by December 31st of the year of transfer or by January 1st of the following tax year. Missing these deadlines can result in lost exemptions requiring reapplication.

Beyond homestead exemptions, other property tax benefits may require attention after trust transfers including senior citizen property tax reductions or freezes (available in many states for homeowners over certain ages), disabled veteran exemptions (for qualifying veterans or their surviving spouses), agricultural use valuations (for farmland or property used for agricultural purposes), historic property exemptions (for properties meeting historic preservation criteria), and various state-specific exemptions or special assessment programs. Each of these benefits may have its own rules about continuation after trust transfers, and each may require separate forms or documentation to maintain. Don't assume exemptions automatically continue; affirmatively verify each benefit you currently receive and complete necessary filings to maintain them.

To preserve exemptions after your trust transfer, immediately contact your county property tax assessor's office (usually accessible online or by phone) and inform them you've transferred property into your revocable living trust. Ask what forms are required to maintain homestead and other exemptions, request copies of necessary forms or links to download them, inquire about filing deadlines to ensure timely submission, and ask whether any additional documentation beyond forms is needed. Complete all required forms accurately and thoroughly, including copies of requested documentation (recorded deed, trustee certification, etc.), and submit them to the assessor's office before deadlines. Keep copies of everything you submit with proof of filing (certified mail receipts, online submission confirmations, date-stamped copies) for your records. After filing exemption continuation forms, monitor your next property tax bill to verify exemptions appear correctly with proper dollar amount reductions. If exemptions don't appear or assessments have increased inappropriately, immediately contact the assessor and be prepared to provide your filing documentation and argue for proper treatment.

The biblical principle of not losing what God has provided through neglect appears in Jesus's parable of the talents. In Matthew 25:18, Jesus describes a servant who received one talent but "went off, dug a hole in the ground and hid his master's money." This servant neglected what was entrusted to him, failing to use or preserve it productively, and ultimately lost even what he had. Property tax exemptions are benefits provided by law—talents entrusted to you by the civic "master" (government)—and neglecting to maintain them through required filings is like burying them where they're lost. The faithful steward actively maintains and preserves benefits entrusted to them, using proper procedures to ensure these benefits continue serving their purposes. File required forms, meet deadlines, provide necessary documentation, and preserve the exemptions that reduce your tax burden and allow more of your resources to serve your family rather than being paid unnecessarily in taxes.

Coordinating with Mortgage Escrow Accounts

Many homeowners with mortgages have escrow accounts (also called impound accounts) where monthly mortgage payments include amounts for property taxes that the lender holds in escrow and pays directly to tax authorities when due. If your mortgage includes such an escrow arrangement, coordinating property tax matters with your lender after transferring property to your trust ensures continued smooth payment processing and prevents disruptions that could cause missed payments, penalties, or confusion. When property ownership changes from individual to trust, several potential complications can arise with escrow accounts if not properly addressed.

First, property tax bills may begin being issued in the trust's name rather than your individual name. If the county assessor sends bills to different addresses or uses different payee names after the ownership change, the lender's escrow department might not receive bills or might not recognize them as relating to your property. This mismatch could cause the lender to fail to pay taxes from escrow, resulting in delinquency. To prevent this, ensure the county assessor knows your lender's escrow payment address and will continue sending bills there. Verify with both the assessor and your lender that tax bill routing will continue functioning properly after the ownership change. Provide the lender with copies of updated property tax bills showing the trust as owner so they can update their escrow records.

Second, if you notified your lender about the trust transfer (as discussed in previous chapters), provide them with updated property tax information at the same time. Send copies of property tax bills, exemption documentation, and assessed value information so the lender's escrow department can verify that taxes haven't increased inappropriately and that their escrow calculations remain accurate for the actual tax amounts. If you didn't notify the lender about the trust transfer, be particularly vigilant about monitoring escrow payments to ensure they continue processing correctly despite the ownership change the lender may not be aware of. Third, review your escrow account statements carefully for several billing cycles after transferring property. These statements typically show deposits into escrow (from your monthly payments), payments made from escrow (to tax authorities and insurance companies), and the escrow account balance. Verify that property tax payments are being made on schedule, that payment amounts match actual tax bills, that no delinquency notices or penalties are being assessed, and that escrow account balances remain appropriate for upcoming payments.

If you notice any discrepancies, missing payments, or unusual escrow activity, immediately contact your lender's escrow department to address problems before they result in tax delinquency or penalties. Fourth, if you don't have an escrow account and pay property taxes directly, ensure you continue receiving tax bills at the correct address after the trust transfer. Update the assessor's office with your current mailing address if it's changed or if you want bills sent to a trustee address rather than your personal address. Set up reminders or calendar alerts for payment due dates to ensure timely payment. Consider whether to establish automatic payments or other systems to ensure taxes are never missed even if you become incapacitated or otherwise unable to manage payments.

The biblical principle of faithful attention to ongoing financial obligations appears in Jesus's parable of the faithful servant managing his master's household. Luke 12:42 asks, "Who then is the faithful and wise manager, whom the master puts in charge of his servants to give them their food allowance at the proper time?" The faithful manager ensures obligations are met at proper times—food is provided when needed, payments are made when due. Managing property tax escrow accounts or direct payments is exactly this kind of faithful management, ensuring tax obligations are met at proper times (before delinquency) through proper means (escrow or direct payment). Don't assume this management continues automatically through ownership changes; actively verify and monitor to ensure faithful fulfillment of tax obligations throughout the transition and beyond.

Dealing with Reassessment Appeals and Disputes

Despite taking appropriate steps to claim reassessment exemptions and preserve property tax benefits, situations sometimes arise where county assessors nonetheless increase assessments or deny exemptions after trust transfers. When this occurs, understanding your appeal rights and procedures enables you to challenge improper assessments and secure the correct tax treatment. Property tax assessment appeals typically follow structured procedures established by state law. Common steps include informal review where you contact the assessor's office to explain the trust transfer and request correction, providing documentation showing the transfer qualifies for reassessment exclusion; formal written appeals filed with the county's assessment appeals board or review board within specific timeframes (often 30-60 days after receiving assessment notices); appeal hearings where you present evidence and arguments to the appeals board about why the assessment is incorrect; and judicial appeals to state courts if administrative appeals are unsuccessful.

The key to successful appeals is documentation proving your transfer qualifies for protection. Gather and organize copies of state statutes excluding trust transfers from reassessment, your recorded quitclaim deed showing transfer to revocable trust, trustee certification proving trust structure and your roles, evidence of continued occupancy (utility bills, voter registration, etc.), prior tax bills showing previous assessed value, forms you filed claiming reassessment exclusion, and correspondence with the assessor's office. Present this documentation clearly and concisely, explaining that your transfer meets all statutory requirements for exclusion from reassessment. Many appeals succeed simply because assessors weren't aware of or didn't properly apply exclusion laws, and providing clear evidence of qualification resolves disputes.

If informal or formal appeals don't succeed, consider engaging a property tax attorney or assessment appeal specialist who understands your state's laws and can advocate effectively. The cost of professional representation is often worthwhile if it prevents long-term property tax increases that could amount to thousands of dollars annually. Additionally, if your appeal is successful and results in assessment reduction, some jurisdictions allow retroactive correction of prior years' assessments, potentially entitling you to refunds for overpaid taxes. Don't hesitate to pursue appeals when assessors improperly increase assessments despite trust transfers qualifying for protection—you're not being difficult or unreasonable but simply ensuring correct application of law to your situation.

The biblical principle of not accepting improper treatment but standing up for what's right appears in Paul's actions when wrongly beaten and imprisoned in Philippi. Acts 16:37 records Paul saying, "They beat us publicly without a trial, even though we are Roman citizens, and threw us into prison. And now do they want to get rid of us quietly? No! Let them come themselves and escort us out." Paul stood up for his rights as a Roman citizen, refusing to accept improper treatment and demanding public acknowledgment of the wrong. While property tax disputes are far less serious than illegal imprisonment, the principle applies: when assessors improperly increase your assessments or deny exemptions despite your transfer qualifying for protection, don't quietly accept improper treatment. Stand up for proper application of law through appeals and if necessary, legal action. This isn't being contentious but pursuing justice and correct application of legal protections properly belonging to you.

Preparing Successor Trustees for Property Tax Management

After addressing immediate property tax matters following your trust transfer, turn attention to ensuring your successor trustee is prepared to manage property taxes when they eventually take over trust administration after your death or incapacity. Property tax obligations continue regardless of trustee changes, and your successor must understand how to receive tax bills, make timely payments, maintain exemptions, and address any assessment issues. Provide your successor trustee with comprehensive information about property tax matters including contact information for the county property tax assessor and treasurer/collector, your property's assessor parcel number (APN) for identifying it in county systems, information about what exemptions apply (homestead, senior, etc.) and how they're maintained, payment due dates and amounts for annual tax bills, whether taxes are paid through mortgage escrow or directly, and where you store copies of tax bills, exemption documentation, and payment records.

Create a section in your successor trustee instructions or trust administration manual specifically addressing property taxes. Explain what the successor should do when they take over: verify with the assessor that trust ownership is properly recorded and bills will be sent to the appropriate address; ensure exemptions continue or determine what steps are needed to maintain them; review assessed values to ensure they're appropriate and appeal if they're not; understand payment obligations and due dates; maintain a system for timely payment whether through escrow, direct payment, or other means; and keep organized records of all tax bills, payments, exemptions, and correspondence. Additionally, alert your successor to potential complications they might face. After your death, property moving from a revocable trust (which was non-taxable during your life because you controlled it) to an irrevocable trust or to beneficiaries might trigger reassessment in some jurisdictions. Your successor should understand this possibility and be prepared to address it, potentially through appeals or by working with your estate planning attorney to structure distributions in ways that minimize tax impacts.

If property will remain in the trust for extended periods after your death (perhaps in ongoing trust for minor beneficiaries or in a spousal trust for your surviving spouse's lifetime), your successor must manage property taxes throughout this period. Ensure they understand this ongoing obligation and have systems in place for tracking, paying, and documenting taxes year after year. Provide your successor with contact information for your estate planning attorney, a property tax professional, or accountant who can advise them about property tax matters during trust administration. Having professional guidance available helps successors navigate issues that arise without being paralyzed by uncertainty about proper procedures.

The biblical principle of preparing those who will follow you to fulfill responsibilities appears in Moses's preparation of Joshua for leadership. Deuteronomy 31:7-8 records Moses addressing Joshua: "Be strong and courageous, for you must go with this people into the land that the Lord swore to their ancestors to give them, and you must divide it among them as their inheritance. The Lord himself goes before you and will be with you; he will never leave you nor forsake you. Do not be afraid; do not be discouraged." Moses didn't just appoint Joshua and walk away; he prepared Joshua, encouraged him, and ensured he understood the responsibilities ahead. Similarly, don't just name a successor trustee without preparing them for the property tax obligations they'll face. Provide information, create systems, offer encouragement, and connect them with professional support. This preparation enables your successor to confidently manage property taxes and fulfill their trustee responsibilities faithfully.

Record-Keeping and Documentation Systems

Proper record-keeping regarding property taxes serves multiple important functions: providing evidence of timely payment if disputes arise about delinquency, documenting exemption eligibility for assessor reviews or appeals, tracking assessment changes over time to identify inappropriate increases, and enabling successor trustees to understand property tax history and current status. Establish comprehensive property tax record-keeping systems that organize and preserve important documentation. Create a property tax file or section within your larger property file containing annual property tax bills (keep at least 3-5 years), payment receipts or bank records showing tax payments, exemption application and approval documents, correspondence with the assessor or treasurer about tax matters, assessment notices showing property values, records of any appeals or disputes and their outcomes, and forms filed after the trust transfer to maintain exemptions and avoid reassessment.

Organize these documents chronologically—most recent year at the front, older years behind—so information is easily accessible and historical trends are visible. Create a simple cover sheet or summary for the property tax file listing current assessed value, current annual tax amount, what exemptions apply and their dollar amounts, payment due dates and methods, and any special circumstances or issues to be aware of. Update this summary annually when new tax bills arrive so current information is always readily available at a glance. Store property tax records with your other trust documents and property files in secure, accessible locations. Keep physical copies in fireproof filing cabinets or safes, and consider creating digital copies stored in cloud services or on external drives as backup. However, preserve original receipts and notices as these may be required to prove payment or exemption eligibility if disputes arise.

Beyond organizing historical records, establish systems for managing ongoing property tax responsibilities. Set calendar reminders for key dates including when tax bills typically arrive (to notice if they don't), payment due dates (to ensure timely payment), exemption renewal dates if any exemptions require periodic renewal, and dates by which appeals must be filed if assessments are incorrect. If you pay taxes directly (not through escrow), consider setting up automatic bank transfers to a tax savings account where you deposit amounts monthly so funds are available when annual or semi-annual tax bills arrive. This approach prevents the financial burden of large lump-sum payments and ensures funds are available when needed. Document your property tax management system in a memo to yourself and your successor trustee explaining where records are kept, what reminders are set, what payment systems exist, and what steps should be taken to maintain exemptions and proper assessments annually. This documentation enables continuity—if you become incapacitated or die, your successor can immediately understand and continue your property tax management system rather than starting from scratch.

The biblical principle of careful record-keeping in financial and administrative matters appears throughout Scripture. In 2 Kings 12:4-15, detailed records were kept of money collected for temple repairs, how it was spent, and who was responsible. Verse 15 notes, "They did not require an accounting from those to whom they gave the money to pay the workers, because they acted with complete honesty." Good records support honest administration and accountability. Your property tax records similarly support honest, accountable administration of trust assets, providing evidence of proper payment and stewardship. Maintain these records carefully as part of faithful trust administration that can withstand any scrutiny or questioning about whether obligations were met properly.

Conclusion: Faithful Management of Civic Obligations

Managing property taxes after transferring homes into living trusts encompasses both immediate administrative tasks—updating county records, filing exemption forms, coordinating with lenders—and ongoing responsibilities that continue throughout property ownership and trust administration. While these obligations may seem burdensome, they're simply the continuation of civic duties homeowners have always borne, with minor adjustments needed to reflect trust ownership structure. The faithful steward approaches these duties not as irritating formalities but as opportunities to demonstrate responsible citizenship, honest payment of legitimate obligations, and wise preservation of legal benefits that allow more resources to serve family rather than being unnecessarily paid in excess taxes.

The biblical teaching about civic obligations and property taxes is clear and direct. Romans 13:6-7 instructs, "This is also why you pay taxes, for the authorities are God's servants, who give their full time to governing. Give to everyone what you owe them: If you owe taxes, pay taxes; if revenue, then revenue; if respect, then respect; if honor, then honor." Property taxes are part of "what you owe" to local government authorities who provide essential services. These obligations continue after trust transfers, and the faithful steward ensures they're met promptly and fully. However, paying what you owe doesn't mean paying more than you owe, and taking appropriate steps to preserve exemptions, avoid inappropriate reassessments, and claim legal protections isn't tax evasion but responsible management ensuring you pay what's properly owed—no more, no less.

As you manage property taxes for trust-owned property throughout your lifetime and as you prepare your successor to continue this management after you're gone, commit this stewardship to the Lord along with all other trust administration responsibilities. Proverbs 16:3 promises, "Commit to the Lord whatever you do, and he will establish your plans." When you approach property tax management with integrity—paying what's owed, preserving legitimate benefits, maintaining good records, preparing successors—you demonstrate the faithful, honest stewardship that pleases God. Trust that this faithful attention to civic obligations, combined with commitment to the Lord, establishes your plans—your property taxes will be managed properly, your estate planning will function as intended, and your property will be preserved to serve your family rather than being eroded by unnecessary tax increases or lost to delinquency through neglect. Walk forward confidently in faithful stewardship of both civic tax obligations and family provision, knowing that excellence in both honors God and serves the common good.

***

Section 3: Keeping Trust Records Current

Keeping trust records current is a core responsibility in estate planning. After assets are transferred into a trust, ongoing maintenance ensures the structure remains effective and legally sound. Document every new asset, ownership change, and beneficiary adjustment promptly. Neglecting updates can create confusion for successor trustees, complicate proof of ownership, and undermine the protection the trust is designed to provide.

An updated schedule of assets is essential. It should list all property held by the trust—real estate, bank and brokerage accounts, business interests, and significant personal property—with identifying details such as account numbers, parcel IDs, and legal descriptions. Each time an asset is added or removed, revise the schedule and have the trustee sign and date the update. Maintain copies of deeds, account titling confirmations, and transfer receipts to preserve a clear chain of ownership.

Organized records enable successor trustees to act efficiently. A comprehensive trust binder (or secure digital vault) should include the trust instrument, amendments, trustee certifications, schedules of assets, recorded deeds, account statements, insurance policies, tax filings related to the trust, and contact information for attorneys and advisors. Clear indexing and version control reduce delays, support accurate distributions, and provide an audit-ready trail if questions arise.

Review and update trust records during major life events and at set intervals. Marriage, divorce, births, deaths, incapacity, relocations, refinances, and significant acquisitions often require changes to beneficiaries, successor trustees, or distribution instructions. An annual or semiannual review—paired with a checklist—helps ensure titling is correct, insurance reflects current ownership, and tax and reporting requirements remain compliant.

Consistency across institutions is critical. Confirm that banks, brokerages, insurers, and county recorders show the trust's exact legal name and trustee capacity. Align vesting language, beneficiary designations, and pay-on-death/transfer-on-death instructions with the trust plan to avoid conflicts. Record deeds promptly, retain acknowledgments of notice, and document all trustee decisions and communications, especially those affecting rights, obligations, risk, or value.

Finally, safeguard access and continuity. Store originals securely, back up digital records, and ensure successor trustees know where to find documents and credentials. Use multi-factor authentication for financial accounts and keep an access log. These practices minimize disruption, prevent administrative gaps, and keep the trust ready for effective administration when it matters most.

***

Section 4: What to Do If You Refinance or Sell

Refinancing or selling a home held in a trust requires careful coordination so the transaction stays compliant and on schedule. Many lenders prefer to process refinances when title is in the borrower's individual name. Practically, this often means deeding the property out of the trust into your name for closing, then promptly re-deeding it back into the trust once the loan funds and records. Confirm timing with the lender and title company, and plan the re-transfer immediately after funding to preserve your estate plan.

When selling a property titled in a trust, the trustee is the legal seller. All sale documents and the deed must be executed by the trustee in their official capacity, using the exact trust name and date as it appears on record. Expect buyers, title companies, and escrow to request a trustee certification or affidavit of trust to verify authority. Provide clear, current documentation to prevent delays and ensure the chain of title remains clean.

During refinancing, lenders may request specific trust pages or, preferably, a trustee certification that confirms the trust is revocable, the borrower's beneficial interest, and the trustee's authority. Respond quickly to document requests and verify that the vesting on the new mortgage aligns with the post-closing plan (i.e., returning title to the trust). If the lender will allow the property to remain in trust, confirm acceptable vesting language in advance.

After a sale or refinance, update your trust records immediately. If you sold the property, remove it from the trust's schedule of assets and retain closing statements, the reconveyance, and final settlement documents in your files. If you refinanced and re-transferred title to the trust, record the new deed, update the trust's asset schedule, and notify your homeowner's and title insurers so the trust or trustee is correctly listed.

Coordinate with your escrow and tax authorities as needed. Ensure property tax billing and, if applicable, escrow accounts reflect the correct vesting after closing. If you maintain homestead or other exemptions, confirm whether any affidavits or notices are required to preserve them following vesting changes. Keep an audit-ready trail: recorded deeds, certifications, policies, statements, and correspondence organized in your trust binder for successor trustee access.

Treat refinance or sale events as checkpoints to verify accuracy across title, insurance, lender records, and trust documentation. Clear communication, precise vesting language, and prompt post-closing updates reduce risk, prevent administrative gaps, and keep your estate plan intact.

Chapter 8:
Legal and Ethical Boundaries

Estate planning is a framework for protection, not a loophole for evasion. Transferring property into a trust must be guided by lawful conduct and clear ethics—protecting your family without misrepresenting obligations or intent. Motive and method both matter: a sound plan pairs accurate documentation with honest communication, reducing risk and preserving credibility.

Fraudulent conveyance is a bright legal line. If a transfer is made to hinder known creditors or evade lawful claims, courts can unwind the deed, impose penalties, and damage your standing with institutions and heirs. Ethical planning faces obligations directly—negotiating, restructuring, or settling when necessary—rather than hiding behind legal structures.

Privacy and transparency must be balanced. Trustees should protect sensitive details (beneficiaries, distribution terms, financial specifics) while meeting disclosure duties. Silence that excludes rightful parties or creates a misleading impression undermines administration and fuels disputes. Selective, timely communication—focused on material facts and rights—prevents conflict and equips successors to act effectively.

Compliance with tax and reporting requirements is nonnegotiable. Homestead exemptions, reassessment rules, and filings tied to trust ownership must be handled accurately and on time. Misreporting or omission can lead to fines, loss of exemptions, and increased scrutiny. Treat numbers, notices, and deadlines as core governance, not back-office afterthoughts.

Trustee authority requires accountability. Fiduciary duties—loyalty, prudence, impartiality—demand organized records, conflict-free decisions, and a consistent focus on beneficiaries' interests over personal convenience. Ethical trustees seek professional counsel when needed, document decisions, and maintain an audit-ready trail that can withstand review.

Timing and intent are part of the boundary set. Transfers during insolvency, active litigation, or delinquency call for heightened caution and professional guidance to avoid the appearance of impropriety. If a transaction could materially affect creditors or counterparties, disclose appropriately and structure the action within legal safe harbors.

Ultimately, legal and ethical boundaries act as protective rails for legacy building. They anchor your trust in orderly records, honest disclosures, and fair dealings—reducing exposure, preserving relationships, and ensuring your plan accomplishes what it promises. Align actions with the law, keep stakeholders properly informed, and let integrity define your approach.

***

Section 1: When silence becomes misrepresentation

Silence is not inherently deceptive, but it can become misrepresentation when material facts are withheld from parties who have a legal or contractual right to know. In estate planning and trust administration, this typically involves beneficiaries, lenders, tax authorities, or courts. If nondisclosure creates a false impression about ownership, authority, asset status, or intent, it functions like an inaccurate statement. The key test is whether a reasonable person would consider the withheld fact essential to making informed decisions.

Intent and duty are the dividing lines. Discretion is appropriate when privacy is lawful and no disclosure duty exists; misrepresentation occurs when a person knows their silence will mislead in a context where there is an obligation to speak. Examples include failing to notify a lender when the mortgage contract requires notice of a title transfer, omitting beneficiary communications that affect their rights, or withholding information in tax filings that changes ownership or valuation.

Fiduciary roles heighten the risk. Trustees owe duties of loyalty, prudence, and impartiality. Withholding material information from beneficiaries—such as asset sales, changes in distribution timing, or significant risks—can breach those duties and lead to disputes, surcharge actions, or removal. Accurate, timely communication, supported by organized records, maintains trust and reduces the chance of litigation.

Legal compliance also sets firm boundaries. Required notices (e.g., creditor notifications, statutory beneficiary reports, lender or insurer updates) must be delivered as specified. Silence where regulations or contracts demand disclosure can result in penalties, claim denials, loan acceleration, or court sanctions. Even if no explicit notice is required, omissions that create a misleading record can complicate audits, refinances, and future transfers.

Practical guidelines help avoid misrepresentation by silence:

- **Identify duties:** Map who is entitled to information

(beneficiaries, lenders, insurers, tax authorities) and what must be disclosed.

- **Define "material":** Treat facts as material if they change rights, obligations, risk, or value.
- **Document communication:** Use dated notices, trustee certifications, and receipt acknowledgments; keep a clear audit trail.
- **Use appropriate summaries:** Provide trustee certifications or memoranda when full documents aren't required, ensuring key facts are still conveyed.
- **Review timing:** During delinquency, litigation, or major asset changes, increase transparency and seek legal advice.

A simple decision framework keeps actions aligned:

1. **Do I owe a duty to this party?**
2. **Would silence create a false impression about a material fact?**
3. **Is disclosure required by law, contract, or fiduciary standards?**
   If any answer is "yes," communicate clearly, limit disclosures to what's necessary, and record the interaction. This approach preserves privacy without crossing into misrepresentation, protects relationships, and reduces legal exposure.

***

Section 2: State-specific laws and lender rights

State-specific laws shape how property transfers into trusts are recorded, taxed, and enforced, and they directly affect lender rights tied to mortgages and deeds of trust. Key differences include recording requirements, homestead and reassessment rules, trustee authority standards, and timelines for notices or challenges. Understanding your state's statutes and administrative practices helps you avoid delays, preserve exemptions, and prevent unintended loan consequences.

Due-on-sale and trust transfers are influenced by both federal protections and state interpretations. While many lenders accept transfers to revocable trusts when the borrower remains a beneficiary and occupant, states vary in how title is vested, how trustee capacity must be shown on deeds, and whether specific affidavits or certifications are required. Some jurisdictions use mortgages; others use deeds of trust with different foreclosure procedures, cure periods, and trustee sale rules that affect lender remedies if obligations aren't met.

Recording and title standards differ across counties and states. Deeds must use precise trust names, trustee capacity language, and legal descriptions that meet local formatting rules. Certain states require additional acknowledgments (e.g., homestead consent from a spouse), trust certifications, or entity authority documents for corporate trustees. Failure to meet these technical standards can result in rejection at the recorder's office, clouded title, or delays in refinancing and sales.

Homestead, reassessment, and transfer tax implications can be state-specific. Some states allow homeowners to retain homestead or similar exemptions after transferring to a revocable trust, provided occupancy and beneficiary conditions are met; others require filings or affidavits to preserve the benefit. Reassessment triggers vary: in some jurisdictions, trust transfers among certain family members may avoid reassessment if statutory requirements and deadlines are met. Transfer taxes or documentary fees may apply depending on the nature of the transfer and whether consideration is exchanged.

Lender notification and consent requirements can be contract- and state-driven. Mortgage agreements may contain clauses requiring notice of title changes or specifying when consent is needed. Even where federal law limits enforcement of due-on-sale clauses for certain trust transfers, lenders may still request documentation to confirm beneficial ownership and occupancy. Providing a trustee certification (instead of the full trust) is commonly accepted, but some lenders or title companies may require excerpts showing trustee powers and revocability.

Insurance and escrow coordination is often governed by lender servicing policies and state insurance regulations. After a trust transfer, insurers may need to list the trust or trustee as an insured party, and escrow accounts must reflect the correct vesting for taxes and premiums. In states with strict proof-of-coverage rules, lenders may impose force-placed insurance if documentation isn't updated promptly—raising costs and complicating future claims.

Foreclosure, default, and cure rights vary widely. In deed-of-trust states, nonjudicial foreclosure timelines can be shorter, with specific notice and sale procedures; in mortgage states, judicial foreclosure typically requires court action and longer timelines. Trust ownership does not shield a property from lender remedies. State law determines deficiency judgments, reinstatement rights, and redemption periods, all of which affect strategy during hardship or dispute.

Practical steps to align with state law and lender rights:

- **Verify local deed requirements:** Confirm vesting language, trustee capacity, and any homestead or spousal acknowledgments.
- **Preserve exemptions and filings:** File required affidavits to maintain homestead or avoid reassessment where available.
- **Review your mortgage contract:** Identify notification or consent clauses related to title changes and respond accordingly.
- **Use trustee certifications:** Provide concise documents that establish authority, revocability, and occupancy without over-disclosing.
- **Update insurance and escrow:** Ensure the trust or trustee is

listed correctly; confirm tax billing reflects current vesting.

- **Document everything:** Keep recorded deeds, certifications, lender correspondence, and policy updates in an organized, audit-ready file.

Because policies and laws vary, coordinate early with a local title company, your lender, and counsel familiar with state statutes and county practices. This ensures your trust transfer respects lender rights, meets legal standards, and keeps your estate plan intact.

***

Section 3: How to protect yourself legally

Protecting yourself legally when creating, funding, or administering a trust begins with competent professional advice. Engage an estate planning attorney who is licensed in your state and experienced with local real property, tax, and trust laws. A qualified attorney will draft documents that reflect your objectives, ensure proper vesting language, and advise on state-specific filing, exemption, and notice requirements that a generic form cannot address.

Use precise, consistent documentation for every transfer and action. Prepare and record deeds with the trust's exact legal name and trustee capacity, obtain signed acknowledgments, and keep copies of transfer receipts, title insurance policies, and closing statements. Where possible, provide trustee certifications instead of entire trust documents to limit disclosure while still meeting third-party verification needs.

Confirm and maintain appropriate insurance and title protection. Update homeowner's insurance and list the trust or trustee as an insured party; verify that escrow accounts and premium payments remain uninterrupted. Review your title insurance and consider endorsements or reissuance that expressly cover trust ownership and successor trustees to guard against future title disputes.

Respect creditor and tax obligations to avoid allegations of fraudulent conveyance. Do not transfer assets with the intent to frustrate known creditors or to evade pending judgments. If you anticipate insolvency, litigation, or creditor claims, consult counsel before transferring assets so transactions can be structured or documented to withstand scrutiny under state fraudulent-transfer laws.

Observe fiduciary duties and institutional requirements. Trustees must act with loyalty, prudence, and impartiality; document decisions, avoid conflicts of interest, and obtain independent valuations for significant transactions. Follow mortgage and lender requirements for notice or consent when title changes occur, and get lender approvals or confirmations in writing when needed for refinances or sales.

Keep organized, current records and an audit trail. Maintain a trust binder—physical and/or encrypted digital—with the trust instrument, amendments, asset schedules, deeds, account statements, tax returns, insurance policies, and correspondence. Date and sign amendments and schedules; record communications with lenders, insurers, and beneficiaries so actions can be justified later.

Plan for continuity and access. Name successor trustees and backup signers, prepare trustee certifications, and provide secure instructions for where originals and digital credentials are stored. Use multi-factor authentication on financial accounts, document access permissions, and give successors a clear checklist for post-transfer duties to minimize administrative disruption.

When in doubt, get written opinions and rely on specialists. Use local title companies for recording checks, retain a CPA for tax consequences, and consult trust litigation counsel if disputes arise. Proactive, documented legal guidance is the best protection—structured advice and careful recordkeeping significantly reduce risk and preserve the effectiveness of your estate plan.

***

Section 4: When to seek professional advice

Knowing when to involve a professional is one of the most important choices you can make in estate planning. Consult an estate planning attorney before you draft or sign trust documents, transfer real property, or make changes that could affect ownership or beneficiary rights. An attorney can ensure the trust language matches your goals, confirm proper vesting, and identify state-specific requirements that generic forms and DIY kits often miss.

Seek advice when your financial or family situation is complex. If you own a business, have significant retirement accounts, hold property in multiple states, or expect contested heirs, professional guidance helps you structure the trust to reduce tax exposure, avoid ancillary probate, and mitigate litigation risk. Complex asset titling, beneficiary designations, and business succession plans almost always benefit from specialist review.

Reach out to professionals at pivotal events: marriage, divorce, birth or adoption, death of a spouse or beneficiary, relocation to another state, or a large asset acquisition or sale. These life changes commonly require updates to trustees, beneficiaries, funding strategies, and exemptions. An annual or biennial checkup with counsel or a trusted advisor keeps records accurate and prevents small issues from becoming legal problems.

Get counsel before refinancing, selling, or re-mortgaging property titled to a trust. Lenders and title companies have precise documentation requirements; without verification you may trigger due-on-sale clauses, force-placed insurance, or title defects. A quick review by your attorney or title professional can confirm acceptable vesting language, advise on deed mechanics, and help coordinate mortgage tasks without jeopardizing the trust structure.

Consult specialists for tax and accounting issues. If transfers may affect estate, gift, or income tax exposure—or if the trust will generate income that requires tax reporting—work with a CPA or tax attorney who understands trust taxation. Accurate filings, timely elections, and clear documentation reduce audit risk and preserve exemptions or stepped-up basis where applicable.

Finally, seek immediate legal help if there is potential conflict, creditor pressure, or litigation. If a creditor claim, divorce, bankruptcy, or lawsuit is imminent or pending, don't rely on ad hoc solutions: prompt counsel can advise on timing, structure, and protective measures to reduce the chance of a challenged transfer or unnecessary exposure. Professional advice at the right moments protects your assets, clarifies responsibilities, and ensures that your estate plan performs as intended.

Chapter 9:

Real-Life Scenarios

Real-life scenarios illuminate common pitfalls and practical responses when a home is placed in a trust. Consider a straightforward transfer where the deed is recorded but the homeowner never notifies the insurer or lender. Months later, a claim is submitted and coverage is disputed because the policy name doesn't match trust vesting. The immediate remedy is documentation: produce the recorded deed, request an endorsement from the insurer listing the trust or trustee, and obtain a written confirmation from the lender that coverage and escrow remain intact. Prevent this by adding a post-transfer checklist that includes insurer, lender, county recorder, and tax assessor notifications.

Refinance matters often create urgent timelines. A borrower who refinanced without confirming trustee certification requirements found the closing delayed while the title company demanded trust excerpts and a new trustee signature page. Best practice is to confirm lender and title company document needs in advance; if the lender requires a temporary reconveyance, schedule a retransfer back to the trust immediately after closing and record the new deed without delay. Keep standardized trustee certification templates and a trusted title contact to shorten response times.

Selling a trust-owned property changes who signs and how title is conveyed. In one example, a buyer's escrow held up closing while the trustee's authority was verified because the sale documents used the trustee's name informally instead of the trust's full legal name. Always execute sale documents in the trustee's official capacity using exact vesting language, provide a notarized trustee certification, and attach a copy of the recorded trust instrument excerpt showing execution authority where required by local practice.

Creditors and contested transfers present higher stakes. A homeowner who transferred the property while anticipating a lawsuit faced a creditor challenge alleging fraudulent conveyance. The court investigated intent and timing; the transfer was upheld only after the homeowner produced contemporaneous counsel opinions, settlement negotiations records, and documentation showing the transfer was part of normal estate planning rather than an attempt to hide assets. When litigation risk exists, obtain written legal advice before transferring assets and preserve an audit trail that explains timing, purpose, and lack of intent to defraud.

Trustee incapacity, death, or removal can create administrative friction if records are incomplete. A successor trustee unable to locate original deeds, account statements, or the trustee certification had to request replacements and wait for record searches—delaying distributions. Mitigate this by maintaining an indexed trust binder or encrypted digital vault, keeping certified copies of recorded deeds, and providing successor trustees with a concise "first steps" checklist and contact list for advisors and institutions.

Multi-state and multi-asset situations add complexity. A homeowner with property in two states discovered differing county recording rules and unexpected transfer taxes after a single trust transfer. Coordinate early with local counsel and title professionals in each jurisdiction, confirm homestead and reassessment rules where applicable, and treat each asset transfer as a distinct administrative task—update insurance, escrow, tax records, and beneficiary designations per location to avoid surprises.

Each scenario yields a common set of preventative measures: plan transfers with local counsel and a title professional, document motives and steps contemporaneously, confirm institutional requirements before closing, maintain an organized, accessible records system, and use concise trustee certifications when full disclosure is unnecessary. These habits turn reactive fixes into routine administration and keep your trust functioning reliably when real life demands action.

***

Section 1: Case studies of successful transfers

Successful trust transfers share common traits: clear planning, precise documentation, timely communication with institutions, and an organized post-transfer process. The first case involves a single-family homeowner who executed a revocable living trust and transferred title before retirement. The attorney prepared the deed with the trust's exact legal name and trustee capacity, the homeowner provided a trustee certification to the lender and insurer, and the title company issued an endorsement listing the trust as an insured party. Because all parties received consistent documentation and the homeowner kept a recorded-deed copy in a centralized trust binder, later transactions—insurance claims and a simple sale—proceeded without dispute or delay.

A second case highlights refinancing coordination. A couple planning a rate-and-term refinance confirmed lender requirements two months in advance. Their attorney drafted a reconveyance plan: deed the property temporarily out of the trust for closing, coordinate the closing date with the recordation of the new mortgage, and have the title company immediately re-deed the property into the trust post-funding. The title company used preapproved vesting language and the lender accepted a trustee certification in lieu of the full trust. The refinance closed on schedule and the trust's asset schedule was updated the next business day, preserving estate goals and lender comfort.

Multi-state holdings present extra complexity, demonstrated by a homeowner with residences in two states. The owner engaged local counsel in each jurisdiction to confirm recording formats, reassessment triggers, and transfer-tax exceptions. Each deed followed county formatting rules; homestead exemptions were preserved via local affidavits; and escrow accounts were updated separately for each mortgage. Because the transfers were staged and coordinated with title professionals, the owner avoided reassessment surprises and preserved exemptions where statutory relief applied.

A fourth case focuses on lender and insurer alignment. After transferring a property, the trustee proactively contacted the mortgage servicer and insurer with a trustee certification and a copy of the recorded deed. The insurer issued an endorsement naming the trust as an additional insured, and the servicer confirmed escrow continuity in writing. When a windstorm claim arose later, the policy and lender records matched trust vesting, preventing coverage disputes and force-placed insurance. That proactive outreach saved time and avoided additional expense.

Succession planning was central to another successful transfer. A grantor created detailed successor trustee instructions, prepared notarized trustee certifications in advance, and stored original recorded deeds in a safety deposit box with a duplicate digital copy in an encrypted vault accessible to the named successor upon proof of authority. When the successor trustee assumed duties, they immediately had authority documentation, beneficiary contact lists, and an indexed asset schedule—allowing fast account access, timely bill payment, and orderly distributions without court involvement.

Across these case studies the recurring best practices are clear: engage local experts early, use exact vesting language, prefer trustee certifications when possible to limit disclosure, notify lenders and insurers promptly, stage multi-jurisdiction transfers thoughtfully, and maintain an audit-ready trust binder. Implementing these steps turns potential administrative headaches into routine procedures, protects title and coverage, and ensures your trust functions as intended when it matters most.

***

Section 2: Common mistakes and how to avoid them

One of the most frequent errors is failing to fully fund the trust. People sign the trust document but never retitle assets—especially real estate—into the trust's name, leaving the estate plan ineffective for probate avoidance. Avoid this by creating a detailed funding checklist, tracking each asset until a recorded deed, retitled account, or beneficiary designation reflects the trust. Treat funding as a project with deadlines, not a single paperwork event.

Incorrect or inconsistent vesting on deeds and accounts creates title defects and delays. Small variations in the trust's legal name, missing trustee capacity language, or sloppy legal descriptions can lead recorders and title companies to reject documents. Prevent problems by using the exact trust name and trustee wording the attorney used, confirm county formatting rules before recording, and have the title company or attorney review all vesting language prior to submission.

Not notifying lenders, insurers, and service providers invites coverage gaps and administrative friction. If mortgage servicers and insurers don't have proof of trust vesting, lenders may impose force-placed insurance or escrow misapplication, and claims may be disputed. Mitigate this by sending a trustee certification and recorded deed copies to lenders and insurers immediately after recording, then request written confirmation that accounts and escrow remain aligned.

Assuming homestead, exemption, and tax benefits automatically transfer to a trust leads to costly surprises. Many jurisdictions require affidavits or filings to preserve homestead status, and reassessment rules differ widely. Check local rules before transferring; file required affidavits or exemption forms promptly; and consult a local title professional to confirm which actions preserve tax benefits and which trigger reassessment or transfer taxes.

Poor recordkeeping and inaccessible documents hinder successor trustees. Originals misplaced, undocumented transfers, and missing account credentials can delay distributions and result in court intervention.

Build an indexed trust binder (physical and encrypted digital copy), keep certified copies of recorded deeds, and provide successor trustees with a clear "first steps" checklist and access instructions.

Overreliance on DIY forms or generic templates can produce documents that don't match state law or unique family circumstances. These templates often miss local filing nuances, trustee powers, or creditor exceptions. Use state-licensed estate counsel for drafting or at least have a local attorney review any template to confirm compliance with recording and fiduciary standards.

Neglecting to update beneficiary designations and successor trustee appointments creates conflicts between account paperwork and trust terms. Retirement accounts, life insurance, and payable-on-death designations take precedence over trust instructions unless retitled or reassigned. During reviews, align beneficiary designations with trust goals or use trust-qualified beneficiary designations where appropriate.

Timing transfers poorly—during pending litigation, creditor threats, or approaching insolvency—can trigger fraudulent-transfer challenges. Avoid last-minute retitling if legal exposure exists; seek counsel before making transfers so transactions can be structured, documented, or postponed to reduce challenge risk.

Selecting an unsuitable trustee or failing to prepare them is a common governance failure. Choose trustees for competence and impartiality, name backups, and prepare trustee certifications and administrative instructions in advance. Offer training or a short orientation packet so successors understand duties, account access steps, and key contacts.

Finally, failing to consult specialists for complex tax, multi-state, or business-ownership issues increases exposure. Work with a coordinated team—estate attorney, CPA, and local title professional—especially when dealing with multi-jurisdiction property, trust taxation, or business succession. Proactive professional input prevents predictable errors and turns a one-time transfer into a durable, administrable estate plan.

***

Section 2.1: Steps and instructions to follow for this chapter

1. Create a funding checklist and timeline

1.1 List every asset to transfer (real estate, bank accounts, brokerage, retirement, business interests, personal property). 1.2 For each asset, note current title, required transfer method, responsible party, and target completion date. 1.3 Assign tasks and set reminders; mark each item complete only after recorded deed, retitle confirmation, or updated beneficiary form is received.

2. Verify exact vesting and deed language

2.1 Copy the trust's exact legal name and trustee wording from the executed trust instrument. 2.2 Confirm county recorder formatting requirements (legal description, notarization, acknowledgments) before preparing the deed. 2.3 Have your attorney or title company review the deed prior to recording; obtain a recording receipt.

3. Notify and document with institutions

3.1 Prepare a concise trustee certification template and a cover letter summarizing the transfer. 3.2 Send the recorded deed and trustee certification to mortgage servicers, insurers, brokerages, banks, and any servicers; request written acknowledgement. 3.3 Save all confirmation emails, letters, and account statements in the trust binder.

4. Preserve tax and exemption status

4.1 Research local homestead, reassessment, and transfer-tax rules or consult local counsel. 4.2 File any required affidavits or exemption forms promptly after recording. 4.3 Track reassessment deadlines; if reassessment is a risk, consider staged transfers or alternative planning with counsel.

5. Maintain an organized, audit-ready trust binder

5.1 Include: trust instrument and amendments, trustee certifications, schedules of assets, recorded deeds, account statements, insurance policies, tax filings, and contact list for advisors. 5.2 Keep originals in a secure physical location and encrypted digital copies with restricted access. 5.3 Implement version control (date-and-sign each update) and an index page for quick reference.

6. Align beneficiary designations and account titling

6.1 Review beneficiary forms on retirement, life insurance, and payable-on-death accounts; determine whether to retitle or change beneficiaries to match trust objectives. 6.2 Where appropriate, use trust-qualified beneficiary designations drafted with counsel. 6.3 Reconcile any conflicts between account paperwork and trust terms and document decisions.

7. Coordinate refinances, sales, and lender requirements

7.1 Before scheduling a refinance or sale, request lender and title company document checklists and timing constraints. 7.2 If a temporary reconveyance is required, schedule retransfer back to the trust immediately after funding and record the new deed quickly. 7.3 Confirm escrow, insurance, and tax billing updates in writing post-closing.

8. Choose and prepare trustees

8.1 Select trustees for competence and impartiality; name successor trustees and backups. 8.2 Prepare a trustee packet containing certifications, access instructions, asset schedule, contact list, and a "first steps" checklist. 8.3 Consider a brief orientation meeting or written guidance to ensure readiness.

9. Implement security and access controls

9.1 Use multi-factor authentication for financial accounts and secure password managers for credentials. 9.2 Maintain an access log for anyone who views or modifies trust records. 9.3 Establish clear procedures for successor access (where originals are stored, how to obtain digital credentials).

10. Engage professionals at key points

10.1 Retain a state-licensed estate attorney for drafting, deed work, and legal advice. 10.2 Use a CPA for tax impact analysis and filings related to trust income, transfers, or estate/gift considerations. 10.3 Coordinate with local title companies and insurers for recording, endorsements, and escrow alignment.

11. Perform periodic reviews and audits

11.1 Schedule annual or biennial reviews to confirm titles, beneficiary designations, insurance coverage, and asset schedules. 11.2 Conduct a post-transfer audit within 30–90 days after major transactions to verify recordings, endorsements, and institutional acknowledgements. 11.3 Update the checklist and binder after each review and retain dated evidence of the audit.

12. Prepare for litigation risk or creditor exposure

12.1 Before transferring assets when claims or litigation are foreseeable, obtain written legal counsel and document the purpose and timing of transfers. 12.2 Preserve contemporaneous evidence (emails, invoices, counsel opinions) showing legitimate estate-planning intent. 12.3 If challenged, provide the audit trail and rationale to defend against allegations of fraudulent transfer.

Follow these steps as a practical workflow: plan and document each transfer, confirm institutional and local legal requirements in advance, maintain organized records, prepare trustees, and consult professionals at decision points. Consistent application of this process minimizes common mistakes and keeps your trust administrable and defensible.

***

Section 3: Lessons learned from quiet transfers

Quiet transfers—retitling property into a trust without broad notification—can be efficient, but they carry hidden risks that surface later. A common lesson is that silence does not eliminate obligations: lenders, insurers, tax assessors, and successor trustees still need accurate records. When institutions discover a transfer only after an event (claim, refinance, sale), the delay often causes complications that could have been prevented with simple, targeted notifications.

Insurance mismatches are frequent consequences. Policies written to the individual owner may not automatically recognize a trust or trustee, leading to coverage disputes or force-placed insurance if the servicer detects a title discrepancy. The practical fix is proactive documentation—recorded deed, trustee certification, and insurer endorsement—sent immediately after transfer to confirm continuity of coverage and avoid unexpected costs.

Lender reactions vary and can be costly if ignored. Some mortgage agreements require notice for title changes or include due-on-sale language that, while often not enforced for transfers to revocable trusts, still prompts administrative holds or documentation demands. Advance coordination with the servicer and title company prevents last-minute hurdles during refinances or sales and avoids emergency reconveyances that add expense and delay.

Tax and exemption issues are easily overlooked. Homestead exemptions, reassessment triggers, and transfer taxes depend on jurisdictional rules; a quiet transfer can inadvertently revoke a benefit or trigger reassessment. The best practice is to confirm local requirements before recording and to file any required affidavits or exemption forms promptly to preserve tax positions.

Quiet transfers can create perception problems with beneficiaries and successors. Even when done for legitimate estate-planning reasons, failing to inform heirs or successor trustees may breed mistrust or lead to contested actions. Provide successors with a concise packet—trust certificate, asset schedule, and location of originals—so they can step in without delay and without needing court intervention.

Documentation and accessibility are the strongest defenses. Maintain an indexed trust binder and encrypted digital copies, record every transfer, and keep a dated audit trail of communications with lenders, insurers, title companies, and taxing authorities. When transactions are quiet by design, this audit trail becomes the proof that proper steps were taken and can resolve disputes quickly.

Use targeted, limited disclosure instead of broad secrecy. Trustee certifications and short cover letters often satisfy third-party verification needs without exposing full trust details. Work with counsel and title professionals to prepare the minimal documentation required by each institution, balancing privacy with the need for clear, material facts.

Finally, involve professionals when risk factors exist. If litigation, creditor claims, multi-state property, or tax-sensitive exemptions are present, obtain written legal and tax advice before transferring. Quiet transfers can be successful when executed with planning, communication to necessary parties, and meticulous recordkeeping—turning a discreet transaction into a defensible, administrable step in your estate plan.

***

Section 3.1: Steps and instructions to follow — Lessons learned from quiet transfers

1. Prepare a targeted notification plan

- Identify the minimal set of third parties who must know about the transfer (mortgage servicer, insurer, county recorder, tax assessor, title company).
- Draft concise cover letters and a trustee certification template that reveal only what each institution needs to verify authority and vesting.
- Schedule notifications to be sent immediately after recording; follow up until you receive written acknowledgement.

1. Confirm insurance continuity

- Contact your homeowner's insurer and mortgage servicer with a copy of the recorded deed and trustee certification.
- Request an endorsement or written confirmation that coverage and escrow will continue without interruption.
- If the insurer requires additional documentation, obtain it quickly to avoid force-placed insurance or claim denials.

1. Verify lender and servicer requirements in advance

- Review the mortgage documents for notice or vesting clauses and call the servicer to confirm acceptable documentation.
- If a refinance or sale is planned, ask the lender and title company for their exact checklist and timing constraints.
- If a temporary reconveyance is necessary for closing, coordinate the re-transfer immediately after funding and record the new deed quickly.

1. Preserve tax exemptions and assess reassessment risk

- Check local rules for homestead, assessment, and transfer tax consequences before recording.
- File any required affidavits or exemption forms at the same time as—or immediately after—recordation.
- Retain proof of filings and confirmations from the county assessor or taxing authority.

1. Create and maintain an audit-ready trust binder

- Immediately add recorded deeds, trustee certifications, confirmation letters, insurance endorsements, and lender correspondence to the binder.
- Keep originals in a secure location and encrypted digital copies accessible to named successors under documented conditions.
- Use an index page and date-stamp each item to create a clear audit trail.

1. Prepare successor trustees and beneficiaries

- Provide successors with a compact packet: trustee certification template, asset schedule, location of originals, and a "first steps" checklist.
- Explain access procedures and who to call for urgent issues (attorney, title company, insurer).
- Encourage successors to confirm receipt of critical documents with institutions to avoid surprises.

1. Use limited disclosure tools effectively

- Prefer trustee certifications, recorded deed copies, and excerpts over full trust documents when institutions will accept them.
- Work with counsel to tailor certifications that meet third-party needs while protecting privacy.
- Maintain signed templates so documents can be produced quickly

when requested.

1. Document decision rationale and timing

- When transfers are quiet by design, record the purpose and timing (estate planning, incapacity planning, succession).
- Preserve any contemporaneous legal or tax advice, memos, and internal notes explaining the transfer to demonstrate legitimate intent if challenged.
- Keep correspondence showing that you checked institutional and local requirements before recording.

1. Audit post-transfer within 30–90 days

- Confirm recordings posted at the county recorder, insurance endorsements issued, lender/servicer acknowledgements received, and tax records updated.
- Resolve any mismatches immediately (re-recording errors, insurer exceptions, lender holds).
- Add audit results and corrective actions to the trust binder.

1. Escalate to professionals when risks exist

- Before transferring if litigation, creditor claims, multi-state property, or complex tax exposure exist, obtain written legal and tax opinions.
- If a creditor or other party challenges the transfer, contact counsel promptly and produce the prepared audit trail.
- Coordinate title professionals and local counsel to correct procedural or recording errors.

Follow these steps whenever you conduct a quiet transfer: plan targeted notifications, confirm institutional requirements, preserve tax positions, prepare successors, and keep an audit-ready record. Thoughtful, minimal disclosure plus prompt documentation turns a discreet transfer into a defensible and administrable action.

Chapter 10:
Final Thoughts and Resources

Estate planning and trust administration are ongoing processes, not one-time events. The work of drafting, funding, and maintaining a trust pays off only when documentation, institutional coordination, and regular reviews keep the plan actionable. Treat your trust as a living file: update asset schedules, confirm institutional records after major transactions, and prepare successor trustees with clear instructions and access to documents.

Prioritize clarity, consistency, and documentation. Use the exact legal name of the trust on every deed and account, keep dated versions of amendments and asset schedules, and store recorded deeds and trustee certifications where successors can retrieve them. A single, well-indexed trust binder (with encrypted backup) reduces delay, prevents disputes, and supports quick responses to lender, insurer, or tax inquiries.

Build a small, trusted team and keep them coordinated. Typical members include a state-licensed estate attorney, a CPA familiar with trust taxation, a local title company, and an insurance agent who understands endorsements for trusts. Share a concise contact sheet with successors and update it whenever advisors change. When issues arise—refinance, sale, litigation, creditor claims—this team shortens response time and strengthens legal defensibility.

Adopt a regular review schedule. Perform an annual check for beneficiary designations, insurance coverage, account titling, and tax filings; conduct a more thorough review after major life events (marriage, divorce, death, interstate moves, large acquisitions). Include a 30–90 day post-transfer audit for any new deed to confirm recordation, endorsements, and institutional acknowledgements are in place.

Use targeted, minimal disclosure to preserve privacy while meeting third-party needs. Trustee certifications, recorded deed copies, and brief cover letters often satisfy lenders, insurers, and title companies without exposing full trust details. Keep signed templates ready so required documents can be produced quickly during refinances, sales, or claims.

Maintain an audit trail explaining the purpose and timing of transfers. When transfers are made quietly for legitimate estate planning reasons, contemporaneous memos, counsel opinions, and confirmations from institutions provide crucial evidence if a transfer is later questioned. Preserve these records alongside deeds and certifications in the trust binder.

Practical resources to assemble now: a funding checklist with deadlines; trustee certification and cover letter templates; a post-transfer audit checklist; an indexed trust binder (physical and encrypted digital copy); and a successor trustee "first steps" packet. If you do not already have these, ask your attorney or title company to supply templates tailored to your state and situation.

Final step: act. Review your funding checklist, confirm vesting on high-value assets, notify your mortgage servicer and insurer of any recorded deeds, and schedule a professional review if you have multi-state properties, business interests, or litigation exposure. Consistent maintenance, clear communication, and prompt professional support keep your trust effective and protect your intended legacy.

***

Section 1: Checklist for transferring your home to a trust

Transferring a home into a trust is a multi-step process that requires coordination, accuracy, and follow-through. Begin by confirming that a properly executed trust instrument exists and that its language matches your intentions for ownership, successor trustees, and distribution. Verify the trust's exact legal name, date, and the trustee capacity language you will use on deeds and certifications so every document is consistent.

Next, obtain a certified copy of the trust and a pre-signed trustee certification template from your attorney. While many third parties accept a trustee certification instead of the full trust, having both ready speeds responses from lenders, insurers, and title companies. Make sure the certification confirms revocability (if applicable), the current trustee, and the trustee's authority to convey or encumber real property.

Prepare the deed transfer using the exact vesting language supplied by your attorney and confirm county recorder requirements for format, notarization, and acknowledgments. Have the deed reviewed by counsel or the title company before recording to reduce the chance of rejection for technical defects such as a misspelled trust name, omitted legal description, or incorrect trustee capacity phrase.

Before recording, check for liens, outstanding mortgages, and any judgments that could affect the transfer. Review your mortgage documents for notice or due-on-sale provisions and call the servicer to confirm their documentation rules. If a mortgage exists, coordinate with the lender and title company to determine whether a temporary reconveyance, a lender's waiver, or a simple notification is required for refinance or sale plans.

Preserve tax positions and exemptions by confirming local homestead, reassessment, and transfer tax rules in your jurisdiction. File any required affidavits or exemption forms with the county assessor or recorder at recording time. If you live in a state with reassessment triggers or special homestead procedural requirements, obtain the specific forms and submit them promptly to avoid unexpected tax consequences.

Notify key institutions immediately after recording: mortgage servicer, homeowner's insurer, title insurer, local tax assessor, and utility or municipal billing offices as needed. Send a concise cover letter, a copy of the recorded deed, and the trustee certification; request written confirmation that policy endorsements, escrow accounts, and tax billing will continue without interruption and retain those confirmations in your file.

Update estate records and asset schedules in a centralized trust binder and encrypted digital vault. Add the recorded deed, trustee certification, insurer endorsements, lender acknowledgements, and any filed exemption forms. Index each item, date-and-sign asset schedule updates, and maintain version control so successors can quickly verify ownership and step into administration without searching.

Prepare successors by creating a compact "first steps" packet containing a trustee certification template, an indexed asset schedule, contact information for your attorney, CPA, title company, and insurer, and clear instructions on where originals and digital credentials are stored. Ensure successors know how to locate the recordable deed, request account access, and obtain replacement trustee certifications if needed.

Conduct a post-transfer audit within 30–90 days to confirm that the county recorder posted the deed, the insurer issued an endorsement, the lender acknowledged the vesting, and the assessor updated tax records or accepted any exemption filings. Resolve any discrepancies immediately—re-recording errors, insurer exceptions, or servicer holds—so small administrative problems do not become larger legal or financial issues.

Finally, involve professionals at critical junctures. Use a state-licensed estate attorney for deed drafting and trust conformity, a local title company for recording and endorsements, and a CPA for any tax concerns. If litigation, creditor claims, or insolvency risks exist, obtain written legal guidance before transferring. Thoughtful planning, precise documentation, and prompt institutional coordination turn the transfer into a durable, administrable step in your estate plan.

***

Section 1.1 Steps and instructions — Checklist for transferring your home to a trust

1. Confirm the trust instrument

1.1 Verify the trust is fully executed, dated, and reflects your current intentions. 1.2 Copy the trust's exact legal name and trustee capacity wording for use on deeds and certifications. 1.3 Request an executed trustee certification template and a certified copy of the trust from your attorney.

2. Plan the transfer and gather documents

2.1 Create a transfer task list with responsible parties and target dates. 2.2 Obtain the current deed, mortgage payoff statement (if any), recent title report, and current property tax bill. 2.3 Collect identification and notarization requirements for the county recorder.

3. Draft and review the deed

3.1 Have your attorney or title company prepare the deed using the exact trust vesting language. 3.2 Confirm the legal description and county formatting requirements (notary, acknowledgments, signatures). 3.3 Review the deed with counsel and get pre-approval from the title company before taking it to recording.

4. Check liens, mortgages, and contractual obligations

4.1 Search for outstanding liens, judgments, or tax liens and clear or disclose them as required. 4.2 Review mortgage terms for notice, due-on-sale, or consent clauses; contact the servicer to confirm documentation requirements. 4.3 If refinancing or selling is planned, coordinate timing and, if necessary, prepare for a temporary reconveyance or lender waiver.

5. Preserve tax exemptions and avoid reassessment

5.1 Research local homestead, reassessment, and transfer tax rules or consult local counsel. 5.2 Prepare and file any required affidavits or exemption forms at recording or immediately afterward. 5.3 Keep proof of filings and written confirmations from the assessor or taxing authority.

6. Record the deed properly

6.1 Record the deed at the county recorder's office with required fees and correct form of acknowledgment. 6.2 Obtain a certified copy or recording receipt and verify the recorded exhibit matches what was submitted. 6.3 If the recorder rejects the deed, correct issues promptly and re-record.

7. Notify and document with institutions

7.1 Send the recorded deed and trustee certification to the mortgage servicer, homeowner's insurer, title insurer, and relevant financial institutions. 7.2 Request written acknowledgements, insurer endorsements, and confirmation that escrow and billing will continue as before. 7.3 Retain all correspondence and confirmations in the trust binder.

8. Update insurance, escrow, and tax accounts

8.1 Ask the insurer for an endorsement naming the trust or trustee and confirm coverage continuity. 8.2 Ensure escrow accounts reflect current vesting for taxes and insurance premiums. 8.3 Verify property tax records and billing address are updated with the assessor.

9. Update trust records and beneficiary coordination

9.1 Add the recorded deed, trustee certification, insurer endorsements, and acknowledgements to the indexed trust binder and encrypted digital vault. 9.2 Update the trust's schedule of assets and sign/date the updated schedule. 9.3 Notify named beneficiaries and successor trustees as appropriate, providing a concise "first steps" packet.

10. Perform a post-transfer audit

10.1 Within 30–90 days confirm: recorder posting, insurer endorsement, lender acknowledgment, and assessor updates. 10.2 Resolve mismatches—re-recording errors, insurer exceptions, servicer holds—immediately and document corrections. 10.3 File audit results and corrective actions in the trust binder.

11. Secure access and continuity

11.1 Store originals in a secure location (safe or safety deposit box) and maintain encrypted digital backups. 11.2 Document who may access originals and how successors will prove authority. 11.3 Keep trustee certification templates and emergency contact information current and accessible to named successors.

12. Coordinate professional support

12.1 Use a state-licensed estate attorney for deed drafting and legal compliance. 12.2 Involve a title company for recording checks and endorsements; use a CPA for tax questions. 12.3 Obtain written legal advice before transferring if litigation, creditor exposure, or insolvency risk exists.

Follow this ordered checklist to minimize title defects, protect exemptions, maintain insurance and escrow continuity, and leave successor trustees a clear, auditable record.

***

Section 2: Sample quitclaim deed template

THIS QUITCLAIM DEED is made this ___ day of __________, 20___, by and between

Grantor: ____ Grantor

Address: ______________________________________

and

Grantee: ____ Grantee

Address: ______________________________________

WITNESSETH: For valuable consideration, receipt of which is hereby acknowledged, the Grantor hereby remise, release, and quitclaim to the Grantee all right, title, interest, and claim which the Grantor has in and to the following described real property situated in the County of ____________, State of ____________, to-wit:

Legal Description: ____ (Include full parcel legal description; attach exhibit if necessary)

Parcel Identification Number (APN): ______________________________

TO HAVE AND TO HOLD the same unto the Grantee, and the Grantee's heirs and assigns forever, subject to all easements, covenants, restrictions, reservations, rights-of-way, and encumbrances of record.

This conveyance is made subject to the following conditions (select applicable items and delete the rest):

- Subject to any and all liens and encumbrances of record.
- Subject to the mortgage(s) described as:

  ____.
- No warranties are given; this deed conveys only the Grantor's interest, if any.

Grantor Covenants: The Grantor conveys by quitclaim and makes no covenants, express or implied, regarding title, possession, or encumbrances, except as expressly stated in this instrument.

IN WITNESS WHEREOF, the Grantor has executed this instrument the day and year first above written.

Grantor Signature: ______________________________ Printed Name: ______________________________

Grantor Signature: ______________________________ Printed Name: ______________________________

STATE OF ______________ COUNTY OF ____________

On this ___ day of __________, 20___, before me, a Notary Public, personally appeared ______________________________, personally known to me or proved to me on the basis of satisfactory evidence to be the person(s) whose name(s) is/are subscribed to the within instrument, and acknowledged to me that he/she/they executed the same.

Witness my hand and official seal this ___ day of __________, 20___.

Notary Public Signature: ______________________________ Printed Name: ______________________________________ My Commission Expires: __________ (Seal)

Recording Information (to be completed by county recorder): Recorder's Fee: $__________ Document No.: ______________ Date Recorded: ______________

Notes and optional provisions

If the property is being conveyed to a trust, use the trust's exact legal name and show the trustee capacity: e.g., "John Doe, as Trustee of the John Doe Revocable Living Trust dated January 1, 20XX."

For transfers involving spouses, community property, or homestead issues, include any required spousal acknowledgments or consents per local law.

If a mortgage exists and lender consent is required, obtain written lender approval or coordinate reconveyance/re-recording steps before recording.

Always attach the full legal description (or reference a recorded plat) and confirm county recording formatting requirements.

Use this template as a starting point. State and county recording requirements vary; have a local title professional or estate attorney review and tailor the deed before execution and recording.

Glossary of key terms

- **Administrator** — A person appointed by a court to manage and distribute the estate of a decedent who died without a will; performs duties similar to an executor but under court supervision.
- **Affidavit of Trust** — A short, signed statement by a trustee that certifies the trust's existence, trustee authority, revocability, and basic trust details for third parties without disclosing the full trust document.
- **Ancillary Probate** — A secondary probate proceeding in a state where the decedent owned property but did not reside; required to transfer out-of-state real property through the local courts.
- **Beneficiary** — An individual or entity entitled to receive benefits, assets, or distributions from a trust, will, insurance policy, or retirement account.
- **Breach of Fiduciary Duty** — A trustee's or executor's failure to act loyally, prudently, or impartially for the benefit of beneficiaries, potentially leading to surcharge, removal, or other remedies.
- **Certificate of Trust** — See Affidavit of Trust; a document used to verify trust authority and basic terms for banks, title companies, and insurers without revealing private provisions.
- **Certified Copy** — An official copy of a recorded or filed document, stamped or signed by the recorder or custodian, often required by institutions as proof of record.
- **Deed** — A written instrument that conveys real property title from one party to another; must meet state and county recording formalities to be effective against third parties.
- **Deed of Trust** — A type of security instrument used in some states where a trustee holds title as security for a loan; foreclosure usually proceeds nonjudicially under statutory procedures.
- **Devise** — A gift of real property under a will; the person receiving the devise is a devisee.

- **Due-on-Sale Clause** — A mortgage provision that permits the lender to accelerate the loan if the property is transferred; enforcement and exceptions vary by contract and law.
- **Durable Power of Attorney** — A legal document authorizing an agent to act for the principal in financial and legal matters, continuing even if the principal becomes incapacitated (if durable).
- **Escrow** — A neutral process or account where funds and documents are held by a third party until contractual conditions are satisfied, commonly used in real estate closings.
- **Executor** — The person named in a will to administer the decedent's estate, carry out distributions, pay debts, and handle probate proceedings.
- **Fiduciary** — A person who owes legal duties of loyalty and care when managing assets or making decisions for another's benefit, such as trustees, executors, or guardians.
- **Funding** — The process of retitling assets into a trust's name (deeds, account re-titling, beneficiary designations) so the trust actually holds the property intended for trust administration.
- **Grantor** — The individual who creates a trust and transfers assets into it; also called settlor or trustor.
- **Homestead Exemption** — A statutory benefit that reduces property tax or protects a primary residence from certain creditor claims; eligibility and rules vary by state.
- **Incapacity Planning** — Legal and financial arrangements (trusts, powers of attorney, advance directives) designed to manage a person's affairs if they lose decision-making ability.
- **Instrument** — A formal legal document, such as a deed, trust agreement, will, or affidavit, that effects rights in property or designates authority.
- **Irrevocable Trust** — A trust generally not amendable or revocable by the grantor; transfers into an irrevocable trust often have different tax and creditor consequences than revocable trusts.

- **Judicial Foreclosure** — A court-supervised foreclosure process required in some states for mortgages, typically slower and initiated by a lawsuit.
- **Lien** — A legal claim against property to secure payment of a debt or obligation, which may restrict transfer or require payoff upon sale.
- **Living Trust** — A trust created during the grantor's lifetime (often revocable) to hold assets for management, incapacity planning, and probate avoidance.
- **Mortgagor / Mortgagee** — The mortgagor is the borrower who grants a mortgage; the mortgagee is the lender who holds the mortgage as security.
- **Nonjudicial Foreclosure** — A foreclosure process allowed under statute for deeds of trust where the trustee sells the property after required notices and timeframes, without court involvement.
- **Notary Acknowledgment** — A formal notarization confirming a signer executed a document voluntarily and was identified, required by many counties for deeds and recorded instruments.
- **Notice of Default** — A formal notice from a lender or trustee indicating a borrower's default and outlining steps to cure before acceleration or foreclosure.
- **Power of Appointment** — A trust or will provision that allows a designated person to choose who will receive certain property or interests under specified rules.
- **Probate** — The court process for proving a will, administering a decedent's estate, paying debts, and distributing assets according to the will or applicable law.
- **Quiet Title Action** — A lawsuit to establish ownership and remove clouds or competing claims on real property, producing a definitive court decree of title.
- **Reconveyance** — The act of transferring title back to the borrower or trust, often used after loan payoff or when temporarily removing property from a trust for refinancing.

- **Recording** — Filing a deed or other instrument with the county recorder to provide public notice and priority against later claims; proper recording preserves rights.
- **Reassessment** — A county or state process that revalues property for property tax purposes after a change in ownership or other triggering event.
- **Revocable Trust** — A trust the grantor can amend or revoke during life, commonly used for estate planning and retaining flexibility while avoiding probate.
- **Schedule of Assets** — A recorded or attached list that identifies property owned by the trust, used for administration and to show what the trust holds.
- **Successor Trustee** — The person or entity designated to take over trust administration upon the initial trustee's incapacity, resignation, or death.
- **Title Insurance** — An insurance policy that protects owners and lenders against losses from defects in title, recording errors, or undisclosed claims.
- **Trustee** — The individual or corporate entity legally responsible for holding and managing trust assets in accordance with the trust instrument and fiduciary duties.
- **Trustee Certification** — A signed attestation by a trustee that summarizes trust authority and relevant facts for third parties while preserving the confidentiality of the trust instrument.
- **Unearned Income** — Income derived from investments, pensions, rents, or trust distributions rather than from employment or services, often taxed differently.
- **Vesting** — The legal manner in which title is held or expressed on a deed; correct vesting language is essential to reflect ownership and trustee capacity.
- **Will** — A legal document that expresses a person's final wishes for property distribution, guardianship, and executor selection after death; must be probated to have legal effect.

Additional terms relevant to transferring a home to a trust

- **Abstract of Title** — A chronological summary of public records affecting title to a parcel of land.
- **After-Acquired Title** — Property acquired after trust creation that may be added to the trust by operation of law or amendment.
- **Assignment of Mortgage** — A document transferring a mortgage from one lender to another.
- **Attestation Clause** — A statement on a recorded instrument that witnesses' signatures occurred as required by law.
- **Beneficial Interest** — The right to benefit from trust property even if legal title is held by the trustee.
- **Chain of Title** — The sequence of recorded instruments showing ownership history for a property.
- **Chattel** — Personal property that may be included in a trust schedule (furniture, equipment, vehicles).
- **Conditional Deed** — A deed that transfers title subject to a specified condition or contingency.
- **Community Property** — A property ownership system in some states affecting how spouses transfer title into trusts.
- **Constructive Notice** — Legal notice to the world provided by properly recording a deed or instrument.
- **Contingent Beneficiary** — A backup beneficiary whose interest takes effect only if a primary beneficiary cannot receive property.
- **Covenant** — A promise in a deed or agreement that creates enforceable obligations affecting the property.
- **Deed Restriction** — A limitation recorded against a property that restricts use or improvements.
- **Easement** — A recorded right for another party to use a portion of the property for a specific purpose.
- **Encroachment** — An intrusion of a structure onto adjacent property that may affect marketability and title.
- **Escrow Holdback** — Funds retained by escrow post-closing to

secure completion of specified obligations.

- **Estoppel Certificate** — A statement from a party (often a lender or tenant) confirming certain facts for a transaction.
- **Fee Simple** — The most complete form of property ownership, subject to governmental restrictions and encumbrances.
- **Fixture** — Personal property affixed to realty and treated as part of the real property for transfer purposes.
- **Grant Deed** — A deed form in some states that provides limited title warranties and is commonly used in residential transfers.
- **Implied Warranty of Authority** — The presumption that a trustee signing in an official capacity has the power to act unless challenged.
- **Instrument Indexing** — The recorder's process of cataloging documents by names and parcel identifiers for public search.
- **Judgment Lien** — A lien placed on property to secure payment of a court judgment against the owner.
- **Life Estate** — An interest that grants possession for the duration of a person's life, with remainder to others.
- **Mechanic's Lien** — A statutory lien that contractors and suppliers can record for unpaid work improving real property.
- **Notice to Quitclaim** — A procedural notice sometimes required when reconveying or correcting title via quitclaim.
- **Partial Reconveyance** — A reconveyance that removes specific liens or portions of security from title after partial payoff.
- **Praecipe** — A clerical request submitted to court or recorder to schedule or process a document or hearing.
- **Quiet Enjoyment** — An implied right that an owner or grantee can possess property without interference from prior claims.
- **Remainder Interest** — A future interest that becomes possessory when a preceding estate (e.g., life estate) ends.
- **Right of Survivorship** — A form of co-ownership where the surviving owner automatically inherits the decedent's share.
- **Search Period** — The timeframe covered by a title search and title

insurance commitment.

- **Shelf Trust** — A pre-created, often undated trust that can be quickly customized and funded when needed.
- **Subrogation** — The insurer's legal right to pursue third parties for amounts paid under a claim, relevant after transfers affecting liability.
- **Tax Parcel Number** — The identifier used by local assessors to track property for taxation and records.
- **Transfer on Death Deed** — A deed that transfers title upon death without probate where state law allows.
- **Trust Protector** — A person granted limited oversight powers over a trust (amend, remove trustee) under specified conditions.
- **UTC (Uniform Trust Code)** — A model statute adopted in many states that standardizes trust law provisions and trustee duties.
- **Waiver of Homestead Rights** — A recorded consent by a spouse or owner to relinquish homestead protections where permitted.
- **Warranty Deed** — A deed that provides express guarantees about title quality and the grantor's authority to convey.

If you'd like, I can group these terms by category (title, tax, lender, trustee, recording) or expand any definition into practical examples and state-specific considerations.

Recommended legal and estate planning resources

Reliable resources make estate planning and trust administration manageable and defensible. Start with professional advisors: a state-licensed estate planning attorney for drafting and state-specific recording rules, a CPA or tax attorney for tax consequences and reporting, and a local title company for recordings, endorsements, and reconveyance logistics. These professionals coordinate filings, confirm lender and insurer requirements, and tailor documents to local practice.

Practical books and guides

- **Practical Estate Planning guides** — Look for recent editions that cover revocable and irrevocable trusts, funding checklists, and state variations; choose titles authored by estate attorneys or recognized practitioners.
- **Real property closing manuals** — Useful for understanding county recorder rules, deed formats, and common recording pitfalls.
- **Trust administration handbooks** — Step-by-step guides for successor trustees covering fiduciary duties, recordkeeping, distributions, and common pitfalls.

Online reference hubs and templates

- **State bar association websites** — Provide state-specific forms, fee schedules, and practice advisories that reflect local law and recording requirements.
- **County recorder and assessor sites** — Essential for local recording forms, fee tables, notary specifications, parcel lookup, and homestead/exemption filings.
- **Title company portals** — Many local title firms publish checklists, trustee certification samples, and endorsement options

tailored to their county practices.

- **Bank and insurer resource centers** — For institution-specific requirements on trustee certifications, endorsements, and escrow handling.

Professional organizations and continuing education

- **American Bar Association (Real Property, Trust and Estate Section)** — Model rules, practicc resources, and referrals to qualified estate counsel.
- **National Association of Estate Planners & Councils (NAEPC)** — Cross-discipline standards, professional directories, and education on coordinated estate planning.
- **Local continuing legal education (CLE) providers** — Offer state-specific updates on trust law, recording practice, and foreclosure differences that affect trust funding decisions.

Practical tools and checklists to assemble now

- **Funding checklist** — Asset inventory, title status, beneficiary forms, responsible parties, and target dates.
- **Trustee certification template** — A concise, attorney-reviewed form trustees can use with banks, insurers, and title companies.
- **Post-transfer audit checklist** — Steps to confirm recorder posting, insurer endorsements, lender acknowledgements, and assessor updates within 30–90 days.
- **Indexed trust binder template** — Sections for original documents, recorded deeds, account credentials, correspondence, and dated audit notes.

How to evaluate and use resources

- Prefer materials and forms produced or reviewed by attorneys licensed in your state; local counsel knows recording quirks, homestead rules, and tax consequences.

- Use templates only as starting points—have an attorney or title professional tailor them before recording or submission to lenders.
- Keep resource links, advisor contact details, and document versions in your indexed trust binder so successors can act quickly and confidently.

Section 1.1 TRUSTEE CERTIFICATION

1. Trust identification

Trust name: ____

Trust date: ____

Grantor(s): ____

2. Trustee information

Current trustee(s): ______________________________________

Trustee address: ____

Trustee phone/email: _____________________________________

3. Authority and status

The undersigned certifies that the instrument identified above is a valid trust that is: (check applicable)

- [ ] Revocable
- [ ] Irrevocable

The undersigned further certifies that: (a) the trustee named above is the duly appointed and acting trustee with authority to convey, encumber, or manage real property owned by the trust; (b) the trust has not been revoked, modified in a manner that alters trustee authority over real property, or terminated as of the date below.

4. Relevant trustee powers (brief)

The trustee is authorized to: convey real property; execute and deliver deeds, leases, and reconveyances; obtain insurance endorsements; and take actions reasonably necessary to manage trust real property.

5. No duty to disclose

This certification is provided in lieu of the full trust instrument for verification purposes only. The undersigned certifies that no further information other than the attached recorded deed and this certification is necessary to verify trustee authority, except as required by law or third-party policies.

6. Governing law

This certification is governed by the law of the state of __________.

7. Signature and notarization

Dated: ________________

Trustee signature: ___________________________

Printed name: _______________________________

STATE OF ___________

COUNTY OF __________

On this ____ day of __________, 20__, before me, personally appeared __________________, who proved to me on the basis of satisfactory evidence to be the person whose name is subscribed to this instrument, and acknowledged that they executed the same.

Notary Public: ______________________________

My commission expires: ______________________

(Seal)

Don't miss out!

Visit the website below and you can sign up to receive emails whenever janice green publishes a new book. There's no charge and no obligation.

https://books2read.com/r/B-A-PIBHE-JOPRH

BOOKS 2 READ

Connecting independent readers to independent writers.

About the Publisher

Janice Green is a legal educator and estate planning advocate dedicated to helping homeowners protect their property and secure their legacy. With years of experience guiding families through trust administration and title transfers, she specializes in making complex processes simple and practical. Her clear, step-by-step approach empowers readers to confidently use tools like living trusts and quitclaim deeds to safeguard their homes for future generations.

Read more at https://thebreakthroughcollective.online/.

www.ingramcontent.com/pod-product-compliance
Lightning Source LLC
LaVergne TN
LVHW052221200926
848481LV00001B/177